2.75

THE NEW SOVIET PSYCHIC DISCOVERIES

THE NEW SOVIET PSYCHIC DISCOVERIES

Henry Gris and William Dick

Prentice-Hall, Inc., Englewood Cliffs, New Jersey

All photos courtesy of the National Enquirer, Inc.

Prentice-Hall International, Inc., London / Prentice-Hall of Australia, Pty. Ltd., Sydney / Prentice-Hall of Canada, Ltd., Toronto / Prentice-Hall of India Private Ltd., New Delhi / Prentice-Hall of Japan, Inc., Tokyo / Prentice-Hall of Southeast Asia Pte. Ltd., Singapore / Whitehall Books Limited, Wellington, New Zealand

10 9 8 7 6 5 4 3 2 1

Library of Congress Cataloging in Publication Data

Gris, Henry,
    The new Soviet psychic discoveries.

    Includes index.
    1. Psychical research—Russia.   I. Dick,
William, joint author.   II. Title.
BF1028.5.R9G74   133.8'0947   77-26085
ISBN 0-13-615823-4

ACKNOWLEDGEMENTS

We would like to thank:

The *National Enquirer* for originating the assignment and dispatching us to Russia on this mission.

The *Novosti Press Agency* for clearing the way for us to do our job, and especially to Natasha Yakovleva and Yuri Shevyakov for putting up with our often impossible demands.

And our dear wives, Mira and Margaret, for letting us go.

CONTENTS

IN THE SHADOW
OF THE KREMLIN

Anna, the buxom bartender in the foreign currency bar behind the crowded lobby of the Intourist Hotel, had obviously been trained to remember faces. As we came up to her counter, she greeted us warmly, readily recalling our first names and beaming: "Welcome back to Moscow!"

"You are looking well, gentlemen," Anna added, addressing us with the plural of 'gospodin,' a word reserved for foreigners.

"So do you, Anna," we responded politely. The bar was empty. We were her only customers. Before we had time to ask, she was busy fixing the espresso while looking in a secret nook under the counter for the special bottle of 5-star Georgian cognac she kept for her better customers.

She had remembered espresso-and-cognac was our favorite way to combat the Russian cold. And on this, our first morning back in Moscow, it certainly was cold outside; the naked lime trees alongside Gorky Street were shivering in the icy wind blowing down the broad boulevard.

We assumed Anna was making a mental note to mention us in her report to her bosses of the KGB, saying that we were in the company of a Soviet citizen she had seen with us early that winter, a scientist by the name of Viktor Adamenko. We didn't think she knew he was a leading Soviet parapsychologist or that she had ever heard of parapsychology. Still, her report would prove adequate. Our three names and our background information would already be on file. Not that we, or Viktor Adamenko, really cared.

We had come a long way. It all started many years earlier—oddly enough, in Hollywood—on the day Valentin Zorin, Russia's leading television news commentator, found himself stranded in a Los Angeles hotel room unable to get the interviews he had traveled halfway around the world to conduct. No one would see him. But before Zorin left Moscow, the head of the UPI Bureau, Henry Shapiro, gave him Gris's phone number for use in an emergency. A few strings were pulled, and Zorin got the cooperation he wanted. He never forgot that we had helped him out of a jam, and readily reciprocated when our roles were reversed.

We had applied for Soviet visas in 1972 for our first trip behind the Iron Curtain. The visas were discouragingly slow in coming, and we obviously needed someone to help us. So, digging up the business card Zorin gave us in

Los Angeles, we called him in Moscow. He remembered us. Two days later we got word that our visas had been approved. Shortly after our arrival, we were having lunch at the Moscow Press Club when Zorin said, "Do you know they actually thought you could be spies?"

"No!" we exclaimed.

"Oh yes. I was asked why I was helping you come to Russia with a minimum of credentials, and I said 'because we are journalists first and last.' I told them that years ago I had gone to Hollywood on a brief visit and found there was a mix-up with the State Department. These people helped me, although they knew nothing about me. So they said if I vouched that you are not spies, you would be issued visas instantly, but I had to assume personal responsibility for your good behavior. I said I would, and this is how you got in. So please, boys, do me a favor and don't spy." On all our visits to the Soviet Union, we kept this plea very much in mind.

We may never know whether Natasha Yakovleva, who then promptly inherited us from Zorin, eventually stuck her neck out as far. She was the rather attractive senior staffer assigned to pilot us around by the Novosti Press Agency, the Government controlled propaganda outlet that normally assists the foreign press inside Russia. Natasha, who was working the North American Department, set up the interviews, took us to the subjects we wanted to see, and stayed by our side through the meetings. She quickly developed an approach that invariably worked. The introductions over, she would dutifully explain that we represented the *National Enquirer,* the best-selling newspaper in America, an American version of two Russian mass circulation weeklies, *Literaturnaya Gazeta (Literary Gazette)* and *Nedelya (Week)* rolled into one. The description didn't really fit, but at least it conveyed an image our subjects could grasp. And the Russians were invariably impressed when Natasha told them the *Enquirer*'s circulation at that time was over five million copies per week—it has since greatly increased. After that, it was clear sailing. We did well, Natasha glowed with delight. Two weeks later, our job done, she saw us off, but we were back twice the following year, and again in 1974, never staying more than two to four weeks.

We reported on everything from old age to life in space, from cancer research to new sources of energy. Each time we kept asking for official backing to do a series on Soviet psychic research. We became friendly with quite a few Soviet newsmen working for publications varying from *Pravda* and *Izvestiya* to *Tekhnika Molodezhi,* a youth magazine, and in Russian radio and TV. On one occasion, we even were interviewed on Moscow television's news program called *Vremya (Time).* For lack of studio space, the filmed interview was improvised on the 17th floor landing of the Intourist Hotel, just outside our rooms.

Newscaster Vitali Beloborodko simply had the hotel elevators halted, and we settled down in armchairs in front of a glass table. The whole thing was filmed in five minutes while we discussed our research into longevity in the Caucasus, from which we had just returned.

At the tail end of Trip No. 4, the one preceding our first all-out psychic venture, this led to a request from the head of the North American Department of Novosti news agency for us to give a talk to their news staff on why the *Enquirer* was such a success in America. It was a summons we could not turn down.

The following day, in the crowded conference room, we found that newsmen other than Novosti staffers had sneaked in. After the talk, the questions came thick and fast. The Soviet newsmen wanted to have the readers broken down as to age, social background, community tastes, etc. Told that American readers actually enjoyed ghost stories, one newsman demanded to know whether we ourselves believed in ghosts. Then, much to our surprise, he proclaimed, "I can tell you a fantastic story about a ghost here in Moscow. It happened to me!"

Others brought up psychic phenomena, astrology, and the occult, clearly yearning to know more about these subjects. "Do you really believe that an Aquarius behaves differently from a Pisces?" one asked. When we agreed, he said, "I believe it also."

After the lecture, a good-looking, well-dressed woman in her mid-forties took us aside. She identified herself as Ludmila Mikhailovna Borozdina, editor of the magazine *Soviet Life* "I'll give you my phone number," she said. "If ever you return here in search of Soviet psychic phenomena, call me. I'll have plenty to tell you. In fact I'd love to accompany you on your journeys." To play it safe, we told our Novosti hosts about the *Soviet Life* offer. A little competition never hurts, even in the Soviet Union.

"Nothing doing," said Natasha Yakovleva, who had just been elevated to the position of head of the U.S. press section of Novosti. "If and when you come again, you work with *us*." For a change, we enjoyed her possessiveness.

In some measure, of course, Borozdina's interest in psychic mysteries helped us when we subsequently applied for Novosti's help with the series. Natasha, for one, knew that if they were to turn us down, we would go to *Soviet Life*—which would cause embarrassment. But we kept our cake and ate it too. Because, when we eventually returned to Moscow to tackle Soviet parapsychology, we called Borozdina.

By then, it had long since dawned on her that we "belonged" to Novosti, and so she did not suggest a switch. Still, she said, "I'll be delighted to help you with the psychics that I personally know." She then gave us a remarkable update on two leading parapsychologists, researcher Genady Sergeyev and medium Ninel Kulagina, both of whom she had met in Leningrad some time earlier. And we were en route to Leningrad.

"Sergeyev is a very exciting man." she said, giving us his phone number. "His experiments with Kulagina are breathtaking. Have him tell you about them."

We spoke several times to her, filling her in on our progress, but she never asked us over to her own office. She was eager not to offend Novosti which could have hurt us.

We grew to like Ludmila Mikhailovna for her total impartiality and willingness to help other newsmen, be they Soviet or from the West. Few Soviet editors, men or women, treated us with such charm and warmth. We reciprocated by treating her with respect and a camaraderie she appeared to enjoy. We made sure, therefore, to always address her with her patronym, Ludmila Mikhailovna, something she appreciated even more coming from foreigners. We used the patronym in all instances when respectful demeanor was in order. We never used it with Natasha, because we hit it off with her right at the start and bypassed the formalities. Her full name was a ponderous Natalia Aleksandrovna Yakovleva, and Natasha is really a diminutive form of Natalia. Curiously, Natasha couldn't care less about *her* patronym, perhaps because she had been abroad a lot and acquired certain Western mannerisms. In any case, poor Ludmila Mikhailovna is no more. She died the same year. While vacationing, she was beheaded in a tragic automobile accident outside Yalta.

There remains no doubt in our minds that in November 1974 when we put forth our first parapsychology investigation request—by cable to Novosti in Moscow—we had reached the point of utter trust with the Soviets. It was eight weeks and an animated exchange of messages later that we were told, again by cable, that our request to carry out a comprehensive study of the Soviets' multi-million-ruble research into parapsychology had been approved. The message from Vladimir Makhotin, then head of the North American Department of Novosti, read that for one month, we would travel throughout the Soviet Union, visiting the people involved in Soviet psychic research. But his cable named only five people we would see! What about the others? We had so many more on our original list, and we were worried. We sent a fast message to Novosti in Moscow.

Two days later, back came a cable from Natasha Yakovleva, "Don't worry. Everything is under control." Our incredible adventure was on. While we realized that we would not be on our own, we were quite happy to resume with the Novosti people where we had left off on our previous trip. By now we knew just about everyone in the North American Department, from the elegant Aleksandr Makhotin to his hard-working, conscientious deputy, Pavel Gevorkyan, to their editors and reporters crowding the rather inadequate offices in an improvised annex on Pushkin Street.

With the exception of Makhotin and Gevorkyan, no one, not even Natasha, had a private office. Natasha shared with two assistant editors. The reporters, about eight of them, crowded into one not very large room. Typically, each reporter had an outside phone on his desk eliminating the need of a general switchboard. But when the phone on a desk rang, others might not pick it up, depending on how busy they were. Some day (and this may take ten years), Novosti will have its own high rise in the same area and things will be different, we were told.

On this particular trip, the Novosti person assigned to us was Yuri Shevyakov, Novosti's excellent senior science reporter. "There's no one more diligent" Makhotin said, introducing Yuri—a pale-faced, earnest-looking young man of medium height, and conservative appearance. He was terribly polite, and nervous. He spoke English slowly but clearly. What about Natasha? "Can't spare her right now." Makhotin said pleasantly, "but she'll accompany you for part of the trip."

Our association with Novosti primarily meant that they could keep an eye on us while assisting us in our work. For some reason, we never had to pay the usual fee for such services, only pick up the Novosti staffers fare, hotel and meal tabs all of which he or she studiously kept to a bare minimum. In return we were provided with a traveling companion, appointment secretary, messenger and interpreter. But the fact that one of us, Gris, spoke fluent Russian meant we rarely had to use the interpreting facility.

We started with the five names promised us by cable from Moscow, five subjects to interview, yet ended up with sixty-two—astrophysicists, physicists, mathematicians, philosophers, space engineers, educators, doctors of medicine, mentalists, clairvoyants, healers—psychics of all dimensions and backgrounds, literate and illiterate. There was world-famous Semyon Kirlian, who developed the technique for photographing the aura, by now copied in universities abroad including the U.S. Access to him had been refused not only to Western journalists but also to Western scientists, including America's respected parapsychologist Dr. Thelma Moss. Yet we were taken to him—all the way to the city of Krasnodar—and shown his private laboratory.

We talked to Dr. Viktor Inyushin who rarely leaves Alma-Ata in Kazakhstan where he is involved in a series of far-reaching discoveries, from diagnosing early stages of cancer with the help of Kirlian photography, to controlling the human mind.

We spent several days with the theoretician, Dr. Genady Sergeyev. Taken into his confidence, we were given the latest, fascinating data on his research into undying bio-energy, the source of immortality.

And, of course, there was Viktor Adamenko, the man we talked to repeatedly, who along with Inyushin and Sergeyev make up the three pillars of Soviet psychic research. Between them, these three remarkable men are responsible for a new scientific nomenclature that pinpoints the various mysterious powers of the human mind in cold, exact terms, and spells out new hypotheses as staggering to us today as Albert Einstein's Theory of Relativity seemed to conventional physicists of 1915. (Significantly, the Russian trio uses Einstein's findings in their own work.)

We watched incredible feats of telekinesis performed by Alla Vinogradova, who has taken over from the well-known medium, Ninel Kulagina. Kulagina suffered a massive heart attack, a victim of science in the fullest meaning of the phrase. Although she was still an invalid, too weak to leave her home, we were allowed to talk to her. We were permitted a glance into a world of dreams, dreams that save human lives, recorded by Leningrad's famous Dr. Vasili Kasatkin, who is also investigating premonitions—something that has baffled mankind for generations.

We were the first Western newsmen to meet face to face with Dr. Felix Zigel, Russia's foremost authority on UFOs, whose research has resulted in widespread investigations into the probable use of telepathy by alien beings trying to communicate with us. Astrophysicists Vsevolod Troitsky and Iosif Shklovsky provided us with additional insights. Dr. Vladimir Raikov and Dr. Pavel Bul took us into the world of our subconscious as revealed through hypnosis. We met Boris Ermolaev, who can float a human being in midair; the renowned telepathist Yuri Kamensky; and the mentalist Tofik Dadashev, who has taken over where Wolf Messing left off . . . All of these, and so many others, talked to us and fully explained their research, work, hopes and ambitions in a scientific endeavor to which they had dedicated their lives.

Crisscrossing the country, we logged more than 5,000 miles by plane, by train, by car, and on foot. We were allowed to collect all the evidence we needed to put the amazing Soviet effort into sharp focus. Besides the interviews, we were shown the laboratories where research is conducted, and were allowed to photograph at will. Time and again we were assured that we were the first professional newspapermen, including their own journalists, to conduct so comprehensive a study, with that many subjects, some of them previously inaccessible to any of the press. On one occasion, when astrophysicist Vsevolod Troitsky had specially come to see us, traveling from the famed radio observatory in Gorky, an installation built primarily to pick up signals from outer space, three Soviet newspapermen had come to the Novosti office and were sitting in the waiting room, eager to seek our approval for them to just sit in a corner and take notes.

"You mean to say that you, as Soviet journalists, cannot see your man for an interview? Can't you ask?"

"It is out of the question. They are serious scientists. Their time is extremely valuable. To be honest, we are terribly envious of you."

"All right, of course you may sit in."

They couldn't thank us enough.

American correspondents stationed in Moscow claim that the Novosti Press Agency, whose twofold official function is distributing features about the Soviet Union for publication abroad and assisting foreign correspondents on the spot, is actually an arm of the KGB, the Soviet secret police. We never actually caught a Novosti staffer spying on us, but we did assume that if they were not actually spying, they were certainly sending back to the head office detailed reports on our behavior and beliefs.

On our first trip to Russia in the summer of 1972, having entered a Moscow hotel room for the first time—we were staying at the giant 5,000 room Rossiya—we began an instant search for hidden microphones. We couldn't find any, which didn't mean they weren't there.

On a subsequent stay at the Intourist Hotel, we actually stumbled onto the 19th floor surveillance center, a room full of electronic gear from closed-circuit television monitors to a huge push-button panel, its colored lights flickering. The man sitting behind the panel was sipping tea. There was a steaming samovar on a side table. The colored lights, he volunteered in a fairly friendly fashion, were three for each room, white, green and red, and helped him watch over hotel guests to make sure they were safe! One was connected to the room's door leading into the hall. Each time a guest opened his door, the light went on. We assumed that another indicated one's presence in the room, and a third possibly activated a microphone.

One evening, on one of our earlier trips, we were followed to the Moscow Circus. God knows why. On one occasion, a man we had come across earlier that night in the bar of the Rossiya Hotel tried to tempt us into a black-market operation by offering us rubles at four times the official rate. We refused.

On yet another occasion, in the middle of the night in the Hotel Azerbaijan in Baku, we were tested for intent with the help of a couple pretending to be dissidents. A light knock on the door, a whispered, "Let us in. We have a message to go out."

We told them to go away, come back in the morning, and bring a witness. They never did. Informed about the incident first thing in the morning, our Novosti companion Natasha became visibly upset. We concluded she had no prior knowledge of the incident. "You didn't do anything foolish?" she asked anxiously. We assured her we knew better. And, of course, we'll never forget Nikolai Sergeyevich Vitrokhin, professor of philosophy, and his bride Lydia Ivanovna, two characters out of *The Maltese Falcon*, Soviet style, who kept popping up all over the map of Russia to bid us a pleasant day. So if we did not have actual, irrefutable proof, we had good reason to think we were kept under surveillance. It did not bother us. Whether we were being tested or not, we were going to make sure our record remained impeccable. No trespassing, no political involvements, no breaking of any laws. As reporters dealing purely with science, we did our job, writing our stories, which appeared in print—first in the *National Enquirer*, then all over the world—without any political bias. The Novosti people were obviously pleased.

On subsequent trips we sensed that they may have personally vouched for us with the authorities, KGB included. If we broke a few rules and regulations, we did so in order to extricate ourselves from Soviet red tape. Nothing wrong with that; in fact, our contacts in Moscow encouraged us to do it. And whenever something denied us was suddenly made available, such as a forbidden telephone number, we knew that someone up there must have given his "Ve poryadke"—"in order," the Russian okay.

Our traveling companions did perform the important task of discreetly keeping contact with the mysterious somebody in the Soviet hierarchy who had approved our mission. He or they continually kept an eye on us, but we didn't mind, for we were in the clear. Obviously, whoever it was knew all about us. We don't think we ever fooled him, even on our "secret" trip back to Moscow later on.

This visit was made to wrap up the loose ends of our extensive probe totally and completely without supervision. We went as tourists. No one in Moscow was appraised of our arrival. We didn't need anyone to help us get around Moscow, which by now we knew quite well. We spoke the language. We hoped we would be totally at ease, and would move all over the city, freely, and call on whoever we felt still needed a checkout these few months later. Most importantly, we could all the time keep a low profile. It worked.

When it was about over, loaded down with information, we called Yuri and Natasha to say hello and goodbye. Yuri wasn't in, and anyway Natasha was much more important. "You sure get around," she chuckled into the telephone. She was genuinely surprised, but she understood: There was no bad feeling. No one took umbrage at our little 48-hour escapade in the Soviet Union, certainly not the Novosti people.

We had arrived in Moscow by plane from Copenhagen. The Aeroflot Ilyushin 62 which shuttles between Moscow and Copenhagen broke down and so never took off for Kastrup Airport in Copenhagen where we were to make the connection. Eager not to slip up, we sensed trouble when the Moscow flight had not yet been designated a gate half an hour before its scheduled departure. We were first in line for whatever seats might still be open on another Moscow-bound plane, the Copenhagen-Tokyo flight by Japanese Airlines.

Leaving in the late afternoon, with Moscow as an intermediate refueling stop, it was the only other flight out of Kastrup on a Wednesday. Two crew seats could be made available, and we grabbed them. All those other passengers for Moscow, mostly Russians, were now stranded in Copenhagen. We sympathized, while overjoyed with our own good fortune: we had just managed, by the skin of our teeth, to stay on schedule. And what an additional break: we would be arriving on board a flight different from the one originally determined for us by the travel agent. Whoever knew our schedule and came to shadow us at Sheremetyevo would have been told: no Copenhagen flight today.

When we showed up—the only Moscow-bound passengers off the Japanese jet—it was well past the bedtime of the airport staff at Sheremetyevo airport. A quick look around revealed no familiar faces. The building was practically empty. The man at the customs checkpoint shrugged us through, too tired or too bored to be bothered with our luggage. In the airport Intourist reception hall, where all visitors must place themselves in the hands of the official government tourist agency, a man sat behind a long table, a row of empty chairs next to him. He glanced at the open page of the book of anticipated foreign arrivals before him and arched an eyebrow.

Our names weren't there. He looked up at us, and back at the book. "I have no hotel for you, he mumbled under his breath, "How come?" We shrugged and looked helpless. Soviet entry visas are valid one day ahead of expected arrival, so there was no real legal problem.

"Let me see what I can do for you," he shrugged, picking up his phone. "Got a couple of dumb ones," he said into the receiver. "Can you put them up anywhere? They have two first-class rooms coming." He listened, nodded, put down the phone. "You're going into the Hotel Berlin," he said indifferently. "I'll give you the number of your driver." Our thanks remained unacknowledged. He was glad to get rid of us so quickly.

The Hotel Berlin has seen better days. Drab and desolate, it belied the claim in the tourist guide that it was a "proud hostelry, one of Moscow's oldest, owing its popularity to coziness, comfort, first-class service, and excellent cuisine." The small vestibule, with a stuffed black bear by the side of the steps leading up the reception desk and elevator, was dimly lit, lifeless and cold. A sleepy receptionist assigned us to our rooms, then turned away, determined to catch up with an interrupted dream. Even before we could summon the elderly porter, his head sank onto his chest.

It was all so familiar. The creaky, undulating floor of the long, dark, and musty corridor, the high ceiling of the rooms turning them into narrow upright boxes, a chandelier in the center of the ceiling barely lighting up the frugally furnished would-be study. We said *"Khorosho,"* fine, and gave the old man a ruble. He waved his hand as if to say, "No tips, please," stuck the ruble in his pocket, and said good night. As he closed the door behind him, we suddenly realized we had made it to Moscow, seemingly unobserved. Great—and now to hit the sack. Both rooms had the same cheaply-made wooden beds in an alcove behind a drape. But as far as we were concerned, we had made it to a perfect haven.

In the morning, we left without finding out about Hotel Berlin's famous breakfast cuisine. We knew that the modern Intourist Hotel, where we had stayed several times before, was just around the corner. Turn right up Marx Prospekt, then up Sverdlov Square past the Bolshoi to Gorky, and cross by the underpass. No need to tangle with the militiaman over crossing Gorky at the wrong signal.

Once out of the underpass, within our reach would be the good old Intourist, comparable to an overgrown, overpopulated, and very much harassed Holiday Inn. Moscow's pride and joy, and our home away from home on at least five previous occasions. We could use our breakfast coupons supplied by Intourist, or the second-floor restaurant that served foreigners only, all for hard currency. The tea was strong, the jam delicious, the hard-boiled eggs, ham, and cheese plentiful, as were the freshly baked bread and the big patties of fresh butter. A foreigner's happy island behind the Iron Curtain as long as one remembered not to sample the tasteless tomato juice.

Still, over our breakfast—well worth the ruble coupon—we faced facts. We wanted very badly to meet Viktor Adamenko again, to check and recheck some of our facts, and update our coverage of the parapsychology research scene. He had given us invaluable advice during our long previous stay, and now could fill in the last holes in our reportage and provide the last remaining pieces of the jigsaw puzzle. We could use a few more solid interviews. If Viktor didn't know the people personally, he knew *of* them. He clearly perceived the value of their work, he could assess the extent of their knowledge and experience, he knew who was phony and who was for real.

We respected him as a brilliant scientific mind in an attractive human being—soft-spoken, earnest, totally sincere. His name indicated a Ukrainian origin, but his dark eyes and black hair, the handsome unslavic features, betrayed the ethnic mixture. Of medium height, well-proportioned, of fastidious manner and well-groomed, he was European to the core. To us he ceased to be Viktor Adamenko; he was simply *Viktor.* To him we represented so many things—from a breath of fresh air reaching him in stifling, oppressive surroundings to outsiders with whom he could relate; friends from far away.

We had to get in touch with Viktor, but how? His work called for him to be in his laboratory at the Institute of Normal Physiology on Tuesdays and Thursdays, and we had the phone number to reach him there. It was a Thursday, but previous experience had shown us that the Institute's secretary, Larisa Fyodor, would invariably say, "Comrade Adamenko is out," and promptly hang up. Viktor rarely got any message. We might have to wait until the next day, when his wife, Alla Vinogradova, would be at her school—and by then, we would already be thinking of leaving.

The sweet hot Russian tea gave us a feeling of optimism, and as we were about to return to the Hotel Berlin and begin telephoning, we felt something would happen to help us. It did. We had just passed through the hotel door and were still inside the protective winter glass enclosure up front when we caught sight of a familiar figure. Incredibly, it was Adamenko.

He was standing down below, on the sidewalk, snow flurries dancing in the air. He must have been there for quite some time, because despite the heavy coat he was wrapped in, he looked frozen. His shoulders hunched, a gray rabbit-fur hat with ear flaps over his ears pushed down into his face, he was shuffling his feet in the snow, his arms deep into his pockets. Because of those ear flaps he didn't hear us call out his name, but we came into his field of vision the moment we stepped out the enclosure door.

"Viktor, in God's name, to find you here like this! How did you know . . . Or did you. . . ?"

He stared at us, his eyes growing round with utter astonishment, then his frozen face broke into a wide delighted grin.

"I did not know," he exclaimed sheepishly. "At least not consciously."

"Have you been waiting for anyone in particular?"

"Not really . . ." Then, a twinkle in his eye, "Unless I've been waiting for you? Perhaps . . ." He paused. "ESP?"

"Come on." We tapped him happily on his heavily-upholstered shoulder. Later we conjectured that he may have been waiting for a fellow scientist, perhaps to receive some unofficial papers that make the rounds of Moscow's parapsychology underground. Hand delivery, safer than mail, was an accepted, much used practice among Soviet intellectuals. The bustling, teaming Intourist entrance was a convenient place for such contact.

By then we were already back inside the hotel, waiting for our coffee and cognac. Viktor agreed to give up whatever his plans had been. We briefly filled him in on the circumstances of our arrival. Our heavy coats dumped in a corner, we settled behind one of the square tables facing the glassed-in inner court, its ground covered with snow. We had sat here with Viktor many times before on our previous trip. It felt as though we had never left.

"Gotovo" Anna called out, meaning "Come and get it." She placed coffee and cognac on a tray. At Anna's place you were supposed to serve yourself despite the stiff prices you paid in foreign currency, be it for an ordinary coffee or an improvised sandwich. She deftly picked up the twenty dollar bill. There would be no change. As he poured the cognac, Viktor grinned and said, "There must be something I can do to help you. Right?"

Right—but before we got down to our long list of questions we had prepared while still in America, questions we needed answered to complete our files on Soviet parapsychology today, we had to fire the one question that troubled us most: Why had we been allowed to gain access to the most intimate secrets of Soviet psychic research? Was there nothing unusual about that—had others been given the same facilities?

Viktor shook his head. "Nothing unusual about it?" he repeated. "Hell, you know and I know how unusual it all was. I hope you realize you have done the impossible. No one—and I mean *no one* coming from the outside before you, and this includes scientists pure and innocent of propaganda—has been allowed to learn what you have learned. No one has been allowed to talk to the people the way you've been allowed to talk to them. Before meeting you, these people were obviously advised to hold back nothing, to be afraid of nothing, and not to worry that their frankness might be held against them.

"You are the first people from what you call the West to meet the top ranks of our parapsychologists. I have helped, but the bulk of it came your way with approval from above. It could not have been accomplished without that, not in Soviet Russia."

"All right, Viktor, the question still is—why?" we asked pointedly. "We assume that somewhere upstairs your people actually decided to trust us, convinced that we'll tell it as we see it. But why are they letting us do it?"

Adamenko had been contemplating the golden liquid in his glass while listening in silence. We waited. He lifted his eyes and said pensively, "I like to believe that new winds are blowing. The powers that be have not all that much confidence in us yet. We are beginning too great a scientific revolution, too seriously challenging the old and established precepts of physics and the way physics has been taught and understood.

"Although they back our research, they are not yet ready to say, 'We believe in you 100 percent.' We are serious scientists who think we can explain the mysteries of the mind with the help of exact equations—and having done so, proceed to formulate a means to control bio-energy and eventually harness it in an organized way. Not today, not tomorrow, but within a foreseeable future. Beyond this new frontier lies the answer to, and the solution of, such diverse objectives as communications with extraterrestrial civilizations, extension of human life, victory over cancer, victory over blindness. . . ."

He faced us squarely across the table. His eyes were firm. This was his vision. Suddenly, a fleeting half-smile crossed his handsome face.

"As for you, gentlemen, let me advance the theory that they want to know how far we the scientists have gone in comparison to the rest of the world by allowing you to collect the data, publish it in the West, and see what the reaction is. They will be watching carefully for that. I think they are as curious as you are." Viktor Adamenko raised his glass of cognac and said: "I drink to your success. You have helped us, too, by giving us outlets for the exchange of information that we would not otherwise have obtained. On behalf of my colleagues, then, our thanks."

Thus, we were able to sit down with him, compare notes, and ask questions that needed to be answered to complete our probe. We asked him for and got his guidance on whom else to see during our short stay. He gave us names, arranged for the appointments, and actually sat in on some of the highly unofficial interviews.

What none of us knew or suspected then was that within months, striking events would put our psychic probe into razor sharp focus and a wholly different light.

Part One

EXTRAORDINARY INDIVIDUALS

1.

BORIS ERMOLAEV, THE RUSSIAN CHALLENGE TO URI GELLER

The office of Luisa Georgyevna Nikitina of the foreign affairs department of *Literary Gazette* was at the far end of a long, poorly-lit dingy corridor on the top floor of a down-at-the-heels Moscow building. It was small, its walls badly in need of a repapering job, the furnishings sparse even by Soviet standards. But it had a visitors' corner of sorts—a low table with a few wooden chairs around it—making Nikitina's an obvious place to welcome guests. Much to our surprise, she was young and rather attractive, although she made little of her good looks.

This occasion was our first visit to the weekly newspaper that had set out to do a hatchet job on Russia's own psychics—especially on its telepathists—and was primarily responsible for Soviet parapsychologists' loss of face at home. While still in America, we had heard about the *Literary Gazette*'s own experiments in the area of parapsychology. We decided to find out what this baiting was all about. Had the paper really managed to discredit Russian telepathists by, for instance, "disproving" beyond a shadow of a doubt their claim they could read thoughts at a distance of hundreds of miles? Our request for a meeting had been instantly approved. Obviously, the orders to accommodate us were explicit.

Nikitina's desk was dominated by a giant old-fashioned typewriter of the kind long extinct in the United States but still very much in use in the Soviet Union. She rose from behind it and motioned us to meet her colleagues Efim Demoushkin and Viktor Ladyshev, both of the science department.

We had made it a point to be exactly on time, having learned from previous experiences that it was expected of us, and of them. The two men had beaten us to the time clock in a similar endeavor to be on time. This is the game you have to play in the Soviet Union: kill each other with precision. Both sides pretend that punctuality is an integral part of their existence. It is only after you miss out once or twice, they being late and in return you being late, that you know rapport has been established. You are friends—friends can afford to be late.

The two men, wearing business suits and ties, jumped to their feet, bland expressions on their faces. "We had been talking about you," she said, trying out a thin smile. It was very formal. We shook hands and sat down.

After the preliminary introductions we fully expected a polite clash. But on that gray, raw morning in Moscow, we hardly suspected that the very government newspaper picked to attack Soviet psychic researchers would help us find Russia's most exciting psychic, whose incredible powers made him possibly the greatest in the entire world—the Soviets' answer to Uri Geller, the West's most famous psychic.

Luisa Georgyevna said pleasantly, "I suppose you'll want to meet Boris Ermolaev?"

"Boris who?"

"Obviously you haven't heard of him. A very remarkable man. Lifts people and keeps them in midair with sheer willpower. We suggested to him we would invite leading physicists to our office so he could demonstrate his amazing powers to them and we, in turn, would write about it. But he turned us down. He said he could do it only in a setting of a home or a club, like our Cinema Club. So, no test so far. We may do it yet. In the meantime, we're reserving our judgment."

"It all started at this very club," said one of the two men. He was the one who identified himself as Ladyshev—studious, in his thirties, rather nondescript in appearance. "I was attending the screening of a movie in the main projection room," he said, visibly warming up to the fascinating recollection, "when a young fellow rushed in, all excited, calling out loud, 'Ermolaev has just suspended Shipikhina in midair and she is up there right now, floating.'

"I'll never forgive myself for not dashing out to see the famous woman film director float in midair. But others did, and they said they actually caught her slowly descending to the divan in the reception room where it all took place. Apparently she agreed to the experiment after he threw a handful of rice into the air. It formed a floating ball which remained suspended for maybe half a minute before falling apart again. To all intents and purposes, the rice had become a miniature planet held together by its own gravitational force.

"As I said, I didn't see it myself, but others did and swore to it. Very soon all of theatrical Moscow was talking about it," Ladyshev smiled. Anticipating our question, he added, "This was several years ago."

Did this Ermolaev live in Moscow?

"Oh, yes," Luisa Georgyevna said cheerfully. "He is a noted film director."

We vowed then and there to find him, First, we requested Yuri Shevyakov our Novosti "aide-de-camp," to scrounge up photocopies of Soviet articles on Ermolaev going back quite a few years. These included full interviews and descriptions of his amazing feats from scientific journals. Viktor Adamenko and others contributed invaluable background information. We also sought information in Moscow's theatrical circles. After all, wouldn't these men and women be closer to a film director than anyone else?

Another well-known scientist, Genady Sergeyev, who holds a doctor of engineering degree and is a consultant mathematician at various Leningrad institutes, met Ermolaev both at home in Leningrad, where Ermolaev spent his youth, and in Moscow. He told us that the extremely talented Ermolaev learned the film business from the ground up and is considered one of Russia's most imaginative young directors. He was currently doing a film *Oblomov* based on the classic novel by Nikolai Goncharov. According to Sergeyev—and Ermolaev later confirmed this himself—he won't do his "mind over matter" feats on stage, nor will he take money for any demonstrations. He will show his unique talents only to serious scientists of his own choosing, or to close friends.

Sergeyev, who has also experimented with Ermolaev, confirmed, "He has the unusual ability of concentrating his energy into a focal point in midair and causing objects to be suspended in the air for many seconds."

Added Viktor Adamenko, "I am familiar with Ermolaev's work with Prof. Venyamin Pushkin, in which he demonstrated his ability to suspend objects in midair. These were carefully controlled tests. Pushkin is a highly respected scientist. Every precaution was taken to ensure that the experiments were scientifically sound. There is no doubt that Ermolaev has remarkable abilities."

Prof. Pushkin is a psychology professor at Moscow University, where he has conducted carefully controlled, government-authorized experiments on Ermolaev. Just as we arrived, he contracted pneumonia and, during the entire length of our stay, was recuperating at a rest home for scientists outside Moscow. As a result we were prevented from seeing him—much to Ermolaev's dismay. He sincerely wanted us to meet Pushkin. Still, we read Pushkin's articles on Ermolaev and we met other scientists who were familiar with his abilities.

"There actually are people," Pushkin wrote in an authoritative monthly, "who possess the capacity of influencing objects so that they remain suspended in midair. I have witnessed Ermolaev suspend objects in midair. I believe that this man is capable of creating a magnetic field that defies gravity."

The tests Pushkin conducted took place in laboratories at Moscow University in 1973 and 1974, with full government approval. In an official report published later, Pushkin said that he started up each experiment with Ermolaev by going through warm-up exercises designed to put the subject in a state of high tension. Ermolaev held his hands over playing cards lying face down and correctly called out their suits and values. Then Ermolaev moved objects on the table in front of him without touching them. Only after this came the most important part of the experiment with "target" objects that included a Ping-Pong ball, a box of matches, and several pencils.

In his article, Pushkin matter-of-factly described what happened: "Ermolaev took an object in his hands, pressed it between his outstretched hands, then slowly moved his hands apart. The object remained hanging in midair. He continued to move his hands till each palm was about eight inches clear of the object. It remained in midair for a number of seconds."

Ivan Guderman, science editor of the newspaper *Evening Sverdlosk*, published in the Ural city of that name and noted for its contribution to psychic research, was a witness to some of the 1973 experiments. He gave a graphic account: "The room is empty except for a table in the middle. On it, a Ping-Pong ball, a box of matches, and several pencils. A man walks into the room, stops in front of the table, stretches out his hand, freezes, but by the expression on his face, by the tension of his body, one knows that he just doesn't stand there, that he is working. A minute goes by, another. Suddenly the ball is jerked from its position and is rolling off the table. The box is moving also, as though sliding across the surface of the table. The pencils seem to have lost their gravity and have risen into the air."

What is the secret of Ermolaev's strange power? Pushkin postulated that one hypothesis to explain his ability was connected with static electricity. In essence, it was assumed that electrical charges affected the object in the vicinity of the human hand, and moved the object or caused it to be suspended. After further experiments with Ermolaev, however, Pushkin concluded that the unusual effect could not be produced by static electricity. "I then considered the theory of one of our scientists, A. P. Dubrov. Its essence is that living systems are capable of originating and receiving gravitational waves. To accept this, one must accept the most unusual assumption that man is able to give birth to a gravitational field and then, with its help, affect surrounding objects. I was able to cross-check this theory with the strong evidence offered in the experiments with Ermolaev."

The noted scientist concluded—although stressing that it was still theoretical—that the demonstrations by Ermolaev were brought about by the creation of gravitational fields! He added: "The tradition of science invokes certain taboos in areas that deal with a violation of fundamental laws of nature. The ability of man to affect objects near him is still considered by numbers of scientists as something pertaining to violation of the basic laws of nature. However, what is essential and should be stressed time and time again is that the feats of moving and suspending objects in air—with all their unusual and mind-boggling aspects—do not contradict the existing framework of physics.

"As for the future," he added significantly, "one should first accept the difficulties and face them squarely. One should not be afraid of the new facts and complicated problems. In our world of jet planes and atomic reactors, there still remains much to be identified. And it is the role of science to keep uncovering the secrets of the world."

The Pushkin report on Ermolaev and his abilities was confirmed by Doctors of Science V. P. Zinchenko, A. N. Leontyev, B. F. Lomov, and A. R. Luria, all members of the Soviet Academy of Sciences, who signed their names to his report. Their findings were published in *Questions of Philosophy,* a scientific magazine, in 1973.

Pushkin reported further experiments on Ermolaev in the newspaper *Trud* in February of 1974:

"I witnessed Ermolaev holding many different objects between his hands, lifting them one by one into midair. It appears that the actual weight of these objects does not matter. It would appear to take the same exertion on Ermolaev's part.

"During one experiment, Ermolaev enlisted the help of his friend,

Maxim Zhukov. By having Zhukov hold a hand above his own hands, as if topping off the object, Ermolaev was able to keep the object in midair for a longer period of time.

"It was as if the object was hanging from a string on Zhukov's hands. But of course, there was no string involved. The experiments were conducted under the strictest controls, and no devices of any kind were used.

"At the beginning of this experiment, Ermolaev was very nervous, showing little confidence in himself, and objects stayed in midair only a second or two. He then demanded absolute quiet, showed a great deal of concentration, and went on finally to regain his confidence. With that, the objects remained longer in midair.

"My conclusion is that the field created by the subject is easier to control when the object is flat. Ermolaev can obviously defy gravity. Obviously, a very special gravity existed in these experiments, and it is not subject to Newton's Law of Gravity. It is something quite different."

Pushkin confirmed his findings again in a 1974 report in *Technology and Science*. He stated that he had been able to verify some of the most remarkable phenomena applied to "what is called parapsychology." As a result of some "very thoughtful, thorough investigations," Pushkin wrote that he had come to the conclusion that many quite unbelievable reports are true.

His examination of conditions surrounding the experiments with Ermolaev showed that his ability totally depended on his mental state, including the attitude of his audience. Each of the experiments caused Ermolaev considerable emotional stress. He fainted on several occasions and on others felt sick.

"The two elements—the fact that very few people have such unusual abilities and that they have problems in retaining full control over themselves —could be used by skeptics to deny the scientific substance of these phenomena," Pushkin wrote. "This, of course, would be totally unfair. It merely means that science has as yet no way to explain fully these mysteries of life. We have merely opened one little door into the micro-world of biological systems."

By the time we first met Boris Ermolaev, therefore, we already knew he was a living legend, a truly superb psychic with amazing abilities. But it wasn't so easy for us to get to him, or to persuade him to talk.

First, we put out official word through Novosti that we would like to meet him. Then we put out the same message through the parapsychology grapevine in Moscow. We were promised action by the latter.

The Soviets don't believe in phone directories, so unless people want you to know their phone numbers, they are to all intents and purposes protected from unfamiliar callers. The phone numbers, in effect, are unlisted. Two days after our request a telephone number of a friend was almost casually passed on to us over dinner at the National Hotel, which once catered to Russian nobility and later to Lenin, who actually lived there during the Revolution. The National had become our second base because it had the best meals in town. We called as suggested, and were given Ermolaev's own number.

We then reached him, only to be told politely that he would meet us, if we could prove that we had official clearance. Apparently we were one jump ahead of Novosti, because when we called there to request that they contact Ermolaev at the number we gave them, we were told that they had already talked to him and that everything was fixed. Five days later we had the first of two long interviews with the incredible Ermolaev.

We met in the lobby of the Intourist Hotel. We knew we would recognize him and we did. Smallish of build, he stood out in the milling crowd of foreign tourists and foreign businessmen with a sprinkling of Muscovites. The forceful face had to belong to someone unusual. His light-blue eyes were studying the crowd with a look of superiority and conde-scension. Ermolaev has incredible eyes—almost magnetic, constantly alert. Above all, there is no doubt that he possesses some kind of psychic power. It oozes out of him. He is surrounded by an aura of mystery. That day, as he talked to a bearded, heavyset man by his side, his fine, articulate hands appeared to be in constant motion. The moment our eyes met we knew we had the right man.

"So you are Gris and Dick," Ermolaev greeted us. Then, turning to the bearded man, he said, "I told you in the car something was wrong with Gris's arm, but I didn't know which. It's the right one."

"Yes, you said just that," the bearded man confirmed, introducing himself as scriptwriter Viktor Gorokhov. "I write stories," he explained, "but I also speak English. Borya doesn't." He was using a diminutive form of "Boris" which the Russians do to denote close friendship. In turn, Ermolaev called his friend "Vitya" instead of Viktor.

What was that about Gris's arm?

"Borya said that Gris has a bad arm. He said that on our way over. I can swear to that." The arm they were referring to was indeed limited in its usefulness, the result of an old injury. But how did he know?

"He knows," Gorokhov shrugged. "He spoke to Gris by phone, didn't he? He senses. It's his special ESP."

"Don't ask me how I do it," Ermolaev said. "I feel it. I know when a person is not well without asking. And I know when a man is wrong, thinking it's his heart when it's really his kidneys.

"There was this director from the Leningrad studios whom I met here not long ago. I looked at him and said, 'You better have a blood test.'

" 'Why?' he protested. 'I'm as healthy as a horse!'

" 'Have it done!' He did, and called Viktor to say, 'You know, Ermolaev was right? I have diabetes.' How could I tell? I don't know. Something clicks in me."

The two men had arrived in Ermolaev's flashy yellow Fiat sports car, quite a sight for Moscow. He left it in front of the Intourist and we walked to the National down the street, to have lunch in the seclusion of the small and dignified second-floor foreign currency dining room. He was visibly pleased to meet newspapermen from abroad. As we walked down Gorky Street, we tried to appraise him. Our first impression was of a dynamic, highly nervous personality, full of theatrical gestures which he used to demonstrate and underline the points he wanted to make.

As he moved upstairs to the dining room we kept watching him, fascinated by his behavior pattern. He was aware of it, and it pleased him. "I'm sorry I can't demonstrate my abilities to you right here and now," he said, "but if one of you has a headache, I'll fix it." Indeed, later, we would take him up on that.

"I can 'see' colors with the tips of my fingers," he said at one point during the meal. "For instance, my fingers tell me that the felt under this tablecloth is brown. I admit it doesn't prove anything. I could have noticed it the last time I was here although I assure you I didn't." For the record, the felt *was* brown, and on the table next to it, it was green.

Then Viktor settled back to exercise his excellent English and, his voice booming across the room, he told us this remarkable story:

Ermolaev loves driving fast cars—it's his way of relaxing. He has been doing so for the last eighteen years. Back in 1968, he was involved in a head-on collision with a cement truck. Thrown clear of his car, he landed unhurt forty-five feet away. His car was a total wreck. The police called him in for an investigation. He was a suspect along with the truck driver, who swore it wasn't his fault.

"The moment Borya sat down opposite the police inspector," Viktor related with obvious glee, "he knew that for some reason the inspector didn't like him. He felt he had better do something quickly to make the man become more friendly. But how? Then he caught sight of a pencil holder full of colored pencils standing on the man's desk. So, as the man wrote out his report, Borya concentrated on the pencils.

"The circumstances were conducive to telekinesis. The room was quiet, the windows shaded, and a fluorescent light in the ceiling was giving out a soothing hum. Borya put out his hand as though holding something invisible and concentrated. Suddenly the pencils rose, one by one, floating upwards out of the container, and began moving through the air forming pretty colored patterns.

" 'He'll enjoy that!' Borya thought. But the man kept writing. Ten, twenty seconds went by and Borya was tiring. He couldn't keep the pencils suspended in midair much longer.

"It was then that the inspector looked up and saw the pencils floating in the air in front of him. He turned to Borya and said in an annoyed voice, 'You there. Stop fooling around, will you?'

"And as he said it, and Borya cringed, the pencils came crashing down. Onto the desk, the floor. 'Pick them up,' the inspector said. 'Yes, comrade,' Borya replied, totally crushed. He went down on his hands and knees, collected the pencils and gingerly put them back into the container."

"There is a postscript," Ermolaev said triumphantly. "The inspector had decided not to like me. But he concluded he had no case against me."

Each of our two lunches lasted a couple of hours, much to the barely suppressed annoyance of the headwaiter, personally serving us special

Soviet-style delicacies. As far as he was concerned, enough was enough. But we frankly, could not tear ourselves away from the man. And indeed, Ermolaev's life story is as dramatic as the image he presents.

We already knew that he was born thirty-eight years ago in Alma-Ata, the city in Central Asia where Leon Trotsky was once exiled by Stalin. We theorized that Boris's father, Dr. Vladimir Ermolaev, may have landed in Alma-Ata under similar auspices. Eventually he was allowed to return and settle down in Leningrad.

He recalled that he had his abilities from a very early age. When he was very young, living in Alma-Ata in Kazakhstan, he would go for long periods without food. He was never hungry. His father, a doctor and professor of medical sciences, kept a careful check on his health but found nothing wrong with son Boris. He developed well physically, although the main part of his diet was a lot of cool, clear water. "Another unusual thing about me was that I had a strange fascination with spiders—even poisonous spiders—and kept them as pets. But they never harmed me.

"I remember when I was about three years old," Ermolaev recounted, conjuring up images from his childhood, "I was given a toy elephant with mechanical legs. My father had already wound it up. Its legs were moving when he handed it to me—but as soon as I touched it, it stopped moving, although it hadn't wound down and was not broken! I clearly remember the surprise on my father's face."

As a young boy, Borya did not yet have the powers to suspend objects in midair. His parents treated him like a normal child and he did not fully realize his remarkable abilities until 1967, when he went to a party in Leningrad. "It's a cute story," he said. "I was staying with my parents when one day the phone rang and a man whom I barely knew called to say there was this party going at his home, and why don't I join them? I said, 'All right,' hung up the receiver, came down, jumped into my car, and drove off.

"I had a friend along, who later corroborated the story to Professor Pushkin. We arrived outside a building and went up the stairs. I had already pressed the bell at the door of one apartment when my friend said, 'Borya, how did you know where to go?' I suddenly realized I didn't have the address. 'Let's go,' I said, and turned to run down when the door opened and a man said, 'Come in. Where are you going?'

"He was the man who had invited us. I told him what had happened and he shrugged, 'Happens all the time. Even if I gave you the address,' he added, 'you wouldn't have found the place the conventional way—the building is being repainted. Can't you see? All the signs, street number, apartment numbers have been removed.'

"The party turned out to be a bore and I was about to leave when the host came up to me and said, 'Let me show you something.' With that he picked a half-open chrysanthemum out of a vase, held it up with both hands, removed his hands, and the flower remained hanging in the air. He said, 'Keep watching.' Suddenly the flower came alive and its curled-up petals straightened out, opening fully.

"In total awe, I complimented him. 'That's nothing,' he said, 'you should see my sister self-levitate.' He introduced me to her, a fat, ugly girl. 'Will you show me?' I asked her. 'I will,' she said, 'but no other audience.' With that she led me into the bedroom next door, stood up on a couch—it sank in under her weight—and she squinted her tiny eyes. Suddenly the couch straightened out under her feet, and then she rose, like a balloon, into the air. She stopped about two feet up. The only thought that crossed my mind was, 'How ugly she is!' then she came down back onto the couch, and I left the room without saying a word. I was stupefied. I asked my host, 'Is your whole family this way?'

"He shrugged, 'Maybe.'

"For the next two weeks I kept coming back to him to see how he was doing it, and to pick up a hint or two. He was an engineer at the waterworks, a lousy one at that, and when I told him he would do much better on the stage showing off his remarkable ability, he eagerly agreed. Since I belong to the theatre, I took him to the right people. At the government talent booking agency, they watched him levitate things, and their comment was 'No one will see it beyond the second row. Now if he could raise and float, say, a large wardrobe full of clothes, that would be different. But this? Sorry, no. Not interested.'

"He was heartbroken. Soon after he quit the waterworks and left Leningrad. I never heard from him again. His name was Senya and my adventure with him is documented. His last name? Let's say I don't remember."

Still, Senya played a decisive role in young Ermolaev's life. Because on the day Ermolaev went home having said goodbye to the man for the last time, he sat down at a table, concentrated on a heavy cigarette box, and with great satisfaction watched it float into midair. From then on, he spent all his spare time, much of it alone, developing his powers.

We specifically asked him about the Pushkin experiments. Ermolaev speaks fast and well. He explained that Pushkin's approach was very scientific. "In order to do it one must be mentally isolated from all other things. You can't be thinking of something else when you are trying to suspend an object in midair. Pushkin, at his laboratory, was able to provide the right conditions of isolation. In one experiment, he attached an electroencepholograph machine to my head. When I was not concentrating, there was a steady beep. When I was concentrating, there was a very fast 'beep, beep, beep.' "

Finally facing him, we were haunted by the report that the dainty body of a famous international film star had slowly risen from a divan to float in midair under Ermolaev's concentrated gaze. "Many people have told me of the levitation of the actress," Viktor Adamenko told us. "The people who witnessed it are solid and upstanding citizens." According to accounts, he kept the woman in midair for some twenty seconds, then gently let her down again. Several people we found and interviewed had attended the party for theatrical people in a Moscow apartment and saw it with their own eyes.

One of the guests at the party was Boris Groshikov, a leading dancer with the Bolshoi theater ballet. "I was there and saw Ermolaev perform the levitations," he said. "I could not believe my eyes, but it happened. The woman was motionless, but floating two feet above the sofa. She left no indentation on the surface of the sofa. We were all around Ermolaev and the woman, as close as we wanted to be. The people at the party included some of the top people of stage and screen in this country. There was no trick. We were not hypnotized, there were no ropes or mirrors. We were not fooled. It was a spontaneous demonstration."

Although Ermolaev himself would not name the actress involved—she had left Moscow for Paris, her actual home—we had no difficulty in identifying her. But for several reasons, we have agreed not to reveal her name. "I was demonstrating my power to make things hang in midair," Ermolaev explained, "when she asked me if I could lift her. She was with her husband, who was cool to her demand. I had never done anything like this before. But she kept on asking, and I finally agreed to do it.

"She was so light that I could have lifted her *physically*. That is very important in leviation. You must know that you can physically lift the object. I can't make houses float in midair; it has to be something fairly light. I told the actress to lie down, because somehow I knew that she would have to be in a horizontal position to levitate. I was right. I've had several experiments with others since, but I usually fail when I try to float people standing up. Apparently this is very difficult. And on this occasion, improvising as I went, I tried to imagine that in fact she was not lying down, but was over my head, as though the ceiling was the floor, and that I was holding her up—that I was keeping her from falling.

"I concentrated on this. My hands were about two feet above her at all times. When she moved upwards, my hands maintained the two-foot distance. Although I was later told that I appeared to be pressing down with my hands, all that was in my mind was that I was supporting her. It is reverse thinking."

Ermolaev demonstrated to us, without a body, how he did it. His face contorted, the muscles standing out in his face and on the back of his hands, pressing downwards with his hands outstretched. Although the effort and energy appeared to be going downward, it was easy to imagine that he was using all his strength to hold up some great weight.

"Slowly she moved up from the sofa. I held her there for as long as I could. But in my mind, I became too tired holding up her weight. I had to drop her. She sank slowly back onto the sofa. At no time did I touch her. I was standing close to the sofa. Afterwards, she did not feel anything unusual."

Later, Groshikov confirmed the details of the event as described by Ermolaev, adding, "At the same party, I saw Ermolaev lift a chair into midair again, using only his powers of concentration. It rose about two feet from the floor, and hung there for at least ten seconds. He also experimented with a spray of carnations, which he had floating in midair for something like thirty seconds!"

Ermolaev's friend, Viktor, threw in an additional thought, "I do not consider this is purely a modern phenomenon. I believe, for instance, that Jesus Christ had such powers." Viktor went on to tell us how one day when he was feeling terribly ill, Ermolaev told him to lie down, then passed his hands close to him, without touching.

"I started to feel warm. Although I was not sleepy, I fell asleep. When I woke up, I felt like a new man, full of energy. Borya explained he had merely concentrated his mind on making me well, and that he had convinced me to take a short nap. Whatever happened, within minutes he had removed my sickness. Borya is like a benevolent vampire—not sucking out the blood, but mentally sucking out the poisons from your body."

Later, up in our Intourist room, he cured Gris of a headache in five minutes. He did it by touching the top of Gris's head, his fingers ostensibly digging deep, fingernails and all, into the back of the skull, as though to remove the pain. Actually he barely touched Gris, but his treatment was very effective.

As a result of repeated reports of Ermolaev's healing power, a well-known Moscow immunologist is now conducting tests on the amazing psychic. He wants his ability analyzed because he feels that once they solve the mystery of his power, they will be able to help other people.

Already the Pushkin tests on Ermolaev were familiar to all of the more than forty scientists whom we talked to on parapsychology. In Moscow, physicist Adamenko commented, "We are used to the unusual in our work, but even we found the results of the Pushkin experiments very exciting." And Sergeyev's comments on Ermolaev were based on tests done by famous Leningrad scientist Leonid Vasiliev, who is now dead. "These tests under laboratory conditions," Sergeyev said, "clearly showed Ermolaev can suspend objects in midair using only the unknown forces of his mind."

He told us, "The fact that it is still difficult to explain this phenomenon fully does not mean that one should negate it. It is the duty of scientists to explore it, to understand it, then explain it. If we have so far not been able to do this, it does not mean that the phenomenon does not exist. As far as I am concerned, it does exist. We have no reason to doubt Professor Pushkin. In fact, in my opinion, Ermolaev has not yet fully developed his abilities, great as they already are."

The flamboyant Ermolaev ended our interviews with a challenge. "I want to meet your Uri Geller to prove who is the better psychic," he told us.

"I have read a lot about him, particularly, how he is your leading psychic. Like Geller, I can levitate objects, I can make them hang in the air, I can read people's minds, I can bend spoons and forks. But I do these things better.

"I don't make a spectacle out of it, and I do not make money out of it, as Geller does. Geller should not be using these powers for commercial purposes. This is a serious subject. It must be treated scientifically. Scientists are studying me to see what they can learn about the human body and mind. That is what should be done. I believe that every man is capable of developing the powers that I have and that science should be able to find out what creates this power. Science has the possibility of discovering something to benefit all mankind. I want to meet Geller to prove I am better. I do not consider him unusual, but by showing I am better, I will help science, which will take the study of this phenomenon more seriously."

When we returned to the United States, we passed Ermolaev's challenge on to Geller, then on a visit to New York. "I've never heard of Ermolaev. I'd like to meet him," he replied, "but I'm neither accepting nor turning down his challenge. I don't care if he says his powers are greater. I don't have to prove anything to anyone."

Sadly, we had to write Ermolaev and tell him it looked unlikely that his challenge would ever be taken up.

2.
TOFIK DADASHEV, SUCCESSOR TO WOLF MESSING

Time and again the standing-room-only audience cheered its appreciation as the dapper man on stage performed astonishing feats of mind reading and thought transference. His small, piercing eyes flashing commandingly from a narrow, ascetic face, he appeared in full control of his audience. The wiry, gray-haired performer could apparently do no wrong.

This was Wolf Messing, the world-famous mentalist whose skill had baffled and impressed even the cynical, egocentric Josef Stalin. Messing was on the road, giving a regular mind reading performance. Aging, but still at the peak of his powers, he looked slightly contemptuous as he correctly answered every challenge hurled at him from the audience. But that night, in the cold drab auditorium of the Radio Technological Institute in Kiev, there was one member of the audience who was not overawed by the great Messing.

Standing alone at the back of the hall was a handsome, raven-haired youth whose face was intent and brooding. He neither cheered nor applauded as his smoldering eyes followed the mentalist's every movement. When the performance was over, he did not wait for the overcrowded bus, but impatiently walked all the way home to tell his uncle, "I've just seen Messing. He is fantastic. But you know what? Whatever he can do, I can do, too."

The year was 1966. Tofik Dadashev was staying with his uncle while attending the Kiev Radio Institute. He was planning to become a radio engineer. But his destiny was sealed when he watched the only performance Messing gave in Kiev. Then and there, the 19-year-old youth from the Caucasus made up his mind to concentrate on the work that came so easily to him and that fascinated him so much. He wanted to probe into the minds of people—and be acclaimed better than Wolf Messing.

By the time we arrived in Moscow, Tofik Dadashev was well on his way to achieving his ambition. Messing had died only months earlier at 75, felled by a fatal stroke as he lived out his lonely last years in a three-room apartment—large by Soviet standards—that had been assigned to him by the city of Moscow for his "accomplishments on the stage," a decorated "Meritorious Artist" of the Soviet Union.

Only two weeks before he died, he had given a lengthy interview to a senior editor of the Novosti Press Agency. Ironically, the man whose incredible abilities had enabled him to predict the exact day the war against the Nazis would end had no premonition of his own death. Dadashev had already donned the mantle of the Soviets' top mentalist before Messing's death. We had not heard of him before our visit, but at our frequent meetings with scientists concerned with parapsychology we constantly were told of the amazing powers of the young wizard from Azerbaijan. Within hours of landing on Soviet soil he had become a top candidate for an interview.

Immediately, we asked our hosts at Novosti to set it up. From earlier experience in the Soviet Union, we had learned never to waste time. Almost as quickly, we were told it would not be possible. During our stay, Dadashev was on tour. He would be thousands of miles away, forever on the go.

We would not give up. At every opportunity, we expressed our disappointment. "If we can't meet him face-to-face, at least give us his phone number," we demanded. Back came the answer: That wasn't the way things were done in the Soviet Union, and, in any case, they didn't have a phone number.

We would shake our heads in disbelief. That was how it was done in the Western world, and why were they—pardon us—so inefficient? Surely they knew a way to find him? But the answer remained an adamant *"nyet"*—no Dadashev.

Then late one night a secretive phone call to our hotel from a government scientist conveyed to us invaluable information: Dadashev's roots were in Baku, the capital of Azerbaijan on the Caspian Sea. He had an uncle who lived down there, who, unlike the majority of Soviet citizens, had a telephone, not just a party line—an encouraging circumstance that could lead to something. The man didn't spell out what this something could be. "Just be patient," he advised.

The following evening, over drinks with our friends in the foreign currency bar at the old National Hotel down the street from the Intourist, the bartender slipped us a folded piece of paper. On it was a phone number in Baku and a name: Eduard Minasov.

The message, however circuitous, was obvious. Although the official response from Novosti was still "no Dadashev," we realized our persistence, our repeated barbs about Western efficiency, had paid off. Without losing face, officialdom had given in, and a top-level decision had been made to let us get the information we wanted.

True, there was a vague possibility that the anonymous source was someone wanting to help us by sticking his neck out. But we would soon know, for sure. In the Soviet Union, even now, it is not wise to talk to strangers from the capitalist world unless one has explicit instructions to do so. If Eduard Minasov talked to us, it would mean he had been given clearance to talk to strangers. If he refused, saying that he had never heard of us and "Please leave me alone," we would know there was no official approval.

We went back to our hotel, dialed the regional operator handling connections with the south of Russia, requested, "Baku 96-87-42, Eduard Minasov. Urgent." We identified ourselves and our whereabouts, settled back, and waited. An hour later our phone rang. A friendly voice said, "Yes, this is Eduard Minasov. I expected to hear from you. How can I help you?"

He had been advised, all right. We were in the clear.

It was thus that we caught up with Tofik Dadashev, who actually was on tour and at this very moment was giving a "concert" in Dushanbe, a city of some 400,000 people, astride the Pamir mountain plateau next to China in the Central Asian Region of the Soviet Union. This was not Tofik's first visit there, his uncle said proudly, nor would it be his last. According to Eduard Minasov, who watches over his extraordinary nephew from the old family home, Tofik takes his bag of miracles wherever he is told to go. His employer, the uncle explained, is a giant government agency called Goskonzert (an abbreviation for State Concert).

We had suspected as much, and as it happened, we had been in touch with Goskonzert while trying to determine whether Tofik worked for them. Goskonzert rules over the professional and personal destinies of some 9,000 traveling entertainers from singers and ballet dancers to clowns, high-wire acrobats, and mentalists such as Tofik. Young and old, liking it or hating it, they go on tours—alone, in pairs, in groups. From Goskonzert's base of operations in Moscow, featuring giant maps of the Soviet Union with thousands of colored pins stuck all over them to represent the entertainers out in the field, it directs these men and women into every nook and cranny of the Soviet Union—in theaters big and small, concert halls, union halls, workmen's clubs, village halls.

There is no retirement age; the demand for performers is too great. When the age for "retirement" is approached, it is marked by a testimonial event of some kind, and the following day it's business as usual. Not that all are kept busy. Whether they are working or not, all of them—be they opera divas or jugglers—receive wages of between 300 and 400 rubles a month, plus traveling expenses. Curiously, the older prima donnas, their voices creaky with age, are doing as well as their young counterparts, because Russians are sentimental by nature. The old lady onstage brings out floods of nostalgia in the audience, so the old ladies keep touring until the day they die.

Apparently this was the fate that overtook Wolf Messing while well into his seventies, failing in his psychic powers, but forced by Goskonzert to go on. When we asked about Messing's death, the Novosti editor Robert Kyucharyants said candidly, "He told me he was looking forward to many more years of peace and seclusion. He had embraced the loneliness and feebleness of old age and was going to enjoy it. Even though he was still busy working—he was back in Moscow between tours—he told me he wanted to stop giving public performances."

Messing was told in unmistakable terms it was his duty to entertain his public. His title of "Meritorious Artist" accorded him various privileges, from a higher fee to riding by first-class sleeper, and he had to keep earning them. Sadly, Messing, one of the greatest mentalists in the world, a living phenomenon recognized by psychic researchers far beyond the Iron Curtain, never disputed his definition as "concert artist." He had surrendered a long time ago, at the very height of his incredible mental faculties, browbeaten into docility by Stalin, his most important Soviet admirer of the time, during the tragic war and postwar years.

He had never been abroad, perhaps because he was ashamed to be equated with clowns and tightrope walkers. Perhaps the authorities wouldn't let him go for fear he wouldn't come back. He was a lonely man, with no family. Be this as it may, Soviet obituaries called him a brilliant entertainer. No one disputed that. When we asked a Goskonzert official in Moscow if certain scientific values involved in Messing's unexplained abilities had not been worth investigating, the man shrugged an indifferent shoulder.

"What science are you referring to?" he asked, then volunteered the answer, "Surely there isn't any. It's simply good entertainment, yes?"

Eduard Minasov obviously regarded Tofik Dadashev as considerably more than a mere entertainer. "He is having a tremendous success, you know," Minasov proudly told us. "He is getting better with every year. I mean his powers are growing stronger and stronger. He can read minds at much greater distances today then he did, say, a year ago.

"Wolf Grigorievich Messing was incredible, but Tofik Dadashev is already better than Messing was in his heyday. That's why they're keeping him on the road so much. He is fantastic."

These days, Tofik's extensive tours take him from one end of the Soviet Union to the other, 9,000 miles apart. They know him in Riga, Tallinn, and Vilnius on the Baltic, but they also know him in Vladivostok on the Pacific, in Fergan within sight of China, Murmansk beyond the Arctic Circle. Tofik is on the road nine months a year.

From Dushanbe, he was going up into Siberia to perform in Novosibirsk, Irkutsk, Bratsk. The tour would eventually take him back to Moscow, where he now lives alone. "No, no steady girl-friend," his uncle chuckled. "That is the price you pay for being famous." The 8,000-mile tour would have yielded, he figured, some 10,000 spectators. But Minasov discouraged us from going to Dushanbe to catch up with Tofik. "You could miss him," he said solicitously, "and get stranded."

We knew he was right. Even if Novosti reworked our schedule and got us the special visa to the Tadjik Republic, we could get cut off from Moscow while out in that faraway and dusty corner of the Soviet Union. It would be much wiser to accept the telephone number Minasov offered us for Tofik's room in the local hotel in Dushanbe, and to interview Tofik this way. We had already done so with other subjects, getting all we needed.

"Call him in his room after midnight," Minasov said. "If there's no one there, keep calling." As with all Soviet hotels, the one in Dushanbe had yet to learn about the effectiveness of hotel switchboards. Every room had its own outside line.

Afraid that we might never reach Tofik, we asked Uncle Eduard for some data on his nephew's childhood. Suddenly he balked. He had been instructed to be friendly and to help us, but being a proud Azerbaijani, he would go so far and no further in his obedience to a Russian Big Brother. "You tell Tofik," he snapped at us, "and if he says it's all right, I'll tell you all you want." How would he know we were telling the truth? He laughed, softening up again. "Don't worry, I'll have talked to him myself in the meantime."

"Above all don't be shy," Minasov advised. "Keep calling. You'll catch him sometime during the night. Tofik goes to bed late. Like all concert artists, he's a night owl."

To be sure, it was exactly midnight—10 P.M. in Moscow—when the phone rang and the operator said, "We have Tofik Dadashev on the line for you."

A confident young voice came through: "Yes, I can hear you. What can I do for you?" The connection was perfect. We had been given the privileged satellite line. Obviously, instructions had been issued for just that. Dadashev's "What can I do for you?" left little doubt in our minds that he, too, had been advised accordingly.

When we said we'd like to ask him some questions, he immediately replied: "Go ahead." Clearly he already knew about us and our mission. He had been out—had he been working? Yes, he had just finished a performance before 400 people in a local workmen's club in a Dushanbe suburb, he explained pleasantly.

What did he do on this occasion?

"In circumstances like these, with simple, unsophisticated people, I make it easy for them. I let them choose a passage from a magazine, have them put it back on the shelf without my being present. Then I identify the magazine, page and passage. It's very basic, really. There was a time when I needed a lot of concentration, and voice contact with the subject, but by now, I do it without any contact at all."

On stage, he explained, he still wears the black hood or black blindfold that has become his trademark. He requires isolation from his surroundings for mental concentration—hence the hood.

"Two years ago I still needed to be close—within one meter—to the subject as I followed him on the search of the object I was to investigate. Gradually I've been able to increase this distance. Today I remain where I am, following the person totally by thought, only stopping and directing him from as far as he can hear me as he wanders out of the room. Most recently I've started using an intermediary from among the judges chosen from the audience so he can pass on my instructions when the subject gets out of earshot."

"What else can you do today that you were unable to do two years ago?"

"Three years ago, a famous parapsychologist, Genady Sergeyev, suggested that I try reading thoughts by long-distance telephone. I told him I wasn't ready for it yet. Today I am. For instance, I could read your thoughts right now, provided I had your photograph in front of me. At this stage, seeing you, maybe on a television screen, or by means of a photo is imperative to me. Maybe later I won't have to . . ."

"Would you like to try a Moscow-New York experiment, then?"

"I'd be delighted."

"How old are you?"

"I am almost thirty."

"You really think you've not yet reached your full potential?"

"I am sure of that."

"Would you be able to find a missing person, possibly one held captive and sending out mental messages for help?"

There was silence on the other end of the line. We realized we'd touched on something he wasn't supposed to talk about. He cleared his throat, then, hesitantly, "People have come to me for help, but . . . I don't like to get involved in these things. After all, this is not my job. I am a concert artist . . . I belong to the stage. Please," Tofik asked pleadingly, "let's change the subject. . . ."

With that, of course, we knew: He *had* been asked and he *can* do it—presumably with success, otherwise he wouldn't have been so reluctant to talk. There was momentary silence. Then, complying, we changed the subject to tell him about ourselves, our work, our mission, our impressions of Russia. He listened attentively, interjecting questions that showed he was at ease again, and the valuable satellite time ticked away. Under different circumstances an impatient Soviet telephone operator would long since have butted in with an annoyed, "What do you think, comrades, you own the telephone line or something?" There was no interruption. Finally we said, "We want to talk to your uncle and grandmother about your childhood, but Eduard Minasov said we need your permission for that."

"You may tell Uncle Eduard that he has my permission," Tofik laughed over in Dushanbe.

It was from his uncle, then, and his grandmother that we learned the story never told before.

Tofik was born in Baku, a large industrial city flanked by oil rigs sunk into the shallow Caspian Sea. His father left his mother after one year of marriage and was never seen again. Neither father nor mother was of Russian blood. Tofik's family on both sides is Azerbaijani, sturdy Caucasian mountain folk akin to Iranians who had spilled into the lowlands and settled there. There are almost as many of them on the Iranian side of the border as on the Soviet side. Tofik was raised by his grandmother, Estera Petrovna Armianski-Grogoryan. His mother, Rosa Bagramovna Dadashev, has not been part and parcel of Tofik's life. In fact, it was grandmother that he called "Mama," and still does. His mother is in Baku, holding down a job, but the family doesn't care to talk about her beyond that.

As a child, Tofik was absentminded, introverted, secretive. "Different," according to grandmother. "We always felt he had some strange hidden powers within him. When he was still very little, I suspected that he was a psychic. In a way, it ran in our family. I had two brothers who were very sensitive, and my own mother and father had the same uncanny ability to anticipate things. Nowadays you call it ESP."

As a young boy, Tofik baffled his uncle and grandmother by showing how he could read their minds. To keep candies from the sweet-toothed Tofik, they would hide them in their home. When they refused to tell him where they were, Tofik would stare at them for a few minutes, then walk to exactly where the candies had been carefully concealed.

"We realized then that he was able to pick up our thought waves," his grandmother said. "But usually, Tofik liked to be alone. He would often sit for hours and brood." When we asked Tofik about his lonely, brooding childhood, he was quick to point out that this was not because he was unhappy. Sitting by himself allowed him to develop his powers of mental concentration. And when he did go out with friends, Tofik quickly found that his mental abilities could come in useful.

Like boys everywhere, he was constantly faced with the problem of not being able to afford the local movie shows. Unlike others, he found a cheap solution. Tofik would lead his friends up to the ticket taker at the local movie house. Then, staring straight into the woman's eyes, he would place in her mind the thought that it would be nice to give some youngsters a break and let them go in for free. Actually, he talked to her about the weather, the price of food, anything except their entry into the theater. And as they chatted amiably, he would watch her nod approvingly at his friends walking in. Then Tofik would salute her with a cheerful "Thank you. Have a nice day" and saunter into the movie for free!

"Not once were we ever stopped!" he chuckled. "I was in complete control of the ticket taker's mind."

When he was in tenth grade, Tofik gave more amazing proof of his incredible powers. He liked the class on Russian literature and admired the woman teacher. But, as in any other classroom in the world, time can drag.

One day in the hot, stuffy Baku classroom, Tofik found that the impeccable speech of the teacher was beginning to grate on his nerves. She was so precise, so self-assured, so exact in her delivery. Tofik found himself mischievously thinking: "Get confused, get confused." He repeated the phrase in his mind, looked intently at the woman, and consciously tried to beam the phrase at her.

Suddenly, the monotonous drone of the matronly teacher began to change. She began to stutter. She became very upset, and stuttered more. "She could not even finish sentences!" Tofik remembered. He stopped beaming the "Get confused" thought message at her. The teacher stopped stuttering, but the experience had so unnerved her that she quickly dismissed the class.

Tofik felt terribly ashamed at what he had done. But how could he explain to her that *he* had caused her temporary breakdown? There was no way she could understand. "I could not tell her," he confided. "To this day I am still ashamed. That has been my punishment, to know I had done such an awful thing to this poor woman."

Even more convinced of his powerful abilities, Tofik felt he could not discuss them with adults until he himself fully understood how to use them. Through concentration and various secret experiments, he began to train himself.

One of the few places the adolescent boys of Baku could gather was the local billiard hall. There was always some small-stake wagering on the outcome of the games going on among the boys. Like the others, Tofik risked his meager pocket money, sometimes winning, sometimes losing.

Then a newcomer started playing in the hall. Tofik got his first introduction to a poolhall hustler. The newcomer lost a few games for small stakes, but never lost when risking larger bets. "He was really like a professional taking on amateurs," Tofik recounted. "He could win when he chose. What made me really angry was that he would gloat over his successes."

One day Tofik decided to punish the hustler. As he watched him play, he settled himself quietly in a corner and concentrated his mind entirely on the hustler's movements. Within minutes, Tofik felt he was mentally playing in the hustler's place. "I then began to order myself to miscue. As soon as I did, the hustler immediately missed his shot! I watched the man get nervous, almost scared, totally unable to understand what was happening to him." The hustler lost the game and his bet, which forced him for the first time grudgingly to pay out a large sum of money. Tofik's was a very private vengeance, because he was still not ready to reveal to adults what he could do.

When Tofik was 15, he went to live with his uncle, Minasov, who had earlier moved to Kiev. He had just graduated from the local Radio Technological Institute when one day posters announced the visit of the famous Wolf Messing.

It was a day that changed Tofik's whole life. As his uncle remembers it, "When Tofik revealed his ambition to me, I already knew he could read minds. He'd demonstrated that he could also influence my mind by directing me to go to various places in the house and bring back certain objects. I had no doubt he could be as great as Messing."

Minasov arranged for local Kiev parapsychologists to test Tofik. Soon the word of Tofik's amazing abilities was spreading along the incredibly fast scientific grapevine that sprawls all over the Soviet Union but always leads back to Moscow.

Typically, before Tofik could even go on stage as Messing's young competitor, he had to take exams before his "peers," Goskonzert-approved magicians, illusionists, prestidigitators. "We are very careful about that," the Goskonzert official explained to us in Moscow. "A mind reader has to be genuine, must not use tricks and deceive the public with false claims."

Called to Moscow from Kiev, Tofik was subjected to tests lasting several days. The first was to transmit thoughts to subjects selected by the panel of judges.

Tofik did that while wearing a black hood over his head so that the subjects could not see his face. The examiners had never watched anything like it! Not even Messing could do what Tofik then did! Invisibly and silently, he caused one subject to sit down on the floor, take off his shoes and tie, dance on his toes. The subject later explained: "Something, a voice from within me told me to do it. I could not disobey the command."

After that came the test of Tofik's ability to read minds. He was brought to a large room and told to pick up an object he was ordered mentally to find. He did. Then came the telephone test: to dial a number and to call by name the person that would answer. He followed the instruction without any hesitation, and was absolutely correct.

On October 21st, 1970, he made his first public appearance, before one of the most critical audiences in all of Moscow, the members of the House of Journalists. More than 1,500 turned out to see "the new Messing." His demonstration was flawless. By then, of course, he was already passed by Goskonzert as well. His career of "concert artist—specialty, mentalist" began when Tofik was twenty-three years old.

Issued a Goskonzert card, he was sent to Byelorussia on his first tour. Despite the triumphant tryout at the House of Journalists in Moscow, the government booking agency wasn't sure Tofik was ready to face large, skeptical audiences.

But Tofik was ready, facing his audiences with a cocky confidence. "Come on, make it real tough on me," he'd call out, then proceed to prove he could do it. His reputation of being a "new Messing" preceded him wherever he went. People flocked to the concert halls where he performed.

Tofik was given his own little apartment in Moscow, and was granted permission to enroll at Moscow University, to study law between tours. He still has the Moscow apartment, visited occasionally by his faithful uncle and doting grandmother, but more often than not, they stay there while Tofik is away on his constant tours.

Here then is a typical Dadashev performance, as described to us by so many eyewitnesses: Tofik appears on stage in a neat dark suit, and with a few words, sets his audience at ease. Then he has a member of the audience tie a blindfold tightly over his eyes and place the black hood over his head. There is no way he can see. More volunteers are called onstage. Tofik exhorts them to "Think . . . concentrate." His hands are outstretched, as if he is attempting to identify invisible mental threads that he can feel in the air.

The audience of about 600 men, women and children watch curiously as Tofik leaves the stage, and—sightless—feels his way up an aisle. Whispers die and the auditorium grows strangely silent as Tofik reaches out and touches the shoulder of an elderly man. He asks the man to return to the stage with him.

The two men quickly join the volunteers on stage. Tofik is still blindfolded and wearing the black hood. Impatiently he tells the volunteer, "I know that I have not yet completed everything. Keep sending me your commands."

Suddenly, decisively, Tofik reaches out and extracts a notebook from the pocket of the old man he had just selected from the audience. Tofik quickly flicks through the book and stops at a page near the end. He hands the open notebook to the volunteer, and then turns to the audience.

"Our volunteer is the son of the elderly man selected to come onstage with me. He mentally commanded me to find his father, take his notebook, and on a certain page select a telephone number that is written there. That number is on line three of the page that I have just pointed out to his son."

Both son and father are stunned. It is obvious that Dadashev is correct. The audience explodes in applause.

But more proof is to come. Before Tofik had begun his performance, a panel of five judges was selected at random from the audience. During his demonstration, the judges have been sitting silently, watching, making sure that no whispers were exchanged between the volunteers and Tofik, and that he did not disturb the blindfold or hood in any way.

Now the foreman of the panel steps onstage and opens up a note the volunteer had given him before meeting Tofik.

"During the interval," the man reads aloud, "I gave my new telephone number to my father, who is in the audience. I want Dadashev to find him, bring him to the stage, take the notebook out of his pocket, open the notebook at the letter 'S' and point to the number."

Tofik had carried out the request to the letter! He had not been asked to read the number, only to point it out! Again the audience breaks into wild applause.

This is only one of many complicated mental feats that Tofik performed that night. And the people of Rostov-on-the-Don still talk about one of Tofik's most remarkable public demonstrations. He stood blindfolded before an audience of nearly 900 people, when a volunteer mentally challenged him to add up the numbers on a passport, a military card, and a travel document concealed on other members of the audience.

After six minutes of total, silent concentration, Tofik announced the number. When the volunteer's three accomplices, all seated in different parts of the room, stood up and totaled up the numbers on their documents, Tofik was proved completely accurate!

Tofik actually prefers these more complicated mental experiments. As he told us, "It becomes more interesting when an intellectual in the audience is mentally beaming instructions to me. Obviously, the complexity of my experiments depends on the mental capacity of the sender. Intellectuals come up with more complicated ideas—and I like these much better." Under strict scientific observation, Tofik has been able to go from order to order, completing as many as 15 complicated instructions sent mentally during a single performance.

From a leading Moscow scientist, we learned that one of Tofik's greatest triumphs was when he was asked to visit a Moscow police headquarters. There, he was ordered to sit down at a table with a stack of 45 photographs and told to find mugshots of three criminals who were being held under lock and key. Reading the thoughts of the police officers standing by his side, Tofik picked out three photographs. These were the men, he said confidently. Then digging into the photos again, he pulled out a fourth and announced: "And this one is being brought in right now."

He was right. The Moscow police were baffled. There was no way he could have recognized the criminals by sight.

Tofik admits that sometimes he fails—usually because the message he receives is scrambled. He also finds mental work more difficult if, for instance, he is near a high-powered radio or television station. Sometimes, other people in the audience try to beam their thoughts at him, making it more difficult for him to receive clearly the commands of his target subject. If he is physically or mentally tired, his ability to carry out complex mental instructions is adversely affected.

His mind also seems to be sharper, more receptive, in the evenings. Tofik believes this is because there is less interference at night. There is less traffic and factories are closed down. Since his success rate is much higher then than during the day, he tries to schedule all serious experiments for the evening.

Tofik trains for his art with the same intensity that an athlete trains for the Olympics. He always eats a light breakfast. Then he heads for the center of whatever city he may be staying in and seeks out the area where the crowds are the thickest. There, strolling around, he practices picking up the thoughts of passersby. In addition, he jogs and exercises to keep in good physical shape and carefully watches his diet. He pays particular attention to exercising his jaw and abdominal muscles and practices proper breathing techniques. And by now in total control of his body, he can assume a state of total catalepsy whenever he wants. His body loses its sensitivity. His muscles contract, his pulse grows weak, he is barely breathing. Experimenters have probed him with needles. He feels no pain. But he is fully aware, and within a matter of seconds he can return his body to total mobility. "I hope it can lead me to new developments in my art," he said.

His only contact with foreign parapsychologists so far was at a Prague conference in 1973 when he demonstrated his prowess. Genady Sergeyev, the Leningrad parapsychologist, was there, and reported later: "Tofik baffled them all. The most remarkable thing that remained unexplained was his ability to read the mind of another person who did not speak Russian. His mind and the other person's mind communicated freely, not only overcoming distance but the language barrier as well. Commanded silently by an English scientist to walk up to a certain man in the second row and to identify him as John, Tofik, who was on stage, smiled, came down, unhesitatingly walked up to the man and said in Russian: 'You are John.' I was present when it happened. Now I know for sure that Tofik does not know a word of English. Apparently, transmitted thoughts use a language of their own."

Robert Kyucharyants, the Novosti Press Agency editor who interviewed Messing two weeks before his death, confirmed the tremendous regard in which Tofik is now held. "Even before Messing's death, our scientists regarded Dadashev as being better—having more amazing powers—than Messing. He has unquestionably now succeeded to Messing's title."

Robert, who has traveled all over the Western world, as well as throughout the Soviet Union, was very impressed by his meeting with the legendary Messing. Living alone and fending for himself, Messing appeared to be in good health right up until the fatal stroke. Kyucharyants quoted him as saying: "I have never been sick in my 75 years of life."

Messing's own story has been told countless times: how he fled his native Poland to escape the wrath of Hitler after forecasting that the Nazi leader would be defeated in a war against Russia and die; how his mental powers were tested by Stalin; how his shows made him a legend in his own lifetime.

Messing explained that one of the secrets of his success as a mentalist was that other people's thoughts became images in his mind. A certain place, a certain action, a certain person—he *saw* them rather than heard them. These images had color and depth.

"We know from studies on the remarkable work of Wolf Messing," wrote Moscow scientist Yuri Filatov, "that he always made a point of either taking his subject by the hand or causing the subject to grab him by the hand. We believe that subconscious muscle movements that accompany human thought played an important part in allowing Messing to read the subject's mind." Indeed, Messing admitted that it was easier for him if he touched his subject, because this helped him separate his thoughts from the extraneous background. But like Dadashev, Messing denied that he read thoughts by studying the barely discernible movements of the facial muscles. As he told Kyucharyants, "It is in fact much easier for me to perform blindfolded, when I don't see the subject or the rest of the audience. The things I see impede my concentration. It's also easiest to read the thoughts of the deaf and dumb—I perceive them more vividly and distinctly."

Messing did not claim to be a faith healer, but on many occasions he relieved headaches by touching the afflicted person's temples lightly with his fingertips. He could also correctly diagnose disease in people, and pinpoint the afflicted organ. His own greatest problem was with thunderstorms. He just could not stand them, and couldn't work if one was close by. He candidly admitted that he was afraid of lightning. But otherwise, because of his amazingly good health, Wolf Messing never underwent a full medical examination, which might have helped explain some of his incredible powers. Once, however, he yielded to the insistent entreaties of a woman neurologist who had watched him perform in the town of Belaya Tserkov, and allowed her to make a cursory examination.

The doctor was surprised to find that the regions of Messing's head and chest radiated much more heat than other parts of his body. But Messing would not stay still long enough to let her find out why.

In his later years, Messing spent most of his free time at home in the apartment, immersed in books. He liked stories about animals and detectives.

Because he was instantly recognizable, he didn't like to walk in the streets or use public transportation, and he had no telephone in his apartment. But he remained exceptionally proud of his correct prediction, during a demonstration in Novosibirsk on March 7, 1944, that the war would end on May 9, 1945—and also of another amazing example of premonition that happened in Ashkhabad in 1948.

"I was due to give several concerts in Ashkhabad," the old man proudly told the young Novosti editor. "But walking along the street on the very first day, I was suddenly enveloped by a sense of alarm. Something began to ache and trouble me. With every minute, the feeling of alarm increased. I was overcome by a powerful impulse to leave the city immediately. It became so strong on me that for the first and only time in my career, I canceled all my local performances and left for Moscow without delay. Three days later, Ashkhabad was leveled by a devastating earthquake. Fifty thousand people were killed."

And what was the explanation of his outstanding ability to predict events correctly, Kyucharyants asked.

"By straining my willpower," Messing replied, "I suddenly see the culminating result of a stream of events. I call it 'direct knowledge.' I don't see anything mystical about it. The future shapes itself from the past and the present, and there are certain models or bonds between them. Understanding the mechanism of this direct knowledge is at present inaccessible to us, because our ideas of the essence of time, of its ties with space, with the past, present, and future are as yet indefinite."

This, then, was Messing's contribution to psychic research; hopefully the young Dadashev will contribute even more.

3.
TWO TELEKINETIC WOMEN

We glanced at each other in dismay. We simultaneously thought, "Poor woman," as the weak, hollow voice on the telephone asked, "Who is that?" Then, with a man in the background prompting her, "Oh, of course. The Americans. . . . My husband has just reminded me. How nice of you to call."

She sounded one hundred years old, yet a few months earlier she was the most powerful and famous telekinesis medium in the world.

"We love you, Ninel Sergeyevna. Scientists the world over respect your incredible accomplishments."

"Thank you." Then, her voice faded to a despondent whisper, "I am not doing so well, you know. It's my heart. No strength in me after the heart attack. I am a shadow of my own self. I can't find any strength. . . ."

How infinitely sad and cruel! We wanted to believe that somehow Ninel Sergeyevna Kulagina, the extraordinary telekinetic medium would survive, and that the energy that has worked scientific miracles had not been drained away forever.

"I doubt very much that I will dare to put her through another experiment, for this could amount to murder," Genady Sergeyev had told us several days earlier. (He was the Leningrad scientist who supervised most of the Kulagina experiments.) "It is questionable if she will be capable of functioning again. It would be a miracle if she does. I keep encouraging her on the telephone to get well fast, that we need her. But I don't think I'd dare experiment with her again. The truth is she is finished . . . Unless, a miracle . . ."

The evening before, her husband, Viktor Kulagin, a civil engineer, told us similarly, "I doubt very much that she will ever be able to regain her strength. Further experiments are out of the question. I think the next one would kill her. In fact, I'm sure of it."

And to our question, "Would you say your wife is a victim of science?" the response was a firm, harsh, pained, "Yes. It is so."

The truth is, of course, that Ninel Kulagina has done more for the scientific study of telekinesis—an awesome ability to make physical objects move by the power of the mind alone—than any other such medium. Carefully documented by Soviet scientists in controlled laboratory conditions, the Kulagina experiments were revealed in detail for the first time in our officially authorized interviews. We learned how Kulagina—whose identity, in earlier years, was protected by the pseudonym of Nina Mikhailova—stopped the beating heart of a frog by merely commanding it to do so. We were told about the mysterious burn marks that appeared on her hands and how on several occasions amazed scientists saw her clothes catch fire—caused, again, by an unseen power source.

Ironically, Kulagina never really knew what it was all about. All she knew was that she endured pain, long periods of dizziness, loss of weight, lasting discomfort, all in the name of a science she herself could not comprehend. But she respected it and its high priests with a complete selflessness—until she suffered a near-fatal heart attack. Significantly, the news was withheld. Even Russia's own parapsychologists learned about it only through the grapevine. Abroad, scientists would still talk about her as they had for the past decade, looking forward to word of new experiments with Kulagina.

In fact, she was high on the list of names we had submitted to the Novosti Press Agency while still in America. We advised Vladimir Makhotin, chief of the North American Department—a congenial, rather westernized Soviet official who had helped us on previous trips—that the scientific West has long taken cognizance of this remarkable woman. A report on "What's Kulagina up to now?" was clearly in order. Her name was not among the five in his final cable approving our expedition, but we resolved to find her just the same.

Before we left the United States, we talked about Soviet parapsychologists with Dr. Thelma Moss, the brilliant researcher at the University of California at Los Angeles. She mentioned Kulagina, but wasn't aware of her illness, and urged us to see her at all costs.

To Dr. Moss, as well as other American scientists, she was worthy of detailed study. They discounted attempts to discredit Kulagina by certain Soviet writers who claimed that she used magnets to perform her incredible feats. Whether the attacks followed directives from above or not, fortunately scientists like Dr. Genady Sergeyev who had witnessed and conducted the tests would not be easily intimidated. A doctor of engineering and a mathematician, Dr. Sergeyev lectured at various Leningrad hospitals and institutes, including the prestigious Medical Center of Leningrad University. On her own visit to Leningrad, Dr. Moss had tried to contact Dr. Sergeyev to discuss his experiments with Ninel Kulagina. She was unable to break through the Soviet red tape, and her efforts to meet him were in vain. But she had strongly advised us to try to get Sergeyev as a "leader in Soviet parapsychology" to tell us of his work.

It was not easy. At first, official sources told us that it was very unlikely we would get to question Sergeyev because he did not like to give interviews. When we reached Leningrad, Dr. Sergeyev was not entirely convinced that he wanted to talk to us, and he made it clear he was particularly concerned about having official permission to do so. We applied constant pressure on our shy yet incredibly hardworking Novosti aide Yuri Shevyakov:

"Come on, Yuri. You always find a way!"

Day after day, he hustled from early morning till late at night, frequently missing meals to cajole recalcitrant officials and scientists into meeting our time schedules.

Yuri was a worrier, and at one point we became so concerned for his health that we strongly advised him to take things easier. The constant traveling, phone calls, interviews, and missed meals had left him pale and worn, with huge dark shadows under his eyes. He was so tired that his English, quite adequate at the beginning of the trip, became garbled and confused. It was only later, after several days' rest at home in Moscow, that his fluency returned.

What mattered to us at this particular point was that Yuri's charm, hospitality, and insistence managed to overcome Sergeyev's hesitancy. Yuri then took the unusual step of inviting the important researcher to be his personal guest at the hotel for private discussions—without us present.

Fortunately, our headquarters in Leningrad was the famous old Astoria Hotel. Built just before World War I as a showplace to impress visitors to Imperial Russia, it had everything the Ritz of Paris, the Adlon of Berlin, the Savoy of London had—and more. Sixty-odd years and two wars, two revolutions, and one siege later, plundered and ransacked by just everybody, it still showed signs of its faded glory. Every room had an alcove, making it a miniature suite. Each had its own color scheme. Old expensive draperies adorned the windows and framed the baroque beauty of the immense St. Isaac's Cathedral, directly across from the hotel in the center of a huge square. Antiques dating back to the Czars had been faithfully restored, placed carefully in the lobby of every floor, to lend the hotel a certain awkward but welcome elegance so badly missing from the pretentious yet inadequate quasi-modern hotels of recent Soviet vintage. Even though the lobby looked naked and the ornate dining room was minus the once-famed exquisitely-worked stained-glass cupola, the brass candelabra and the Gobelin tapestries, there was faint glamour in the high-ceilinged rooms, corridors, and lobby.

The Astoria was prestigious enough to impress even a scientist of Sergeyev's standing. He accepted Yuri's invitation. We learned later that Yuri, out of his own pocket, had plied the doctor with coffee and cognac, lemonade, sandwiches, chocolate bars, and—oranges. It was something the young Novosti Press Agency correspondent could not afford, and there was no chance of reimbursement from his Soviet Government employers. But he would not let us pay. He had adopted our project of psychic research as a very personal mission, and although he would not let us meet Sergeyev at this point, his sincerity and hospitality paved the way for our subsequent warm friendship with the famous scientist.

And so one morning, Yuri borrowed our rented car and picked up Sergeyev at his home. We met outside the Astoria Hotel and journeyed to the local Novosti office, where our interviews could take place in officially-controlled conditions.

Outside the building, the Neva River was swollen and black from melting snow, with huge chunks of ice rushing past, but the welcome in the bare rooms was warm and friendly. Soon Sergeyev, who during the car ride had kept his observations to small talk, was warming to his favorite subject, science—in particular, his scientific experiments over the years with Kulagina.

Serious and businesslike as were most Soviet scientists we met, the dark-haired Sergeyev was neatly dressed in a dark suit, white shirt, and conservative tie. He seldom allowed a smile to cross his strong, weathered face.

He soon left no doubts in our minds about Kulagina's skill. "Before a recent heart attack," he announced, "she was unquestionably the most powerful telekinesis medium in the world."

Kulagina, now 58, was a young girl in Leningrad when the Nazis laid siege to the city. Despite her age, she became a tank radio operator and served in the armored train that fought its way in and out of Leningrad with supplies. Seriously injured by an exploding shell, she recovered to lead a normal healthy life, becoming a happy wife and mother.

Even before her talents became known to scientists, Kulagina was aware she had unusual powers. For instance, she could "see" items concealed in people's pockets. A picture of the hidden objects seemed to flash into her mind. She was also able to diagnose disease, often without really trying. When she met sick people, an image of the illness, such as an aching head, or a swollen kidney would appear to her mentally.

Her abilities first came to the attention of the scientific world in 1964, after she was taken to a hospital with a nervous breakdown. While recuperating, Kulagina did a lot of sewing. Doctors were amazed to see her reach into the workbasket and select any color of thread she wanted without even a glance. Local parapsychologists were notified of her "blind sight" abilities. The following year, when she had fully recovered, she agreed to take part in various experiments.

First the parapsychologists ascertained that she could genuinely perceive colors just by touching an object with her fingertips. Then they found she had the power to heal by merely laying her hands on the affected site. Dr. Sergeyev conducted many of the faith-healing experiments, using patients who were dissatisfied with their doctors' efforts to cure them, and were only too happy to try something different. The experiments, Sergeyev said, were highly successful. Kulagina showed that her strange powers were particularly effective in making open wounds of accident victims heal more quickly. To effect an improvement, she had only to place her hands near the injuries for brief periods of time. She was also very successful in treating pneumonia by placing her hands on the patient's sides. A 26-year-old man who was brought to Kulagina with partially paralyzed legs was able to walk again after only three months' treatment.

Kulagina was also successful in limited demonstrations of telepathic powers. But when the scientists directed her into the field of telekinesis, they found Kulagina was outstanding.

Kulagina found that to move items successfully with the power of her mind, she must cast all other thoughts from her head. She concentrated solely on the target object—to such an extent that only its image filled her mind. Just before the target object moved, she told the researchers, she would feel a sharp pain in her spine, and her eyesight blurred. Doctors found that her blood pressure rose significantly.

Kulagina needed no special diet to maintain her abilities, but would not conduct experiments after a heavy meal because it unduly strained her heart. She did not drink alcohol or smoke cigarettes.

Best results were obtained when the weather was dry and cool. Following each experiment, a minimum of five minutes' rest was needed to prevent her blood pressure levels from rising dangerously.

The story of the remarkable feats of Kulagina, or Mikhailova as she was then referred to, were first officially broken in the West in 1968. The stories were carried by newspapers and magazines all over the world. Just as quickly came the allegations that she was a fraud. Despite the official attack, the Leningrad scientists quietly continued with their experiments.

Sergeyev then went on to tell us that it was possible to record the tremendous energy emanating from Kulagina: "In experiments in Leningrad, we placed undeveloped photo film in a black envelope. By looking at the envelope, she was capable of exposing the film inside!" He showed us some snapshots that had been developed from the film used in the experiments. They clearly showed irregularly-sized white dots scattered all over the photos. "She never touched the envelope, just looked at it!" Sergeyev insisted.

During one experiment, when Kulagina was in a high emotional state, moving a table tennis ball on a table, the scientists again placed undeveloped film in a black envelope and passed it close to her head. They found that the film was again marked by light. The largest area of light marks was made when the envelope was passed near the back of her head. The energy emanating from Kulagina marked three pieces of film, one behind the other, sealed in the envelope! Every precaution had been taken in placing the film in the envelope and in developing it. There was no chance that the film could have been affected by light from any other source than the energy from Kulagina.

Sergeyev believes that this is another way of registering the "auras" that have been shown in what is known as Kirlian photography. The light marks on the film were caused by Kulagina's electrical discharges. In further tests, using the same film procedures, scientists found that Kulagina could direct this power. Through a black envelope, she was able to "draw" light pictures on undeveloped film. The envelope with the film was placed in front of her. She stared at it, and with her eyes tried to create an image. She was repeatedly able to draw a cross by moving her eyes up and down, and then sideways. "When she did it over and over again on the same envelope, we had multiple images of the cross. She could also draw letters on the film with her eyes. It was like using a laser beam," Sergeyev reported. He showed us the results of this test. The snapshot-size prints clearly showed multiple white crosses. They were roughly "drawn," but easily recognizable.

Sergeyev's voice swelled with pride when he spoke about Kulagina's power as a telekinesis medium. He carried out repeated experiments with her in controlled laboratory conditions in Leningrad, and found that she could move objects weighing over one pound.

"The object was put on the flat surface of a table. By concentrating on this object, she tried to move it without touching it. She preceded this with a long period of concentration, as if she was filling herself up from some invisible energy source—like priming a pump. During this period, she told me, she tried to remove every other thought from her mind. The only thing she thought about was the object and its movement.

"When she reached her highest emotional stage, she looked as if she were about to lose consciousness. At that second, an invisible hand seemed to touch the object and move it. It moved in separate jerky movements, although to the human eye, it appeared that it was rolling."

Attending scientists proved this jerky motion by placing a piece of film in a black envelope under a ceramic cylinder on the table. Then they asked Kulagina to move the cylinder with her mind. She did. When the film was developed, they found clear impressions that it had moved in six separate jumps. In other words, there was a light mark on the film, then a blank, then a light mark, then a blank. Each leap of the object was about one inch. The scientists believe that the imprint was caused by the energy that Kulagina discharged into the object.

The scientists also measured the energy field of electrical discharges around her body. They found that when Kulagina was concentrating on moving an object, the energy field diminished to half that of a normal person. They believe that Kulagina absorbed the energy from around her into her body, then discharged it at the target object to make it move.

Electrocardiograph tests showed that her heartbeat increased very measurably during the experiments. A sprinter when running his hardest has a heartbeat of 110. Yet Kulagina's heartbeat raced to 160, even as high as 180. "In no case during these experiments were we thinking of mysterious forces," Sergeyev told us emphatically. "Everything was explainable. We felt that every method known to science should be used to investigate the ability of a human being to focus his or her will."

The most unusual experiment of all with Kulagina took place in the Leningrad laboratory on March 10, 1970. It was then that Kulagina used her energy to stop the heart of a frog! The experiment was conducted by Dr. Sergei Sarychev, and Dr. Sergeyev was one of the many scientists present.

"As is known, frogs' hearts continue beating for some hours after being removed from the body," he said. "The beating heart of a frog was placed in a glass jar. Kulagina sat down about two and a half feet from the jar, and concentrated her mind on the heart. Cardiogram readings of the frog heart were taken throughout the experiment.

"She gave commands to the heart—go slower, go faster. The cardiograms showed that the heart responded to her commands! In the first experiment, she stopped the heart five minutes after the experiment began. "Then another frog's heart was placed in another jar. And this is what happened." Sergeyev produced the minutes of the experiment, quoting Kulagina:

10:28 P.M.	I am beginning to slow it down.
10:30	Slower . . . .
10:34	I am beginning to stop it.

10:35	I am stopping it.
10:39	I cannot stop it.
10:41	I will try again . . . I am beginning to slow it down again.
10:50	I am using all my strength.
10:51	I have stopped it.

The record of the cardiogram showed that the frog heart stopped beating at precisely 10:51 P.M.!

As Sergeyev summed it up: "It was as if the hearts had been struck by tiny bolts of lightning. Both hearts should have continued beating for hours after the experiment."

A Leningrad psychiatrist who heard of these amazing experiments refused to accept their validity. Through Sergeyev, he challenged Kulagina to try the experiment on him. It was an interesting way to find out, under strictly controlled laboratory conditions, what effect Kulagina had on human beings, so Sergeyev arranged the experiments. Both Kulagina and the psychiatrist were seated three yards apart in the same room, under the full observation of a medical team. There was no contact, no words were exchanged. At the start of the experiment, both subjects, attached separately to ECG machines, showed steady heart rhythms. Kulagina, her brown hair tied up in a bun, stared into space, her unblinking deep black eyes seeming to cut through the very walls.

Within two minutes, serious changes were shown in the psychiatrist's heart condition. His ECG graph went far above normal, showing great emotional stress. Kulagina's heartbeat, too, was faster than normal, but the psychiatrist's heartbeat increased at such an alarming rate that the scientists feared for the safety of the psychiatrist's life! Sergeyev had to stop the experiment five minutes after it had begun. Sergeyev acknowledged to us that had the experiment continued, they were certain the psychiatrist would have been killed.

Several times during the telekinetic experiments with Sergeyev, Kulagina became unconscious. Instruments measuring the electrical field around her showed that when she took electrical energy from around her and sent it to an object, it apparently drained her completely of energy. On several occasions, an electrical force from the surroundings rushed back into her body, usually through the arm, and left burn marks on the skin. These were easily seen, for Kulagina preferred a short-sleeved dress for such experiments.

"I have witnessed this startling phenomenon," Sergeyev said simply. "No object could have caused the burn marks other than the reentry into her body of some powerful energy. On one occasion she exclaimed, 'I am burning!' and collapsed unconscious. A burn mark appeared on her hand. On several occasions, these burn marks were four inches long! I have been with her during this return of energy when her clothing caught fire. When these incidents happened, Kulagina became unconscious and very ill, and we had great difficulty in reviving her."

Eventually it wore her down. One more jolt and her heart would cave in. Possibly the scientists should have known that, but they were too eager to experiment to think about it. The crisis came with the sudden death of her father.

Ninel loved him—not passionately, Sergeyev told us, but dutifully, like a good Russian daughter. Still, it came as a shock. The family was attending his funeral when she collapsed, right there in the cemetery. An ambulance rushed her to a hospital.

It wasn't mere grief, but a massive heart attack. She was placed in intensive care. Subsequently her life was saved, but "We were told not to expect miracles," Sergeyev said sadly. "She would remain an invalid for the rest of her days."

It was Yuri who came up with her phone number, swearing us to secrecy on how we got it. We assumed that his immediate superiors might not know, as he indicated, but someone very high up *had* given approval. It was actually four days after we'd learned from Sergeyev what had happened to Kulagina. Now that we knew the truth, we would do our best with it.

The question was how much would the Kulagins tell us. We also realized that in view of the world's interest in the Russian medium, we might have to prove that she had been written off, a woman with a heart damaged beyond repair. Taping the interview with Kulagina, was essential. We wanted to bring the irrefutable proof home with us.

It was Viktor Kulagin, Ninel's husband, who advised us that a visit was not possible. She had not been receiving any visitors. We had dialed the phone number Yuri had obtained for us, and Kulagin answered. Obviously he was in, tending to his wife. Was Ninel Sergeyevna bedridden, we asked solicitously? Yes, he said. She's been in bed continually, for the last three months. Could he take the telephone to her, then? No, he said she was too weak to talk right now, but maybe she could in the morning.

The next morning she answered the phone herself. She was waiting for our call, yet her mind failed to register fast enough who we were.

"Ninel Sergeyevna!" We used the patronym to convey our respect and admiration. "Can you hear us?"

"Yes."

"Tell us what happened."

Haltingly, she recounted the story of her collapse at her "papa's" funeral. "I almost died, you know."

"But you'll be well soon."

"Oh, I hope so. I hope so."

"Wouldn't you like to resume those experiments?"

"Oh, yes!" she cried out. "They tell me the experiments were very important."

"Indeed, yes, and you have contributed to science. Do you know that?"

"I know and I am so glad. That's why I want to be of more use to them."

"You've been doing it a long time, haven't you, Ninel Sergeyevna?"

"Ten years. No, longer. Ever since the late Dr. Leonid Leonidovich Vasiliev first discovered my ability to recognize color by touch of hand rather than by sight."

"Which was . . . ?"

"After I had that nervous breakdown in 1966. Or was it 1964? The doctors at the hospital where I was being cared for called him to come see it with his own eyes."

"You've enjoyed the experiments?"

"Oh, yes."

"Which did you prefer?"

"Oh, those with Genady Sergeyev."

Her voice began to falter. Kulagin came to the phone to say, "One more minute. She tires very fast."

"Wouldn't you like to resume your work with him?"

"Oh yes. As soon as I am well again." Her eagerness was pathetic.

"Have they told you when this will be?"

"No." Her voice sank to a doleful whisper. "I don't like it, you know. I was in ill health even before the heart attack; since early 1974. But at least Genady Aleksandrovich calls me every so often. He is such a dear man."

"You rest now, Ninel Sergeyevna. One day you'll come to see us in America."

She managed a chuckle: "Oh, yes. For sure. For sure."

We had bugged our phone, and after we replaced the receiver we checked the tape. The recording was perfect. It was all there, her agony and despair, her eagerness and hope, the pathos and humbleness of a conscious sacrifice.

As we caught the famous Red Arrow night express back to Moscow, we were haunted by the memory of the famous Kulagina's feeble voice. Would she recover? And if she did, would her incredible powers still be available to her? Who would dare to find out? Certainly not Sergeyev, her most dedicated researcher. In any case, we had already been introduced to her successor as the top telekinetic medium in all of the Soviet Union.

Alla Vinogradova is not a very impressive person—until she starts to demonstrate her telekinetic powers. We first met her, with her husband Viktor Adamenko, in the conference room of the Novosti Press Agency in Moscow.

We were delighted when the Soviet authorities told us that Adamenko and Vinogradova were to be our first interviewees. The meeting itself was remarkable, and we were impressed that an official Government agency should agree to have its premises used for a parapsychology demonstration. It was a clear-cut indication of the great interest the Soviet Government now has in parapsychology research.

Back in Los Angeles, Dr. Moss had told us about Dr. Adamenko.

"He is young, he is dedicated, he is brilliant," she said. "I admire his work." A physicist anchored at the National Institute of Normal Physiology in Moscow, he donned the mantle of leading parapsychology researcher in Moscow after the official attack on Eduard Naumov, who was exiled from Moscow for getting too much publicity out of parapsychology work.

Adamenko, with whom we became very friendly subsequently, turned out to be a young, good-looking man in a dark business suit, who favored neatly laundered shirts with flashing cuff links.

His wife Alla, a slightly built brunette, at first struck us as very dry and colorless. It turned out, however, that she was just rather hesitant to meet strangers in such an official setting. It did not take her long to prove to us why she is acclaimed as the successor to the ailing Kulagina. We ourselves tested Vinogradova's abilities, in the Novosti conference room where we first met and later, as our friendship grew, at our hotel.

They had brought an experimental plastic cube, two feet square, to the conference room especially for the official demonstration. We watched as Adamenko placed an aluminum-foil cigar container in front of her. Vinogradova sat with her back rigid, her feet firmly planted on the floor. She rubbed the tip of the clear cube, then took the cigar container in her hands for a few moments before placing it back on the cube. The container was absolutely still. She then placed her right hand very close to it, fingertips outstretched, the side of her hand running parallel to the container . . . first one side, then the other, never touching the container, but within an inch of it.

Slowly it began to rock, then move. Then she pointed her fingertips at it, an inch and a half to two inches away from it, and it rolled very quickly to the side of the cube. She then put her fingertips about two inches in front of it. The container stopped, then ran back. She repeated this time and again.

We examined the cube and the container very closely and were satisfied there were no wires, magnets, or other devices. Vinogradova was at first wearing a long-sleeved pantsuit, but she later did it again without the jacket and with her arms bare. We made sure there were no devices of any kind hidden on her. At all times, Vinogradova was seated beside the cube, but never touching it. Even had her fingers touched the container, we could not figure out how one could make it spin so quickly, nor how one would stop or start it at will.

As a test, we gave her a British cigarette not common in Moscow. She placed it in front of her, and made it move in exactly the same way. A cigarette, obviously, would not be affected by a magnet. We further checked that the cigarette had not been tampered with by asking her to smoke it, which she did with obvious pleasure. Then we repeated the experiment with an American cigarette, which she proceeded to roll across the cube with apparent little effort.

Yet Vinogradova told us afterwards that she found the cigarette much more difficult to move because it was quite different material. "There are problems in psychologically tuning in to some objects, particularly if they are nonmetallic," she smiled. "All it means is that you have to concentrate even harder. It is possible to move any object if you try hard enough."

With that, she took one of our red plastic pens, and made it roll incredibly fast. Then she made a Ping-Pong ball spin like a top. At no time was she touching or blowing on the objects. It was a classic demonstration of telekinesis.

Our friendship with Adamenko and Vinogradova was to be a vital part of our success in probing the Soviets' psychic secrets. At first we thought they would not be able to help us. Following our first meeting we were happy, feeling we could learn much more from Vinogradova and Adamenko on other aspects of parapsychology behind the Iron Curtain. We tried to bombard them with questions over lunch at the famous Aragwy Restaurant on Gorky Street. Service was slow, but the Caucasian menu superb. Strangely, the pair stonewalled our eager questions, although they gave every appearance of being friendly. We quickly realized that it was the presence of a Novosti editor that was inhibiting them.

So, instead of parapsychology, we talked of food and clothes, their homes and families. It did serve the purpose of establishing a mutual friendship and trust between Vinogradova, Adamenko and ourselves. We obtained their office telephone numbers, they had no phone at home but later that night Adamenko called us. We arranged for both of them to meet us at our hotel the following day.

When they came and we met in the lobby of the Intourist, Vinogradova did not hesitate to go upstairs for more photographs while demonstrating her telekinetic talent. We offered to keep the room door open. She shook her head: "It is not necessary." Was it not in contravention of a rule to visit a foreigner in a hotel room? Her answer was ambiguous: "It is a rule, but not a written rule and it used to be much stricter." She shrugged. It appeared that she was taking a chance.

Subsequently, as we became increasingly aware of the good standing the couple had with Novosti and Soviet editors in general, we concluded that in their case such risks were minimal. Also, word must have come down to all we met that we had been accorded special privileges, and that bending the law a bit in our favor was therefore quite in order. On this particular occasion, though, Vinogradova's quiet pluck impressed us. After the couple left we settled back to evaluate this strange, rather mousy woman, who spoke only when spoken to.

Vinogradova is a teacher and psychologist who works with the problems of psychology of school children at the Research Institute of the Academy of Pedagogical Sciences in Moscow. She considers psychology and parapsychology very closely related. Fellow schoolteachers once felt that she would not be able to control large groups of kindergarten children, aged between three and six, in the classroom. However, although she is very emotional, a mental empathy made control of children very easy for her, and colleagues were amazed.

She first started experimenting with telekinesis in 1969, after seeing the now-famous film of Kulagina moving matches and other small objects. Interestingly enough, there is now a similar film of Vinogradova that was shown to us at a government TV studio the day after we had met her, and it's an impressive demonstration of how she uses her mind to move objects. The fact that official approval was given to allow the TV studio to show the film again proved to us that the Soviets take the subject of telekinesis very seriously.

"Before I saw the Kulagina film, I sensed something unusual in myself," she recounted to us. "I had wonderful dreams, colorful dreams, which I always remembered. And sometimes I had the ability to prophesy through these dreams. For example, my brother died some time ago. Two days before it happened, I had a dream in which I saw myself and our whole family, all our relatives, on a train—except my brother. We were on the train to go to a funeral. I had not seen my brother, or communicated with him, for a long time before the dream. Two days after it, I got a telegram telling me of his death."

There were other unusual psychic experiences before she moved into the field of telekinesis. Vinogradova first tried some experiments at home, but they didn't work. She was sure that she could move objects by the power of her mind, but she had not yet mastered the required technique of concentration. Over a period of weeks, she began to get limited success. At first, it was with lightweight objects, such as matchboxes or the aluminum-foil container for a cigar. But they distinctly moved. And as she became more confident, they moved further. Then she began to move heavier objects, until now she can move objects weighing up to 200 grams.

As her husband Adamenko helped her with the research, she achieved such expertise that by now she can not only move the objects, but control them. She can make them move in one direction, stop, then move backwards! She can make a heap of wooden matches fly outwards in every direction as if hit by an explosion. Out of a dozen objects lying in front of her, she can pick a target object and make it move while the others remain still. Lately, she's been trying to develop her mental powers through meditation. Unlike Kulagina, she is not exhausted after demonstrations. Her husband Adamenko, who has published many scientific papers on his telekinesis experiments with her, said solemnly, "She has clearly shown in these experiments that she does have the ability to move and control the movement of objects without touching them."

Experiments were carried out when Vinogradova was in different emotional conditions—for example, when she was under stress, or after she had drunk a glass of cognac. The husband and wife team also investigated what effects atmospheric conditions had on her ability to move objects. Vinogradova was tested during a rainstorm or standing on her bare feet on wet ground. Basically, they found that Vinogradova was far more effective in good weather, when she was well-rested, had taken no alcohol, and felt in a good mood. The research has shown she must be close to an object, about two inches away, to start it moving. But once it has been started,

Vinogradova can keep the object moving from a distance of several feet. "I think only of the object and that it must move," she told us. "I concentrate on it, I must tune myself in to the object. I feel as if some kind of energy is pouring from my fingertips, and from the sides of my hands."

In 1971, Adamenko reported to a conference in Alma Ata, Kazakhstan, "Upon my demand, Vinogradova was able to move the objects backward or forward, to accelerate the objects' motion, and to start or stop the motion of the objects. With objects such as Ping-Pong balls, she was able to make them rotate at a distance according to my signals. When Kirlian aura photography was taken as she was concentrating on moving objects, the aura of her fingertips burst out with a new pattern of great activity, not only on the hand that she was pointing at the object, but also on the other hand.

"My scientific conclusion on this ability is that the object to be moved lies in an electrostatic field, and the added energy from the telekinetic medium causes electrical activity in the field and triggers movement. However, the object will move only if the forces are greater than friction. Usually —with a nonmedium, for example—the forces of friction are greater, and the object does not move. The telekinetic medium is able to provide the necessary additional energy to overcome the friction."

Adamenko detected the electrostatic field by using voltometers and simple indicators, such as a flashlight bulb. The experiments with Vinogradova were performed on the same clear plastic cube, two feet square, that they brought to our first conference. It is easy to create an electrostatic field by rubbing the surface of the cube. "The key is the ability of the medium to concentrate fully on the object while in a good mental state," Adamenko told us. "Familiar objects are easiest to move. When we increased these in weight without telling Alla, the movement was not impaired."

After her first demonstration for us, we both tried to emulate her feats ourselves, but failed miserably. Nothing moved. Determined not to be beaten, we took turns trying to move the objects in the same way we had just witnessed. We screamed our frustrations at the objects—"Come, come, come . . . go, go, go"—but to no avail. When we gave up, there was even no electromagnetic field left. Adamenko placed a small flashlight bulb on the table and it failed to light, although it had done so after Vinogradova finished her demonstration. During the experiment with the cigar container, Adamenko demonstrated the electrostatic field he had spoken of earlier by placing the light bulb close to the surface of the plastic cube. The bulb flashed briefly, as if there were an electrical discharge.

In Leningrad, when we asked Sergeyev about Vinogradova he acknowledged, "She is without a doubt the successor to Kulagina as the top telekinetic medium, although she does not yet have the power of Kulagina. I am fully familiar with the experiments conducted under Viktor Adamenko's supervision. To say that I am impressed would be putting it mildly. I still hope that a miracle will happen and that the two women will get a chance of working together."

The miracle, if one may call it that, took place in Moscow in

March 1977 when both women demonstrated their telekinetic abilities for film cameras. Kulagina was brought down from Leningrad and, while looking pale, wan and aged, was able to perform feats of telekinesis that, to quote Vinogradova, "showed me that she is still the pastmaster of a remarkable power.

"Ninel Sergeyevna," she added, "is like the soldier determined to die with his boots on. We fully expected her to live out her days as an invalid, cared for by her family. But nobody reckoned with her amazing recuperative ability not even the doctors attending her. Her incredible will won out—it's as simple as that."

The documentary filmed in Moscow may well have been in line with the Soviet reevaluation of parapsychology and so contributed to the official stand taken later, declaring Soviet parapsychology out of bounds to foreigners. According to Vinogradova, whose share of performance in the film was quite substantial, it became the latest proof of the validity of telekinesis. Both women moved objects with sheer will power. Kulagina also demonstrated her ability to see objects concealed from view. Parapsychologists call this ability "introvision."

Dr. Inyushin who attended the Moscow filming sessions confirmed that Kulagina appeared to have come forth with a sudden burst of her previous psychic strength. She looked "normal, quite well," and "proved to be remarkably effective." However, Kulagina did not attempt her other famous feats, such as stopping the heart of a frog. Quite obviously, she did not have the strength to do that. Still, this was the first time since her heart attack that she tried her hand at telekinesis again—and succeeded. "A miracle did happen," Sergeyev said later, "and it took a load off my mind." What next, Ninel Kulagina?

"What next? Next, the end," she spoke up bitterly announcing her retirement. She was home in Leningrad, it was evening, Saturday, September 24th, 1977. This then was her message to the outside world:

"Unless Soviet scientists recognize telekinesis as fact, not fiction, and are willing to accept it as a valid phenomenon, useful and important to our science, I shall not go out, I shall not travel anywhere, I shall not do anything to demonstrate my abilities. This is it. Besides, my health is gone. Let's face it."

She had agreed to the Moscow experiments against her better judgement, she said, because she was not quite up to it, but she would have gladly put her life on the line if the cause was worth it. "It was not," she said sadly. "None of the scientists who are acquainted with the phenomena of telekinesis and clairvoyance and know my work had been asked to supervise the filmed experiments."

For the record, Adamenko was there, but Sergeyev was not invited. "So, while I did what I was still able to perform, and we were successful, our efforts were really wasted. And after four strenuous days at the Ostankino television studios, I was exhausted. I barely made it home. I stayed in bed for weeks after that, I had headaches that wouldn't go, and fainting spells. I paid a heavy price. For what? To show magical tricks? I resent that."

The statement was brought out of Russia recorded on a tape which is now in our possession. Analyzing the voice on the tape we found it listless, drained of vitality although stronger than when we spoke to her in Leningrad, only a few months after her near-fatal heart attack. She was talking in the monotone of one who didn't care anymore. Later, we were able to determine that the Kulagins had their phone number changed, in April 1977, one month after the filming at Ostankino.

Why would they do that? Were they trying to hide? Have they had enough of a curious yet ungrateful world? Or were they being hidden away by someone who didn't want to unnecessarily expose Kulagina and whatever precious powers were left within her—in a country where parapsychology is rapidly becoming a secret weapon? In Soviet Russia, where private telephones are still as scarce as private automobiles, it may not be too hard to give up one's phone number. But it takes pull, a word from someone high above, to be given a new number in its place—especially an unlisted one.

4.

THE GREAT TELEPATHY CONTROVERSY

The story occupied the entire outside page of the Soviet weekly newspaper, *Literaturnaya Gazeta.* The two-line headline, big by Soviet standards, screamed: "Effect of Telepathy Not Found." An inconspicuous subtitle read: "Control Test, Moscow-Kerch."

This was the way that in early June, 1968, some three million readers of the powerful weekly *Literary Gazette,* learned about the alleged failure of a major Soviet telepathy experiment. The readers, who picked up their copies at newsstands across the length and breadth of the Soviet Union, were given a clear, authoritative message: "Forget it—telepathy doesn't work."

It was clear to all that the article was intended to harm a research project growing in prestige in the Soviet Union. Back in Moscow, the two telepathists involved, Yuri Kamensky and Karl Nikolayev, cringed as they read the paper. So did Viktor Adamenko, then a young, enthusiastic biophysicist who had followed the two-city experiment with bated breath. His cry of "foul" was heard far and wide. His indignation was shared by Professor Venyamin Pushkin, a respected Moscow scientist with a definite stake in parapsychology. Dr. Vladimir Raikov, a noted psychiatrist who had been probing the human mind with the help of hypnosis, made it known that his faith in telepathy would remain unshaken. Dr. Genady Sergeyev, the pioneering Leningrad researcher, simply swore, then busied himself with more telepathy experiments.

Now, nine years after the Moscow-Kerch "debacle," observers recording the ups and downs of telepathy research in the Soviet Union have little doubt that it is still very much alive. In fact, the Soviet researchers are probably well ahead of their Western counterparts.

The hatchet job done by the know-it-all "Literaturka," as the organ of the Soviet Writer's Union is referred to colloquially, has remained a single operation. There were no follow-up attacks except one in the paper itself one month later. An indifferently displayed collection of letters from readers, both for and against telepathy, it contained interwoven editorial comment that went to great pains to appear impartial while in reality it was not. After that, silence. Not even the *Literary Gazette,* the self-appointed guardian of Communist morals and champion of "scientific truth" in its "struggle" against "superstition and old wives' tales" could expect to dispose of telepathy in a single coup. The uproar of the so-called exposure died down all too quickly. The reason is obvious: serious research is continuing, approved at an official level, and totally unhampered by the *Gazette*'s allegations.

On our last trip to Moscow, however, the Great Telepathy Controversy was still raging. When we sat down to discuss it with the staff of *Literary Gazette*, we were already well armed with the facts, both pro and con, of the Moscow-Kerch experiment. We said we were interested in the details of the organization of the test because we felt a similar experiment might be set up between Moscow and New York. But even then, the reception was cool. The *Gazette* editors were still adamant about the outcome of the experiment.

Efim Demoushkin, the science editor, made this clear with his opening remarks: "Let me clarify our role. It is not the function of our newspaper to sit in judgment. We are not a tribunal. However, we conduct periodic scientific tests of phenomena worthy of investigation, and our editors in these cases are not even moderators. We invite the author of a new scientific exploration to demonstrate his findings before a panel of scientists whom we pick on merit, and merit only. They are the experts. We bow to their wisdom."

Demoushkin looked rather like a Russian intellectual—thin-faced, a quizzical look in his eyes—as he tried to assess our reactions. "These scientists are not anonymous," he stressed. "Their names are published in the paper, and it is they who sign the findings. It is they, too, who suggest the circumstances for the demonstration, where, what, how. All scientifically justified. Before we start, both sides agree on a procedure. Eventually, we at the paper only report what happened."

His statement was not entirely accurate. The *Literary Gazette* places its "seal of approval," rather like that of *Good Housekeeping,* on the results of such experiments. The report of the Moscow-Kerch experiment, for instance, carried this seal. To one side of the two-column, bold-type introduction was the word "Laboratory" and the initials "L" and "G." It is accepted throughout Russia that this seal attests to the fact the newspaper approves the quality of the product—in this case, the results of the experiment—and vouches for the veracity of the report and the procedures adopted.

Before we had time to challenge Demoushkin, Luisa Nikitina of the newspaper's foreign affairs department, cut in: "You must understand that where new things are concerned, we are as curious as anyone else. But we don't believe in hocus-pocus. We like to get to the bottom of that, and expose it. Checkmate it, I call it. We don't believe in miracles. Physics has its established set of laws. We accept these laws, and go by them; we have to. On the other hand, we like to keep an open mind to all that is genuinely new. If we think there is something there, we leave it to the scientists to figure out what it is. We certainly don't want to mislead our readers." The pretty Nikitina probably sincerely believed what she said. But we had learned several disturbing facts about the way the experiment was conducted. Her intervention gave us the perfect opportunity to start raising these points.

We understood, we said, that the final conclusion of the panel of scientists who supervised the experiment was that such controlled experiments should be continued, and that the publication of results should take place, be they positive or negative. We had heard that the committee appointed by *Literary Gazette* had felt the next two-city experiment would be a success. But had *Literary Gazette* ever offered a second chance?

We smiled. Nikitina's face was stern, Demoushkin was emotionless; and both were silent. We pressed home our advantage. "We understand that in fact two objects were identified, although not in the correct order?" There was still silence, though Demoushkin's lips pursed thoughtfully. "We also understand that it is common with telepathy experiments to record the right images in the wrong order. Critics of your techniques say that steps should have been taken to avoid electrical interference. Why was that not done? In our country, a single test would not be regarded as sufficient to establish the important conclusion you drew. What standards do you have on the question of multiple tests?"

We were getting nowhere. The two *Literary Gazette* staffers shifted rather uneasily, then pointed to a photocopy of the story that was lying on one of the desks. "We had that made specially for you. You may take it, and find all the answers in our story," Nikitina said tartly.

When we picked up the copy, we found that, certainly for a Soviet newspaper, it was quite attractively laid out. In the upper-right corner was a photograph showing a dark-haired man, his hands in midair, groping over the surface of some kind of object. His face showed tension and all-out concentration. The picture was a very dark halftone, the details washed out, and it was difficult to see whether he was sitting or standing, or what equipment was shown. It was captioned "Moscow Laboratory of Psychophysiology. In the photo—inductor Y. Kamensky."

The picture diagonally opposite, at the bottom of the page, was a lot clearer, and showed a man similarly concentrating. But his hands, also in midair, were seemingly touching an object that wasn't there. He wore a plaid shirt and a large watch on his left wrist. In the background two men in shirt-sleeves with their elbows resting on a table, and their hands cupped against their chins, watched intently. On the extreme right, a woman secretary was taking notes. The caption read: "Kerch. Rehearsal hall of the city theater. Percipient K. Nikolayev (foreground)."

It struck us that *Literary Gazette* had enough faith in its readers' knowledge of telepathy not to bother defining "inductor" (a person transmitting thoughts telepathically) and "percipient" (the recipient of a telepathic message). The editors did not explain the nomenclature anywhere in the article, as certainly they would have had to do if they had been dealing with Western readers.

To the extreme left, the broadsheet-sized page carried a story headed "Objectives of the Experiment," which gave an elaborate history of earlier telepathic experiments in the Soviet Union reported in its own press. The midsection was devoted to "Program and Methods" of the test, and also listed the names and academic titles of the ten scientists on the investigating committee. Beneath that was a section headed "Course of Experiments," describing the procedure. This was flanked on the extreme right by pictures of the ten objects handed to Kamensky for "transmission," counterbalanced by pictures of objects Nikolayev thought he received. The bottom of the page carried a section "Findings," and gave opinions of Soviet Academicians A. Kolmogorov, E. Kreps and E. Asratyan, whom the paper had picked to judge the results on merit.

It was an impressive presentation, but it obviously did not answer the questions we had raised with the *Gazette* staffers. We changed our tactics, and again sat down to discuss the coverage of the experiment without raising difficult, controversial, issues.

The seeds of the trouble had been sown in the early 1960's, when telepathy research began to be recognized as an important field. But the showdown with the establishment, in the form of *Literary Gazette,* did not come until December 1967, when "parapsychology enthusiasts" approached the newspaper with a request to publish an article entitled "Parapsychology—A Science of the Future." The researchers spoke of parapsychology as if its various aspects, including telepathy, telekinesis, clairvoyance, had already been proven. They called for all-round research, and spoke of the practical applications this could bring.

They told the *Gazette* editors, "The results of parapsychology research not only present a purely theoretical scientific interest, but also make it possible to solve a number of applied problems, such as the use of bio-telecommunication—that is, the transfer of information by media other than the existing technical means of communications. It would also bring an improvement in the efficiency of educational processes and extraction of information from the depths of human memory." However, the *Gazette* staff took the stance that the very existence of parapsychological effects evoked serious doubts in many scientists. The suggested article was rejected, but the editors suggested an "unbiased, completely scientific experiment" on telepathy and promised to publish the results, whether negative or positive.

Arguments on telepathy have been going on for many years. The *Gazette* publicly noted "A section of our press regularly publishes material on the subject, and does not let the public lose interest in it. It persistently even rouses new interest. Many popular scientific magazines generously lend their pages to discussions on telepathy. Physiologists, physicists, cyberneticists, psychologists, journalists, and even 'telepaths' themselves are offered wide opportunities for expressing their opinions. From time to time, the papers publish sensational information on the results of telepathic experiments conducted both in our country and abroad. Then the supporters of telepathy use these results as if they were authentic facts. As a rule, however, these reports offer no opportunities for objectively estimating the results of the experiments."

The editors of the *Gazette* stated they were aware, however, that there was now appearing information on telepathy that looked more reliable. In 1965, the Popov Scientific and Technological Society of Radio Engineering and

Electric Communication in Moscow founded a Department of Bio-information for the purpose of investigating parapsychological phenomena, and conducted several well-reported experiments. A number of them involved the famous telepathic pair of Y. Kamensky and K. Nikolayev, who were said to have realized distant telepathic communication under test conditions.

In its July 7, 1966 issue, *Komsomolskaya Pravda* reported in an article entitled "Transfer of Thought from Moscow to Novosibirsk" that "two kinds of transference were tested: Zener cards (five cards bearing five different geometrical figures) and visual images of random objects. During the experiments, Nikolayev received rather clear images of dumbbells and a screwdriver.

"When receiving other images, there appeared to be much interference. However, the experimenters believe that in the future, when the experience of the first experiment is taken into consideration, it will be possible to reduce the interference. The experiment with the Zener cards has not yet been analyzed completely, but already it is clear that the number of coincidences in the transferred and received images is greater than the number of possible occasional coincidences calculated according to the theory of probability."

The author of the article said in conclusion, "I want to note that I had the chance of checking the telepathic abilities of K. Nikolayev and Y. Kamensky. This allows me to share the opinion of those Soviet scientists who believe that all people are capable of thought transfer, only to a different degree, and that this ability can be developed by training."

On April 9, 1967, Moscow *Pravda* published an article on telepathy, headed "Report of a Seance of Bio-Communication Between Moscow and Leningrad." The experiments on thought transfer over 390 miles between the two cities were conducted in January and March 1967, and the researchers said they had taken into account the experiences of the 1966 Moscow-Novosibirsk experiment.

The description of the Moscow-Leningrad experiment, which also involved the famous duo of Nikolayev and Kamensky, was very dramatic. "A light flared at Kamensky's closed eyes," the researchers reported. "The flashes of a bright lamp followed one after another. Even through his closed eyelids Kamensky could feel the brightness of the ray. He tried to see Nikolayev with his mind's eye and to convey to him his sensation of light.

"Nikolayev 'saw' Kamensky and screwed up his eyes, but he had nowhere to hide from the rays. Then the second test began, which was easier and more familiar to the two men. Yuri Kamensky in Moscow looked at different intervals at a plastic brush, an empty box of 'Yava' cigarettes and another object whose name he did not know because before the beginning of the experiment, all of them had been brought in a sealed package from the Polytechnic Museum. Kamensky had to transfer the images of the objects.

"Kamensky opened the cigarette box and pictured Nikolayev taking a cigarette out of the empty box. At this moment Karl was writing in his notebook, hardly keeping pace with the images, 'I seem to see a cigarette somewhere . . . having to write distracts me. There is a cover of a box, but nothing inside. The surface is not cold. It is cardboard.' And lastly, on the second day of the stay in Leningrad, something took place that could have been done only by radio, except no radio was used—words were transferred over great distances through the air."

The editors of *Literary Gazette* were not impressed by such apparently promising experimental results. In editorial conferences, they discussed the fact that researchers working in any field that gets a lot of publicity usually receive wide support for their work. However, even after many publications had carried stories on parapsychology, the leading scientific institutions did not change their skeptical attitude to telepathy and were in no hurry to develop parapsychological research on a wider scale, to finance it, or to set up special research institutes. Parapsychology researchers countered that this showed a biased attitude, a lack of scientific objectivism, and an unwillingness to consider facts. They claimed that Soviet science was consequently being damaged. The article they wanted published in *Literary Gazette* demanded that parapsychology should receive every possible support, and it listed a large number of what they considered "facts" that had been published in both the Soviet and the foreign press.

The *Gazette* editors were not satisfied. First, they refused to accept any evidence published in other countries, because it was impossible for them to verify it. Then they invited science experts to examine the minutes of experiments such as the Moscow-Novisibirsk, and Moscow-Leningrad telepathy experiments. They concluded that proper methodological requirements had not been observed during the experiments, and that the minutes showed serious violations of the rules existing for scientific experiments.

Since, in their opinion, the papers did not contain any proof of the existence of telepathy, the editors said they did not wish to misinform the readers and refused to publish the "Science of the Future" article. Instead, they decided to organize a controlled telepathy experiment of their own, with the cooperation of the parapsychology researchers.

A special supervisory committee of ten was set up under the chairmanship of V. F. Turchin, doctor of science (Physics and Mathematics) at the Institute of Applied Mathematics of the Soviet Academy of Sciences. Among the other nine members were a radio engineer, a psychiatrist, a chemist, and a computer expert. The committee met with Nikolayev and Kamensky and agreed on the procedures.

According to the two telepathists' wishes, the committee agreed that images, rather than words, should be transmitted. The number of items, the method of transference and reception of the telepathic signals, the method of determining which image had been transferred, and the places of transfer and reception, were all approved by Kamensky and Nikolayev. It was also mutually agreed that the choice of the image to be transferred would be made by drawing lots just before the beginning of the experiment. A test would be considered successful only if the number of the object mentioned by the sender corresponded to the number of the object given by the receiver.

The committee chose fifty pairs of objects. These pairs were given numbers and divided into two identical sets. Each object differed from any other in the same set by several characteristic features and had a duplicate, bearing the same number, in the other set. Nikolayev and one half of the committee, forming the "receiving group," then went to the city of Kerch, 700 miles away, while Kamensky and the other half of the committee stayed in Moscow.

Two telepathic seances were held. Each consisted of the transmission and reception of the images of five objects. According to the accepted methods, before the beginning of the experiment, the recipient and the sender were asked whether they wished to put it off. If either Kamensky or Nikolayev had expressed such a wish thirty minutes before the moment fixed for the beginning of the experiment, it would have been postponed.

At 6 P.M. on May 10, the Moscow group of the *Gazette* committee gathered at the laboratory of psychophysiology of the Moscow Research Institute of Psychiatry. Kamensky gave the go-ahead. Information provided by the meteorologists indicated the condition of the Earth's magnetic field was normal—which the parapsychology enthusiasts claimed was necessary to prevent undue interference with the telepathic transmissions.

The first experiment officially began at 7 P.M., and the numbered lots were drawn at 7:10, when the first object—number 30—was handed over to Kamensky. At 7:15 P.M., he indicated that he had begun telepathically sending the object's image.

In Kerch, Nikolayev was ready in the rehearsal room of the city theater. At 7:15 P.M. he was told that Kamensky had begun transmitting, and almost immediately began orally describing the object he received. The description was recorded on tape and a handwritten report was also made. Each transference lasted ten minutes, with a five-minute break in between.

At 8:25 P.M. Moscow time, the experiment ended. Nikolayev and his assistants then carefully compared the handwritten notes and the tape recording. The committee members showed Nikolayev duplicates of the fifty objects, and he was asked to write down which objects he had received, and in which order.

These notes were then signed and sealed, and in Moscow, the correct order of transmittance was also written down, signed and sealed. On the second day, transference began at 11:15 A.M., Moscow time, and was over at 12:25 P.M. Again, the minutes were signed and sealed.

On May 13, the full committee gathered at the *Literary Gazette*'s Moscow editorial offices and opened the sealed envelopes containing the minutes of the experiment. Kamensky and representatives of the editorial board were present. A comparison of the minutes of the Moscow and the Kerch groups produced results represented in the following table:

First Day

(Transmitted)	(Received)
Lead cable tied in a knot—No. 30	Cooling radiator—No. 19

Rubber eraser—No. 9   China saucer—No. 32
Motor launch model—No. 46   Champagne bottle cork—No. 3
Aluminum plate with holes—No. 37   Hacksaw—No. 41
Jubilee one-ruble coin—No. 12   Motor launch model—No. 46

Second Day

(Transmitted)   (Received)

Motor launch model—No. 46   Brown plastic wheel—No. 36
Axe—No. 13   Wooden toy soldier—No. 26
Insole—No. 34   Lead cable tied in knot—No. 30
Ball bearing—No. 31   Leg of plastic doll—No. 27
Spoon—No. 1   Electrolytic condenser—No. 42

In the opinion of the committee, "not a single one of the ten transferred images of objects was received. We conclude that there was no telepathic communication in this experiment." At the same time the committee expressed its firm belief that "it would be worthwhile to continue such experiments for the purpose of checking the existence of telepathic communication, which should be conducted under strictly controlled conditions and followed by compulsory publication of both positive and negative results."

Wrote Academician Kolmogorov: "The control experiments on the transfer of information over a distance (telepathy) organized on the initiative of the *Literary Gazette* resulted in complete failure. The conclusion drawn by an authoritative committee under the chairmanship of V. F. Turchin testifies to that. Of course, the failure of one series of experiments does not refute the possibility of telepathic transfer of information in general. This is an age-old problem, and quite naturally attempts are made in some places to find in the stream of doubtful and even fantastic reports on telepathy at least something authentic. Such attempts should not be forbidden.

"However, the *Literary Gazette* is quite naturally worried by the atmosphere created around telepathic experiments by our press. The wide circle of readers should be told in unmistakable terms that there has not been a single case when the transfer of thoughts or images was established without doubt. The information concerning telekinesis, when a person moves inanimate objects by the power of his mind, appears even more fantastic. Unfortunately, our press sometimes presents such experiments as authentic.

"It would be very important if an even more representative committee of scientists set up by corresponding departments of the Soviet Academy of Sciences explained to the public the true state of things in this area."

Academicians E. Kreps and E. Asratyan, the latter a corresponding member of the Academy of Sciences, wrote in a joint report: "Why are the results of the control experiment in contradiction with the results of the experiments Moscow-Novosibirsk and Moscow-Leningrad? A comparison of the minutes of these experiments with those of the control experiment permits us to draw certain conclusions. In the first instance, the methods of estimating the results may differ, but they must be decided upon before the beginning of the experiment, since when different methods are applied different results may be obtained.

"This condition was observed during the Moscow-Kerch control experiment. Another important condition was carried out, too. The correct drawing of lots directly before beginning the transfer ensured an equally probable choice of any of the fifty objects prepared beforehand. And lastly, there was no communication between the transferring and receiving groups up to the very end of the experiment. The minutes of the preceding experiments between Moscow, Novosibirsk, and Leningrad do not allow one to maintain that all these conditions were observed, and this is sufficient to give rise to doubts as to the correctness of the results.

"The problem of telepathy was discussed at our Department of Physiology of the Academy of Sciences some ten years ago. No exact facts were revealed at the time. However, it is to be regretted that as soon as it seems that certain progress has been made in the field, the press immediately informs everyone about it, while negative results are never published, even in scientific literature. Quite naturally, a false impression is created in the wide circles of readers that science has already received many proofs of the existence of telepathy. Therefore, it is very important to publish the negative results of strictly scientific experiments conducted under controlled conditions.

"But let us try to imagine what would happen if the results proved positive in these investigations, in which quite a number of people are engaged at the present time. Following the wise advice of Anatole France, we 'are ready to accept the supernatural when it takes place.' However, the authenticity of such a case must be proved without fail and not cause any doubt."

Six weeks after carrying the results of the experiment, *Literary Gazette* published an article under the headline: "Telepathy: Opinions and Doubts," reviewing and answering a selection of letters from readers. It took up one third of a page and began with this *Gazette* commentary: "Following the publication of the report on the control Moscow-Kerch telepathic communication experiment conducted by our laboratory, the editorial board received a great many letters. The report evoked a lively interest. Most of the readers hold that it was a useful experiment because it dispelled the erroneous concept of many uninitiated people that telepathy was allegedly an established scientific fact."

Reader opinion followed. Prof. V. Uspensky of Moscow University wrote, "A precise aim was set and brilliantly achieved, the purpose of which was not to establish whether telepathy existed or not—that goes beyond the confines of journalism—but to check the reliability of contradictory reports on the success of telepathic experiments. With its publication on telepathy the *Literary Gazette* earned itself the status of an authoritative arbiter in the field of parapsychology."

Dr. V. Malnakhov of Volkhov, Leningrad, said that in his opinion "the fact that the 'telepathic effect' was not disclosed is not a sensation. It is the quite explicable and legitimate result of a well considered scientific experiment. Had the same conditions been painstakingly observed in the Moscow-Leningrad and Moscow-Novosibirsk telepathic communication experiments, there wouldn't have appeared reports in many esteemed and serious newspapers on the transmission of thought and images of different objects at speeds faster than light."

However, other readers stopped to wonder and voiced doubts. Prof. F. Tarasenko of Tomsk University, then working as an UNESCO expert with the Physics Department of the University College in Dar es Salaam, Tanzania, wrote: "I would like to discuss briefly the organization, course, and result of the experiment you arranged to ascertain the possibility of telepathic communication. The problem of telepathy has become so overgrown with numerous rumors, prejudices, and superstitions, that many scholars just smile ironically even at the mention of telepathy. Advocates of telepathy, however, insist on the absence of any reliable scientific refutation of its existence, and justify their efforts and expenditures by the prospects the mastery of this phenomenon would open. That is why any attempt to probe telepathy without prejudice and verify facts experimentally should be applauded.

"Your experiment resulted in an apparent defeat for the 'telepathists,' and the committee's calm conclusion that 'it might be worthwhile to continue experiments to verify assertions of the existence of telepathic communication' seems but a sugarcoated, bitter pill. I would, however, like to draw attention to the fact that the very planning and organization of your experiment from the very outset proceeded from the assumption that telepathic communication would readily make itself apparent, and that the probability of the correct reception of a transmitted image greatly surpassed the probability of an accidental correct guess. Were this really so, champions of telepathy would have proven the correctness of their claims long ago. The point is, however, that even the most optimistic evaluations of the results of a number of experiments have shown that the telepathic communication channel if it really exists is a very poor one compared even to the worst of those we are normally accustomed to using. Putting it technically, the noise level in the channel is very high: that is why the probability of a correct reception of a symbol is but slightly higher than the probability of a correct guess, and the channel's transmissive capacity is very small. That is why any experiment like the *Gazette*'s is doomed to failure from the very start.

"How do we convincingly disclose the possibility of telepathic communication? It's first of all necessary to establish whether the probability of correct reception really exceeds that of an accidental guess. This can be accomplished by conducting a sufficiently long series of experiments in the transmission of two or three images. And, of course, no less trouble should be taken than you took to keep the conditions of the experiment unpolluted. I wish you success."

Other readers firmly believed in the existence of telepathy on the basis of their own "personal experiences" and they did not hesitate to tell the *Gazette* they did not accept the reportedly negative Moscow-Kerch results.

"I have personally no doubts as to the existence of telepathic phenomena, because it has happened in the case of myself and close friends," wrote L. Premirov from Karaganda. S. Demkin in Khovrino, and A. Suglobova from Lugansk voiced approximately the same view. They recounted instances from their own lives when they or their friends had a premonition of events occurring far from them, or even influenced the course of these events by an effort of their own will.

The *Gazette* answered, "Such conclusions are most frequently based on accidental, apparent coincidences of events, but it goes without saying that no coincidence, even the most improbable, can serve as proof of the manifestation of telepathy."

A number of readers took the opportunity to voice their doubts about the methods used in the experiment. For instance, were the direct executors of the experiment, the inductor and the percipient, chosen correctly? A. Zisman, of Moscow, wrote: "If the matter in question was whether a weight lifter could total 580 kilograms in the three lifts, the committee would have invited not the rank and file weight lifters to ascertain this probability, but such outstanding sportsmen as Vlasov and Zhabotinsky. Otherwise such a probability would not have been established. In the same way, only the very top telepathists should have been involved in the Moscow-Kerch experiment." The *Gazette* replied that Kamensky and Nikolayev were generally considered "record holding" telepathists.

Some readers criticized the selection of objects in the experiment, saying they differed in too many ways to allow ready telepathic recognition. That's exactly what the two telepathists wanted, the *Gazette* rather smugly countered.

S. Levitsky, of Rostov-on-Don, argued that the location of the telepathists and the time of the experiment "were not very happily chosen." Pointing out that even the most sophisticated radio receiver operates better at a distance from a big city and late at night when there is less interference, he asked: "Why was Kamensky in Moscow, and why was the transmission begun at 7 P.M. when there is so much interference in the city?" And journalist K. Karpov of Stavropol was among several readers who held that the experiment was doomed to failure from the start because of the great distance between the transmitting and receiving points.

"These same readers and Prof. F. Tarasenko do not take into account the fact that our laboratory conducted not an experiment of research or quest, but a controlled one, in which the results of the Moscow-Novosibirsk and Moscow-Leningrad experiments were methodically checked with fitting methodological severity. The distance from Moscow to Kerch is greater than that to Leningrad, and less than that to Novosibirsk, and interferences were probably the same, for in all three experiments transmission was effected from Moscow," the *Gazette* pointed out. Muscovite G.

Maksimov, a mechanical engineer, submitted that the experiment described by *Literary Gazette* was methodically deficient. He wrote: "According to the 'hypothetical laws of telepathy,' bio-telepathic communication is possible only when one of the participants is in a very tensed, emotional state, but this was not the case in your experiment. In addition, much too complicated information was transmitted, and the repetition of the experiments reduced the emotional potential of the inductor and percipient."

Unfortunately, said the *Gazette*, nothing was reliably known about the true laws governing bio-telepathic communication, and there was no point in discussing these laws. "Some of our readers object to the publication of the negative results of the experiments," the *Gazette* continued. "They voice sundry apprehensions. For instance, one reader, L. Premirov, suggests that 'all of us suffered sufficiently in our day from all kinds of taboos imposed on such fields of science as the gene theory, cybernetics, and the theory of the expanding universe. We should not repeat such errors in the future.' But telepathy, the existence of which has not been scientifically proven, is an absolutely different thing.

"It would at this point be fitting to remind the reader that science does not know of a single reliably established instance of telepathy. Besides, no one forbids quests in this field. Muscovite A. Getsov believes that the negative results of the experiments are of absolutely no interest to the public at large. He is hardly right.

"The abundance of readers' letters engendered by the publication of the documented account of the control experiment showed that the public at large did not ignore the negative results. One should also remember it is not only a reliable positive result that is of value to science. A no less authentic and reliable negative outcome of experiments helps change the direction of the quest or leads to the conclusion that the contemplated phenomenon does not exist. For example, attempts were made in the course of many centuries to build a perpetual-motion machine. The results were negative. But knowledge of the entire chain of setbacks led to the emergence of the principle of the conservation of energy and the second principle of thermodynamics—cornerstones in the modern natural sciences."

The *Gazette* ended its comments on the readers' reactions by saying, "Columbus headed for India, but discovered America. . . . In the meantime, however, let us stick to facts regarding parapsychology." Considering that the newspaper claims it receives some 7,500 reader letters a month, all dealing with issues debated by the newspaper, and bearing in mind that telepathy had been the issue of that month, the selection was pitifully meager. Who picked the letters used? How representative were they of the mail response? Were they all genuine? These were questions we could not get answered. The *Gazette* gave its verdict: telepathy did not exist.

However, the scientists and telepathists involved in the experiments had other opinions.

5.
THE CONTROVERSY CONTINUES

We had been looking high and low for Yuri Kamensky and Karl Nikolayev, the famous Russian telepathists. We knew the parapsychology grapevine had told them we could be trusted. We waited, but nothing happened. Nikolayev had shown enough courage to continue with the experiments after the *Literary Gazette* attack, and we thought he would be the first to surface. Much to our surprise, he went into total hiding. Nothing would induce him to emerge. We were repeatedly told he was out of town performing with a repertory theater and could not be tracked down.

By contrast, Kamensky did surface briefly, although after the Moscow-Kerch disappointment he had officially "retired" as a telepathist. He sent word he'd meet us, then changed his mind at the eleventh hour to say he had "the grippe, the flu." In Russia, "flu" has the same connotation as the American businessman's "in conference." "Sorry, he has the flu," equals our, "Sorry, he is in a meeting." While the illness does wreak havoc with Russians, and is a genuine threat winter after winter, resulting in desperate preventive measures, it is also a great excuse. On the two occasions Kamensky ducked under the cover of a sudden flu, he never bothered to explain when the first bout ended and the second began. Who cared? A Russian would understand, and lay off. Reluctantly, we did.

"You have to understand," we were told. "These men have suffered a lot since the *Literary Gazette* experiment. The criticism has affected their public and private lives. They are reluctant to be put in the limelight again."

But on a quiet Saturday morning in Leningrad, something—it might have been telepathy—made us try once more. For a change of pace, why not call Kamensky long-distance? We had his home number in Moscow.

We were sitting by the window in Gris's "red suite" facing the snow-covered park outside the Astoria Hotel when we got through to Kamensky's phone. We heard it ringing. Once, twice. Again, once more, but no answer. Should we give up? Then there was a clicking sound. Somebody picked up the receiver, and a voice said: "Kamensky speaking."

Somehow the memory of our subsequent conversation has remained intertwined with the view of a wintry Leningrad outside the window, the huge, baroque St. Isaac's in the background. It replaced a visual impression of a man we could not see and so could not appraise. We collected our wits fast enough to turn on the tape recorder we had kept attached to the telephone, and said pleasantly:

"How do you feel, Yuri Ivanovich?"

"Everything is normal. I feel fine. Who is this?" the voice said, a bit brusquely.

"We are the American newsmen who had been trying for the past two weeks to reach you. We are calling you from Leningrad."

Would he hang up? Below our windows, a man was trudging along the snow-covered path next to the huge flat wooden covers protecting the flower beds from frost. They were painted a bright green. The man was wearing a heavy fur cap, its earflaps down. He cut a lonely figure, his hunched shoulders giving the impression he was bowed under by years of hardship.

"Oh, yes. I know. How are you?" Kamensky replied. He would talk to us. But he also sounded like a man very much on guard. So we had to be careful.

"We are well, thank you. Did you know, Yuri Ivanovich, that your experiments with long-range telepathy are well-known outside the Soviet Union."

"Really?"

"They've attracted a lot of attention. So, if you wouldn't mind, would you talk about that a little bit?"

Careful . . . we must not scare him away. Outside our windows, the man trudging through the snow reached a large flower bed under a huge round green wooden flat and now had to skirt it to the left or to the right. Without slowing down, he turned right.

"For instance, Yuri Ivanovich, do you intend to continue this type of experiment?"

There was brief silence, then he spoke up, his voice hesitant but at least half-trusting:

"I have sort of drifted away from this type of work. Actually, these were experiments conducted on my own private time, and my present work, of course, is of a very different nature. Because I have to work hard and long hours, I don't have that much free time left."

"But since you possess this very unusual ability, don't you think you should continue to conduct this type of experiment?"

He hesitated. Then: "Absolutely. As a matter of fact, this work is very important." His voice, pained at first, seemingly fed on a growing defiance as he went on. "What is equally important is that the experiments be conducted on an even higher level than what we have already attempted. I feel that our experiments, imbued with genuine enthusiasm, were somewhere halfway between amateurism and professionalism."

"We are not sure you are being fair to yourself, Yuri Ivanovich. We spoke about you to Sergeyev, to Inyushin, to Adamenko. They are serious scientists. They were full of praise for your experiments and they approach the problem of telepathy on a high scientific basis."

There was a sigh at the other end of the phone. "It is true, what you are saying about them. Still, the subject has been in the hands of enthusiasts. You have to realize that in our country science is approached on a governmental level and, because of this, serious scientific work can be conducted only in government institutions. As there are no government institutions of this kind in our country at this time, we have nowhere to turn. A person must work on his own, with the strength of his personal enthusiasm, beliefs, and conviction."

His defiance was surfacing, we thought to ourselves, and he was growing in strength. And at least it seemed we'd gained his confidence. We looked at each other and nodded. Keep those fingers crossed. Below the windows, the man had crossed the little snowed-in park and was now walking faster, toward the street, his shoulders straightened out.

Should we try to get Kamensky to open up some more? "How did you start doing it? During childhood?"

"Yes, in my childhood. Actually, it began when I was about ten years old. I can't single out any particular occasion. The incidents were rather insignificant. Our family was on the go all over the Soviet Union at the time, but I could say that I spent more time in Moscow than anywhere else. We also lived in Siberia and Mongolia. We traveled with our father."

"Did your father transmit thoughts to you?"

"No, it was usually my friends when we were together, such as in the same room. I could pick up certain sensations. My friends would be talking about a certain author, and I would receive an impulse. I would walk up to the bookshelf, pick out a book by this author, walk over and hand it to a friend, who automatically would pick it up, open the page, and read the quote he wanted. Then he would look at me and say in surprise, 'How did you know I wanted this book? I never said anything.' The point is that I didn't know either. I merely received an impulse and obeyed it." He was now sounding quite at ease.

"How did you meet Nikolayev?"

"He was interested in telepathy before I met him. On one occasion, when I and some of my friends were discussing telepathy he simply came and joined our discussion. So we agreed then and there to try experiments together. That is how it began. All I can say right now is that I hope that the work we have done will not have been in vain."

"What actually do you do, Yuri Ivanovich? We mean, what is your profession?"

"I am a biochemist by training. I work as a biochemist in a government laboratory."

"So telepathy has nothing to do with your profession."

"No."

"But you've enjoyed it?"

"Yes."

"Have you, on a private level—that is, at home, on your own time— carried out telepathic communications with, say, a member of your family? We understood from Sergeyev that you have done that on at least one occasion."

"What he means is not my family but others, friends who may be as close to one as family members. Yes, with them, with people who like me have been interested in telepathy, I have experimented. Colleagues."

"Successfully?"

"Oh, yes."

"Have you ever had a sensation that someone is trying to communicate with you? Spontaneously? A sort of sudden voice in the dark?"

"No, nothing like that. We have only worked these things after prearranging signals. It has to be done this way to assure meaningful success. Circumstances have to be established first, then worked out in detail. There has to be a plan. One has to work according to a carefully worked out procedure. I have never worked without such a plan. Spontaneous telepathy does happen, but it is of no use in scientific experimentation.

"Without the proper controls, you cannot tell if it was a genuine telepathic contact, or merely coincidence. The spontaneous occurrence, therefore, does not interest me."

"The Moscow-Kerch experiment was a very important one, was it not?"

"Yes, it was a serious experiment. However, we did not think out the entire methodology, which then brought about a negative result. As you probably know, our experiment was labeled a failure, but this happened because we did not sufficiently study all the elements of the experiment before we made the attempt."

"Didn't the *Literary Gazette* jump too quickly to the negative conclusion?"

"Formally, they were correct because formally the connection had not been proven with regard to what was sent and what was received. In fact, the percipient described in detail all his sensations, and said much more than was necessary. He actually said so much that he himself couldn't distinguish between the necessary and the unnecessary. The descriptions were wrongly selected from the unnecessary material, and did not fit. This was one circumstance which we had not thought out, but should have. The other was that next to the percipient was a person who actually did know the object being sent. This was a cardinal error, but the error was our own. He could have unintentionally conveyed his thinking to the percipient and confused him. He had been present earlier at the sending place when the objects were selected. I seriously think these two circumstances were the reason that the results were so confusing."

In view of their realizing the errors, which were actually minor, shouldn't this experiment have been repeated after a while?

"Well, I wouldn't really try a second time unless I was totally convinced of success. Frankly, this failure has compromised me as an inductor."

"In the United States, it is not expected that a scientific experiment will succeed the first time. The chances are much too slim. The history of science is rich with the number of successes that came as a result of hundreds of experiments, yet here success is required after Number 1?"

"Yes, that is quite true. But you see, we already had successes. It was not really the first time. It was just one very important official test. We were fully hopeful that we would have succeeded this time as well. After a fiasco like that, however, no one wants to risk it again. After all, the repercussions are too broad and painful. You see, one has to distinguish between a public presentation and a test that one conducts with one's own colleagues, in one's own circle. There you train, you try, you work out one method and then another. But when you submit to a test like this one, you have to be absolutely certain."

A group of schoolchildren had appeared down below and was scattering through the little white-clad park. There was enough snow there for a lot of snowballs, but Soviet kids are too disciplined to let their hair down in so important a place as St. Isaac's Square. They just quietly ran about in the snow. Even so, they made a delightful picture.

"But would you say you are going to continue this type of experiment in your own circle of enthusiasts?"

"I can't say that I myself know. It is very difficult for us. Whether I will have an opportunity or not, as the years go by, I don't know. When one has to spend so much time on one's actual job, it is really difficult. But I still remain convinced of telepathy as a means of thought transference. Of course I do."

We were hoping he would say all that. He had made his choice. He did not beat about the bush, but told the truth, stood up for his convictions. It is something so easy for us, so difficult for them.

A militiaman had appeared in the snowed-in park and was motioning to the children to be on their way. They obeyed. One always obeys authority in Soviet Russia. Suddenly, the park was empty, the militiaman standing watch to make sure the children didn't return.

"You were saying, Yuri Ivanovich?"

"That is really all." His voice, vibrant a few moments ago, had grown solemn and dark. We could almost feel him wondering if he hadn't told these Americans too much. "I will bid you goodbye," he said. The early agony was back in his voice. "I am sorry that I will not be able to meet with you. Maybe the next time you come to the Soviet Union." He waited for our acknowledgment and thanks, then hung up.

Silence. Suddenly the phone rang. It was the long-distance operator to say the call lasted fifteen minutes.

How did these fifteen minutes stack up against the fifteen or so years of the Great Telepathy Controversy? We felt they summed it all up, as a tortured man bared his soul as much as he dared—to the voice of a stranger on a Soviet telephone. Yuri Kamensky mustered more courage and conviction than we had thought there was in him. Good luck, Yuri Ivanovich. You may win yet.

We wished we had spoken to Nikolayev as well, but realized the man must be troubled, and we respected his desire not to go on record with anything that could eventually be held against him. Both obviously needed their jobs—for as basic a thing as survival. Kamensky as the biochemist, Nikolayev as the actor.

Nikolayev, though, had spoken up on other occasions. It was our faithful Yuri who delivered to us a photocopy of a Nikolayev interview with an East German journalist. The story read:

"Nikolayev is an actor with the regional district theater in Moscow. The troupe he belongs to travels from theater to theater, has no actual home stage. Acting is his profession, telepathy is his hobby.

" 'Do you believe in telepathy?' he was asked.

" 'Where telepathy is concerned, one is either convinced or not convinced. I am convinced of telepathy. Just as night follows day, it is just as obvious to me that telepathy exists as a means, as a science. Every fiber of my body knows it,' Nikolayev replied.

"Nikolayev went on to describe what he sees when receiving telepathic messages. 'I see before my inner eye something like a screen of a small TV set,' he said. 'On it appears, very faintly at first, the outline of the object, as if the TV set has not been tuned too sharply. Then the picture travels into my hand. I feel as though I can touch it to determine its shape and size, and the temperature of the surface. The longer I am touching it, the clearer is the image on this inner TV screen.' "

As we read, we remembered the photographs in *Literary Gazette* during the infamous Moscow-Kerch experiment, where he appears to be grasping an invisible object.

" 'Like a Yogi, I keep pushing all sounds and light out of my consciousness. The fewer people in the room I am in, even though they are beyond my field of vision, the better it is for me. I need less energy to focus the image. The ideal for me is a room with a muted, diffused light.

" 'There is nothing unusual about what I am doing. Every human being possesses the faculty of telepathy to some degree. We don't all develop these faculties because we have not comprehended the mechanism of the ability. After all, the first telephone was magic to man when it was first invented . . . for a voice to come out of such a thing! I believe that in twenty to fifty years, telepathy will be as much part and parcel of man's every day life as the telephone is today.' "

It was Dr. Genady Sergeyev, the man who picked up the gauntlet so contemptuously thrown at Russia's parapsychologists by the editors of *Literaturnaya Gazeta,* who provided us with the most convincing evidence of the recent successes of Soviet telepathy. Totally undaunted, and challenging his opponents to do something about it, Sergeyev helped organize several subsequent long-distance telepathy tests. We had three meetings with him, all in his home city of Leningrad. Sergeyev first analyzed for us the experiment that preceded the Moscow-Kerch affair by one year:

"Nikolayev is the greatest percipient we have, very sensitive. We have worked many times with him, under tightly controlled laboratory conditions, and he has proven his ability to receive telepathic messages on many occasions.

"In the 1967 experiment with Kamensky and Nikolayev between Moscow and Leningrad, we set out to see whether the feelings of physical excitement, fear, and pain could help in the transmitting of telepathic messages," Sergeyev reported. "In this experiment, Kamensky merely induced these emotions in his mind—he just thought about fear or pain and tried to beam these emotions to Nikolayev.

"Both men were wired to electrocardiographs and electroencephalographs. Nikolayev had no idea what pattern would be sent, nor that the experiment was to last one hour. We made no attempt to transmit images, just the emotions. Kamensky sent two different types of messages—one lasting 30 seconds, one lasting 45 seconds—carefully timed. Meanwhile, we had Nikolayev register his reactions.

"During the period of one hour, seven messages were sent—two long, two short, two long, one short. Nikolayev recorded it as three long, one short, two long, one short. In other words, he was only one reaction wrong. We regard that as highly successful, proving that telepathic communication did take place between the two men. Also, Nikolayev's cardiograph showed that the heart reacted four seconds ahead of the brain being stimulated by the message. The changes of heart rhythm in Nikolayev took place seven times, coinciding with the sending of the messages by Kamensky.

"On June 27, 1973, we conducted an even more precise experiment on the sending of emotions. Nikolayev sat in an open room in Leningrad's Medical Institute. The inductor, in Moscow, was this time Anatoly Arvaskin, who had participated in other experiments with us.

"In accordance with a program not known to Nikolayev, Arvaskin sent telepathic messages of real emotions—pain and burns. A teakettle, boiling, with steam pouring out, was placed in front of Arvaskin. Arvaskin deliberately either touched the metal of the kettle with his fingertips or placed his hand in the steam, while thinking at the same time of sending the telepathic messages of pain to Nikolayev.

"Arvaskin felt real pain, but was not injured in his contacts with the kettle and the steam. He also concentrated on the size, shape, and color of the kettle.

"Nikolayev, during the sending of these telepathic messages of pain, exclaimed, 'It burns . . . it is a candle . . . yes, it burns.' And although he did not say the object was a kettle, he also said he was receiving 'an image of something round like a ball, with a nozzle . . . it could be a utensil . . . it has a handle.' The kettle did have a handle and a spout.

"We again concluded that telepathic communication had taken place."

At the conclusion of this meeting, Sergeyev handed us the minutes of this truly incredible experiment. The minutes were in Russian. He wanted them back.

Would the Leningrad office of Novosti make up photocopies? "Not only that," came the reply. "We'll translate the minutes for you and deliver the translation before you are ready to leave for Moscow. How's that?"

"Great," we said thankfully.

"Don't worry, I'll take care of all the details." Yuri said, receiving the minutes from Sergeyev.

Right or wrong, we read into this helpfulness a message that new winds are indeed blowing; whether its chief detractor, the ponderously powerful *Literary Gazette*, liked it or not, telepathy has emerged from the doghouse. Novosti would certainly not patronize an unpopular cause.

After the minutes were delivered to us and we had read them we decided that if at all possible we would reprint relevant parts of the impressive documents.

It was headed "Minutes of an Experiment of Transmission of Information by Means of Telepathy, Leningrad, June 27, 1973." The exact record follows:

1. The percipient Nikolayev was in the room of a brick building.

2. An ECG of the Elkar type was used during the whole length of the experiment. It recorded the signal at the exit of the analogous installation determining all 'possible resistance.' The entrance of the analogous analyzer was connected to two meters registering electric and magnetic low-frequency fields of the brain within the area of 0.2 to 10 hertz. The recorders were set up at a distance of 1.5 meters from the percipient.

3. A special recorder registered the beginning and end of the transmission of a signal as identified by the percipient. The active phases of the reception were spread out in the following way. At 8:46 P.M., the percipient identified the transmitted object in the shape of a burning wax candle. At 8:50 the signal was interrupted. In five other cases of signal pickup the percipient called out identifying peculiarities of the objects without identifying the objects themselves.

The time of pickup by the percipient of the signals:

8 P.M.   Beginning of experiment. Percipient is being prepared.

8:05 to 8:11   He receives Object No. 1.

8:15 to 8:20   He receives Object No. 2.

8:22 to 8:29   Object No. 3.

8:33 to 8:42   Object No. 4 (Comment by percipient: "They have discontinued to transmit while I am still receiving it.")

8:46 to 8:50   Identifies Object No. 5 (a candle).

8:57 to 9:04   Receives Item No. 6.

The full minutes, in Nikolayev's own words, revealed that after he relaxed at the beginning of the experiment at 8 P.M., he spoke as follows:

8:05   "Hard...not large ... slippery in your hand ... prolonged."

8:07   "Small ... something thickening ... not large ... round."

8:08   "Conic object ... blue-green."

8:09   "Metal ... and something else ... with a thickening on one side."

8:10   "Opening."

8:11   "Small object ... smaller."

8:13   "I don't see anything ... that's all."

8:14 "I am feeling with my hands."

8:15 "It has angled ribs, flat surface and corners . . . plastic . . . light color . . . almost transparent . . . something sharp from one side . . . it could be a utensil . . . it had a handle."

8:17 "Could be a plastic object . . . a utensil."

8:19 "Ashtray . . . No . . . difficult to see . . . if it has a cover or no cover . . ."

8:20 "No more . . ."

8:22 "Reception resumes."

8:23 "Round like a ball . . . maybe a ball? resilient, not hard."

8:25 "Smooth surface . . . yellow . . . looks like it's resilient . . . rubber . . . no, it isn't."

8:27 "There is a ball with a protruding element."

8:28 "A ball has become elliptic . . . it is rough . . . but the protrusion is still there . . . could be plastic."

8:29 "It has gone."

8:33 "Hard . . . a square box . . . some design . . . letters."

8:36 "Metal and wood . . . a flat square above it . . . something two . . . square has a top . . . becomes round."

8:36 "Has some lettering."

8:38 "It is slippery . . . slips away . . . covered with wax."

8:39 "Still slippery . . . cold."

8:40 "It reduces in size then it widens again, as if . . . like it had a nozzle . . . but it is not round . . . there are inscriptions."

8:42 "That is all . . . stop."

Nikolayev adds, "I was still receiving when they stopped sending."

8:46 "It begins . . . I think it is wax."

8:48 "It is like a candle . . . and it burns . . . yes, it is a candle . . . I don't think I am wrong . . . candle is round . . . clearly cylindrical."

8:50 "Yes . . . cylindrical . . . stop."

8:59 "Empty . . . no, a cup, a thimble."

9:01 "In this cup . . . it has a rim."

9:04 "It is all over."

9:05 " . . . End."

"Another interesting point we found," Sergeyev told us, "was that during the Moscow-Leningrad pain experiment, the ECG's showed that the two men's hearts beat in perfect unison. They showed the same deviations from usual rhythms. When the experiment ended, the heart rhythms changed to different beats.

"The following day, Arvaskin came from Moscow to Leningrad, and we performed another experiment with the two men. Arvaskin sat in an adjoining room and suggested the feeling of fear to Nikolayev. As soon as Nikolayev said he had the sensation of fear, we stopped the experiment and took Nikolayev into a nearby darkroom. There we placed undeveloped film in a black envelope near his head. On developing it later we found large light spots on the film, indicating that at this time, when Nikolayev was under emotional stress, there were increased electrical emissions from his head."

In another experiment on June 21, 1973, which had never been reported, Sergeyev told us telepathic messages were correctly sent by a man in Leningrad to his daughter in the Ukraine. The man was Aleksei P. Sysoletin, 48, an artist and famed telepathic medium, and his daughter was Ludmila, aged 15.

"Under controlled conditions, between the hours of 8 P.M. and 9 P.M. Sysoletin pulled six cards from a possible 60 and telepathically transmitted the objects depicted on the cards to his daughter. The girl had merely been informed by telegram saying that 'On June 21 at 20 hours your father will communicate several messages. Try to receive them.' Her father was away over a period of two weeks and when he arrived in Leningrad, it was spontaneously arranged, so the girl had absolutely no knowledge of what would happen.

"The day after she received the telegram, the selection of the sending of these items was determined without any preparation—a complete random picking of the objects on the spot. Her father arbitrarily drew the cards, and prior to the experiment did not know what the cards would depict.

"The transmission was from a room in a medical institute here in Leningrad," Sergeyev said. Sysoletin sent the following images: ball, envelope, ball, stick, envelope, envelope. "Every image was transmitted for five minutes over a total period of one hour. His daughter identified the time when she was communicating with her father, and this was done in front of witnesses who then recorded her observations. She wrote down, 'envelope, stick, ball, stick, envelope, envelope.'

"She therefore got four correct out of six. However, she had no idea that six objects would be sent."

Ludmila had not been told the session would last one hour. Consequently, she could not work out a system dividing the hour in her mind. Six objects with a period of five minutes each would take up only 30 minutes.

"We concluded that this was a successful experiment proving telepathic communication."

Dr. Sergey V. Sperunksi of the Novosibirsk Medical Institute conducted another remarkable experiment in November 1974. He kept 500 white mice together in his laboratories before dividing them into two groups of 250 each.

One group was kept on the ground floor, the other was placed on the third floor. There was no way they could see or hear one another. The group in the basement was then killed. The second group, on the third floor, immediately went into a high state of agitation. The mice reacted to the death of their fellow mice. But how did they know?

"Some type of telepathic communication took place between the two groups," Sergeyev concluded. "Bonds were established when the two groups were together. During the trauma of death, a telepathic message flashed the warning of danger to the group that was not scheduled to die, causing fear and anxiety." Later we learned from another scientist that to heighten the emotional state, the first group of mice was actually tortured before being put to death—since then researchers have known that tension greatly increases telepathic abilities.

Significantly, Sergeyev was able to round out his own experiments with a first—a recorded transmission of telepathic signals received in the brain of percepient Karl Nikolayev during a history-making session in April 1977. The way Sergeyev subsequently relayed the details to us, the unnamed inductor was taken to a place 80 kilometers outside Moscow. Nikolayev, the percipient, took up his position in a laboratory in Moscow. A new element was the recording device he was connected to. The instrument had been invented by Sergeyev, who named it the "Sergeyev Bio-Pelengator."

"It was the first time," Sergeyev said with quiet pride, "that we were able to actually register an entire telepathic transmission on the receiving end and thus present visual proof in objective terms. The experiment was unique in that we were not concerned with Nikolayev identifying the thoughts beamed at him. All we were concerned with was his receiving the signals."

And this, he did. Each and all, exactly on time, Sergeyev reported, as the transmissions were monitored at the transmitting point and Nikolayev's brain was sending impulses to Sergeyev's "Bio-Pelengator." "Its needle wrote out the exact pattern of Nikolayev's brain waves which in themselves were recordings of messages from 80 kilometers away," Sergeyev said. "He could not know the time when thoughts were directed at him, nor did anyone know it beforehand. It was left to the inductor to pick the time when to start sending and when to stop." To Sergeyev this latest experiment was the beginning of a new chapter.

After we completed our work in Leningrad we returned to Moscow and there, in the foreign currency bar of the Intourist, we reported to the man who had so expertly served as our Russian sounding board, Viktor Adamenko.

He listened carefully. Then he launched into an appraisal and reappraisal of the telepathy scene in Russia—from the scientist's point of view. He reminded us that he had conducted his own share of experiments into telepathy.

"I have been involved physically, and have witnessed many of the experiments with Sergeyev, Nikolayev, and Kamensky. They were sound, scientifically controlled tests. The team of Nikolayev and Kamensky is the greatest telepathic combination in the world. They have been tested rigorously and proven without doubt to be able to send telepathic messages. The Moscow-Kerch experiment which *Literary Gazette* found so negative had, in fact, positive results. Nikolayev did identify two objects, even though not in the correct order.

"In experiments with telepathy, it is common to have the right images but the wrong order. One tends to forget that a time gap in reception is not as important as the basic fact that the percipient *did* receive the correct object."

Adamenko feels there may be a special "ESP language" which we must learn to translate. "It is rather like hearing two people speaking foreign languages you can't understand," he reflected. "We hear something, we know an exchange of information is taking place, but we can't understand it or translate it. It is, I feel, the same thing with ESP—we are hearing a different language, but we can't translate it. Perhaps this is why some people are skilled psychics—they do have the ability to translate this language into something we understand.

"I believe that high-energy particles, which bathe the earth from outer space at all times, carry information from brain to brain at speeds faster than sound, causing reactions which we don't yet fully understand. I urge that scientists everywhere try to translate this particle into the language of our senses. In other words, find exactly what this particle changes in our brain, what human emotions it triggers."

Adamenko theorized that the carriers of ESP information and tele-pathic exchanges are the neutrino particles that constantly bombard Earth from outer space. These particles, unseen except by sophisticated scientific equipment, constantly pass right through the Earth and everything on it. In passing through one person's mind, he believes, they pick up information and deposit it in someone else's mind.

"I would like to see experiments carried on in outer space or on high mountains, where there would be less interference from other objects and perhaps more of these particles carrying information. We may do this in the future."

He pointed out that U.S. astronaut Edgar Mitchell, on a U.S. moon flight, reported flashes of light inside his brain. All the astronauts reported this phenomenon, believed caused by particle streams from space. But Mitchell, who is deeply involved in psychic research, reported more. "This may well be that his psychic abilities are greater than those of others, allow-ing him to recognize the light flashes caused by these particles passing through his brain. I would like to see a testing system whereby such people could be identified and subsequently used in psychic research." Although everyone has the capability of being a psychic, and the bombardment of neutrinos affects everyone, some people just have better abilities to translate the information than others, making them better psychics.

About a year ago, Adamenko conducted a series of experiments that pertained to the same subject with the famous hypnotist Dr. Vladimir L. Raikov at the Psychoneurological Clinic in Moscow. Twelve students, all excellent hypnotic subjects, were put into deep sleep and connected to EEG machines. Adamenko and Raikov then sent telepathic messages to the sub-jects. The EEG machines registered unusual brain activity by the subjects at the exact moment the telepathic messages were beamed at them. "It was obvious that the telepathic message was being received, although the subjects had no knowledge of it when they were brought out of the hypnotic sleep," Adamenko recalled.

One subject who registered a great deal of brain activity during these telepathy experiments showed no reaction in subsequent tests. Nobody could understand why, until it transpired that the subject had since married. Incredibly, marriage had changed his psychic abilities.

"The man did not believe in premarital sex," Adamenko grinned. "His morality made him very tense, which enhances psychic abilities. When he got married, he relaxed."

He was dead serious. It never occurred to Viktor that his reasoning would sound archaic anywhere but in Soviet Russia, whose society, despite the rule of communist doctrines, still clings to Victorian precepts.

Sex versus telepathy . . . ? We made a note of it—for whatever it was worth.

6.
THE KIRLIAN EFFECT

In a little cemetery on the outskirts of the city of Krasnodar in the Russian steppes stands a touching tribute to one of the pioneers of Soviet psychic research.

On a headstone are carved the buds of lilacs surrounded by auras! An anthropologist stopping by the grave, seeing flowers with haloes on a graveyard stone, may well rub his eyes in bewilderment. An ancient relic? No, the grave is recent. And the name on the stone reads Valentina Khrisafovna Kirlian.

The keeper of the little cemetery will be proud to inform the visitor that "Comrade Kirlian" died an untimely death in 1971 and was laid to rest here by her husband, Semyon Davidovich Kirlian, who visits the grave every Sunday, bringing fresh flowers. There's another headstone in the storage shed bearing his own name, and featuring a similar spray of lilacs with haloes around them. Kirlian carved both headstones himself. When the time comes, he'll be buried next to his wife, with the lilac buds signifying the achievement of their lives' work—the photographing of the aura surrounding all living things.

One day, the names of the Kirlians of Krasnodar may well live in history and enter our vocabularies like those of Alessandro Volta of Como, George Simon Ohm of Erlangen, André Marie Ampère of Paris, and the many other great inventors who centuries ago prepared the scientific foundation for our world of today. The name of Kirlian already offers deep meaning to scientists around the world, scientists who had never even heard of Krasnodar. They know and are genuinely impressed by what the Russians have termed "The Kirlian Effect."

We call it Kirlian photography or aura photography, a method of recording on film, in all its luminous, vibrant colors, the very spark of life that animates all living beings from plant to man. Parapsychologists call it bio-energy. Ever since the Kirlians announced their incredible discovery and the word about it spread, at first very slowly but eventually gathering momentum, students of psychic research have been holding international conclaves to discuss the new phenomenon and its seemingly endless applications. Indeed, a recent such international gathering took place in Bucharest, Rumania, in May 1977. Significantly, the man who caused all the excitement wasn't there. He stayed behind, too busy to bother, too self-conscious to take bows. Besides, without Valentina by his side, he didn't feel entitled to accept the acclaim.

When we went to Krasnodar in the south of Russia to see him, the first journalists from the Western world ever to meet him face-to-face, he was getting on in years, yet at seventy-eight he was as spry of body and agile of mind as others half his age. Even though he had never been abroad, and only a couple of times had journeyed to Moscow, he was fully aware of the impact the "Kirlian Effect" has made in the hallways of the scientific world around the globe. Yet fame has not corrupted him.

He has done without recognition most of his life. Now that his invention is seemingly opening a door to a new universal understanding of what life and death are all about, offering in passing a new scientific explanation to many miracles of past centuries, he is happy to have done his share. He made a point of this as soon as we met. He himself did not matter, but his discovery did. "The Kirlian Effect," he declared, as if he personally had nothing to do with the "Kirlian" of the Effect, "deserves universal approval." Then he added, "After all, the whole world will be able to benefit from it." His voice lowering almost as if he were talking to himself, he whispered, "If only Valya were here today." Valya, in Russian, is an affectionate form of Valentina.

Semyon Kirlian spent most of his life with his wife Valentina in a dingy two-room apartment on the corner of Gorky and Kirov Streets in Krasnodar. The wooden two-story house in which they lived has been swept away by progress—a building program that has turned a quiet provincial town slumbering under the poplar and maple trees on the bank of the sluggish Kuban River into a bustling industrial city and an agricultural trade center. Today, Gorky Street is a busy thoroughfare, featuring five-story concrete and brick buildings. He was a mechanic by trade, she a schoolteacher. His was the practical mind of the born inventor. She was the intellectual, a university graduate who served as his apprentice.

During the day she taught Russian literature at a local high school. But the rest of Valentina's time was his. She helped with his experiments, which consumed every evening late into the night, every weekend, every holiday, every vacation. Because they were so totally engrossed in their experiments with the aura of living things, which they first began in 1939, they worked long and hard. Their only relaxation was an occasional stroll, hand in hand under the trees and past the colorful flower beds that even today distinguish Krasnodar from other Soviet cities.

The Kirlians' most prized possession was their laboratory. They shared their tiny bedroom with their equipment. Every evening, before they could settle down for a night's rest, they had to move photographic plates, developer pans and induction coils from their bed. A black monstrosity in the corner was a rebuilt Tesla high-frequency generator. At night it served as coat hanger. And it was here that Valentina died in December 1971, paying a terrible price for her part in the experiments. The cause of death was simply the deterioration of a body encountering too much stress.

"Beyond a shadow of a doubt," a friend of the Kirlians told us on our visit to Krasnodar, "Valentina gave her life to science. Yet she never hesitated. She went on even after realizing that the experiments, particularly exposure to high-frequency, 200,000-volt electricity, were destroying her physically. But, she must have reasoned, who else would help Semyon? He was much too engrossed in their work to stop to think."

Another friend, a leading scientist, who visited the Kirlians during Valentina's last days, offered the following details of the tragic story: "She paid the price that science sometimes demands. It doesn't always happen, but in her case it did. Her long years working continually with high-voltage electric currents affected her nervous system and caused a deterioration that, once it began, could not be stopped.

"Valentina's was a horrible death. Her nerves had become supersensitive, causing excruciating pain whenever her body came in touch with anything. In all, she spent two years bedridden, her body slowly disintegrating until she was little more than a living skeleton wreathed in pain. During the days preceding the end, even the slightest noise caused her physical suffering. We had doctors come from Moscow, Leningrad, Kiev. She was beyond help. She was offered the best hospital care, but she turned it down. Semyon would not hear of her being taken away from home. He was going to take care of her—and he did, until that day in December, 1971 when she passed away.

"Her death ended a nightmare. Still, it proved a terrible shock to him. At first he seemed in a daze, unable to adjust to the thought that she was gone. Valentina had been his companion through life. They had no children. He blamed himself and his experiments for her death. 'Let's face it,' he told me again and again, 'I murdered her. I should be tried and convicted and made to pay the supreme penalty.'

"He wouldn't accept our premise that this wasn't so. After all, the experiments had not affected him, however much he had exposed himself. 'She was always in greater danger than I,' he insisted. He stopped going to the local agricultural institute, where he was carrying out some very important work that he had begun a year before Valentina's death, on the auras of plants. He spent most of his time at the cemetery sitting beside her grave. Almost overnight he became a bent old man.

"The next thing we found out was that he was in the cemetery shed, chiseling a granite headstone for Valentina. One day it was taken out and put over her grave and we, their friends, came to the cemetery to offer a prayer for Valentina's soul. Semyon had never been religious, but his experiments gave him faith in life after death. He realized it, he said, as he watched so many times the last flicker in the aura of a dying leaf. He had become convinced that bio-energy, which produces those vibrating auras of living beings, is never extinguished, even as it leaves a dying body in a last burst of flame—to travel on into the universe. Hence soul is immortal. And on her stone he carved buds of lilacs with auras around them—not so much for himself as for us, to remember him and her in the time to come when he, too, is gone."

It took Semyon Kirlian two years to snap out of it. Since he was past retirement age, he could live quite comfortably on his pension. Then, on February 1, 1974, the Presidium of the Supreme Soviet of the Russian Republic recognized him as "Meritorious Inventor." With the title came additional privileges. It was one day soon after that, Krasnodar scientist Ruben Stepanov remembers, that his friend Kirlian came to his door. Dr. Stepanov, a Kirlian disciple, had been dabbling with the Kirlian Effect in the research laboratory of the Krasnodar city hospital, trying to obtain auras of medical students subjected to different kinds of mental stress.

"Semyon asked how I was doing. I said, 'So-so.' My pictures were all muddy. Results were inconclusive. He had one look at my equipment and threw his arms up in despair. 'You are doing it all wrong,' he said, took off his coat, and went to work."

This episode heralded Semyon Kirlian's return to life—and work. Apparently, he's been at it ever since, his strength and agility back to what they used to be. His latest work, though, at the Agricultural Research Institute outside Krasnodar is shrouded in secrecy. . . .

When it all began half a century ago, Kirlian was the local jack-of-all-trades, a self-taught repair man with a magic touch. Some people in Krasnodar still remember his little workshop in the heart of town. With only four years of school behind him, he could fix any type of electrical equipment, from burned-out fixtures to bicycle lights. When summoned, he came with toolbox and rolls of wire to put in new electrical wiring, fuse boxes and fixtures. As years went by, he graduated to repairing photo cameras and microscopes. Whatever he didn't know he figured out. He did his own schematic drawings, spent nights reading up on whatever it was he needed to learn. By the late 1920's, he was sufficiently proficient to dismantle and put together the most intricate generating equipment. He was in love with electricity and the machines it powered.

Those were hungry and turbulent years, during which the USSR was emerging from total chaos. A city called Ekaterinodar (Catherine's Present), handed to the Kuban cossacks by a grateful Empress of All Russians back in 1794, was renamed Krasnodar in honor of the Red Army. As a sleepy town was waking up to a new rhythm initiated by the Bolshevik regime, a young mechanic working out of a little workshop was fixing machinery for a new world. When a new hospital went up, and its electrical equipment refused to function, Kirlian went over and got it going. He could fix anything a hospital would put in, from electrical massage machines to X-ray equipment. As word about his amazing prowess spread, he became the visiting repairman at every medical installation in town.

With the job secured, young Kirlian gave up his workshop, married, and was granted his request for the tiny two-room apartment that he and Valentina would occupy for the next forty years. "At that time," says Viktor Adamenko, who grew up in Krasnodar, "Kirlian was working at the hospital as a maintenance man, taking care of all electrical machinery. One evening, as he was repairing the high-frequency generator of an electrical massage machine, an electrical discharge accidentally passed through him. He felt no pain. Instead, he observed beautiful pyrotechnics he thought were worth recording.

"The idea fascinated him. But how could he photograph an occurrence like this? He needed total darkness. They were still using glass plates then, which meant that the object he would photograph would have to be pressed against the plate.

"So, now for the object. Obviously himself. What part of him? Why not his hand? And that's how he rigged it all up. He planned to use an insulated table as a base, with the photographic plate wrapped in black paper sitting on top of an electrode. He would attach the other electrode to his hand, press against the plate, throw the switch and push it back. Done. To prevent disaster, he would stand on a rubber pad for insulation.

"He returned to the hospital the following day and proceeded as per plan—with one improvement. He asked a young medical student to stand by and throw the switch for him. It was the first time, after all, and he wasn't sure of himself. As advised, the student threw the switch, heard the click he was warned he would hear, and disengaged it again. Kirlian raised his hand from the plate. Nothing had gone wrong. Later that night, a frantic Kirlian watched wife Valentina develop the photographic plate. What appeared on it was a silhouette of a human hand, its bones firmly outlined, a mysterious aura surrounding the fingertips. They didn't sleep that night."

By all reports, Kirlian's original equipment was pathetically primitive. He built it from scratch from rejected supplies hauled home from the hospitals. The most expensive items were the technical books he bought to study at home. He was later to engage their authors in scientific controversies by mail. Valentina, a photography buff, loved to do her own developing and printing.

One day the hospital where he was doing repairs got in a new Tesla high-frequency generator and let him have the old burned-out one. He carted it home and, after figuring out what had gone wrong and improvising replacement parts, Kirlian got it working again.

"Once it was repaired," Viktor Adamenko recalls, "they could continue their experiments at home, under controlled conditions. Their first objective was to obtain sharp images. Early images were very blurred. In order to get better results, they had to find the proper exceptionally thin material to be placed between hand and plate. They tried a variety of materials, from fabric to tinfoil. Solving the problem took them an entire year, but once they got the sharpest possible image, they were on their way to complete success.

"By then it was 1940. They started systematic research and expanded it when they discovered that leaves also emanated auras. Not only that—each leaf photographed like a sea of shimmering lights. They didn't know what it was but they went on, feeling they were eavesdropping, perhaps on life itself."

Adamenko clearly remembers himself as a little boy living around the corner from the Kirlians. "I was one of the children they would ask in on a Sunday, treat to a candy, and allow to watch them operate their mysterious machinery. But only from the doorway. They didn't allow us close to the machines, and under no circumstances to touch anything. They would then tell us to go out to play and pick some leaves for them. They always wanted the leaves in pairs. We would race one another. Whoever brought the largest and prettiest pair of leaves won. Little did I expect to find myself, years later, working with the man as a fellow scientist. But it pleases me to know that I was among those who supplied the Kirlians with some of the very leaves that helped them pinpoint the Kirlian Effect."

On one occasion, working with what appeared to be identical leaves, the Kirlians got very different results. "They already knew that live leaves off the same shrub would photograph identically, revealing the same brilliant array of twinkling lights. This led them to the discovery that the two leaves had photographed differently because one had been infested by micro-organisms that, two days later, became visible to the naked eye. One leaf was dying; the other was healthy. The second stage of their research resulted: diagnosis. Then the war broke out, and all their laboratory research stopped. It was not until five years later that they were able to resume where they had left off."

Not until 1948 did the Kirlians reach the stage where a working model could be sent to Moscow for approval. It took the State Patent Office one full year to get around to issuing a patent, but a full ten years after Kirlian had stumbled on it, his invention had become official reality. Over the years, as the Kirlians probed deeper and deeper into the mysteries of the spark of life, they were awarded some twenty more patents. They had come a long way from their original primitive appliance. Making a switch to color film—which in itself opened exciting vistas—they translated their procedure to observations under a microscope, images on the luminescent surface of vacuum tubes, and finally, nonoptical procedures. Years of experience turned them into scientists and inventors of the highest order, who could meet the challenge of the most learned members of the Soviet Academy of Sciences.

Not that this led to fame and fortune. Still very little was said and written about the Kirlians. The reason, probably, was the fact that they had come into the limelight following a series of technical discoveries that had managed to confuse the issue. As early as 1898, an electrical engineer, Y. O. Narkevich-Iodko, exhibited at the Photographic Exhibition of the Russian Imperial Technical Society some unusual "electrographic" photographs of coins, leaves, and human hands. To create these "mystical" photographs, actually all he did was to place photographic paper between object and elec-trodes. A Czech physicist, B. Navratil, had discovered similar phenomena some years earlier. At that time, the circumstances of electrical discharge itself were still being investigated. The photographs were very unclear and proved nothing.

For years after that, others toyed with a similar type of "photo-graph," never accepted as a serious scientific discovery until 1945 when, according to Adamenko, Prof. G. Spivak of Moscow State University came up with quite good "electrographic" pictures of inorganic objects obtained by means of an electric discharge.

"There was no point in any of this," Adamenko says today. "All it did was to cause an initial indifference to the Kirlians. If by now hundreds of scientific articles have been published on the subject of 'aura photography' and the 'Kirlian Effect' enjoys world-wide reputation, it was not for lack of obstacles in their way.

"It was their dedication, their fighting spirit, their belief in the importance of their discovery that finally won out. We should have long accepted the fact that they had succeeded in opening to us a bird's-eye view of the exciting inner structure of life as exemplified by expected but also unexpected biological phenomena. Leaves showed auras around their contours to include a section recently cut off and hence nonexistent. The human mind expressed itself through the tips of the subject's fingers, to become an open book as the aura's flickering 'flames' differed with the nuances of the subject's emotions. I remember how on one occasion I myself served as a Kirlian guinea pig to measure the influence of alcohol. I fortified myself with a glass of wine between picture sessions. The aura coming off the tips of my fingers was clearly different before and after.

"Love, hate, fatigue, stomachaches, sexual desire—as faint as might be caused by a fleeting kiss—all registered to lead to important biological conclusions.

"And yet, as late as March 27, 1974, a skeptical Vladimir Lvov would refer to the Kirlians in an article in *Evening Leningrad* as 'that idle Krasnodar couple who waste everybody's time with harmful photographic hocus-pocus!' "

The attack misfired. An outspoken foe of Russia's parapsychologists, Lvov made a double fool of himself that evening in Leningrad. He ignorantly attacked a woman long dead in the service of science. And he cast doubt on the credibility of Kirlian as an inventor not two months after he was officially named "Meritorious Inventor" of Soviet Russia.

Actually, Lvov was far behind the times. The 1960's saw the Kirlians handed recognition from many scientific quarters. First, Kishinev biologists V. Lusikov and V. Mikhailevski spoke up in praise of the Kirlian method and its usefulness in biology. Then in Leningrad, physicist K. Frantov went on record with similar observations. Finally in Alma-Ata, in the spring of 1968, Dr. Viktor Inyushin called to order the first conference on bio-energy, with its main topic "The Kirlian Effect." The Alma-Ata conference, emerging from four years of concentrated study, subsequently led to the city getting an official nod to go all out to research the effect and evolve practical applications. Simultaneously, vivid descriptions of various aspects of the Kirlians' work appeared in many Soviet medical and scientific journals. Here is one clipping we picked up, at Dr. Stepanov's office the author reporting:

"Obtained on the photos is the surface structure of live objects, surrounded by a halo of a high-frequency discharge. According to the physiological condition of the organism the size of the halo and the luminescent brightness are apt to vary. Man's skin photographed on colored film reveals that different sections are distinguished by different colors. For instance, the cardiac area photographs a deep blue, the armpit area is greenish blue, the hips photograph an olive color. Emotional sensation, such as pain and fear, causes an immediate change of color."

The author waxed ecstatic at what he saw. "Under magnification, against the background of skin, the discharge channels break out in dots, crowns, torches in the nature of luminescent concentration. They are of different hues: blue, lilac, yellow, bright and dull; continually burning and flickering, periodically flashing, stationary and weaving. ... At the fingertips, the discharge channels turn outward like torches while strictly following the pattern of the skin. At some skin sections, golden and blue spots suddenly flash up, while clusters in other colors continually spill over from one point of the skin to another, to be absorbed there."

We could see Semyon Kirlian shrug at reading this, to say impatiently, "Of course, of course. This is not the point, though. What matters is, what does all this mean? That is the crux of the issue."

It was Dr. Thelma Moss whose wistful, "How I wish they would have let me see Kirlian. He may be sick, or dying, or dead, you know!" caused us to push his name high up on the list of interviews we had put together for submission at Novosti in Moscow. We were relieved when no attempt was made to turn it down, and when eventually a cable arrived from Moscow listing approved subjects, the name Kirlian was among them.

The old embargo had been lifted—for us! Was it because it was felt in Moscow that it was time to produce Kirlian for an outside world to see that he did exist? We decided we weren't going to fuss over it. To show extreme enthusiasm over a breakthrough could be imprudent. When told by a Novosti official at our first meeting in Moscow, "You are extremely fortunate that Kirlian agreed to be interviewed by you. We cannot even get him to talk to our own newsmen!" we merely nodded appreciation.

"Mr. Kirlian has obviously shown good judgment," we joked purposefully. Even before we left America, the visit to Krasnodar had been marked in by Novosti's Natasha Yakovleva for a Sunday arrival, with the Kirlian interview set for Monday. A special visa for Krasnodar had been requested and approved, all as part of the preliminaries. None of this actually meant we would *see* Kirlian, only that all necessary moves had been thought of beforehand. "I am going to take you there myself," Natasha said now, on that first day in Moscow.

"That's very nice," we replied, holding back our genuine delight.

On our previous trips throughout Russia, Natasha's energy and ingenuity in removing obstacles had served us in very good stead. Her efficiency matched that of the best press relations person in the West. The price—her watching over our movements and making sure we didn't stray—was not that high. We had no inclination to stray anyway. Her plan, as she explained it to us, was for the three of us to check in early on Sunday at a Krasnodar hotel, so that she could set the stage for the interview the following morning. The rest of that Sunday we could spend visiting a huge new artificial lake everyone was talking about, and later have dinner at a place Moscow was raving about, a replica of an old Cossack village, what is known as a *Kuren*, a Kuban Cossack-style recreation area. And, as a minor pièce de résistance, taste there the Soviet Pepsi-Cola that is now being produced in neighboring Novorossisk. It sounded fine, but it was not to be that way. That Sunday morning, things went utterly wrong.

A heavy blizzard was wreaking havoc all through Moscow's Vnukovo Airport as we arrived to board our flight to Krasnodar. When we caught sight of passengers trudging through the snow toward waiting Aeroflot jets, we heaved a sigh of relief. The snowstorm notwithstanding, it seemed the airport was fully functioning. All the flights were departing, except the one to Krasnodar!

We were well past the departure time and the passengers huddling in the waiting room had not been called. "Let me snoop around," Natasha said, and departed. Twenty minutes later, she returned, looking disappointed. The news was bad. Ironically, it was not the blizzard over Moscow that caused the cancellation of our yet-to-be-announced flight, but fog at Krasnodar, brought on by the new artificial lake. As a result, the flight from Krasnodar that was to take us back had never taken off.

"We may not be able to leave at all today," Natasha said. "It could mean you are losing Kirlian."

For a while we sat in the red plastic chairs of the sparsely furnished passenger lounge not saying a word. It wasn't fair. "We could try to get to some other city," one of us said, "and hitchhike from there."

It was meant to be a stiff-upper-lip joke, but it caused Natasha to look up, say, "Rostov-on-Don. Let me find out," and disappeared, leaving us without an explanation.

We pulled out our map of Russia. There was Krasnodar, just above the Caucasus to the right of the Black Sea. And there was Rostov-on-Don at the estuary of the Don River in a far corner of the Sea of Azov. A friendly red line, denoting a major highway, was emerging from the dot of Rostov-on-Don heading south, and at a place called Pavlovskaya curved slightly to the west, to hit—Krasnodar! Eagerly, we measured the distance. It came out at a solid two hundred miles.

"Two hundred miles of illegal travel by train, or rented car, or cab," we said. "Why not?"

Natasha was back, looking composed. "All right, boys," she said. "The 3:45 P.M. flight for Rostov is fully booked, but I've put us on the 6:45 P.M. flight. Takes two hours. We arrive too late for the train that gets to Krasnodar in the morning, but we might try something else. Shall we risk getting stranded in Rostov-on-Don?"

"If you're game, Natasha, so are we," we said hopefully. And we added a note of wisdom, "Since we don't know when or where or if at all we may be eating down there, why not go back into town and grab a decent meal?"

Back at the National, we surveyed the situation. Natasha kept disappearing to make phone calls. We had no visas for Rostov, so we would be breaking a law by going there. Nor were we permitted to travel two hundred miles across Russia's Kuban steppe, be that by cab, hired car (if we could get one), or any other means of transport. However, as long as we had Natasha along—she was well aware of the illegalities—it was not our responsibility.

Suddenly she was back, her face registering triumph. "There's been a cancellation. I've managed to switch us to the 3:45 P.M. flight." In our circumstances, "cancellations" meant she had applied pressure where pressure could be applied, even on a Sunday, and some poor locals had been bumped off the flight to make room for us. "Let's eat and then go back to Vnukovo," Natasha said. Things were looking up.

It was pitch dark when we landed in Rostov-on-Don and found ourselves in a small provincial airport where, for a change, we were not expected. The Intourist waiting room reserved for foreign travelers was empty. Natasha parked us under a huge imitation-marble plastic plaque confirming the bestowal of the title "Hero City" to Rostov-on-Don for its role in the war against the Nazis, and left in search of help.

Minutes ticked by. We were getting worried, seeing ourselves stranded in Rostov by the Sea of Azov when Natasha returned. She found a taxi driver, she announced in a businesslike manner, who would take us to Krasnodar for 80 rubles—one hundred and ten dollars. Was that too much?

"Too much?" we said grandly. "We'd pay three times that much to make it there on time for the Kirlian appointment."

"Then," she said, "let's not waste time."

The white Volga outside was the latest model, which was encouraging. The driver, who was young and friendly, didn't ask questions. We piled in and set out across a dimly lit city, every so often stopping at taxi stands to talk with other drivers. "He is borrowing coupons," Natasha explained.

The coupons were vouchers for gas that the driver needed to get him to Krasnodar and back. Finally, he jumped back in, adjusted himself in his seat, turned around and exclaimed happily: "That's it. We go."

"You see?" Natasha said knowingly, "Now relax. We have ahead of us a long journey through the night."

There were no more stops except at the wayside gas stations, where the omnipresent heavy-set woman in her fifties—who seems to be doing all the menial jobs in the streets, on the highways, along the canals of Russia—presided over the rusty old-fashioned pumps. We did slow down for the militia checkpoints, each time expecting the man with the khaki greatcoat and peaked cap, a huge gun in his holster, to signal us to halt for inspection. In our particular circumstances, such a stop could have landed us in serious trouble. Each time our hearts sank. Each time we were waved on.

We zoomed at a respectable clip along a paved and monotonously straight road flanked by what appeared to be endless fields. "This is the Kuban," Natasha explained, "the black earth of Mother Russia. Wheat, wheat, and more wheat. Our richest land." At one point she became involved in a discussion with the driver on who makes more, a Soviet editor—she had told him we were newspaper people, but omitted to say from where—or a

Kuban wheat farmer. They figured for a while in the darkness. Five and six hundred rubles per month were mentioned. They ended up agreeing that both earned good money.

After we set out from Rostov-on-Don, it was three hours before the pitch darkness around us began to show signs of life. A blurred light here and there multiplied gradually into a carpet of dim lights and, eventually, a cluster of lights ahead of us. "Krasnodar," said the driver. Our taxi swerved around a dark bend. Suddenly we were rolling along a wide, double avenue, flower beds along the middle strip, and the two avenues flanked with shadowy trees. Behind them loomed buildings, all looking alike and five-storied.

The avenue, which was poorly lit, was empty. The buildings, too, looked vacant, unless everything in there was fast asleep. Only an occasional window was lighted. At a corner, the taxi driver swung around and came to a stop in front of the only building showing definite signs of life. Most of the windows in the five-story facade were alight—with the typical 25-watt power of a Soviet window. There was a big sign over a six-story tower behind, too dark to make out.

"This is the Kavkaz Hotel," said our cab driver, "all important visitors to Krasnodar stay here." He was gambling on our having rooms there, because we didn't know where we would be staying. Our hosts were to advise us upon arrival at the airport. But he was right.

The receptionist lifted an indifferent eyebrow, found our names in the register, requested our passports and visas, but asked no questions. We had just enough time, he said, warming up to Natasha, to have dinner at the hotel restaurant—if we hurried. We did as told, left our luggage in the lobby, and turned up on the balcony of a huge noisy dining room with a Sunday dance in progress. The dance floor was jam-packed with couples jitterbugging to a glaring Russian band—heavy-set men and women, descendants of the Kuban Cossacks, giving themselves a strenuous workout.

"Thank you, Natasha," we said, raising our glasses of champagne, local Krasnodar vintage, "for getting us here. And here's a toast to the success of our interview with Semyon Davidovich—as planned."

7.
KIRLIAN IN PERSON

As is typical for a man who had spurned hundreds of invitations from scientists and journalists at home and abroad to discuss his invention, Semyon Kirlian met us without any fanfare.

Early that morning, two men from the Krasnodar Novosti office had come to our hotel to see if by any chance we could have slipped into town unnoticed by anyone.

They and a girl from Intourist, all apprised of our coming and agog with anticipation, had spent the entire day at the Krasnodar airport. Told our plane would be late, they waited. Typically for a Russian airport, no one told them the flight had been cancelled. Eventually, as no plane arrived, they went home—about the time we were checking into our rooms at the Kavkaz Hotel. The rooms were small, bare, sparsely furnished in a cheap quasi-Danish style, with flimsy flowered curtains over the window and a single 25-watt bulb for light. Each room had a telephone, but it was out of order. The Novosti men hadn't thought of checking the hotel—how would we know to go there if we had come by any other means? But they dropped by in the morning on an off chance, to be told we were there, all right.

They looked and felt embarrassed. "Never mind," we said. "It's all Natasha's doing. She's quite a girl!"

The two men, Yuri Dyachkov and Yuri Zenyuk, eyed her in awe. "Honored to meet you, Comrade," they said. We thought we heard a clicking of heels. They shook hands, and when the men turned, she winked. We really had good rapport with her.

"Where do we meet Kirlian?"

"At the Institute," came the reply. "He is coming over especially. We had better hurry." The men were making up for yesterday. We were ushered out into the street and to a waiting car.

It was a beautiful morning, a warm sun suspended in a light blue sky caressing the "black earth of Russia" outside the windows. En route out of the new city with the broad boulevards, past the picturesque old wooden houses, presumably homes of the old Kuban Cossacks, the men filled us in on the Institute.

It's really the Research Institute of Agriculture, the two Yuris explained, a Soviet horticultural mecca where the best Soviet agricultural experts had crossbred the latest and most formidable species of wheat, yielding two to two and a quarter tons per acre. The new strains, Aurora and Kavkaz, produce almost twice the normal yield. Noted Soviet Academicians Pustovoit, Lukyanenko, and Khadinov have carried out similar breeding and crossbreeding at the Institute with sunflowers, corn, and rice. Yet the most important man at the Institute is Kirlian, whose study of the aura of these and other plants has just prevented a serious blight that could easily have reduced the Kuban's crop by half. He caught the disease just in time, and was now regarded as a "miracle man."

"Semyon Davidovich," they intoned respectfully, "has been very busy at the Institute ever since his return to work after the death of his wife."

What was his function—could they spell it out?

"Actually, we don't know the half of it," they said, exchanging glances as if saying, "Haven't we said too much already?"

"Much of it is secret, you know, but the Director may tell you."

Astride a country road below Krasnodar, the sprawling white four-story building of the Institute was slowly coming into view from behind a long, straight line of poplar trees beyond the upturned black earth of the fields. We had arrived exactly on time. But when our car pulled up at the front entrance, there was no one there. "Follow us," the two Yuris said, leading the way up the broad steps past the elevator. Possibly it wasn't working. Reaching the upper floor, slightly out of breath, we stopped in front of the ornate door facing the stairwell. One Yuri knocked respectfully while the other beckoned us to follow him.

Sure enough, the reception committee was all there. The burly, bullet-headed head man introduced himself with a heavy handshake as Timofei Semyonovich Dubonosov, Institute Director. He was flanked by two aides. We were motioned to take seats at the large conference table. This was obviously the "board room," quite lavishly paneled in what seemed to be maple, with glassed-in sideboards in the same wood. A large plaque on the wall featured a spray of wheat, the Institute's pride and joy, as it was the strain Kirlian saved from untimely disaster. There were the usual batteries of soda bottles and upturned glasses on neat little round tablecloths on the table. The coffee, cognac, and cookies, we knew, would come later. We pulled out our portable tape recorders and placed them near the empty chair next to Dubonosov's. "Good," he said approvingly, "Nice. Strong microphones?"

"Yes."

"Good," he said and pulled the tiny Sony-55 closer to himself. He settled back in his chair.

"Before you begin," said Yuri No. 1, "would you mind very much if we, too, took notes? You don't know what it means to us. It's quite an event."

"Be our guests," we said. They whipped out their notebooks. Then we sat in silence. Two, three minutes ticked by and then, suddenly, silently, the knob in the door turned. The wide, ornate door opened a crack and a face peered in as if making sure it was the right place. Then, recognizing the men around the large conference table, the newcomer beamed, entered the room and almost apologetically took a few steps toward us, a slightly-built man, his receding hair a pure white, hornrimmed glasses accenting an ascetic, scholarly, face. He was wearing a neat double-breasted gray suit and black tie.

"I am Semyon Kirlian," he said softly, a sensitive hand outstretched. We had met a living legend.

Comparing notes later that day, we tried to think who it was that he reminded us so much of at the time he came into the room and shyly took the empty seat next to Dubonosov. He was self-conscious and ill at ease, yet there was quiet dignity in his posture. We decided there was something faintly Chaplinesque about him, in the noble sense of the little man striving to help the world. Later the scientist, the engineer, the brilliant inventor in him took over and the original impression was gone.

The conversation started out with our "We're so glad you exist! Back in America we had begun to doubt it."

"Now you know!" he replied, amused.

We talked for two and a half hours. He took the floor to describe his work, but also to touch on his disappointments, his hopes, his fears. He grew a bit anxious as he described how his invention was now being used in so many scientific fields all over the Soviet Union and was, presumably, beginning to make a similar impact on the outside world. As he surveyed the grand scene, from a bird's-eye view that was very much his own, his voice grew firm, authoritative, and confident. He was proud—but not ostentatiously so—of his accomplishments. Thereafter, he remained in easy, courteous command, to describe, not without humor, the "Kirlian Effect."

"I have lost count of the areas where Russian scientists today are applying the Kirlian Effect," he was saying. "Applying it with amazing effectiveness while, mind you, moving on all the time." He adjusted his glasses, then went on. "Space technology, geology—Soviet geologists have started applying it while looking for ore. It's certainly more effective than dowsing. We've started using it in metallurgical research, especially in the study of metal fatigue. It can be employed for safety checkouts in every conceivable industry. Recently, in Moscow, they even tried out the Kirlian Effect in checking a murder weapon in a court case. They used it as they would in a ballistics test for the aura to show what they wanted to know. Has this particular gun been fired using this particular bullet?

"The Kirlian machine will tell whether one is lying or telling the truth much more conclusively than those lie detectors of yours. Which means that criminologists can—if they want to and the law permits—have a field day. In a very different area, that of our past, historians are enlightened by our discovery. For there is no longer any doubt as to the origins of the haloes observed and recorded around the heads of martyrs by their contemporaries who watched in awe."

He shook his head in wonderment. This was an area he obviously didn't feel he wanted to discuss here and now, yet. . . .

"Anyway," he went on, "the greatest value of the Kirlian Effect to the world, I think, lies in the help it offers us in dealing with the problems of human beings. Which takes us back to medicine—all medicine. For example, a sick child was brought to our city hospital, but no one on the medical staff could diagnose the illness. They then fell back on their aura equipment and photographed the child's abdomen, where the trouble seemed to lie. What showed up was similar to the aura of a patient suffering from scarlet fever. A corresponding conclusion was made, and the child was treated for scarlet fever. Days later, typical scarlet fever spots broke out on the child's body to confirm the aura finding."

Kirlian paused and then, throwing back his shoulders, said proudly, "Do you realize that work on the Kirlian Effect's diagnostic properties alone is being conducted not only in Russia but in Rumania, Bulgaria, Hungary, Czechoslovakia, and East Germany by over 1,000 high-level scientists, physicists, biologists, medical doctors, with a total staff of as many as 50,000 laboratory assistants. We've come a long way in helping emotionally disturbed people. By comparing their auras to those of the mentally healthy, we see where and how they differ. We keep aura files on the patients as they are being treated. The Kirlian photos show when a mentally disturbed person has grown worse, even when there are no other symptoms by which a psychologist could discover it. Different types of mental illnesses show up in different auras. This offers the attending physician invaluable clues.

"Mental fatigue shows up as clearly as do a great variety of quite harmless emotions. The Kirlian Effect can measure emotions to a fine degree, even determine when people are genuinely in love or merely think they are in love. Can you imagine what this can do to our institution of marriage? It can also help in treating alcoholics. The Kirlian Effect will determine whether the cure is taking effect, whether a patient is faking or cheating. Drug users can be similarly helped."

He caught the question in our eyes. "No, never in my wildest dreams did I expect anything like this to happen." His mind traveled back in time, conjuring up sights that were no more. His work, he mused, had been everything to him, the whole meaning of his life.

"As long as I could remember, I always had some sort of workshop where I could tinker with old instruments and machines that others had abandoned, from electric meters to old microscopes. When I was a child, I had some musical talent and I was told that I could become a pretty good musician. Then came World War I and suddenly I was thrust into grim reality. They made me a soldier.

"I survived. Then came the Civil War and I survived that, too. After I returned home, I tried myself out at everything, from being a shop salesman to a piano tuner, to a shop window decorator, until I settled on being a repairman. This I loved. This, I felt, had promise for me, a progression.

"Mind you, I've always been imbued with an untameable fantasy. Always full of dreams. Because I didn't get to finish school, I taught myself everything I knew by reading. I was the only youth in Krasnodar who gobbled up textbooks instead of novels. I was fascinated by mental calculations. And equations. I was lucky because I had an unusually easy understanding of highly complicated mathematical problems. Whatever others learned at the universities, I learned in a corner of my workshop, textbook in hand."

Did he remember his first experiment with auras? The birth of the Kirlian Effect?

"Of course I remember," he said simply. "I was carrying out repairs of a high-frequency generator and I happened to have a scratch on my hand. It had healed. There was no visible sign of it. Yet in the high intensity field around the generator, it showed up clearly."

He was amplifying on Adamenko's account we had heard earlier: "I am a curious man, and I set out to find what this phenomenon was all about. The following day, as it happened, I experienced a double electrical discharge and it didn't bother me. So, between my curiosity and self-confidence, of which I had plenty, I decided to go ahead with an experiment. I took the picture of my hand that everybody seems to know about, and Valentina developed it. It looked very much like an X ray, but we both agreed that it was not, because it was not bone structure that was outstanding in this picture, but the contours of my hand, of each finger, with thicknesses at their tips. That was the aura, but we didn't know it at the time.

"That's how it all began. We had some wonderful days, days of discoveries. But, if you ask me which gave us our greatest thrill, it was when we stared at our first picture and saw the aura. We were ecstatic; that is the only way to describe it. I was not sure I knew what I had accomplished, but I knew I had hit on a discovery that could have an enormous impact on the future of the world.

"For a long time, our equipment remained rather simple. We had no money to buy or build expensive machinery, so we kept going as best we could. The equipment was all over the bedroom," he recalled with a pleasant smile, "but we felt that we were in *its* way, not the other way round. We took aura pictures of each other, only to find out that we were different in color. My wife's aura background was orange and mine was bluish. We then found out that everybody has his own color. We still don't know why. Maybe it's as simple as fingerprints—no two match.

"But it wasn't always smooth sailing. Especially during the early stage. We had several accidents with the high-frequency high voltage. We suffered shocks that sent us stunned to the floor. We accepted that as part of progress. But one day, after a series of shocks hit me so hard I was knocked unconscious, my wife said, 'Can't you do something about it?' and I said, 'Of course I can.' I replaced the switch with a pedal. The current remained connected as long as my foot remained on the pedal. Whenever a shock knocked me back, my foot automatically kicked off the pedal and the current was cut off, exposing me to much less shock." He shot up an eyebrow: "It was that simple.

"For years, as you know, we worked in our little apartment, and then in 1962 the authorities gave us a much larger place to live in and we continued our experiments there."

This, for the record, was the apartment on Karl Libknecht Street that the city of Krasnodar assigned to them—very possibly out of a growing embarrassment. By 1962, word about the Kirlians had spread and scientists were traveling to Krasnodar to have a look at their discovery. They would knock on the door of the dilapidated, cramped quarters to find equipment and the inventors in the bedroom because there was no room elsewhere. By contrast, the apartment on Karl Libknecht has 600 square feet of "living space"—enormous in size by Soviet standards for a family of two. There was a living room, a bedroom, and a kitchen. Typically, the Kirlians turned the, living room into a laboratory, which it still is. At least there's no more equipment in the bedroom, and enough room in the lab to sit down.

The coffee—thick, heavy, strong Turkish coffee—had arrived, and he was sipping it slowly and deliberately. "Science has long taken cognizance of my early finding that cancerous tissues show up very muddy in aura photography, whereas unaffected tissues photograph sharply. The doctors have made far-reaching conclusions. On this basis, Soviet oncology is developing a new technique, and its future is bright and exciting. As part of a five-year plan, it is being applied in oncology in many medical centers throughout the country.

"Photographs of cancerous tissues are very specifically different from those of other diseases, and different types of cancer have different auras. So our medical men will have their hands full separating one from the other and tackling each as an enemy on its own—and licking it. Quite a job, this. Still, progress is being made."

A satisfied nod. Then—"A hospital in Rostov-on-Don has started a unique program so ambitious in scope that it will have to attract world attention—if they succeed. The hospital recruited the help of one hundred mothers who gave birth to children at this hospital in 1973 and 1974. The children's auras were photographed at birth, and the program calls for the children to visit monthly so they may be photographed. So far, obviously, the children are still very small and their files are slim, but as time wears on, the progression of monthly photographs of the children's aura will yield case histories that should prove staggering as future guidelines.

"Now I'll tell you something else. This program has been given a fifty-year span, meaning that each child as it grows to adulthood will continue to be photographed using the Kirlian Effect twelve times a year for the next fifty years—ending up as middle-aged men and women. The hospital fully expects some of them to fall out of the program as they move away, but those that will remain in Rostov-on-Don will keep returning every month for another session. Gradually, their files will become invaluable. Obviously, not all of us will be around in fifty years," he went on, a twinkle in his eye, "which also applies to the doctors at the Rostov-on-Don hospital. But we'll all be watching from wherever we are."

He gave out a good-natured chuckle and beckoned to Yuri No. 1 to refill his coffee cup. "How safe the Rostov-on-Don experiments are is another question," he said, growing pensive. On a recent visit to Krasnodar his good friend, biophysicist Viktor Adamenko, reminded him of the inherent dangers. Not long before, a Moscow hospital asked Adamenko to take charge of a Kirlian Effect unit to conduct experiments on how to recognize different illnesses by their auras. He turned down the offer because he did not feel that Kirlian photography has yet enough safety standards built into it. Also, Adamenko felt that wide-scale use would be too dangerous to the patients.

"I don't think Viktor is right," Kirlian reflected cautiously, "but I respect his point of view." He feels that between the two Viktors—Adamenko and Inyushin—the fate of the "Kirlian Effect" is in good hands. He had known Adamenko many years, remembering him as a child in the neighborhood—"a nice little boy, but a little too curious for my liking." He didn't meet Inyushin until 1964, when the Alma-Ata scientist paid him his first visit. Ever since, Inyushin has been among his most faithful disciples. Meanwhile, Kirlian and Adamenko write scientific papers together, "for the fun of going on record with new hypotheses. And Inyushin includes them in science books he publishes in Alma-Ata.

"It depends on the others now. This I do know: I myself have not much time left. I am helping Comrade Dubonosov here by carrying out tests that not even I have done before. For once it has to do with plants, not man. In a way, I've made one big circle and in the evening of my life, still useful, I again tinker with plants.

"Except that nowadays I am dealing with giant problems of wheat and corn. I am exploring such problems as what effects frost or extreme heat have on wheat. At the critical point when the wheat can take no more frost, there is a bursting aura, a cry for help—then death. You may say I am conducting survival tests."

"Absolutely invaluable," Dubonosov said. We had watched Dubonosov straining at the leash to interrupt, but he didn't take over, microphone and all, until now, when we were well into the second hour.

We didn't particularly care for the presentation that followed. While paying Kirlian compliments, Dubonosov also conveyed the clear-cut message that Kirlian, a man without an academic degree, had merely triggered a chain reaction. His discovery has been taken over by Soviet scientists who knew a lot more and better than the old man—who, Dubonosov reminded us gently, never even finished high school. He spoke of the work at the Institute and again, "with the invaluable help of Semyon Davidovich, it was the current leadership" that was carrying the ball in creating better wheat and plants.

We listened politely. Dubonosov never returned the floor to the old man, nor did Kirlian try to recapture our attention. He just sat there, appearing to listen, courteous, kind, and generous. The innuendos passed his ears leaving ostensibly no reaction. Still, as the "Kirlian Effect" might have shown, deep down they had to register. We glanced at the two Yuris. After first eagerly making notes of what the burly boss of the Institute had to say, even they had stopped writing.

"We should be going now," Natasha spoke up. "We have taken up enough of your invaluable time." We knew Natasha was unsurpassed in her sense of timing—when and how to offer one's goodbyes, the Soviet way.

Dubonosov cleared his throat as if to say, "What's your hurry?" But Natasha was up on her feet, and we followed her.

Kirlian smiled meekly, "I enjoyed your visit." Could we, before we left, see his lab, the inner sanctum of an inventor? He shrugged a frail shoulder and turned to Dubonosov.

"Why not?" the burly man said grandly. "But don't be disappointed in what you see. Anyway," he added, "the main equipment isn't there; it's being repaired. Isn't that so, Semyon Davidovich?"

Kirlian didn't answer. Maybe he didn't hear him, or maybe he didn't want to. We proceeded down the flight of stairs to a ground floor laboratory. It was locked. Dubonosov called for the key. An attendant wearing a white smock came running to unlock the door.

Indeed, there were plants, instruments with meters, panels with switches, and some not very large machinery that we didn't understand and no one seemed eager to explain. In the Institute lab we took pictures. Dubonosov tried to be in all, but we kept him out of some.

Three hours after we had met him, we parted from Kirlian by the reflection pool, in the courtyard below. There, once again, the self-conscious smile was back. His face had grown wistful and mischievous at the same time, as if saying. "Ah, we're all trying to do our best for a world going to the dogs." We said our last goodbyes by the side of the empty pool and got back into the car. As he walked off, up the steps of a terrace and around the corner, we felt a tinge of nostalgia and compassion for the Kirlians of the world.

Later in the day, with Kirlian's permission, we visited the apartment on Karl Libknecht Street to see much of the same equipment we had viewed in the Institute's locked room. Adamenko had warned us, "The truly sophisticated equipment is in Alma-Ata, behind guarded doors." So we were not really disappointed.

We hoped Kirlian might take a picture of our auras, but possibly he was too embarrassed by Dubonosov's treatment and so failed to show up at his own home. A neighbor conveyed his apologies. He had left us a souvenir, though—a book for each of us titled *Our Land, the Kuban*. On the flyleaf he wrote, "In memory of your visit, Kirlian," and under that, "Semyon Davidovich, Krasnodar."

"You know," Natasha said, "if we plan the day right, we may still have a Cossack dinner at the Kuren. And I'll pick up a six-pack of our very own Pepsi-Colas to take home to Moscow. We don't have any up there."

Several days later, back at the Intourist Hotel in Moscow, we decided to call Kirlian to thank him for a memorable visit in Krasnodar. Suddenly we realized he didn't have a phone in his apartment.

"We'll call the Institute but ask for Dubonosov," was our next thought. We had better not upset a Soviet chain of command. Dubonosov might never forgive the old man if we spoke to him over the boss's head.

A male voice answered, "Comrade Dubonosov? No, this is not he."

"May we speak to him, please?"

"And who are you?"

"We are the American journalists who visited you several days ago."

"Oh, yes," said the voice. "I remember you. I am sorry, you cannot speak with Dubonosov. He has been replaced."

"Replaced? Why?"

"It was nice of you to call," said the voice. "Have a good stay in the Soviet Union."

Click. "He hung up," said Gris.

We looked at each other in bewilderment, then burst out laughing. There had to be supreme justice everywhere. Incredibly, Dubonosov had gotten what he deserved. By whose hand and why we could not understand—from the way he had thrown his weight around, it certainly didn't look as if his position at the Institute was shaky.

Whatever happened, a Soviet axe fell. Was it Kirlian speaking up? Was it Natasha? Was it because of us? We'll never know, but we hope it is to the benefit of a real gentleman, Semyon Davidovich Kirlian.

8.

THE HEALING HANDS OF THE
KRIVOROTOVS, FATHER AND SON.

"You might as well know the truth," said Natasha Yakovleva, looking terribly officious.

Whenever Natasha—who is really very feminine and rather pretty, with a willowy figure and a beautiful, sculpted face—became stern and her light blue eyes suddenly turned gray, we knew that something had gone utterly wrong with our schedule. This was one of those times.

"We are not going to see the faith healers," we groaned. We had arrived in Tbilisi from Krasnodar the night before by a rickety, turbo-prop Antonov-24 which had long seen its better days. Coming in, we had a few anxious moments wondering whether our pilot would find his way into the narrow Kura Valley without slamming into the mountain range above the city. But we landed all right.

"I told you not to worry," Natasha intoned with a mock sigh of relief. However, the car that was to take us into the city wasn't there. "It will be here," Natasha said confidently, and the next moment an old gray Volga came to a screeching halt in front of the airport building. "You see?" Natasha said with a shrug. "Everything's okay."

The Iveria Hotel, a 22-story green quasi-modern high rise that was Tbilisi's pride and joy was being remodeled.

"This," the man at the reception desk told us, writing in room numbers on our guest cards, "is the best I can do for you." We were taken upstairs to the 12th floor and into a hallway crammed to the ceiling with furniture.

"Watch your step," the attendant said, piloting us in-between mountains of commodes and dismembered beds, "You'll get used to it," he added encouragingly. "Your rooms are behind these wardrobes. Just don't step on the drapes." We looked at Natasha.

"Leave it to me," she said, "Go into your rooms and wait." We were moved to another floor before we had a chance to unpack.

"Now we eat," we said, and Natasha concurred. As we reached the glass door the upper floor restaurant had just closed. "Sorry, Comrades!" said the stern-faced doorman.

"Comrades, our foot," we told Natasha, "we want our dinner."

"Patience," she said, and flapped her eyelashes at a swarthy Georgian coming out the door, obviously the maitre d'hôtel.

"We've just arrived, and we are hungry," she said sweetly, her big blue eyes coquetishly pleading with him. He looked back at her approvingly and grinned with obvious delight.

"Why, of course," he said, clapping his hands at the man behind the door. It instantly flung open. "Please. It will be my pleasure to serve you personally."

The lights inside the restaurant had been turned off. Now they blinked on again as the amorous Georgian maitre d'hôtel hovered over Natasha, smacking his lips. His greasy cheeks quivered with joy as he stole a glance into Natasha's bosom. He disappeared, to return with a bottle of red wine. "This comes from the Oteyashvili cellars," he said grandly. "With the compliments of Prince Elgudzhe Oteyashvili. That's me," he added in a conspiratorial whisper.

"Flirt with him, Natasha, flirt," we muttered under our breath. "We're famished."

"Relax, boys," she muttered back. "Leave it to me. Keep your shirts on." For the record, Natasha had spent several years in London, working for a Soviet press service, which accounted for her excellent English and a thorough acquaintance with English idioms. We had a feast. At the end the prince slipped Natasha a scribbled note while ceremoniously kissing her hand.

"We have a busy day tomorrow," she told us in the elevator, throwing the note away. Before we turned in for the night, she had confirmed that today we would meet the Krivorotovs, the famous father and son healing team, the next day.

Now, facing us over the breakfast table a few hours later, she was very unhappy. "You are right—you are not going to meet the Krivorotovs. The father is attending a reunion of officers of the tank corps in which he served during the war. He is out of town, and we don't know when he'll be back."

"Natasha," we said stubbornly, "we came here to see the Krivorotovs and to find out how they heal people. The visit has been approved by your head office in Moscow. We couldn't care less about the tank corps. Call Krivorotov back into town. Do anything, but produce him. We depend on you, Natasha."

She shook her head. "You are crazy, but I think you know that. However, I shall go to the local Novosti office and make a few phone calls. Why don't you go sightseeing or something?" This was not the kind of busy day we had expected. But while Natasha tried to straighten things out, we did go sightseeing to kill time.

We had visited the picturesque city—a quaint mixture of ancient, old, and new—the year before, and we observed that slow progress had been made in constructing some landmark high rise buildings. We took a ride in a cable car to a mountaintop restaurant for only 5 kopeks (6 cents) a ride, and we wrapped up our "lost day" by taking in a play at a local theater—a topical comedy on Soviet black marketeers.

We were more than amply rewarded the next morning when Natasha said, "I am taking you over to see the Krivorotovs. And please, don't ask me any questions."

How she did it we will never know. Unless we face her again, in her office of Assistant Deputy Director of the giant news service in Pushin Square in Moscow (she was handed the promotion at year's end). If she is in a talkative mood, she may tell us the story behind our very own Tbilisi miracle. In the meantime, thank you, Natasha! You made us very happy that day in Tbilisi, when we finally met the two Krivorotovs, possibly the only father-son psychic healing team in the world.

The meeting took place in the Novosti office in Rustaveli Boulevard, Tbilisi's busy tree-lined main street, on the third floor of an old gray four-story building housing several newspapers and press services. Only too happy to meet them on purportedly neutral territory, we never asked why we were not taken to the Krivorotovs' home, nor what had happened to the tank officers' reunion. The colorful carpets on the parquet floor of the roomy Novosti office, the cozy armchairs with little throw pillows, and a smaller carpet on the wall reminded us we were at the gates to the Near East. Iran and Turkey were just around the corner. We were in Georgia, not in Russia, and Tbilisi was its 1,500 year-old capital founded by a Georgian king named Vakhtang Gorgasali.

Even though we were exactly on time, they were already there, waiting for us. We shook hands. The father, Lieutenant-Colonel Aleksei Krivorotov, was a graying, chunky man of rugged build. He reminded us of a Khrushchev in a positive frame of mind, his benevolent blue eyes surveying us from beneath bushy eyebrows. By contrast, son Viktor, almost a head taller than his father, was black-haired and slender, with a long, angular face. His complexion and the shape of his face betrayed an ethnic mixture. He had the looks of an American college kid. The local Novosti boss, a high-strung, wiry, bald-headed man—who, hopefully not on our account, suffered a heart attack the following day—discreetly disappeared, leaving Natasha in charge.

"You're not really a Georgian, Colonel?" we asked in Russian.

Aleksei Krivorotov smiled, realizing that translations would not be necessary. Son Viktor grinned, happy he didn't have to serve as interpreter.

Natasha smiled knowingly. "Yes, you can talk Russian to them," she said, "Let's all sit down and be comfortable."

"No, I am not a Georgian," Krivorotov senior said gently. "But I do speak Georgian."

"May I ask you how it is that you know about us?" We said that actually we knew very little about him, which was the reason for our visit. We had heard about him and his two sons in Moscow. We knew that Viktor, who first planned to be an engineer, is now studying to be an artist, and that the other son, Vladimir, was a psychiatrist and also a gifted faith healer, although authorities would not allow him to practice the "laying on of hands" because of his medical position.

Such serious scientists as Viktor Adamenko and Dr. Vladimir Raikov strongly advised us to go to Tbilisi to meet them, we informed the Krivorotovs, but before that, also, in America. . . .

"Don't tell me they know about me in America!" Krivorotov senior said, his eyes growing round and full of wonder. "You don't mean it?" "We do mean it," we said. At least one American parapsychologist— Dr. Thelma Moss, in Los Angeles—had mentioned him to us, The knowledge about him back there was very slight but enough to cause curiosity about his remarkable faculties of healing the sick by the touch of his hand.

Might we look at their hands, please? They readily obliged. The hands of Krivorotov senior were small, fine, and sensitive, his fingers slim and long, the hands of a piano player. Viktor's hands were larger and seemingly stronger than his father's, but as soft.

"Tell them about yourself, Colonel," Natasha said, "but let's open the door to the balcony. It's so warm and beautiful outside." Son Viktor jumped up and thrust open the double door leading to the balcony. Outside, a tall chestnut tree showing early spring buds was reaching to the balcony railing. The garden courtyard below was sweet with the early Caucasian spring. Moscow and its blizzards were worlds away.

"All right," Krivorotov said and cleared his throat.

Alexei Eremeyevich Krivorotov was born in Borisov, Byelorussia, and moved to Tbilisi in 1931. Evidently this man, like many other Russians, liked the lovely city in the lush Caucasian valley inhabited by friendly, proud, and beautiful people, and decided to stay.

After settling in Georgia, he married a local girl, who became Viktor's mother. Eventually, when Georgia once again became an entity under Soviet rule, Georgians grew rather nationalistic, if not chauvinistic, and Russians going there to settle today are no longer so welcome. Since they represent the Bolshevik philosophy of life and Moscow, the capital and figurehead of the Soviet Union, they are treated with respect, but when the time comes they are expected to go home. The average Georgian is proud of Georgia having given the Muscovites its Iosif Dzhugashvili, alias Joseph Stalin, to rule the total land in war and peace. This pride has given them a feeling of superiority over the average Muscovite, a feeling shared by Armenians in Armenia to the south and Azerbaijani in adjoining Azerbaijan to the east. With the snow-capped Caucasus range isolating their lush land from the north and from Muscovy they are almost an island on Soviet land.

It is this "island" that has become the chosen spot for Krivorotov's home, office, and waiting room as he heals people who have heard about him and his healing powers by the most reliable communication—word of mouth. People who have found the medical profession unable to help them, travel from all over the Soviet Union to seek the aid of the amazing Krivorotovs— and most return healed to their homes in Leningrad, Sebastopol, Moscow, or a hundred other towns and cities.

The Krivorotovs never ask for a fee. That would be totally illegal. But grateful patients give gifts of money which, in the cases of politicians, actresses, or authors, can be quite substantial. For the less wealthy, a gift of the ruble equivalent of five American dollars is common. In America, the Krivorotovs could be multimillionaires. But they seemed genuinely happy with the standard of living and genuinely more concerned about helping people.

Krivorotov senior shares his small apartment with son Viktor. Most of the healing is done in the apartment, situated near the fast-flowing Kura River that cuts through the heart of the picturesque town. As the father took the floor he explained that his healing was particularly effective when the patient had limited paralysis, such as after various operations, or in some cases of polio. But he and Viktor could also dramatically help people with varied cases of functional disorders of the nervous system, with psychological disturbances, and with many of a large number of internal illnesses. Children's and women's ailments occupy a large amount of their time.

To be most effective, they start their healing by first making sure the patient is sitting or lying comfortably. The surroundings should be quiet, so as not to distract the attention of the patient or healer. The patient then spends several minutes settling into a complete state of rest, consciously relaxing the muscles of the face, then gradually relaxing the tensions in the muscles right down the body to the feet.

The healer then takes up a comfortable position next to the patient, either sitting or standing. The sick person should fully concentrate on the process of the treatment. As he and the healer concentrate on the source of the ailment, the healer pours new energy into the body of the sick person, creating a sensation of heat in the affected organs. A healing session can last from one to twenty minutes, depending on the nature of the sickness and the healer's degree of preparedness.

Krivorotov paused for a while to make sure he was describing his method accurately. We had the feeling that he was trying to do more than just tell his story—we should carry the word to others who might take up this work to help people. Then the two Krivorotovs told of their case histories with the pride and sincerity of successful doctors or surgeons.

"One of my most successful treatments," Krivorotov senior reported, "involved a 72-year-old lady from Krasnodar. She was brought to me with her left arm terribly swollen, the skin an angry red. She was in terrible pain and could not hold the arm out straight. Doctors had told her that there were blockages in the blood vessels, that the blood flow was stopping, and that they feared the arm was totally poisoned. They wanted to amputate the arm to stop the spread of the blood poisoning. And to further complicate matters, the lady had bronchial asthma.

"I sat her down and passed my right hand over the arm—not touching the arm, just moving my hand parallel to it about a quarter-inch or an inch away from the skin. The swelling started to go down almost at once, and the red coloring began to fade. In ten days, the arm started to work freely. Each treatment lasted from 10 to 15 minutes, once a day. After a month she was 100 percent healthy. Even her asthma had disappeared after the 30 treatments."

Krivorotov's eyes twinkled with satisfaction as he went on to recount other cases.

"When I was on holiday in the resort of Sochi on the Black Sea," he continued, "a mother heard about me and brought her child, an eight-year-old boy who was almost totally paralyzed with polio. The boy had no movement in his arms or legs. He just lay there, unable to react to anything.

"I applied what I call light massage—passing my hand close to the skin but not touching. At first I concentrated on the head and the spine, then moved on to the rest of the body. After a month of daily treatments, I obtained some muscular responses, and the boy started to become interested in the activities around him. The mother was delighted, and took the child home. But when she brought him back a year later, he still had only limited muscular movement. I applied head and spine massage for another 30 sessions. At the end of this, the boy was able to walk. It gives me tremendous satisfaction to help people in this way."

Sochi is only a few miles across the Russian border, just north of where Georgia ends. It's a giant rest home, sprawling high rises flanking the blue sea—the Black Sea is such a misnomer!—in Miami Beach fashion. Each is owned by a different trade union, and each serves thousands of vacationers who flock to Sochi the year round.

Later, when we visited Sochi, we discovered without surprise that Krivorotov is actually well known in town. According to a local Soviet journalist whose name had been passed on to us in Moscow, Krivorotov goes to Sochi regularly, tending to whoever needs his help. "He has quite a reputation here," the journalist said. "People swear by him, and even the medical staff at our sanatoriums often request his services, unofficially."

Another incredible case in the files of the elder Krivorotov concerns a five-year-old girl, who was brought from the town of Tambov to the healer's Tbilisi apartment with a tumor behind her right eye. The tumor had grown so large, it was forcing the eye out. Her mother was an eye specialist, and she decided to have an operation performed to remove the tumor. However, under the anesthetic, the child's heart had stopped beating. The medical team managed to get the heart started again, but surgeons refused to continue the operation because of the close brush with death.

"The mother started looking for another method of helping her daughter, and heard of my work," Alexei stated. "By this time, the child was suffering great pain and was unable to sleep at night inless injected with a strong sedative. The mother told me, 'I don't believe in faith healing, but I'll try anything to save my child.' After seven treatments, the child was able to sleep peacefully at night without sedatives. By the end of the month, the eye had returned to its proper position, and there was no pain."

The mother continued to disbelieve Krivorotov's powers as all he had done was to place one hand over the child's eye and the other at the back of her head for periods of up to 15 minutes. Still, for the next three years, even though the tumor had not reappeared, she returned with the child for more healing sessions. Finally she told him, "I believe in you"—whereupon he went on to treat the mother successfully for a liver complaint!

Krivorotov senior discovered his incredible healing powers in 1929. He had a very bad migraine headache. Doctors could do nothing for him. But

Krivorotov, who was already experimenting with hypnosis, was convinced that the powers of faith and the mind were limitless. By placing his right hand on the top of his head, he made the migraine disappear, and it never came back.

Although an accomplished hypnotist, he does not use this skill during treatments because he believes it suppresses the person's will, and he wants the person to help him fight the illness in the body. Over the years, he has also found that to heal, he must himself feel very healthy and strong. In fact, as he passes his hand close to the patient, he concentrates on feeling strong and healthy. If for some reason he can't get himself into that mental condition of well-being, he won't treat anyone.

As we sat sipping coffee in the large room of the Novosti office, Krivorotov explained: "When a person is ill, his whole organism is weak. Scientists who have studied us think we reach the affected part of the body with high-power bio-electrical currents that help the affected organs, such as liver or kidney, to win over the disease."

When he is performing healing, he must not drink alcohol. Even one glass of wine can rob him of his fabulous powers for up to three days. Shaking his head he said: "I found that after a drink, when I put my hand near a patient, absolutely nothing happened! When the patient told me he felt nothing, I felt as if he had insulted or struck me!" The Krivorotovs also insist that a patient give up smoking and drinking during the period of treatment "so that the body is not poisoned."

The Krivorotovs try to eliminate the cause of the pain, as well as the pain itself. That way, they can give long-term relief. "We are not interested in just diagnosing illnesses, or in getting the diagnosis of a doctor before we give treatments," Krivorotov senior said proudly. "If a patient reports that a large area of the body is painful, I can pinpoint the source of the pain by merely passing my hand over the area. No matter what ails a person, we first pay special attention to the spine and the back of the head, then move to the particular site of the pain. My hand never touches the person. It always remains a fraction of an inch away. When I massage the spine, the person always feels the pain in every sick part of the body, and can tell me exactly what is affected—often they didn't know that such an area was affected by disease."

The people who are treated say that they feel an "electric current" going through their bodies. Many feel dizzy; their heads start whirling, and they want to sleep. People with insomnia often need only one short, fifteen-minute treatment by Krivorotov senior to enable them to begin sleeping again. But other patients say they can't stand the healer's hands being too close: their heads start rolling as if they were drunk, and he can only treat them for a minute at a time.

Not every treatment is successful, he continued. "If, for instance, a person has a small blood clot near the surface of the brain, we can almost always dissolve it. But if it is a larger blood clot, and much deeper inside the brain, we face difficulties. What we do is give the body additional energy so that it is able to cure itself. Sometimes it is too late to help." As he spoke, we had to think that a battle-scarred former tank commander like Krivorotov would of course categorically deny that this was *faith* healing. Yet there was so much compassion in his voice, such benevolence in his eyes, that whether he admitted it or not, faith did play a key part in his methods.

Krivorotov's powers to heal have been repeatedly tested and proven by Soviet scientists. In 1956, as the Krivorotov fame grew, the Georgian Republic's Ministry of Health ordered a full probe into the claims made about his healing hands. A special commission of seven doctors, headed by Academician Pyotr Kavtaradze, was set up, and Krivorotov was ordered to report to the Republic Hospital in Tbilisi.

First, the commission diagnosed thirty patients with various illnesses—light paralysis in arms and hands following surgery, chronic headaches, serious back complaints, diseases of the nervous system. The commission was concerned that in fact the healer might be "talking" his patients back to health—curing by autosuggestion—so they deliberately chose some patients who did not speak Georgian or Russian. During a one-week period, these thirty patients were placed fully under Krivorotov's care. They received no medical treatment from the hospital at all. "We found the results in all cases, including those patients who could not converse with Krivorotov, were positive," the commission later reported. "All showed improvement in their conditions, and several were cured."

When Viktor was 18, he discovered he had powers similar to those of his father. His girl friend complained of a violent headache. Viktor told her he didn't know if he could help, but he'd seen his father at work. Making himself sound as convincing as possible, he told her to relax and put one hand on her forehead, one at the back of her head. His hands began feeling as if they were burning—and after 10 minutes of this treatment, the girl's headache was gone.

His girl friend told her friends, and soon youngsters were calling at the apartment asking for help from the young Krivorotov. The famous Krivorotov father-and-son faith-healing team had been founded! From then on, Krivorotov senior treated the older patients, and Viktor the young. Like his father, Viktor concentrates on feelings of strength and health when he is healing and tries to direct power and energy to the palms of his hands. Although very capable of doing direct healing, Viktor likes to handle the cases that involve mental diseases, phobias, or psychosomatic diseases.

Viktor recalled a typical case which he was treating at the time of our visit. "The patient is a local man who feels a 'heart attack' every time he sees a funeral procession. Immediately he has a tremendous pain in his chest, collapses, and has to be treated by doctors. But although he suffers all the symptoms of a heart attack, the doctors say his heart is quite healthy.

"When he finally came to us, my father and I discussed it, and agreed that either of us could easily take away the chest pain for a limited period. That would not have taken us to the root of the trouble, which was obviously in his mind. So I agreed to take him on as a long-term patient."

Viktor found that the sudden death of the patient's mother, eight years earlier, had left terrible impressions in the man's mind. The patient had seen psychiatrists, but they had been unable to erase the dreadful memory. Each time the man saw a funeral, the remembrance was too much—he fell in shock, as if strikcen with a heart attack.

After a few weeks of treatment, in which Viktor applied his hands to his patient's head while the patient discussed his mother's death, his condition significantly improved. For the first time the power from Viktor's hands gave the man the ability to talk about death without getting agitated. In a letter which we received six months later, Viktor confirmed that the man was now completely cured.

Both the Krivorotovs feel tired and drained after each treatment—again, as if their bodies had passed energy into the patient. "We believe that may be how our feelings of health and strength are passed on to the sick people," Viktor said simply.

The famous Semyon Davidovich Kirlian told us earlier, "Aleksei Krivorotov unquestionably has the power to heal." Kirlian had had a personal experience with Aleksei in 1965, and in our interviews in Tblisi, Krivorotov senior was delighted to discuss his treatment of Kirlian.

"Kirlian worked too hard and when I saw him he was suffering from extreme nervous exhaustion. He felt weak, and everything was wrong with him," Krivorotov recounted. "He had a badly infected right kidney, and bowel movements were troubling him."

His kidney had been infected some time before the treatment, but he thought it had cleared up. Kirlian said that when Krivorotov came to the area of his kidney, he suddenly felt very hot inside and had difficulty breathing. After the Tbilisi healer passed his hand over it, the feeling of heat in his kidney remained for a period of 24 hours. "Following 15 treatments, in which I concentrated my hands mainly on his spine, Kirlian told me 'I feel 20 years younger.' His kidney was healed, his bowel movements were normal, and he felt as if his 'energy battery' had been fully recharged."

The scientific-minded Kirlian, even under treatment, could not let a chance go by to investigate such a phenomenon as Krivorotov's healing ability. Kirlian was fascinated by the healer's hands, particularly the palms, which he found to be very different from a normal person's. "The skin looks like that of a child," he remembered, "but in fact the palms are very strong, very hard underneath."

When Kirlian photographs were taken of Krivorotov's hands, it was found that at the time when he was concentrating on healing, an energy aura several times larger than normal appeared around his hands and fingers. Physicist Viktor Adamenko, who investigated Kirlian's healing, described it graphically.

"A cold blue flame was spurting from the pores and canals of Krivorotov's hands. Protuberances like herds of amoebas wriggled from one place to another, sometimes merging into a blazing cone, sometimes splintering into bits." When Krivorotov became excited at seeing this incredible photography, the aura changed to orange, violet, and blue flickering stars. Kirlian formed the opinion that the change in mood in Aleksei had changed the electrical state of his body, and the skin, like a mirror, reflected the change in the inner, bio-electrical processes. "Interestingly," Krivorotov recalled, "before and after his treatment, Kirlian took photographs of his own fingers. At the end of the treatment, the aura was clearly more brilliant and larger!"

Viktor Adamenko, who has also tested Krivorotov senior, reported in a privately circulated scientific paper:

"As Krivorotov slowly passes his hands at some distances along the patient's body, there arises in the patient approximately at the site of the sick organ a strong subjective sense of heat, at times almost unbearable. Krivorotov also feels at this place an intensification of heat in his hand. Stopping his hand, he says: 'You feel pain here.' Krivorotov's hand remains at the sick organ until the sensation of heat becomes annoying—the signal for the session to be terminated.

"As a rule, Krivorotov has no knowledge of diagnosis in advance. Perception of 'heat' is different in different people and is apparently related to whether the disease is more or less serious. In the case of a serious disease, the treatment session takes less time, while as the patient makes progress, the treatment increases in length.

"Sometimes the patient's subjective sensation of heat at the site of the sick organ persists for up to two days. In some patients, the subjective feeling of heat is accompanied by the sensation of vibrations, whose frequency differs from person to person.

"Academician Nikolai Zelinsky experienced a very strong sensation of 'heat' and in order to allay the sensation, he suggested that Krivorotov should keep his hands at some distance.

"Occasionally, slight discharges of electricity take place between Kirvorotov's fingers and the patient's body.

"The sensation of heat corresponds to a temperature of 40 to 50 degrees Centigrade. Some people experience the feeling of light prickling, uneasiness, intoxication, or on the contrary, heaviness."

In July 1974, tests were conducted on both Krivorotovs at Tbilisi University. The scientists wanted to find out what type of energy might radiate from their healing hands. Academician Gregor Komitiani, a member of the Georgian Academy of Sciences, took charge of the experiments, which lasted several weeks.

As we studied the complicated charts and reports resulting from the experiments, Krivorotov senior explained that Soviet scientists working in Novosibirsk had apparently shown that ultraviolet rays carried information, just like radio waves. These scientists had placed living cells in two hermetically sealed tubes, with a "field" of quartz between the two tubes. Only ultraviolet light passes through quartz. When the living cells in one tube were deliberately killed, the cells in the other died immediately, leading the scientists to conjecture that the second group of cells had received the "death information" via ultraviolet light from the first group. So, the scientists wondered, was there any link between the ultraviolet emissions and the Krivorotovs' healing hands?

The two healers were tested under different temperatures and in different emotional states, while they attempted to heal. A variety of scientific instruments were used to gauge the ultraviolet radiation emitted by their hands. At the end, the scientists announced the incredible facts. When the Krivorotovs were in a normal condition, their hands radiated very little ultraviolet emissions. But when they concentrated on healing people, the ultraviolet emissions increased 1,000 times! "It was interesting" the father added, "that when we made these experiments during the late part of the day, when we were very tired, little ultraviolet radiation was recorded. When we were fresh, after a good sleep, the results were very positive!"

At the end of Krivorotov's narrative, we suggested that we move onto the balcony. It was so beautiful outside, and out there he might like to "work on us." He glanced inquiringly at Natasha.

She smiled and nodded: "Why not?"

His face lit up. "All right," he said. Viktor brought out a chair for us to take turns playing patient. Nothing ailed Dick, but at least Krivorotov could send a charge into his arm, and he did it by moving his outstretched hand up and down over Dick's sleeve, without touching it. His hand, its palm facing Dick's arm, moved slowly, maintaining the same distance, about an inch away. Dick reported an instant sensation of warmth penetrating the sleeve of his jacket and the shirt below. He looked up to catch Krivorotov's eye. The man's face showed no effort or tension.

Krivorotov repeated the same experiment with Gris. His eye had noted the shorter right arm and he inquired solicitiously about the cause. Told it was a childhood injury not properly attended at the time he shook his head.

"I wish I could treat you over a period of time. I could not restore your arm to full use, but I know I can help you. I could give partially atrophied muscles and a possibly degenerated nervous system at least 30 percent of additional normal use. Let me show you."

As he moved his hand up and down Gris's sleeve, keeping within an inch of it, soothing warmth seemed to ooze into Gris's arm. "You feel it, don't you?" Krivorotov asked.

"And how," came Gris's amazed reply. "May I touch your hand?"

Krivorotov's hand had to be hot to convey so much warmth through the sleeve, yet when Gris touched it with his left hand, Krivorotov's hand was cold. Not just cold. *Ice* cold.

It was an incredible experience. But as Adamenko told us: "The Krivorotovs are no ordinary men. They have incredible healing power. It is our duty as scientists to find out more about this power, so that we may help other people." And indeed, the latest word we have received from Georgia is that tests are still continuing on the famous healing hands at Tbilisi University.

9.

VARVARA IVANOVA, THE "STORMY PETREL" OF SOVIET PSI

"Varvara Ivanova is incredible—you must try to catch up with her," Viktor Adamenko had said early in our trip. Later, other parapsychologists brought up her name, speaking with obvious awe, to further heighten our curiosity.

Varvara Ivanova, they said, controls such a wealth of psychic abilities that she is unmatched by any person in the Western world. While holding a university degree in philosophy, she is a healer, clairvoyant, telepathist, telekinesis medium, hypnotist, and authority on reincarnation. Scientists recognize her as a skilled practitioner and top researcher in nearly every aspect of parapsychology. Ivanova is particularly known for her outstanding ability to diagnose and cure illnesses by telephone at virtually any distance— in one documented case, at the range of 8,000 miles.

"Yes, we know," we'd shoot back at the parapsychologists who praised her gifts, "so why don't you locate her for us?"

"It isn't as easy as you think," they retorted. Patiently, they'd explain why. What emerged was the image of a dogged rebel in the name of science, but also probably the most elusive person in the vast network of Soviet psychic research. She is nicknamed "General Psi" because of her commanding attitude and forthright leadership in psychic research. Journalists covering the field of science told us that Ivanova had probably written more "open letters" to editors championing parapsychology than all her learned colleagues put together.

But from our earlier inquiries we knew that Ivanova had recently lost her job as an interpreter at the Soviet Ministry of Foreign Affairs because authorities felt she was too outspoken on psychic matters. In her fifties, she was asked to accept early retirement rather than be summarily dismissed for her overenthusiastic "propaganda" in the psychic cause. It would have given her a livable pension and a small apartment. But Ivanova wouldn't bow, and she was kicked out of her job without pension or home.

Ever since, she has been on her own, proudly independent. She is helped by an unofficial mutual-aid pool set up by Russian parapsychologists for their own in need. Unemployed and homeless, Ivanova flits from city to city, the honored guest of whatever parapsychologists she happens to drop in on. Ivanova gets five rubles here, ten rubles there. Train tickets materialize almost as if by magic and she rushes off to lecture, teach, or consult in some distant city. There is always a couch on which to lay her weary body. At this point in time, for instance, she was rooming with another well-known woman parapsychologist, Larisa Vilenskaya, who was also single and had a tiny two-room apartment.

It was Adamenko who showed us a carbon copy of Ivanova's bi-monthly reports, *News of Psychoenergetics* and *Psychoenergetics Abroad.* One had fifteen legal-size, single-space pages, the other had eight. Carefully translated into Russian, these were articles from various Western periodicals, including the *National Enquirer* and *New Scientist.* "Compiled by Larisa Vilenskaya" read the bottom line of each. This, we were told, was camouflage. Even though the two women have been working together and Vilenskaya has been a colecturer at the Popov Institute, her name was used because she's been on better terms with the Soviet authorities than Ivanova.

"It's really Ivanova's doing," Adamenko said admiringly. "All of it. I worry about her because she's a typical stormy petrel, and an indomitable, fearless woman." Yet apparently she accepted her nomadic life-style without showing any bitterness. She was like the seasoned old fighter shrugging off adversity. For a number of good reasons she expected to be spied on by her own government: this was part and parcel of her existence.

When we finally encountered her—or rather when she came face-to-face with us—it turned into a dramatic exercise in evading the Soviet secret police. Told to stand by in our Moscow hotel room, we didn't know what to expect. Suddenly, at exactly the prearranged time, she burst into the room, looking very much a typical, robust, waddly Soviet housewife.

"I am Ivanova," she called out in a rather melodious voice that didn't seem to fit her plump body atop short, stocky legs. A well-worn handbag was firmly clenched under her arms. She thrust out her hand to pump ours vigorously. Nobody could have guessed that this plain, if not downright shabby, Russian woman was a famous researcher of a fascinating, barely explored world beyond a newly breached frontier. Yet she was just that—a top-ranking Soviet parapsychologist.

"Nice day," she exclaimed, ignoring our attempts to welcome her. "We will now wander past the Historical Museum and Revolution Square" she went on commandingly. "A big crowd is there now. You will enjoy a little walk."

Her English, heavily accented but easily understandable, allowed no contradiction. "Later we stop by the Metropole Hotel for a glass of tea." She winked a knowing eye. The wink translated into: "Keep the KGB out of our hair; they are probably listening to us now. Okay?"

We grinned in acknowledgement. She turned, motioning us to hurry and we followed her, grabbing our overcoats and fur caps on our way into the hallway. While we mentally approved Ivanova's strategy, we also had to admit to ourselves that in the past week or so we had allowed ourselves to be lulled into a feeling of false security. Since the incident in a Baku hotel a good two weeks earlier, there had been no attempts to trip us up, and we had taken refuge behind a seemingly foolproof system of checks and cross-checks.

We refused to confide in strangers, to get involved with strangers, unless they had been approved by people in authority. The latter would be either representatives, official or not, of the state—personified by Natasha or Yuri of the Novosti Press Agency. It was their responsibility to keep us out of trouble. This way we turned a dependency into an advantage. We also accepted the authority of science, as exemplified by such men of prestige as Viktor Adamenko and Genady Sergeyev. Only if they said, "Yes, good idea you should talk to so-and-so," did we proceed with the interview arrangements.

We had begun to accept things at face value—not a particularly prudent attitude in the Soviet Union. Now we were all too aware of the possibility of another "Professor Vitrokhin"—whom we suspected of being a KGB agent—cropping up again. Vitrokhin kept popping up like a jack-in-the-box when least expected, on all our trips to Russia. It would be relatively easy for such a man to pose as a parapsychologist with a view to entrapment by letting us accept information deemed secret.

We came out into the street without having exchanged a word. Flecks of clouds hung in a pale-blue canopy above the rust-colored walls of the ancient Kremlin. The omnipresent line for the Lenin Mausoleum patiently snaked its way up the broad avenue toward Red Square, its wiggly tail coming into being on the sidewalk opposite the bloody-red facade of the Historical Museum. With Ivanova in the lead, we set out across an empty huge square toward the mass of humanity. Still not a word was spoken until we reached the other side. The milling crowd outside Revolution Square Metro was obviously Ivanova's objective. The sidewalk was full of people streaming in and out of the subway station. This was Moscow's counterpart of Times Square and Piccadilly Circus. Ivanova grinned as we marched silently beside her to submerge in the crowd outside Moscow's busiest subway below us. Obviously she felt safer in the crowd. Curious passersby would catch only snatches of conversation. We would be aware of anyone who paid too much attention to us.

"Welcome to Moscow," she now said. "I hate 'bugs'—hidden micro- phones, you know." We nodded understandingly. The bustling, noisy crowd would make it almost impossible to record our conversation, even with a long-distance directional microphone.

To Varvara Ivanova, though, on this springlike day in Moscow all this cloak-and-dagger stuff was simple, contemptible reality. She had lived with it all her adult life. Amusingly, she had checked us out as carefully as we had checked her out. She knew, she told us, that we had been to Krasnodar to see Kirlian, had gone to Leningrad to talk to Kulagina, had spent some exciting time with Ermolayev; that we knew Adamenko, Vinogradova, Ser- geyev, the Krivorotovs.

We were now talking in Russian. "You are doing fine," she was saying, as she piloted us through the crowd in Revolution Square. "It is fortunate that we could get together, because tomorrow you would have missed me." Ivanova was about to leave for Leningrad, where she planned to stay and lecture while getting reinforced with rubles from understanding Leningrad scientists.

"And this would have been a pity. Because, and I don't want to brag, I combine more areas of parapsychology than any of my colleagues. For instance, I practice telekinesis, but I am also a clairvoyant. I am a telepathist, but I also heal by long distance. I am a medium, I have ESP, I regress people, and I talk to animals. And I don't let myself be bugged."

Her mouth broke into a huge grin. "Before you tell me that I do brag, let me add that my research of the phenomena of parapsychology has been discussed by international scientists, and references to my work have appeared in science journals all over the world."

We remembered what Aleksandr Kazantsev, the noted Russian author and historian, said when he urged us to see her: "Varvara Ivanova is also a 'Vedma,' a real-life Soviet witch!"

She shrugged. "Kazantsev is a good man, I don't mind being called a witch. But I won't confirm it, because here in Russia one doesn't really like to admit such things. However, put it this way. I am glad I am living in the twentieth century this time. I was burned at the stake twice, in previous lives."

Viktor Adamenko had warned us, "Varvara Ivanova is a bona fide researcher, but she is also an eccentric, no doubt about it. Still, don't get thrown off by that. What matters most is that she possesses most unusual psychic powers begging to be explained. However incredible her accounts, believe me, they are true." However eccentric, she is held in high esteem by both scientists and Soviet writers. Indeed, her apparent eccentricities may be one way she copes with the grim realities she must face. Ivanova has had more than her share of trouble with Soviet authorities, it seems, ever since she decided to dedicate herself to psychic research.

She grew up in Moscow, and found she had a great ability to learn foreign languages. "I have studied eight foreign languages," Ivanova said proudly, "but can use only six of them. English seems very difficult to me, and it has taken me twenty years to master it. I studied the Czech language for three years, and could not even read a newspaper. But Portuguese I knew fluently after having studied it only four months. I was even able to work as a translator after that period. I loved this language. Two years after I first started to learn it, people from Brazil, where they speak Portuguese, as you know, believed that I must be from there. I never felt I was really studying this language, it was like remembering it after some twenty or thirty years of not having used it. Later, I began to deal with hypnotic regressions. I found out that I did live there once in a previous life."

Ivanova once taught a man the German language. The man often said, "Yes, that is right," as if he were not learning new things from her, but remembering old ones. He explained, "I feel that I have it dimly in my memory, and there is nothing new for me in German. You are only confirming and reminding me of it, not teaching me." He had extremely good results in studying this language. When regressed, he saw himself as a German. He had indeed lived in Germany—a century ago. . . .

"One man told me that he found studying Arabic was very easy," she continued. "He could not understand why people said it was so difficult. I regressed him to his previous life, where he saw himself as an Arab, and gave many details of his family, home, actions, work and fights. He 'saw' that he could read and write this language. When he was brought out of hypnosis, he was told the reason for his being so facile with Arabic. The man is a psychiatrist and he never believed in regression. He does now."

Skills learned in previous lives can explain a great deal about why some people show unusual talents in their early life, Ivanova believes. It can explain why some people are geniuses in particular fields. When Ivanova herself was regressed, she saw she had not only been a Brazilian but also a German in previous lives.

"I have known German," she said, "since my childhood." And of course she speaks Portuguese perfectly. "Spanish and Italian I know, but not well. I have since found during other regressions that I lived in these countries a very long time ago. I was never born in an English-speaking country, which I blame for the difficulty I have with that language."

After graduating from university, she made her living as a language teacher in higher grades, eventually joining the staff of the language school at the Soviet Ministry of Foreign Affairs. This is the elite school where Russia's fledgling diplomats learn the language of the country they plan to concentrate on in their foreign service careers. She taught Portuguese, and later served as translator, dealing with foreign publications. Although the latter was a demotion, she probably welcomed it, as it gave her the opportunity to read material normally banned to the Russian public. An inveterate data collector, she has managed to open channels to the West—only God knows how—to obtain not merely information on the progress of parapsychology elsewhere in the world, but to lay her hands on recent foreign publications none of which are actually allowed into the Soviet Union: *The Journal of Parapsychology, Parapsychology Review, Psychic, Nature,* plus many others published anywhere from the U. S. and Great Britain, to Italy, Brazil, and Japan. How does she do it? Is it her former ties at the Soviet Ministry of Foreign Affairs? She won't say; we didn't pry. It's healthier that way.

The switch also gave her more time for active work within the so-called Popov Institute or Popov Group, the parapsychology unit that came into being back in 1965 under the name of "Department of Bio-Information" on the premises of the Moscow Radio Engineering Institute.

This was the time of a brief honeymoon between a new science probing the mysterious powers of the human mind and Soviet authorities hoping to profit from their discoveries. The scientists needed a place to hang their hats, and also needed to receive official sanction for their work. The latter, as the telepathist Yuri Kamensky had sadly reminded us only a few days earlier, was imperative in Soviet Russia, the difference between legality and out-and-out illegality. But by the time Ivanova joined the Popov

Group in 1972, it was barely in existence, still smarting from the prestigious *Literary Gazette*'s "exposures" as lowly hocus-pocus. "We were relegated to a basement," Ivanova recalled bitterly, "too small to hold all those interested in parapsychology. At least we were allowed to exist."

At this point in time, though, the group may well be homeless—as implied by the telepathist Kamensky. Indeed Ivanova, who prided herself on being an important and permanent Popov Group lecturer—her twice-a-week subjects dealing with ESP, diagnoses of illness, transmission of physiological effect on human subjects, regression, and clairvoyance—had just switched to lecturing "under the open skies."

"I had to do that," she told us, "because they forbade me to continue my work with my group on our premises."

"Why was that?"

"Because I was holding a clairvoyance class and they said I was using hypnosis, which I was not authorized to do. The accusation was false." Shrugging off her clash with the authorities, she went on to describe her most interesting cases.

A girl student of Ivanova's insisted that she be regressed by a co-student, a young man who had never done such a thing before.

"She submerged so completely that, although her eyes were wide open, she did not recognize anybody." Ivanova recounted. "She saw only the world of her previous life, and acted like a completely different person. She performed a classic Persian dance . . . yet, normally, she does not dance at all. She behaved like a very shy Eastern girl of no more than fifteen, although she was a young, independent modern woman of twenty-six. She went down on her knees, addressing the boy as if he were a prince and she his loving slave. She kissed his hands, cried.

"It was like a very beautiful legend come to life, and it lasted at least an hour," Ivanova said. "Shortly after it began, her co-student phoned me, frightened, asking me to come immediately, to help to bring her back. I rushed over by taxi, very much alarmed. It took me two hours to return the young woman to normal. Later, we discussed the experience together. With the help of my clairvoyance, I was able to describe some of the scenes even better than the girl. The golden bracelet with which she played, the exquisitely carved windows and walls, the soldiers who dragged her from her prince to a prison tower, how she fought and cried. The key which she searched for beneath a nonexistent carpet, finally finding it and trying to escape. The girl recalled everything I said."

As she was about to come out of her trance, she was asked her name. She replied "Saida," and said her country was Persia, although it was obvious that she was a Russian girl, fair-complexioned, blue-eyed, with long blond hair. Later, she was asked what country she liked best, and she replied, "Iran,"—the present-day Persia— although at that time she could recall nothing about her actions during the trance.

"After all we went through that day, I forbade her to take part in such experiments without my being present. Regressions can be highly dangerous." She glared at us as if to say "you better believe it," then fell silent and for a while we kept walking without saying anything. She was gathering her thoughts. Slowly, she resumed, "Let me amplify on regressions. Whatever people think, their previous lives are not individual experiences. They are interconnected; the impressions of former lives are stored in the subconscious. Hence you will do well to be attentive to inexplicable habits in yourself and in others. They will tell you a great deal. Let me give you a few examples.

"A woman, when walking up stone stairs leading from the Black Sea to a sanitorium at Yalta, which was once a palace, behaved very strangely. She lifted her short modern dress as if it were a long and heavy one and was encumbering her ascent. She could not understand it—it was a completely unconscious gesture. But after being regressed to one of her previous lives, she saw herself as a noble lady wearing a heavy velvet dress, which she had to lift to be able to walk on the stairs of her palace.

"Another woman, this one in Leningrad, had the strange habit that when she rose from her writing table with her head bent, she sometimes made a movement with her fingers, near her forehead, as if jerking the brim or the peak of an invisible cap and bringing it back to the right position. When regressed she saw herself as a Czarist Imperial Guard, wearing a parade helmet which fell off each time his head was bent.

"I have many experiences of this type with the different psi-effects, which I teach—healing, clairvoyance, prognostication, regression. We think that it is very important to understand the facts of reincarnation, the purpose of 'far memory flashes,' to know how they influence our lives," Ivanova said.

Birthmarks are particularly significant. A secretary 'saw' her death from a bullet, which a man had shot at close range into her chest in a previous life. She had a jagged birthmark in the same spot, yet she had never heard about reincarnation and birthmark coincidences.

A young engineer, when regressed, 'saw' his death from an arrow in Asia. He felt a sharp pain in his chest, where the arrow hit him, and was feeling it even after he had been 'brought back' to the present time. People at the experiment wanted to see if there was a birthmark, and asked him to show the spot where the arrow hit. He said there was no mark there. But on closer scrutiny, he found a pale round mark, a half inch in diameter, that he had never noticed before.

"There are too many examples of this type of birthmark for it to be ignored," Ivanova said with conviction. She told us of a schoolteacher who was terrified when somebody walked close behind him in the street. He always stepped aside in such cases, to let the others walk past him. After being regressed to an earlier life, he saw his death by a bullet fired by a person close behind him.

She was once asked to treat a young man for mental illness. She had never met the patient, but had a vision of him as a French soldier killed in battle, with a saber stuck into his side. The boy's mother then revealed that her son had a birthmark exactly at the saber entry point!

Ivanova went on to describe how she became a healer. "I wanted to heal. I felt a strong urge. I prepared myself for the task by studying books on the subject, fasting, dieting, and meditating. However, even after several years I had not enough courage to try to heal anyone. Sometimes I felt the pain of others who were near me. Healers call this an 'echo sign.' My friends told me that this ability meant the possibility of diagnosis in cases where the sick person could not answer the doctor's questions. I took their advice and went into healing by doing just that, helping make a diagnosis when the patient was unconscious.

"As with many healers, I accidentally discovered the curative effect of my touch. I had a headache at the same time as one of my students. I asked the boy where he felt the pain, at the same time touching his head at the places where I felt my pain. He answered, 'Yes, exactly, here and here.' Suddenly he exclaimed, 'Oh! It doesn't hurt anymore. I feel no pain.' But now the pain I felt was worse. I had picked up his as well. A few minutes later though, it was gone.

"After this case, I began to seek out people to heal. At first, my body absorbed the pains from the sick people, making me quite ill. However, I now rarely feel any pain when healing."

Her research has found that there is often a connection between the profession or job a person was employed in during a previous life, and the one he or she prefers in this existence. Similarly, many ailments are caused by incidents in previous lives. "I have had very good results healing people under hypnotic regression," Ivanova said. "My first experience was with a very bad stutterer. After I put him into a half-trance, he spoke for an hour, describing a life in Spain which was in total contrast to the one he now led as an ordinary worker in a Moscow factory. He never stuttered when under hypnosis.

"During the second seance, he experienced some other incarnations, and visualized his life in the future. When he saw that he did not stutter in other lives, he thought, why should he stutter now?

"The tape recording of this makes a deep impression on everybody, by the way."

But Ivanova was not totally satisfied. She wanted to know the *reason* for the stutter. She regressed him to another life, this time finding him with a pastoral people in an Eastern country, in an ancient time, there he had committed an evil crime. "In his half-trance, I asked him, 'Have you suffered enough for what you had done?'

"His voice was low and sounded guilty, 'No.'

"He began to cry. 'How can you get free from this curse?' I asked. He replied, 'Only by doing much good to people, by healing them.'

" 'Will you do enough of that in this life?' I probed.

" 'No,' he answered. 'Only in the next one.' "

When the young Russian worker came out of the trance, he did not remember anything. That happens, Ivanova said, when the person submerges more deeply than in average cases. This method is akin to psychoanalysis, but directed to a deeper level, the extracerebral memory submerged in the subconscious.

"Nevertheless after my regression treatment, he began to speak much better. He had the confidence to go out shopping alone, something he had dreaded before because of his stutter. He spoke fluently in front of 150 people, participants in our bio-energy seminar. It worked almost 100 percent." Interestingly, the man has developed into a good healer. Ivanova told him "healing heals the healer," and he uses that as his motto. The regression experiences have made him very eager and happy to help people.

Many phobias are caused by experiences in past lives, she reflected. For example, claustrophobia may be the result of being locked up for years in a tiny cell hundreds of years ago. The fear of heights may have been instilled when one met death by being pushed from a high rock. One of Ivanova's friends did not like cats. She feared them and was in a panic when she saw even tiny kittens. Ivanova had a clairvoyant flash, and said, "In one of your incarnations, you were killed by a black panther."

"How did you know?" the friend cried out. "I often have a terrible dream about a giant black cat attacking me, killing and eating me! I never mentioned it to anybody!" It was no coincidence, but her "far memory," which surfaced in her dreams, Ivanova said. She caused her friend to change her attitude about cats, and the woman became a different person. The dream did not appear again.

There is also an educational purpose in far-memory regressions, which is perhaps the most important part of it. According to Ivanova, people can see in their previous lives the source of their illnesses, misfortunes, and tragedies; the real purpose of all their sufferings; and the educational goal of their "chain of life."

"A quiet, placid housewife, blond and fat, was regressed," she recalled, "and saw herself living in the Orient as a 'free' woman, tall, proud, indifferent to others, content with her errant life, her many lovers, expensive dresses, rich houses. Then I showed her the end of her life. She was old and ugly, ill and lonely, with no friends around her. Asked what she learned from that life, the housewife answered, still in the trance, 'It was not a good life. Never again. I want a simple home, a good husband, children.' In her present life, she has all this."

The subjects of her experiments could not only see their previous and future lives, but could make conclusions from them and from their behavior. "They see the reasons," Ivanova said, "the ways, the main objectives of their life, the 'why' and the 'because.' It is something like a broadened form of clairvoyance, sharpened by the bio-energetical field of the inductor. This is very important for our research."

Many cases seem to emphasize the intrinsic goodness in man. For example, a soldier was very unhappy and lonely. Regressed to one of his past lives, he saw himself betraying a friend. Asked what he had learned from that regression, he answered, "I have to suffer now, because I have to understand and feel what a treasure a friend is, and how bad it is to be betrayed."

A girl student told Ivanova about a recurrent dream that troubled her very much and made her nervous. She saw herself lying on railroad tracks with a train fast approaching. But despite terror gripping her heart, she did not stir.

"I told the girl," Ivanova continued matter-of-factly, "that what was happening in her dreams was a replay of an incident in a previous existence, in which she committed suicide. She felt that she could not master the difficulties, could not fight them. Therefore, her present attitude, when face-to-face with personal problems, has been to accept the inevitable. I told her she had to understand that suicide, as with every form of avoiding decisions, is not a way out of problems.

"After this experiment, her mood changed radically. She became more cheerful and stronger as a person. She brought order into her life and started to handle her problems. The dark, recurrent dream vanished. Everybody should know that such an attitude does not help, and one will get the same situation in the next incarnation, until one learns to fight adversity. The type of difficulties are always the same. You have to solve them. If you don't solve them in this lifetime, they appear again and again in different forms and situations in the same life, and in other ones, till you learn to master them in the right way."

She paused to glance around quickly, her trained eye taking in the people wandering alongside us in a stream of humanity. No, we were not being followed.

"It was by accident," she went on, "that I discovered I could help people over the phone."

She has been doing this with considerable success and as recently as the previous week when she cured a man in Novosibirsk, 1,200 miles away, of heart spasms. It took her two telephone sessions, each lasting two minutes.

"I can't tell you how many I have helped in Leningrad, which is 390 miles away, all by telephone. I fail in 20 percent of the cases, and then only whenever my subjects do not trust me, can't relax, or actually resist me."

She shook her head as if saying, "Poor people."

"There was this peasant woman," Ivanova went on, "who called me from the village hall after probably waiting six hours to get through to me in Moscow. She had been given my name by someone I had helped before. She said she was suffering from pains, stiffness, and cold in her body, mainly in the neck, shoulders, and hips. She had had it for years. Nobody could help her.

"As we talked, I had a vision of her in a previous life. I saw a young girl with fine features. In the first scene I glimpsed, the girl was kneeling in prayer. In the second scene I had visions of her being chained to a wall in a medieval cellar. The stone wall was cold and damp. She was cold all over.

"Then I saw her being taken down and thrown onto a wooden bench. I could feel the sting of cold. In my mind I covered the girl in the vision with a blanket, and instantly the woman on the other end of the telephone felt better.

"I told her to call me again in a week's time. She did, and once more I had the same vision and I again mentally covered her with a blanket, and again she felt better. At the end of our third conversation, another week later, the woman's pains had gone. They have not returned.

"Again, I am convinced they stemmed back to the experience of a previous life. By being able to go back into that in my vision, I was able to cure the ailments at the source."

Ivanova halted dramatically in mid-stride, stared at us, and said proudly, "I assume you have heard about my attempt to help a young woman in Cleveland, in America, also by telephone." This was the case we hoped she would tell us about. A visiting American parapsychologist had called on Ivanova and, impressed with her accomplishments, suggested the experiment.

"They wanted me to keep all names secret and I respect their request, but my colleagues here have been given all the particulars. This young woman was 23 years old and recently married. The poor girl had been in an automobile accident that killed her parents. Pulled out of the wreck still alive, she was rushed to a hospital, where it was ascertained that she had lost one kidney and most of the other kidney. She was placed on a dialysis machine. By the time I was approached, she had been in the hospital six years.

"At the request of this American parapsychologist, I conducted three telephone conversations with the patient in Cleveland, each time attempting to relay bio-energy. Each time I received enough bio-information via ESP to know what was required. I knew she was in a bad state—I could feel cold waves. After the second call I was told that the patient was able to urinate for the first time in years. But the effect of bio-energy in her case did not last long. The damage had been too severe. All I could offer her was temporary relief. I am sorry I could not do more for her."

The distance from Moscow to Cleveland is 4,800 miles. She has tapes of the three sessions, which have been studied by Adamenko and others. The tapes could be made available to us when we meet again, she said earnestly, and she herself was ready to undertake additional international experiments by telephone. We could see what the success of such an international experiment could mean to medical science. Even if it were limited in time and effect, it could attract enough attention to make nonbelieving scientists on both sides of the Atlantic sit up and start revising their attitudes to parapsychology. What would the authorities say to that, we countered? How legal was it? Would one have to request permission somewhere?

Strangely, Ivanova ignored the question. Later, we were told there was nothing strange about it. This was simply not the time to seek official sanction, and she knew it. Her offer was merely to implant this possibility in our minds for the time of the propitious opportunity—some time in a shaky future.

As we thought of it, we also became uneasily aware that should such benevolent transmission of bio-energy by telephone across huge distances be possible, then the same power could similarly be used to produce negative results. The equivalent of the medieval curse transmitted over the modern satellite telephone was perhaps an outlandish thought, but we had to accept it as potential reality in the light of Ivanova's experiments. Much later, in the wake of disclosures about secret Soviet tests, we thought of Ivanova's transmission again, only to conclude that in the newly developed circumstances, official Soviet permission was not about to be given at all.

But on this day in Moscow, wandering around Revolution Square, we thought "good thoughts" only. And Ivanova was plodding along totally engrossed in the subject. She was saying, that while the telephone is her bridge to reach the patient, she may use different means of crossing it. One of her most famous cases concerned the same principle of long-distance transmission of healing energy—but without involving a phone! She was only too happy to tell us about it.

"A mother came to beg me to help her son. He was suffering from hallucinations that his late stepfather, whom he had loved, was trying to destroy him for some unknown reason. The poor boy was taken to a mental institution here in Moscow and became so violent that he had to be placed in a padded cell. I spoke to the hospital. They diagnosed his case as acute schizophrenia. I asked them if they minded if I tried a long-range experiment, under medical supervision. They said, fine, they had heard of me.

Ivanova's first move was to try to communicate with the stepfather's spirit, since she was not going to rule out that it was possibly affecting the boy. She went into a trance and said, "I assume you are angry with the boy over something, but the boy is suffereing very badly. Please leave him in peace. The boy's been punished enough." Two days later, the boy's mother called her to say that the hallucinations had not recurred for the last two nights. She told her it meant that this part of her boy's mental illness had been alleviated. But he was still suffering from mental exhaustion. She then concentrated on treating this with the help of her long-range bio-energy radiation.

"In the case of this boy, I reached him direct. That means I was at home, he at the mental institution about five miles away. Each time, his mother and an orderly were with him," she went on.

"His mother knew the time of transmission and made sure the boy assumed the necessary position—sitting upright, legs about one foot part, hands spread out palms down and resting on his knees, body very loose. She assumed the same position. So did I, of course, back at home, sitting very upright on a hard chair, concentrating on the boy. Each time, his mother told me, she felt prickling in her fingertips. In other words, she too was getting some of the bio-energy I was sending to the boy.

"On at least one occasion she called me to say that both she and the boy began to receive my transmission a whole half-hour later than had been prearranged. I reassured her everything was under control. What actually happened was that I had been detained elsewhere and started the transmission half an hour late. Accidental as it was, the incident was additional proof that they were actually receiving me. Eventually, the boy regained his mental strength and was discharged."

Where other healers such as the Krivorotovs need to be within inches from the patient, she does not. It is well known, and has been verified by Soviet parapsychologists, that she works mostly by telephone, if need be over a distance of thousands of miles. She can also do it at a distance of several miles within the same city. Even though the area of her effectiveness is widening with time and experience, she treats only certain illnesses, the ones she knows she can handle: heart spasms, severe headaches, nervous tension, loss of energy through illness, anxiety, heartaches, stomachaches, toothaches. . . .

"Let me qualify that I am not using the word 'treat' as a medical term," Ivanova hastily added. "You can't call bio-energy medicine. I've conducted quite a few demonstrations of this in the presence of scientists. We do not have a scientific explanation of the phenomenon yet, but my own hypothesis is that we are dealing with bio-energy radiation. It is transmitted directionally and instantly onto the person on the other end of the line, the distance as such not having an effect on either sender or receiver.

"I am convinced by our 4,800 mile experiment that no delay, however brief, occurred, meaning that transmission of bio-energy is faster than light. We have yet to measure it. How much faster? If it is many times faster, or, incredible as this may sound, truly instantaneous, the consequences may be staggering. The world may be within reach of instant extraterrestrial communications, a breakthrough for which scientists have been hoping."

Out in Revolution Square Varvara Ivanova was about ready to wrap it up. "As for healing by bio-energy," she was saying, "speaking in parapsychological terms, I am of the opinion that life is mutual exchange of energy with our environment. Illness is caused when this exchange is interrupted. An introduction of outside bio-energy restores this exchange.

"The points of energy exchange coincide with the points of acupuncture, which are also points of highest conductibility. By pouring bio-energy into a human system in need of regeneration, we assist the process of biological energy inflow—a life-giving function.

"Let me add that many people can be trained to transmit bio-energy into others. I myself have been responsible for training about one hundred such psychic healers, who currently work in hospitals around our country under strict medical supervision. I have similarly taught ESP and clairvoyance to my pupils—a total of as many as three hundred. It took me one year to teach it to myself with the help of textbooks, and it takes me one year to teach my groups. As I said, I was teaching a class when they came in to close us down.

"So, I took my class into the park. Come on, let's have a glass of tea."

She slung her bag under her arm and set out toward the curlicued turn-of-the-century facade of the old Metropole.

"At the Department of Bio-Information, where I am a member of the Council, I teach, train, and study clairvoyance in its various forms with a 'spontaneous prognostication' group. I will soon begin to teach 'image diagnosis,' as I call it, training people to have 'pseudovisual images' of the sore and ill parts of the body. They will be able to see what is wrong with the patient, and how the healing is progressing."

The tea break with Ivanova didn't take long. She liked to keep on the move.

Before she departed, we did ask her what would happen next. She didn't know. And she didn't care. Her psychic healing classes were closing down, but she hoped it would be possible to reopen them again at some point. She hoped she would learn to heal better, and be able to teach many others to use their abilities to the utmost. She believed that some of her pupils were already better healers.

For example, one of her pupils deliberately cut himself on the finger and closed the wound with his healing powers. The next day, there was no scar. Yet Ivanova cannot heal her own illnesses, and wounds that she heals always leave little scars. Her pupils, in their turn, teach others, and so the healing movement grows, although she is officially not allowed to conduct her classes.

"Nobody will stop me," she snapped.

There was no doubt about it in our minds; she will continue classes wherever and whenever possible, expecting that after a while her good name will be restored and she will be given an official nod of approval. "After all," she flared, "I am a scientist, not a charlatan, and our high-level authorities know this all too well. Even if so few of them comprehend parapsychology."

But wouldn't she get in serious trouble in the meantime? She shrugged a stubborn shoulder. "When at war, do as at war! One must take things as they come."

"Okay, Varvara Mikhailovna, one last question. What advice can you give to people who want to become psychics or healers?"

A broad grin carved her face. "I knew you would ask that," she said. She reached into her bag, and brought out a sheaf of papers. "Here—take these. I prepared them for you. Tell your readers to follow my advice and they may become as good as me."

10.

IVANOVA'S ADVICE ON
HOW TO BE A PSYCHIC AND HEALER

It was early rush hour, and while the bulk of Moscow was headed for the subway, the rest was lining up at the busy bus and trolley stops. Dusk was fading into early night and in the distance, huge five-pointed stars impaled on the spires of the Kremlin's towers lit up with a ruby glow to remind us where we were. As Varvara Ivanova stumped off into the dark, she certainly left us with a memory that we will treasure: a warm, honest woman who wanted to help people and was not afraid of political consequences.

She melted into the crowd and was gone. There were hundreds of Varvara Ivanovas with similarly stoic faces, heavy coats and fur hats, grimly pushing in the direction of the subway entrance on the corner facing the Bolshoi Theatre's pseudo-Greek facade. There were the men, the Ivanovs, who also looked alike. One great mass of humanity brought down, at least outwardly, to the common denominator of life in the Soviet Union. We could visualize her riding the unusually long escalator down to the subway station, built so deep to be safe from conventional bombs—as it surely was in World War II.

We have never seen Varvara Ivanova since that day when we drank tea at the Metropole Hotel in Moscow. She is probably still living the life of a gypsy, traveling the country, lecturing, teaching, training people in psychic endeavors. "Is she in danger?" Adamenko had repeated our question. "To some extent, yes. Maybe they won't touch her because she has so many genuine admirers among important Soviet scientists and powerful newspaper editors. Only yesterday one of them told me, 'We respect Ivanova. She is a fanatic, of course, but shouldn't a dedicated scientist be just that?' She will have her ups and downs, more so than any of us. What matters in the long run, however, is her contribution to Russian parapsychology research and this, make no mistake, has been tremendous."

We wondered what she had thought of our encounter. We were sure that it would not be an exaggeration to say it was equivalent to a rendezvous with visitors from another planet. We knew how Adamenko felt. We detected in the eyes of Vinogradova, Sergeyev, Kirlian, all of them, a mixture of wistfulness and sadness, yet also reassurance, at having touched the world outside their walls. In Ivanova's case, obviously, it had to be so much more.

The fact that she did not show it was perfectly in character. She came to us, talked, and left, all with the businesslike manner of one with a purpose. In a way, she was the classic dissident, meaning the dissenter, the freethinker. Not a dissident by creed or political philosophy, she was fighting to make her science as important as space flight, or the task of harnessing the atom. She unquestionably wanted Mother Russia to extend its lead in psychic research, and felt the power of the mind could solve the myriad problems facing the world.

Perhaps that is why she had prepared the advice for "our readers" —she knew they were in the West—on how to be a psychic or a healer. Obviously, other parapsychologists had told her that we were the ideal "messenger service" to the West. Not until a quiet afternoon two days later, when a promised interview had not materialized, were we able to sit for a couple of hours and digest the material she had given us. We read with avid interest. Ivanova had prepared the material carefully, which is perhaps the reason it had taken so long for her to contact us.

Her advice was not based just on her own experience as a psychic. Ivanova headed the experimental unit on clairvoyance that had been organized by the Popov Group—the first such training unit in the Soviet Union: "We no longer ask if people can be trained to be psychics—we have proven it can be done," she wrote in her opening remarks. "Most men and women have the ability. I have trained people as young as 18, and as old as 75. All have shown remarkable precognitive skills. All you need is the will power, the desire, and a few good friends to help you develop your hidden talents." In great detail, Ivanova then outlined the regime of preparations she had developed over the years, stating, "It invariably brings good results." We know she will not mind that we have condensed and simplified her remarks. In essence, they still carry the message she took such great pains to write for us—and you, the reader.

Ivanova firmly believes that personality plays a role in obtaining good results. There are, quite simply, some people who have character traits that are more suited to this type of work. Expansive, positive-thinking people are the best, while people with a constricted, negative attitude have little success. She has shown in her experiments that people who really believe in extrasensory faculties, who think that research into ESP is really important, score better than those who merely think it is an interesting phenomenon. The former appear to be more highly motivated to score well because they feel that a demonstration of extrasensory abilities will prove an unrealized potential in themselves. The whole idea is to them more real and meaningful.

To be a good psychic, first relax physically. Choose a favorite chair or a quiet spot in a park. Let the muscles unwind. Make sure that you are totally comfortable, and that there is nothing in the surroundings to disturb you. Then empty your mind of all thoughts. If you are particularly preoccupied by something—a child's progress at school, a family illness—you must deliberately and specifically cast this thought out. Generally, it is sufficient to try to visualize a blank sheet of paper or the emptiness of space. The object is to create a vacuum in the mind.

The next step is to recall a familiar symbol or object. Examine it, mentally, from every angle, until you know every detail of its size, shape, texture, and color. Finally, brush that image from your mind. You must consciously make it disappear. You are now ready to receive precognitive information. You have created the perfect vacuum, the blank screen, that will suddenly fill with unexpected images giving information about the future. However, like an athlete, you must then train your mind to achieve even better results. It is best to start this training simply. Having completed the buildup exercises, have a friend set up a simple situation in which the predictive choice is yes or no, left or right, black or white.

There is general agreement that a cheerful, friendly, informal atmosphere favors the operation of all aspects of psychic training. It is therefore very important that the person who is supervising is carefully chosen. Domineering, narrow-minded people can change and even completely spoil all the results, just by being present. Their bad vibrations seem to affect everyone. This type of person should not be involved in psychic training or research, and any results obtained when such a person is present should be ignored as unreliable.

Once you have achieved a high success ratio at these either/or questions, make the test more complicated. For instance, use playing cards, where the choice also can include red or black, picture cards or nonpicture cards. In other words, you are trying through precognition to give *two* identifying features—a *black picture* card, or a *red nonpicture* card. The targets should be changed after every three to five attempts, since boredom has adverse effects on people with psychic talents.

From there, more sophisticated training tests can be devised with three, four, or five factors being introduced. A competitive atmosphere is good in training—everyone likes to be able to score higher than another person. But you must not overemphasize this aspect, as some people become disappointed and lose interest if they feel they have been constantly "beaten." It should always be remembered that the main goal is to expand and develop the mind.

Psychic ability can appear and disappear, without any particular reason, but it will always return to a properly trained psychic, the person who is willing to regularly exercise his or her mind properly. When you have achieved a high success ratio in these more sophisticated tests, you will find that you have become an accomplished psychic who is also able to "see" and predict future events with great accuracy.

The psychic should be physically and mentally fresh before attempting precognition. Experiments have shown that fatigued people achieve lower marks. The intensive concentration needed should not last more than 45 minutes. There are pitfalls a beginning psychic must avoid, such as two answers flashing into the mind in quick succession. In that case, the very first image that appears should be recorded. It will invariably be the right answer. There are other problems people must be aware of. At times, a psychic will receive information indirectly—he or she will visualize a familiar object or symbol, but it is merely a *clue* to the real information. This clue has to be expertly interpreted.

And so, beginning psychics should always speak out. Never be shy! If an image is received, tell people about it. Choose the right surroundings and serious, well-informed and open-minded friends, so that there will be no hesitation in recording psychic information that may not be easily understood.

How do you know you have received a genuine psychic message? Ivanova gave us a simple "checklist" she had devised, which psychic trainees should run through after an impression has been received. Have you picked up telepathic vibrations from another person? You will find, for instance, that a person who is thinking of suicide emanates energy beams relating this desire. It is possible that your mind will pick this up in an example of "automatic telepathy." This is not truly precognitive information. Was a warning or prediction unfulfilled? For example, you feel you should not fly on a certain airplane, because you see your own death in a flaming crash. You give back your ticket, and in fact there is a disaster involving this plane. But the incident in the premonition has not come true because you changed the pattern of events. Since it *did not happen,* it is not a true example of precognition.

Could it be that you have unconsciously *calculated* an answer? For instance, you might see a car crash, a building falling, or a train derailment. However, your mind is like a computer. You must examine your memory and find out if you have fed this computer with information you have read—that car traffic at a certain junction has reached an impossible peak, that faults have been discovered in a certain construction technique, that the weather has affected railroad tracks. Information such as this could lead your mind to reach a calculated conclusion. Again, this is not a psychic effect.

Was it intuition, which again is not regarded as a true psychic insight? Intuition, Ivanova explained, is when you don't hear, don't see, don't know how information has reached you, but are convinced that something will happen. In the professions, the sciences, business; there are many examples. For instance, a physician recognizes an illness without the presence of any outward symptoms and without having all the necessary data. The engineer finds a solution to a problem without conducting controlled experiments. Mathematical ideas, physical conceptions, philosophical constructions, are born in a flash of genius, as if a light has gone on in the brain. In art, good taste, and even the talent exhibited, is often a demonstration of intuition. It must be remembered, however, that all these phenomena appear generally after a good deal of work, or certain physical preparations for the acceptance of these "flashes of insight." But they are not psychic precognition.

Properly trained psychics can help solve many world problems if taken seriously and asked serious questions. Ivanova believes that more and more people of the caliber of famous seer Jeane Dixon will develop as correct training procedures are used. Ivanova's statements on healings were equally lengthy, and we have again condensed them without, we hope, losing any of the information.

She is convinced that bio-energetical healing was an art widely practiced by ancient man, who knew and valued the laws of nature. However, as we evolved into an industrial society, these values were lost, and with them the widespread ability to heal. There are very few cases in the modern world of spontaneous healing, because there are too many mental distractions. The healing gift is a complex of many things, difficult to study and understand. Potentially anyone can heal just as anyone may be able to paint or play the piano. But the efficiency is different. If you have some knowledge and training, you can do it even if you do not have much talent for it. In any case, it takes rigorous training and steadfast dedication. Ivanova firmly believes that the key to using it properly and fully is to master your own desires and thoughts, and devote your total existence to helping others.

Keeping fit is very important. A healer must follow a proper diet, which should have little fish or meat, and must not imbibe alcohol. Meditation is very important, for it improves the mental powers. Her advice to students is that if they wish to be successful, they must try to visualize close links with the forces of nature. It is a very important part of preparing to be a healer. Before trying to heal someone, put all other thoughts aside and concentrate your mind, the inner eye, on examining the miracle of a flower or a tree or a bird. Think of its purpose in life, its beauty, its role in the universe. This will stimulate the latent talents, the knowledge of nature and healing, that we have pushed into the dark recesses of our minds as we developed from a simple existence so many thousands of years ago.

In healing, it has been found that people with kind hearts, open minds, and a positive attitude to people and animals are better patients and better healers. A person with a closed psychological system allows neither information nor energy to flow in, and cannot be healed with bio-energy. Ivanova warned that beginning healers should not be disappointed if they come up against such people. It is not possible to penetrate their shield. These are people who don't believe in bio-energetic healing, and in fact do not want to be healed. They are actually afraid of the healer. Unless the healer is prepared to spend a great deal of time changing their whole attitude, it is better to tell them immediately that they cannot be given assistance.

Everyone emanates invisible bio-energetic rays. It is the healer's task to beam these rays at the affected organs of the patient. You must consciously send them out, as if you were directing a searchlight beam. There is no need to touch the sick person. The rays of bio-energy that pour from a healer's hands are more effective at a distance of between three and four inches. Experiments conducted by Ivanova, using Kirlian photography, show that although the healer is directing the energy rays at a particular organ in an individual, the rays often scatter like a machine-gun burst. Most patients will feel the rays as an unusual heat on the target area, but others report that it feels like a light pressure, or a slight electrical shock, or the soothing touch of a cool wind.

Healers find that the pain in a patient will sometimes disappear from one area, only to affect another. This is quite normal. In such cases, the pain may return after a period of some months, and the healer may have to schedule treatments for regular intervals before finally accomplishing complete success. The healer must continue to work on the ailment, literally "chase" it from the body, till the patient reports he is healthy again. The more you practice, the more effective the healing beam will become.

As his abilities expand, Ivanova explained, the healer passes through five easily recognized stages. First, you will find that you feel the pain of sick people who are near you, but you can do nothing to help them. Next, you will be able to draw that pain into your own body, which can cause you great temporary suffering. This is one reason that the beginning healer must be very careful. It is advisable to deal with cases of slight illness at first. The pain you have absorbed in healing does disappear, but it is not a pleasant experience. As you heal more and more people, you will pass to the third stage, in which you initially feel no pain. But the stress of constant healing is too much for your body. You will feel sick, with strange pains in the middle of your spine. You will be nervous and very tired, yet you will have great difficulty in sleeping. Ivanova reached this level after treating six patients at once; but each individual has a different stress plateau. She was eventually able to heal 45 persons in one evening without feeling ill. Everyone must experiment to find out what is his or her ideal number.

Once trainee healers can do this, they pass to the fourth stage, in which they are able to stop at their limit: in other words, if they find they suffer adverse affects on mind and body after treating 20 people, they must set the limit of 19 in one evening. The totally accomplished healer—one of the few people who ever reach stage five—is able to prepare himself for any amount of patients, if he knows how many there will be in advance. He can organize and store the necessary quantity of energy.

There are occasions when merely talking to a healer has resulted in relief for sick people, Ivanova recorded. Many people are too shy to ask for individual healing treatments. She finds that some of these people follow her, trying to get near her or brush against her. They have told her that afterwards they feel free of pain, have more energy, and feel calm and happy. The same effects have been noticed when people merely enter her apartment. Her explanation is that a true healer is at all times radiating bio-energy, which is absorbed by those close by. People near the healer or selected patient often benefit, particularly those who have complete faith in the healer. After the sessions, they frequently report that they have also been healed. Objects such as a favorite chair also become saturated with these rays, and it is frequently enough for a sick person just to sit in this chair to be cured.

Ivanova ended with a stern admonition. "To be a good psychic or healer means a great deal of hard work. You must not be disappointed if you fail to achieve the desired results at the the first, or even the tenth, attempt. You must remember that the ability is there, and it is your duty to help all of mankind by using it to the utmost."

We know she will be happy if even a single reader in the Western world will one day say, "I have healed someone—thanks to Varvara Ivanova."

The question is: Where will she be—to be told about it?

When we tried to contact her in Moscow in late 1977 we could find no trace of her, anywhere. She had disappeared. "We haven't heard from her in several months," was the way Viktor Adamenko put it, "but I wouldn't worry. Not yet, at least."

Part Two

THE SEARCH FOR
NEW LIFE FORMS
ON EARTH AND BEYOND

11.
THE SEARCH
FOR EXTRATERRESTRIAL CIVILIZATIONS

At any moment, a breathless teletype operator in Moscow may dash to his machine and flash to the West a message that will change the world. It will read simply: "Soviet scientists today announced they have recorded signals from intelligent life in outer space."

We will not be surprised. For, on our many visits to Russia, we uncovered a vast Soviet effort to be the first to intercept signals from space civilizations. The Soviets are convinced that Earth is being bombarded by these signals. As a result, twenty-four hours a day, teams of researchers are relentlessly monitoring the universe with sophisticated equipment in an all-out race to record the first contact. They believe they could be successful at any moment.

It took us three years to document the incredible facts of what one scientist described as "the most fantastic adventure man has ever been involved in." When we first asked to talk to the top space scientists, the key men on our list were Prof. Vsevolod Troitsky, head of the famous radio astronomy observatory at Gorky; Prof. Viktor Ambartsumyan, head of the Byurakan Observatory in Soviet Armenia; Prof. Iosif Shklovsky, head of the Department of Radio Astronomy of Moscow University; and Prof. Nikolai Kardashev, a leading member of the Space Institute at Moscow University. When we telephoned from the United States to Moscow prior to our trip, Natasha indicated that we might be able to see all of them.

But when faced with the reality of our presence in Moscow to do just that, Natasha sighed, "Actually, we have a small problem. The men you want to see are attending a seminar in Gorky. You can't go there: the city is very strictly out of bounds, and the men you want will be tied up there until long after you leave."

Gorky, 300 miles east of Moscow, is a military staging area from which all foreigners are barred. But there had to be an alternative to Natasha's suggestion to drop the interviews. What about the observatory in Byurakan? It turned out that the deputy director of the Armenian observatory was a very famous astronomer, Dr. Ludvig Mirzoyan. He had remained behind to continue operations. Couldn't we see him?

Natasha shook her head sadly. "It isn't that simple. You have no visa for Soviet Armenia." Her tone of voice told us she would go through the official motions, but her heart was not in it. She expected to be turned down even before she started.

It was time to use up another favor. From our room at the Rossiya we placed a call to Valentin Zorin, the all-powerful Soviet television commentator who had helped us to get into the Soviet Union in the first place. He listened attentively, then said: "Sit tight. Apply for the visas for Soviet Armenia, even if they tell you it can't be done."

We made the application to the girl at the hotel desk, and, as expected, were told it was out of the question. We persisted. Wouldn't she at least try?

"Didn't you hear what I just said? It can't be done." We showered her with compliments on her looks and efficiency, and begged her help. Finally she agreed. "Come back in a few hours, and then I'll have it officially that it is not possible."

It was almost 6 P.M. when we returned. As we approached, she pulled out a stack of forms and said reproachfully, "Why didn't you tell me that you knew the right people?" Our request had been granted. A few phone calls from friend Zorin, and the red tape had been cut. We were on our way to Yerevan, Armenia, a city in the Caucasus foothills only about one hour by car from the Byurakan Observatory. We really didn't know what we might find there, but Professor Mirzoyan's Moscow colleagues had highly recommended him as one of the Soviet Union's leading researchers.

As our overloaded, well-worn turbo-prop Ilyushin 18 groped its way down for a bumpy landing outside the reddish-brown city of Yerevan, we caught a brief glimpse of the famous observatory against the backdrop of Mount Ararat. Two sets of cupolas, half-hidden in clumps of trees atop a hill, clearly marked the site. According to legend, Noah's Ark came to rest on the smaller of Mount Ararat's twin snow-capped peaks. In fact, what are claimed to be fragments of the Ark are on display in the nearby town of Echmiadzin. Yerevan is a sprawling but pretty city, nestled in vineyards. Its treelined streets are broad and clean, with fountains of sparkling pure drinking water every few hundred feet. The people were quite well-dressed and seemed happy and relaxed.

In Yerevan, we were assured that the astronomers at Byurakan had done well, not because the giant Leningrad-built telescope was the largest in the Soviet Union, nor because its East German Schmidt camera had the finest prismatic lens in the country. No, the reason for Byurakan's success was that it was run by Armenians, who "have done well by astronomy over three thousand years of our civilizations." Ancient tracts do document an interest in astronomy going back into antiquity.

The Byurakan observatory is almost on the Armenian-Turkish border, and the area is tightly guarded, with many sections completely off limits. When we set out on the narrow winding road from Yerevan to Byurakan, we found armed soldiers manning frequent checkpoints. We were stopped at each.

Who were we, and how was it possible for foreigners to have been issued passes to proceed to the observatory? Not only were we suspect, but so were our passes. The fact that we had Natasha, an escort from Moscow along with us, loaded down with official credentials, left them unimpressed. Every time, the situation had to be explained carefully and in detail. From the guards' reactions, it dawned on us that we were among the very few Western journalists that had been granted permission to visit a sanctuary of scientists involved in a top-priority Soviet project—the search for life in outer space.

We finally reached the entrance gate to the observatory, only to be confronted by more guards. They couldn't care less whether we were expected or not. They denied any knowledge of instructions to let us in. We had reached an impasse. Eventually Akop Ekakyan, a Soviet photographer whom we had hired in Yerevan and whom the guards knew well, was allowed in to find Mirzoyan. Some twenty minutes later, he was back, beaming. Suddenly we were free to enter—to meander our way to our host all by ourselves.

We wandered from the guardhouse to the main building. A mild sun hung high in the clear blue sky. The cloudless heavens above Byurakan are the reason that the observatory was built on this hilltop, 4,600 feet above sea level, and why it has since been expanded into a formidable monitoring post. The guards were on the outside. Inside the sprawling complex, a small colony of some forty scientists had been left to their own devices.

It was a self-contained community, with housing for the scientists actually on the grounds of the observatory. We could see that at least the director lived well. Professor Ambartsumyan's two-story pink villa, sitting on a slope in the back of the compound, was a mansion worthy of a dyed-in-the-wool capitalist anywhere. But its proximity also allowed him to get to his telescope in three minutes flat.

Obviously this was the main reason he and the others lived here. They slept by day and worked by night, unless they were off duty, or on the rare occasion that the star-filled canopy was overcast. Half a dozen women, all middle-aged and heavyset, were clearing weeds from the flower beds in front of the main building.

The door was ajar, but there was no one around. Eventually a man peered out, then conducted us to an office on the second floor of the main building, knocked, and retreated.

That was how we found Professor Mirzoyan, a soft-spoken, mild-mannered man in his mid-forties. He opened the door, said cheerfully, "So here you are," and motioned us to a low table by the windows. His English was halting but precise. He went straight to the books and charts spread out on the table. There, too, were cognac and cookies—for the weary travelers who had made it to Byurakan. He was careful to offer us a welcoming toast before he got down to business.

"I am certain that we are on the threshold of a major breakthrough in interplanetary communication." He was speaking with obvious conviction. "It is no more a matter of wondering if there *could* be somebody out there, but *how* to establish the first interplanetary dialogue. A study of life in the universe, up to now a subject of fiction writers, has begun. We are working round the clock to gather and sift data."

Later, Mirzoyan showed us the observatory tower containing the main telescope. He paused thoughtfully as he pressed one of the buttons that electrically open the viewing doors in the cupola's roof. A multiple echo picked up his words and seemed to throw them back at us. "What we propose to discover will affect every aspect of life on Earth. Signals from outer space sent out by other civilizations should be coming our way with increasing intensity and frequency as other planets pick up evidence that Earth is inhabited by intelligent beings.

"If we haven't been watched before, we are being watched now. Our presence has been revealed by our development of radio and television emanations that have increased radio-wave radiation of Earth about one million times in the last thirty years.

"We are making an all-out effort to capture these signals—and we could do it today, tomorrow, or the next day."

The team of men in Byurakan became known as "the world's lookout" for lights in outer space after their 1962 discovery of stars that flared up at certain intervals.

Right from the start, they felt strongly that another civilization might be flashing a light beacon at intervals—in addition to radio beacons—to attract attention from civilizations like that on Earth.

A year before our visit, the Byurakan observatory recorded a celestial flare-up that did not fit the pattern of observed natural phenomena. The astronomers at first conjectured that they had picked up a signal from another civilization. They carefully analyzed it and concluded that it was a natural occurrence. However, the time was not wasted; the experience allowed them to extend their knowledge of conditions in space. It also reinforced their hopes that some time in the future they would pick up a flare artificially created as a space beacon.

"A civilization of a higher degree of development than that of Earth," the Armenian astronomer pondered aloud, "would deliberately use an obsolete means to attract our attention, while having much faster means to observe us. The obsolete means are both light and radio waves, whose speed is terribly slow when applied to the distances beyond our own solar system. A civilization existing 100 light years, or roughly 600 trillion miles away from us, might be able to 'see' us instantly, but a signal sent to us from such a planet today would be picked up by us with the help of our present means only a full century from now. Conversely, a signal we may receive and log sometime this year would have left that particular planet a century ago." He was reconciled to this hundred-year lag because he believes that the nearest civilization is actually that far away—100 light years.

"There can be no other living worlds closer to us" he said solemnly. "Those closer worlds are dead; planets of extinct civilizations that man will visit some day to find monuments and other relics, but no signs of life." There are 100 billion *known* stars, or suns, in our own galaxy, and quite a few, obviously, have their own satellites and planets, Mirzoyan stated. He rejected as unrealistic the thought that conditions of life had not been duplicated on some of them. There might be as many as 10,000 "Earths" within a distance of 1,000 light years.

"The question is, how many of them approximate our age?" he continued. "By our age, I do not merely mean the existence of man but also his technology. It is a matter of scientific record that we have advanced further technologically in the last hundred years than in the thousands of years prior to that. In a sense, our civilization is one hundred years young, rather than ten thousand years old. The next hundred years will put us in a stage of technological development beyond present-day comprehension.

"Not all astronomers agree with me, but all of us are equally aware of the desirability of contact with a civilization whose concept of life and technology is within our grasp. This could lead to a mutually beneficial coexistence. One could envisage an interplanetary alliance based on the same stage of development.

"The ideal would be to find a civilization that today is the age of Earth, plus no more than another hundred years. But I don't think this probability exists. On the other hand, we must not assume that technology habitually develops at the pace it has now reached on Earth."

A shadow of concern darkened his face as he went on: "Our finest astronomical theoreticians are of the belief that after another hundred years, our technology will reach a plateau, a golden age, and thereafter remain on the same level of development for several thousand years. And then? Is ten thousand years the span of a technological civilization before it begins a decline? This is an opinion to which many of us subscribe. In the light of these considerations, then, a coexisting civilization may be ten thousand years older than ours, and still be at a communicative stage. I would say that a number of such planets situated within a reasonable distance from our solar system do exist."

The immediate challenge to man—one that Soviet scientists have picked up with alacrity—is to contact beings on such a planet and to go on from there, Mirzoyan explained as he closed the doors of the observatory and we strolled back through the gardens. The assumption is that it is exactly this type of civilization that will want to attract our attention in the first place. If our problem is to train our telescope on the minutest section of the sky, at exactly the source of an infinitesimally tiny signal, at the right time, the task of the other civilization is to make this possible.

His voice growing stronger with every word, he confirmed, "I am certain that as more evidence of growing radioactivity on Earth is picked up, there will be increased efforts to break through to us.

"The pulses we shall hopefully pick up and log within the next years will most probably be nondirectional beacons, ones not actually aimed at Earth when activated about a century ago."

He did not rule out the possibility that these space beings multiply their signals by bouncing them off "dead" space bodies, such as the Moon, and therefore we should also carefully monitor such objects. His swarthy face lit up with a smile as he told us of his dream. "More than anything, we need an observatory on the moon. I hope to be the one chosen to build it and thereafter to run it. This may take another twenty years, which is regrettable, because we could use it right now. It need not feature the most powerful telescope in the world. Even a medium-sized telescope on the moon will pick up interplanetary beacons that at this point we on Earth only think we can see or hear."

As we solemnly shook hands to depart, the deputy keeper of man's lookout post issued a warning: "Our lives are too short to expect much more than initial contact. But our children will have an excellent chance of starting an interplanetary dialogue and to request and receive information.

"I do not anticipate physical interplantary contact for them or the next generation, but after that, who knows? We are on the brink of exciting discoveries almost beyond the realms of our imagination.

"I hope and believe that one day soon you in the West will read that we at Byurakan have been the first in the world to pick up and confirm a message from another civilization in outer space!"

He said it with sincerity. It is obvious that he and the other members of the observatory team have dedicated their lives to this search. Not until a year later, on another visit to Russia, did we get the opportunity to fit another piece into the puzzle.

There was still no word from Professor Troitsky. However, Shklovsky and Kardashev, the two space experts at Moscow University, were in town. "Would you like to interview them?" Natasha smiled, knowing full well what our answer would be.

She set it up for two days later. We got as far as the door of the Space Institute on the grounds of the huge university, when a military guard barred our way. "Passes?" he demanded.

We had none. He shrugged. No passes, no entrance. We stood wistfully looking up at the space insignia over the door of the Institute. It looked as if that was as close as we were going to get to two of the most important men in Soviet space research.

Then, word came on the guard's phone: "Professor Shklovsky is coming out in just a minute to express his personal regrets."

It gave us just a glimmer of hope. If the famous scientist was prepared to leave his office to say he was sorry for us, then perhaps we could conduct our interviews outside the Institute? It was a beautiful, warm, sunny day, and the newly mown grass of the lawn outside the Institute smelled invitingly.

Shklovsky, a round-faced, barrel-chested man wearing a brown jersey sweater and glasses, grinned as he listened to our proposition: Since we couldn't go in, would Kardashev and he come out? He nodded encouragingly and disappeared. Minutes passed, then the guard's phone rang again: Wait for five minutes. The two scientists will be right down.

Ten minutes later, we were all sitting on the grass of a patch of lawn separated from the building of the Space Institute by bushes and clumps of trees. Shklovsky was lounging back in the grass, chuckling: "I love it here—it is the best interview setting ever!"

Chewing on a blade of grass, Kardashev was just as happy. A boyish-looking 40-year-old with ruffled black hair and a carefree smile, his white shirt open at the neck, he looked like the typical image of a Russian poet rather than a famous scientist, an international authority on radio astronomy, engaged in the study of space sciences.

Shklovsky, whose credentials included membership in the Soviet Academy of Sciences, the American Astronomical Society, and the Royal Astronomical Society of Great Britain, wasted no time in getting to the heart of the matter. "Despite a probably very low frequency of life in the universe, I agree with my colleagues that we are not the only intelligent beings in existence. Other civilizations exist, for at least two reasons. First, there is such a vast number of star systems in space. Second, we know that chemical building blocks of life exist out there just as they do here.

"I would place them at the distance of several hundred light years from Earth, even though I would not rule out the possibility that the nearest may be one hundred light years away. To an advanced technology, the exact distance doesn't matter that much. What matters is that they are most probably out there, and that the level of technology on some of these planets is close to ours. The living beings and their span of life need not necessarily be similar to us. Those ahead of us in development could convey to us an enormous wealth of knowledge."

"I too have studied the subject very closely," Kardashev joined in. "While I don't rule out the possibility that such planets exist, I believe that where our own galaxy is concerned, there are few such civilizations left. The bulk of them have already joined the supercivilization that I would definitely place within the very nucleus of our galaxy, 40,000 light years away. This supercivilization is millions and possibly billions of years older than we are."

He stopped for emphasis, then went on: "These are circumstances obviously far beyond our comprehension. We would have to take leave of what we would call normal reasoning to assume such things as a progression from natural life to life with artificial bodies and from there to fully artificial life controlled by artificial brains and an eventual parting from mass. However fantastic this may sound, modern science is quite willing to apply this progression to humanity and to expect Earth to be eventually inhabited by automatic, computerlike machines. It would take between 450 and 1,000 years for man to go through this evolution and presumably reach immortality. The ultimate machines would be immortal, but programmed to have emotions, and thus would function like human beings. These machines could eventually leave our solar space to join the supercivilization in the nucleus of our galaxy.

"The area in the nucleus of what you also know as the Milky Way is the most promising location for such a civilization made up of migrations at different times from dying planets. It's an ideal spot. From the center of the galaxy, a civilization could easily be in touch with many other galaxies. We also find a tremendous amount of energy radiation in this area that such a civilization could profitably put to use."

The two men exchanged knowing glances. Then, using the stem of grass as a pointer to emphasize his remarks, Kardashev went on to discuss the black holes that astronomers have discovered in space but have not yet fully explained. "I believe that these black holes can be widely used by a supercivilization nearby to give its begins an opportunity of traveling through time. Theoretically, if the fundamental laws of modern physics hold up, a man in a spaceship who flies into a black hole is bypassing time. He can not go back in time, but he can advance into the future. We believe that these black holes offer an exit to the next space. The theory is that the universe consists of many separate spaces and that the black holes are the linking 'passageways.' "

He furrowed his forehead. Then, pensively, he said: "The beings of this supercivilization, who are on a so much higher level of intelligence than we, are most probably machines, immortal, possessing artificial intelligences. It is impossible to guess their physical shape, if mass still applies, which I doubt."

Shklovsky, who had been nodding encouragement while Kardashev expounded his extraordinary theory, took up the theme. "I fully subscribe to the hypothesis of machines ultimately inhabiting our planet. The machine beings of the supercivilization Professor Kardashev describes may be small, may be large, may have no physical shape whatever and have turned gaseous, into the shape of a cloud.

"Such a supercivilization does not inhabit a planet—a planet would be too small. Possibly, instead, it's a system of machines. Obviously, it is beyond our comprehension to communicate with this type of ultimate civilization. To them we would have the minds of insects, or less. They could not be interested in us. I do not believe that it would want to communicate with civilizations like ours. There is no level on which we could meet.

"But on the other hand, I can see how thousands of years from now, by which time we will have run out of energy and space, we would want to join this supercivilization Professor Kardashev is talking about. By then, obviously, we'll be superbeings ourselves. Ours should be a planned, conscious migration to the one ideal spot in our galaxy where we may continue to exist, in whatever shape we may have by then. This won't be, though, until well after our civilization leaves the plateau our astrophysicists expect us to reach in one hundred years. I am confident that the fantastic developments of our technology, now racing ahead, will slow to a crawl before the end of the twenty-first century. Whatever man will be by then, his interest for more technology will have died down. It won't resume for several thousand years."

It was Kardashev who brought us back to the reality of the present. Soviet scientists are manning posts all over the country in a "very determined and scientifically programmed effort" to probe the universe for signals from space, he stressed. These signals are expected to be short impulses sent out far apart at exact intervals, maybe once a month, even once a year. They will be short because of the vast amount of energy needed to have them picked up at distances of many light years away. Their precision and regularity would prove them to be artificial, the products of intelligent life in space.

"We assume that contained between the short impulses are weaker but more complex transmissions containing real information," he continued. "Once we succeed in receiving the simple impulses and determining that they are arranged in an artificial pattern, we will know what point in the sky to examine for more information.

"One problem we face is that we do not have the key to their units of time. Does one year also mean one year to them, or one minute in their life, or an eternity? They could be the equivalent to Gulliver's Giants, or Lilliputians." He glanced at Shklovsky. There was agreement between them on that.

Shklovsky added his own final observation: "We in Russia expect the signal to be a television transmission. Scientists agree that it would be easiest to decode—which, after all, would be its purpose. But even if not, cipher experts have assured us its deciphering will present no problem. A civilization capable of sending such signals would know how to design them for reception by underdeveloped civilizations like ours."

By now we were strolling back to the Space Institute, the interview nearly over. Kardashev had a final word. "We must be prepared to fail in our efforts as long as we remain earthbound. Experiments with the most powerful radiotelescopes have shown that existing radio noises in our atmosphere garble reception. So far, the ratio of signal to noise has been against us. I feel that not until we set up our first space observatory will we be able to read the messages. Whatever information we expect to receive will come this way rather than visually. After we eliminate the noise problems, we may look forward to a wealth of computerized information flowing in from outer space. We have started on the most fantastic adventure that mankind has ever been involved in!"

We had just received another fascinating insight into the Russian space scientists' thinking. Despite their differing descriptions, they believed these space beings have two things in common: intelligence far beyond our own, and a desire to communicate with other civilizations, such as Earth. But were these fascinating, intriguing personal views, or the considered opinion of the Soviet scientific hierarchy? We needed to know. And until now, the one man who could confirm it—Prof. Vsevolod Sergeyevich Troitsky, the dean of Soviet space scientists—always had eluded us. Again, time ran out on our visas before we could meet. We had almost gotten together on one occasion. Natasha Yakovleva of the Novosti Press Agency, our friend and traveling companion, had borne the brunt of our complaint that Troitsky was the only man in the Soviet Union qualified to analyze the information we had received. Finally she told us, "He will meet you in Moscow tomorrow."

Early the next morning, she phoned to say, "He has cancelled out." No reason was given.

Our basic training in Soviet setbacks served us well. "We'll interview him by telephone," we told Natasha. "Can you give us his phone number in Gorky?"

There was silence. Then: "You'd better come over to our office."

At 11 A.M., keyed up with expectancy, we gathered round the

receptionist's telephone in the waiting room of Novosti at No. 2 Pushkin Square. We had been given permission to bug the Novosti phone, and a curious Soviet electronics expert came in to watch it in operation. A few minutes later, Gorky came through—on a different line, rendering our phone bug useless. There was no time to change it to another phone. The electronics expert, who probably expected it, grinned: tough luck!

We tried to go ahead with the interview, taking notes instead of taping. The reception on the phone was terrible, weak and overloaded with static. Troitsky was on the line, but we could barely hear him and he could not make out our questions. We hung up and tried again. It was useless. After twenty minutes, we gave up. It was too important a subject to risk a misunderstanding because of a bad telephone connection. And Troitsky was too busy a man to stand by the telephone until we got it right. Disappointed, we asked Natasha, "Next time, let us meet with the Professor. We'll go anywhere." She promised she would do her best.

Now, on our most recent trip, Natasha had called our Moscow hotel with startling news. "Professor Troitsky is in Moscow. He will see you this morning."

"We'll believe it when we sit down with him," we said to ourselves. But our hearts were beating faster as we ordered our driver to take us to the Novosti office. This should be the culmination of our probe into Soviet space research. Now we would have the opportunity of confirming all we had learned.

As we climbed the steps to the Novosti conference room, the buzz of activity around the door indicated that all was well. Novosti, taking another opportunity to meet otherwise unobtainable scientists, had allowed three Soviet newsmen to join us, provided we approved. Natasha was also present to introduce us.

Two desks had been pushed together to make a long conference table. Seated behind it in comfortable lounge chairs were three men: Prof. Troitsky, Prof. Nikolai T. Petrovich, director of technical sciences at Moscow University, and Prof. Vadim V. Kazytinsky of the Institute of Philosophy, the Academy of Sciences in Moscow.

As we were introduced, we could hardly control our excitement at finally meeting Professor Troitsky. He was a dignified, solemn-faced man, his dark hair swept back severely from a broad forehead, accentuating his academic bearing. "We have sought you here, and there, and everywhere, but finally we have caught you," we told him to break the ice.

He smiled wanly. "It has just not been possible until now," he answered. "I understand you have many questions. I hope that my colleagues and I will be able to answer them."

As he relaxed in the chair, his hands folded in his lap, we briefed him on what we had learned from Mirzoyan, Shklovsky and Kardashev. "What is your opinion, Professor Troitsky?"

His statements were crisp and definite. "Of course there are civilizations in outer space. Obviously they differ in age and in conditions in which

William Dick inside the Kremlin. In background, Russian tourists file past the historic Czar Bell, supposedly the largest in the world. Dating back to 1733, it was never hoisted to the belfry in front of which it still rests

Henry Gris inside the Kremlin. In background, tourists examine the historic Czar Cannon which, cast in 1586 to defend Moscow against Tatar invaders, was never fired

The late Wolf Messing, considered the world's greatest mentalist, displaying his powers on a stage in Russia

Yuri Shevyakov (left) of the Novosti
Press Agency assigned to Gris
and Dick (right) as their "aide-de-camp"
to set up many of their interviews

Boris Ermolaev, during lunch with
the authors at Moscow's Hotel
National, demonstrating the
"passes" he makes while
suspending objects in mid-air

Wolf Messing, duplicating a drawing
sent to him telepathically

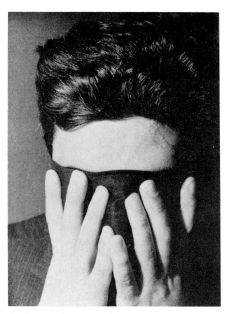

Tofik Dadashev, who has inherited Messing's mantle and his place on the Russian stage, photographed before a recent demonstration at a Moscow television studio

Dadashev first blindfolds himself, pressing the cloth tightly against his eyes

Over the blindfold goes a black hood. Dadashev's hands seem to serve as antennae to provide mental contact with his audience

At the conclusion of the demonstration, Dadashev's face shows the effects of strain and intense concentration

Dr. Genady Sergeyev, Russia's top parapsychologist, who supervised experiments with psychic medium Ninel Kulagina

Ninel Kulagina, moving a matchbox by telekinesis.
Recovering from a near-fatal heart attack she was able to repeat this experiment during a filmed demonstration in Moscow in March 1977

Alla Vinogradova, considered Kulagina's successor, demonstrating her own telekinetic abilities for the authors in the
Novosti office is Moscow

Viktor Adamenko, Vinogradova's husband, holding the small bulb that lit up when placed near an object his wife had moved. A leading parapsychologist and theoretician, Adamenko was an invaluable contact during the authors' investigation

As a research assistant looks on, Karl Nikolayev concentrates on objects he is receiving long-distance telepathically, from his partner, Yuri Kamensky. The men came under attack by the prestigious *Literary Gazette* but Nikolayev has been allowed to continue his work as a telepathist

The view outside the Astoria Hotel during Gris's and Dick's telephone interview
with Yuri Kamensky. St. Isaac's Cathedral is at the rear of snow-covered
Leningrad square

Outside Krasnodar's Research Institute of Agriculture, where Gris and Dick were granted an exclusive interview with Semyon Kirlian. *From left*: Timofei Dubonosov, the head of the Institute, Dick, Kirlian, Gris, and a Soviet reporter allowed to attend the meeting

New buildings in Krasnodar, home of Semyon Kirlian, the inventor of Kirlian photography

Inside laboratory, where Kirlian
is currently engaged in secret
agricultural work. *From left*:
Dubonosov, Dick, Kirlian, Gris,
and Natasha Yakovleva of the
Novosti Press Agency

Semyon Kirlian, examining one of
the plants he hopes to strengthen
and improve through Kirlian
photography's diagnostic methods

The Krivorotovs, Tbilisi's father-and-son healing team, being
interviewed on the balcony of the local Novosti office

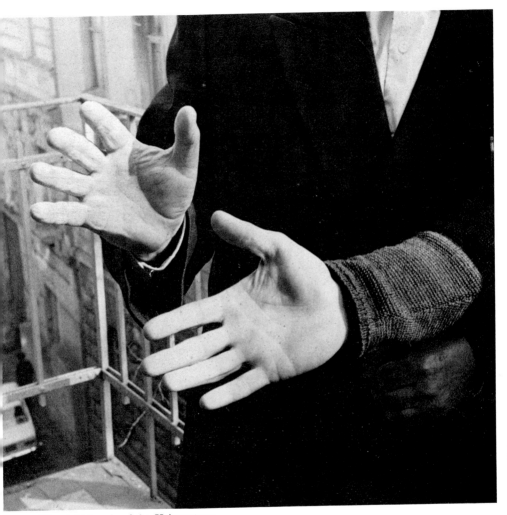

The right hands of the Krivorotovs

Viktor Krivorotov (*right*), and his
father, Aleksei, (*below*) "operate"
on Henry Gris's headache and
old arm injury

Dick, Natasha Yakovleva, and Gris en route from Tbilisi to Sochi on the Black Sea where the Krivorotovs tend to patients at local sanatoriums

Varvara Ivanova, the eccentric psychic researcher, during a stop in Moscow

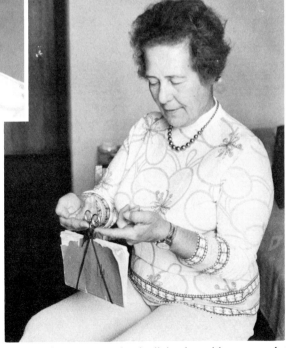

Ivanova demonstrates simple divination with a suspended scissors and book

The authors meeting with Prof. Ludvig Mirzoyan, deputy director of the Byurakan Observatory near Yerevan in Soviet Armenia

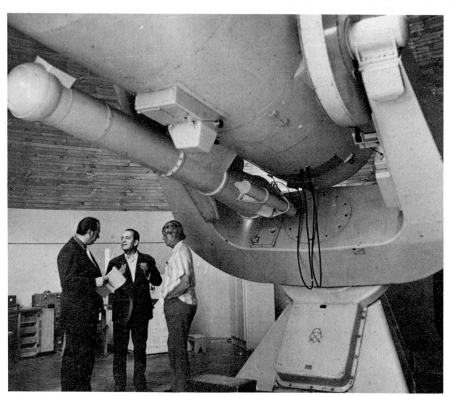

Dick, Mirzoyan and Gris before the giant telescope that searches for visual flares from outer space

The authors with Professors Iosif Shklovsky and Nikolai Kardashev on the steps of the Space Institute at Moscow University

Since the building itself was off-limits, the two astrophysicists agreed to be interviewed on a nearby lawn and discuss their speculations on the nature of extraterrestrial life. *From left*: Gris, Shklovsky, Kardashev, Dick, and Natasha Yakovleva

An early photo of Prof. Vsevolod Troitsky, head of the secret radio astronomy observatory at Gorky

From left: Prof. Vsevolod Troitsky, astronomer; Dr. Nikolai Petrovich, astrophysicist; and Prof. Vladimir Kazytinsky discussing in Novosti's Moscow conference room man's inevitable colonization of space

Part of the radio antenna installation at Gorky, actually a vast forest of antennas set to pick up signals from many light-years away

Aleksandr Kazantsev in his Moscow study, showing the authors an 8,500-year-old Japanese statue that, he is convinced, represents a cosmonaut from Phaeton, a hypothetical planet that once orbited between Mars and Jupiter

Dr. Felix Zigel, Professor of Cosmology at the Moscow Aviation Institute, and a leading and controversial authority on UFOs and extraterrestrial life

Dr. Aleksei Zolotov has sworn not to shave his beard until he proves conclusively that the Tungusky "meteorite" was actually a nuclear-detonated device sent by an extraterrestrial civilization

Prof. Zigel exhibiting to a Soviet reporter the cross section of a tree that stood two miles from the epicenter of the 1908 blast over Tungusky; 97 years old at that time, the tree was stimulated—probably by radiation— to increase in circumference almost four-fold within half a century

Prof. Igor Bourtsev, curator of Moscow's Darwin Museum, Lt. Col. Karapetyan, and Viktor Adamenko examine the footprint cast of "Big Foot" which is used to compare footprints of the elusive Russian *Almasty*

A Moscow back street, en route to the interview with Lt. Col. Vargen Karapetyan, who was called out to "interrogate" a captured "Abominable Snowman"

Paris-born Dr. Jeanna Kofman, who dedicated her life to investigating the wild primitive men of the Caucasus

Henry Gris at the Piskarevskoye War Memorial for the 500,000 Russians who perished during the Nazi siege of Leningrad in World War II

At Novosti's Leningrad office the authors met Dr. Vasili Kasatkin, whose research demonstrates that patients' dreams can alert doctors to impending health problems

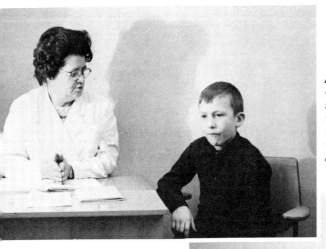

At Leningrad's Poliklinika No. 26, doctors have pioneered hypnosis as a tool to cure children's ailments. Dr. Aleksandra Chernopolskaya with Vasya, her star pupil, who regained his speech after a childhood trauma left him mute

Dr. Vilen Garbuzov in the hypnosis room, where children are hypnotized in groups

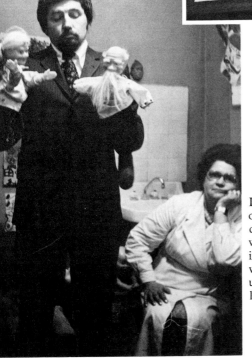

Dr. Aleksandr Zakharov in his office at Poliklinika No. 26, demonstrating the hand puppets whose "dramas" give him insight into children's psyches. On the wall are paintings done by children under hypnosis; Dr. Chernopolskaya looks on

In a sitting room at Leningrad's Astoria Hotel, professor of hypnotherapy, Dr. Pavel Bul, shows Dick his "magic wand" on which he focuses a patient's attention to induce hypnosis

Authors flank Dr. Vladimir Raikov and Prof. Artur Petrovsky, who employ hypnosis to release talents and abilities untapped in a subject's waking state

Dick, Dr. Raikov and Gris, pose with paintings done by untrained artists who were hypnotized into believing they were accomplished Russian painters

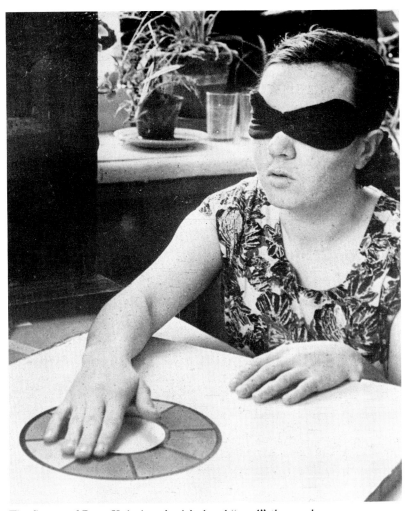

The fingers of Rosa Kuleshova's right hand "read" the numbers on the card—even though there is a piece of glass between the card and her fingers

The formidable Dr. Natalia Bekhtereva, granddaughter of the
pioneering parapsychologist Vladimir Bekhterev, is head of
Leningrad's prestigious Brain Institute, where doctors working
under her probe and map men's neurological functions

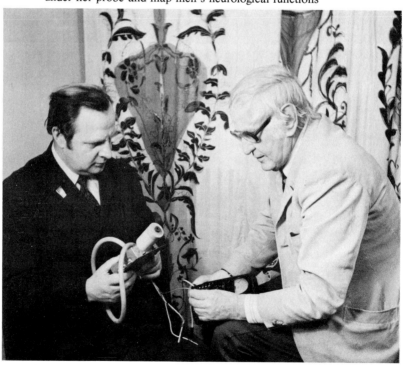

Dr. Genady Sergeyev shows Gris his model of a "time machine"
which, in its later stages, will be able to recover the emotions and
thoughts of people long since dead

they have been allowed to develop, but among them there are planets just like our Earth. These planets have gone through the same evolution of life that Earth has. I am convinced that they are inhabited with beings with brains like ours."

As he spoke, even his two colleagues leaned forward to listen avidly. Behind us, the team from Novosti was frantically taking notes. Obviously they had never heard a noted Soviet scientist talk so freely on such a controversial subject.

We asked Troitsky what the inhabitants of such planets would look like. He paused for a moment, then answered, "It is difficult to say whether they have man's ways, shape, and size. They very well could be like us, since man is nature's most perfect instrument and goals of perfection would be equal here and on planets with circumstances close to ours. More importantly, they would have been subject to similar laws of development. That is why I am inclined to assume that inhabitants of these worlds would not be giant insects or little one-eyed green men, or other creatures envisaged by science fiction writers. I believe they will be beings somehow resembling man. Their functional characteristics should be the same. This would also apply to the flora and fauna on these planets."

Soviet astrophysicists, he went on to say, are being encouraged in their search for life in space by a number of new, important discoveries. Not long ago they detected the presence of a great number of complicated organic molecules in the universe, voiding earlier theories that such units could not exist in space. Obviously, the cosmos contained a lot of unexpected and unpredicted elements. Its wealth was far beyond expectations. Therefore, in his opinion and that of his fellow scientists, the existence of other populated worlds was not only probable but logical. These worlds just had to be there—and indeed, the Soviets hoped to be the first nation on Earth to make contact with them.

"There must be several hundred worlds that provide conditions for intelligent life, and which are located 100 to 1,000 light years from Earth. Some of these worlds have probably detected our existence through our increased radioactivity, and are probing us with signals."

A faint smile crossed his austere face. His Gorky team has already had heart-stopping moments, he said, when they thought they had actually intercepted signals from another world. They picked up and logged impulses that could have been emanating from radio beacons, or could have been flareups of radioactivity signaling other civilizations. The scientists figured that it would be tantamount to Earth turning on all its radio and television in an all-out transmission.

The radio flare-ups they detected caused them to concentrate the Gorky radio equipment on these particular areas of the sky in the hope they could establish a pattern of signals. However, they subsequently found that these particular emanations were due to the effect of the sun on Earth's ionosphere.

Troitsky shook his head. "We were terribly disappointed. We were forced to discard our earlier hopes that these were artificial signals, indicating intelligent life in outer space." His team has not given up, however. His men were able to determine certain patterns, and arrived at important scientific conclusions. They didn't find another civilization, but they did learn more about the cosmos.

They are still scientifically analyzing radio impulses received during the same period but at night, and therefore not affected by the sun. These experiments were reported in the West and interpreted as a failure.

Asked about this, Troitsky commented, "We still think we are on the right track. We would not agree that our work has been a complete failure."

He then calmly answered out next question. No, they are not concerned that establishing contact with another civilization might be harmful to Earth.

"The question is frequently raised," he shrugged, "even by some of our scientists, as to whether we shouldn't leave well enough alone, rather than risk attracting attention and possibly put Earth in deadly danger of having outer space forces descend on us to destroy or conquer. I firmly believe this is nonsense.

"The distance between any other populated world and our own will prove so vast that physical contact will be impossible for eons. A spaceship, or fleet of spaceships, could never carry a threat of force at such a distance." Eventually, he foresaw man going out into the universe to colonize it. It would only be when this happens that man would have his first face-to-face rendezvous with citizens of other worlds.

Until then, the dean of Soviet astronomers expects only unmanned probes to visit Earth. "As I see it, for some time to come the only form of contact will be via unmanned space probes sent for the purposes of obtaining information and close-quarters observation, rather than landing. In relation to actual interplanetary travel by living beings, the distances are so incalculable that whatever space civilizations can exchange by way of spaceships will have to remain limited to measuring devices. In fact, these probes might have already visited us, for it would not be necessary for such probes to have the physical shape we most envisage, and it would not be necessary for them to enter our atmosphere."

He added firmly, "It is my considered opinion that only good can come from Earth's contact with another world because, for one thing, any kind of knowledge is good for mankind. I am not really worried about supercivilizations, although these are of course possible. I am more concerned with the existence of other civilizations whose level of development is close to ours. Man should make the greatest possible effort to seek out such worlds. Since they function within the processes of our understanding, we will know what they are doing and saying.

"I can easily see our starting a dialogue across space and exchanging information, using television images and computers. What we may learn from them by way of accomplishments in all sciences, in medicine in particular, will benefit all mankind."

As our Sun dies, making Earth uninhabitable, Troitsky believes these civilizations will help save us: "The death of the Sun is inevitable, and as it burns itself out, Earth will be a doomed planet. We will be faced with the prospect of freezing to death, and will realize that the flow of life-giving energy from the Sun into the bottomless pit of space is too wasteful.

"There is only one alternative—a mass migration into space. An enormous sphere will be built to enclose the Sun, catching every last photon of its waning energy. This enormous sphere will contain islands of humanity in perfectly controlled artificial conditions," he went on. "We will be like people huddling round a fire, making sure that none of its warmth is lost."

Soviet astrophysicists have already figured out how such a giant sphere will be constructed. Octahedral building blocks made of steel rods one meter long and one centimeter thick will be linked together to form a giant cobweb round the Sun. Then the gaps between blocks will be filled in. Once the population has been moved into the partially completed sphere, the Earth's tremendous core of molten iron, some 4,000 miles in diameter, will be tapped to use in completing the space colony. At a certain point, this will cause the planet to break up, spewing out huge chunks of the molten iron into space, where it will solidify and be retrieved. If need be, additional building material will be taken from elsewhere in the immediate solar system. The inside surface of the sphere, closest to the warmth of the sun, will be used as living space.

Troitsky showed little emotion as he spoke, not even when describing the death of Earth. "I am convinced," he continued, "that such colonies exist in other solar systems. We will benefit from the experiences of other space civilizations that have already been forced to flee their doomed planets. When the time comes, they will tell us how to escape to a space colony built round a dying star to conserve its energy. They will share their technological secrets with us, enabling humanity to add millions of years to its life expectancy."

And so life will go on. . . . He believes that the nearest "sphere civilization" is tens of thousands of light years away from Earth, but that we will have made contact with it long before it is necessary to evacuate the planet. Scientists estimate that the Sun still has five billion years of life left, although it is already five billion years old.

Professors Petrovich and Kazytinsky had been content to allow Professor Troitsky to deliver the main answers to our questions. Now they joined in, Professor Petrovich to explain the technical aspects of the search for life in outer space and Professor Kazytinsky to tell how philosophers were aiding the space scientists in assessing what type of intelligent life might signal from space.

"Could an advanced supercivilization use telepathy to make contact?" we asked.

"Of course," Professor Kazytinsky replied. "It is something we have seriously considered, and it is an interesting concept." For whatever reason, telepathy was not a topic Troitsky, the senior scientist wanted discussed, and a quick frown at his colleague ended the conversation. We were not concerned—we had already been briefed on this by other sources.

Time and again we were told that Soviet researchers firmly believe advanced civilizations on other planets will have totally mastered the art of thought transference, making all other types of communication obsolete.

"Telepathy is an ideal method of transmitting a message from outer space," Dr. Genady Sergeyev said confidently when we interviewed him in Leningrad. "It is fast, and it bypasses the barriers of language and culture by going straight into the mind of the receiver." He pointed out that U. S. astronaut Edgar Mitchell, had already experimented with telepathic transmissions while in moon orbit.

We resisted the temptation to press questions on the constantly veiled suggestions we had received that Russian cosmonauts were making similar experiments. The scientists had a definite reluctance to discuss this possibility, and since military secrets could be involved, we did not pursue the matter. We knew that no one would answer our questions at KGB headquarters in Lefortovo Prison or the Lubyanka Prison, the famous spy "hotel."

However, it was made clear that the possibility of incoming telepathic messages from other civilizations is one reason the Soviets are so intent on discovering the secrets of telepathy.

"We already have evidence that telepathic messages are being sent by whoever or whatever controls UFOs," Yuri Fomin, the Moscow UFO investigator, revealed. "Many witnesses involved in close encounters with strange flying craft in the Soviet Union tell of clearly 'hearing' in their minds a voice saying 'Do not fear us. We come in peace.' These are sober, outstanding citizens, and we can only conclude they have received a telepathic message from the UFO."

If telepathic messages can be sent clearly and accurately at relatively short ranges, the Soviet scientists reason that it is entirely logical that an advanced civilization would use it for sending long-range messages. "Look back into history," we were instructed. "Over the centuries, every civilized nation in the world has had visionaries who have been ahead of their time in ideas and concepts. Men such as Leonardo da Vinci have been able to design machines that could not be built until hundreds of years later. How were they able to conceive such ideas? Could it be that they were unconsciously receiving telepathic signals from some advanced culture?

"We accept that such civilizations exist and can be hundreds, even thousands of years ahead of Earth in development. Just as advanced nations on Earth have shared their technical and scientific advances with less fortunate nations, is it not reasonable to assume that a superspace race would want to do the same with the primitive beings on our planet? It is entirely feasible, and telepathy is a valid method of transmitting this knowledge."

Since it was obviously pointless asking Professors Troitsky, Petrovich, and Kazytinsky anything further about telepathy from space beings, we quickly changed the subject. Why did they believe any intelligent life would be so far from Earth? Why was there none closer? Because, came the answer in the last three years, Troitsky's radio listening devices have completed the investigation of the area within 16 light years of Earth. No signs of intelligent life capable of emitting signals have been discovered. Now his team is probing beyond this area using the fixed observation technique of a monitor "glued" to a star for months on end.

"We are moving into space, slowly but surely and systematically," Troitsky said. "To give you some idea of our task, there are 10,000 stars within 100 light years of Earth, and 10 million stars within the range of 10,000 light years. Luckily, not more than one in a thousand may be considered as likely to have planets supporting intelligent life.

"We believe we can safely exclude all double stars, systems revolving round twin suns. Life there is not possible. The same applies to stars of the spectral class which are not hot enough to sustain life on planets orbiting around them. We may similarly disregard stars that are too young and stars that are too old, and those with potentially too light a mass for animal life on their planets."

By eliminating all these stars, the Gorky observatory is now monitoring "suspected" stars within the 100 light-year radius. All monitoring equipment is tuned to the space "life frequency" or 21 centimeters. "There are two reasons that we expect word from outer space on this particular frequency," Troitsky said. "One is that this is the frequency of hydrogen radiation, hydrogen being the element most common throughout the universe. The second is that on this frequency there are fewer static noises originating in the universe, or for that matter in Earth's atmosphere and ionosphere, than on any other. In fact, the frequency is relatively quiet, making it a sort of window in a seemingly impenetrable wall.

"We must assume that if this fact is known to us, it must be known to other civilizations smarter than we are. They would, therefore, use this frequency for space communications. The surest way to catch word from outer space is to lie in wait and intercept it when it comes."

The Soviets, who lag in the production of their own computers, are using new American computers to concentrate and analyze their results. Sophisticated television techniques are being used. We were told the space researchers have the go-ahead to try any method possible, whether it has been fully tested or not, to locate the signals from space. They have high-priority clearance for obtaining the latest equipment. It is an all-out effort similar to that which resulted in the launching of the Earth's first Sputnik satellite.

"We are still facing one important technical hurdle," Troitsky said, sounding what amounted to an appeal for help from abroad. "Even though we are equipped to pick up flashes of radio beacons from outer space, we need very wide band frequency equipment to pick up signals that are probably emitted, at super-high speed, during the intervals between the slower beacon flashes. No country has equipment capable of picking this up. But after we get the first signal verified internationally as being of artificial origin,

I hope the public will agree with the scientists that we need to know what messages these civilizations are sending out into the universe. We feel that it will be information of the greatest value to mankind. I am sure we will band together very quickly feeling very much like single-purpose earthlings, rather than individual countries. We will want the recording equipment in a hurry!

"One of the first things we will want to know is the age of the civilization we are talking to. It would be most reassuring to a civilization such as ours to know that others have existed tens of thousands, maybe hundreds of thousands of years longer, perhaps in their ultimate home, the sphere—without having destroyed themselves or having regressed after reaching a high plateau of knowledge. The answer, in fact, is probably contained in their identifying signals, which—unfortunately—must be passing our monitors at this very moment without being detected."

Like many other scientists, Troitsky has a dream, and his eyes glow and his voice acquires unexpected warmth when he talks about it. He would like to see all nations pooling their resources to build a giant network of huge telescopes on Earth, in space, and on the moon. Linked by computer, it would be run by not only the world's leading astronomers, but top anthropologists, biologists, and other specialists in the origins of life. The single object of the network would be to seek out life in space.

We asked the obvious question: When did he expect a breakthrough? Troitsky straightened his angular frame and stared at us intently. "My answer to that is, it's a matter of luck. If we are very lucky, we may be able to confirm a signal from outer space within this year. If we are unlucky, we may wait another hundred years. What we are certain about is that the signals are there to be intercepted and interpreted.

"Remember, we are scientists, not science fiction writers. Even our theories must of necessity be based on observations and findings. Some findings may be in error or be proven erroneous in time. All we can do is relentlessly continue our efforts to set up our first contact. I am confident we will do it. But we have yet to intercept our first signal."

12.

THE MISSING PLANET PHAETON

One day in January 1975 a young geology student walking through the Karakum Desert northeast of Ashkhabad noticed what appeared to be little lumps of glass glinting in the yellow sand. Dark green in color and the size of walnuts, they struck him as being most unusual. The pieces of once-molten glass could have been manmade remnants of an ancient civilization, since not long before, a 4,000-year-old city was found in the sands of Karakum just east of the Caspian Sea.

The student collected six pieces of the strange glass and back at base camp handed them over to the expedition's leader, prominent Soviet geologist Pavel Florensky.

"I took one look at the little glass 'eggs' and my heart skipped a beat," Florensky recalled later. "I recognized them immediately as tektites, tiny meteorites from outer space, which had never before been found in the Soviet Union." Florensky immediately sent the pieces of glass to Moscow for analysis and within days his opinion had been confirmed. They were tektites, comprising several known metals including beryllium, which had melted in silicic acid while exposed to a temperature of millions of degrees Centigrade. The tremendous heat had turned them into glass.

The discovery was hailed as of inestimable importance by Soviet scientists who have been trying to solve the "Mystery of the Missing Planet." For years they have theorized that this planet—almost a duplicate of Earth—orbited the Sun just beyond Mars before a massive explosion tore it apart. Soviet Academician Sergei Orloff named it Phaeton.

A major part of the theory of the exploding planet was based on the finding of tektites in Australia, the Philippines, and Czechoslovakia. The scientists reasoned that only such a tremendous explosion in space could create the heat needed to make these glasslike tektites and send them shooting through space to hit the spinning Earth. But if the tektites arrived in one single cosmic hailstorm, they should also have been found in the lower areas of the Soviet Union. They had not been until Florensky's discovery, and as a result, other scientists argued that the Australian, Philippine, and Czechoslovakian tektites were all individual showers caused by separate cosmic explosions.

While in Moscow, we learned that Soviet scientists, bouyed by the Karakum Desert finds, had reopened the investigation into the missing planet Phaeton and its fate. We wanted to find out why and—surprisingly—were given immediate permission to talk to Professor Yevgeny Krinov, head of the Soviet Committee on Meteorites. The committee has been established as a branch of the Soviet Academy of Sciences to probe into the mystery of heavenly bodies that every so often come crashing down on our Earth. Professor Krinov did not normally give interviews, we were told, but was prepared to make an exception in this case because of the excitement over the tektite find.

We also interviewed Dr. Genady Vdovikin, a young Russian geophysicist with an international reputation, and Krinov's most trusted lieutenant; Dr. Felix Zigel, Professor of Cosmology at the Moscow Aviation Institute, whose work is held in high esteem by scientists around the world; and Aleksandr Kazantsev, noted historian and lecturer on space and author of a dozen books on space exploration. They presented a fascinating scenario pointing to the death of an inhabited planet in a nuclear holocaust.

Professor Krinov was ill while we were in Moscow, but authorities permitted us to visit his home for the interview. We settled down in his study, a large room with a view to the courtyard. Its walls were lined with bookcases, and the ubiquitous television set—as much a part of Soviet culture as it is of ours today—in a corner. "The reason that Florensky's discovery caused much excitement," Krinov explained, "is that tektites travel to us from the Asteroid Belt—a ring of debris that circles the Sun at a distance of some 400 million kilometers. The Asteroid Belt is positioned between the orbits of Mars and Jupiter, about 2.8 times the distance from the Earth to the Sun. According to a theory which has never been fully confirmed, but which has neither been effectively denied, asteroids circle the Sun along the orbit of a planet which, according to some of our astronomers, should have been there, according to the theory known as Bode's Law."

Johann Bode was a German astronomer who, back in 1772, published the theory of a numerical relationship governing the relative distance of our planets from the Sun. They fitted into a pattern, a progression of numbers arrived at by doubling each number except the first two, thus: 0, 3, 6, 12, 24, 48, 96, 192, 384. Bode added the figure 4 to each and so obtained the series: 4, 7, 10, 16, 28, 52, 100, 196, 388.

Much to the bewilderment of astronomers of that time, Bode's progression was remarkably correct. These figures proved to match the relative distances of the known planets from the Sun: Mercury fitted 4, Venus 7, Earth 10, Mars 16, Jupiter 52, Saturn 100. But there were three spots vacant: 28, 196 and 388.

Astronomers were still debating the theory when, in 1781, Uranus was discovered. Its relative distance from the Sun—191.8—was too close to 196 to call it a coincidence. True, Bode's Law suffered a setback in 1846 when Neptune was discovered at distance 300.7 for which there was no corresponding number on Bode's scale.

But when Pluto was discovered in 1930, Bode's Law found itself vindicated again. The distance was 394, too close to 388 not to be taken seriously. This discovery, reviving the credibility of Bode's Law, reaffirmed the belief that the Asteroid Belt, orbiting around the Sun at the exact distance of 28—that of the missing planet—actually *was* the planet, now decimated, strewn into a circular stream of debris in the cosmic winds.

"We have reason to believe," Krinov went on, "that at a certain point in history this planet disintegrated following an explosion. The explosion sent some of the rubble out of the Solar System. The remainder—some 4,500 fragments at the present count, ranging in size from chunks 700 kilometers in diameter down to 1.4 kilometers—has remained in the planet's orbit.

"Asteroids in this ring of space debris continue to break up as a result of forces exerted upon them by the planets. As fragments are hurled into space, some enter the Earth's gravitational pull, breaking up as they encounter our stratosphere, and again on impact. The majority of these are iron and rock, but some that are composed of more complex substances have puzzled scientists. There have been claims of discovery of petrified vegetation such as the one-cell hydrophytes: seaweed. More ambitious claims by scientists outside the Soviet Union insist on the discovery of traces of animal life of the trilobite genus."

Some of the most remarkable Soviet research in this field was carried out by a member of the Meteorite Committee, Prof. Aleksandr Zavaritsky. The importance of his contribution to science earned him a full membership in the Academy of Sciences. He worked with Prof. Krinov and until his death in 1963, was regarded as one of the leading experts on meteorites.

"Aleksandr Zavaritsky devoted the last years of his life to a theoretical reconstruction of the missing planet that Academician Orloff called Phaeton," Krinov recalled. "Using the meteorites that landed in our country as the basis for his theoretical building blocks, he came up with an estimation that the missing planet was larger than Mars, and possessed both a hydrosphere and a biosphere. Convinced that many of the meteorite fragments found on Earth were pieces of this very planet, he reconstructed it, layer by layer. He eventually saw it as an iron core enclosed in a narrow layer of iron-silicate, in turn wrapped in a wide layer of peridotite, all surrounded by a subcrust of basalt lava. Finally, a thin outer crust and mantle.

"The missing planet, he concluded, had all the external characteristics of our Earth, with oceans, mountains, and an envelope of atmosphere. There had to be life on it, he insisted. Since it revolved around the Sun along an orbit beyond Mars—on the outer border of what we call the Belt of Life, it *was* possible for life to have evolved there.

"If we accept the Phaeton theory," Krinov said, "life on such a planet should have existed there, but this would have been considerably earlier than life on Earth. We know that as time goes on, the Belt of Life, the temperate zone that supports life, keeps moving closer to the Sun. At some time, Phaeton would have been closer to the middle section of this belt, as Earth is now, and so fully support life."

Krinov stopped for emphasis. Obviously what he meant to say was that Zavaritsky believed not only that life had existed on the missing planet, but that its own humanoids, very similar to man, could have started a civilization preceding ours by millions of years. And assuming he was correct, this civilization would have been well ahead of ours when Phaeton perished.

"Unfortunately, before Professor Zavaritsky could present irrefutable proof of the planet's existence—or, for that matter, of its destruction—he died very suddenly, taking his findings with him. After he died, we searched for papers but couldn't find any. His death was a tremendous loss, because we feel that he had evolved a viable theory that could have become the basis for future research." He shook his head. "And so, we still don't know definitely, although Professor Zavaritsky may have found an answer. What caused the planet to perish? When was it? We all agree that it could not have been later than one million years ago. We also agree that when we find the answer, it will be with the help of meteorites. Will our latest find of tektites bring us closer to solving the many riddles?

He wished he could be more positive, Krinov said, as he escorted us to his entrance hall. "Speak to Professor Zigel. He can tell you more," Krinov assured us as he closed the door.

The following afternoon, too excited to stop for a meal, we met the balding, stooping, sad-eyed Professor Felix Zigel in author Aleksandr Kazantsev's apartment. There was another Moscow courtyard outside of Kazantsev's windows—this one with planted trees and beds for flowers that would bloom come summer. The reason for our meeting in Kazantsev's place was simple: the two men were not only very close friends involved in complementary research, but they agreed with each other's theories. If the ailing Krinov was still in doubt, Professor Zigel and Kazantsev were not. As far as they were concerned, Phaeton *did* exist, *did* suddenly disintegrate—and what happened to Phaeton should be a poignant and awesome warning to all of us on Earth.

"The life and death of Phaeton explains a lot of what is contained in these books," Kazantsev said on that first day we got together. He had surrounded himself with a large number of volumes, mostly in Russian, and almost all were scholarly translations of ancient literature, preserved legends, mythology, paleontology, and the like.

"But we won't waste our time on that," he dismissed them pleasantly. "Writers like Erich von Däniken have already dwelt on visitors from outer space and on what, apparently, they left behind for future generations of earthlings to ponder over. What these writers failed to consider is that some of these space visitors came from Phaeton. I am certain of this. They did not come of their own free will. They had not come to our Earth to colonize a planet which, they knew from earlier explorations, was a primitive and forbidding place, still in an early stage of development. They came because they had nowhere else to go."

Zigel didn't want us to use a tape recorder, nor did he like the idea of our taking notes. The ascetic face of the true scientist registered wonderment. "Can't you memorize?" he asked almost reproachfully. "We can," we reassured him. This, then, is what he said, reproduced to the best of two reporters' abilities.

"Phaeton disintegrated as a result of a chain of explosions originating on its surface. Had this destruction been of volcanic origin, the planet breaking up from within, the debris would have been hurled in all directions, eventually settling down into an elliptic orbit around the Sun.

"Another possibility: collision in space. Collisions that can cause destruction of a planet the size of Earth are most improbable, yet they must not be ruled out. What matters, though, is that a collision, head-on or even at an angle, would have thrust the debris into yet another oblong orbit, one even longer than the one caused by a volcanic explosion from within. On the other hand, the planet breaking up from without, through its crust, would have caused the resulting debris to remain on a near-circular path.

"Any astronomer will tell you that the Asteroid Belt has an orbit that is nearly circular; that in this respect it is remarkably similar to that of our Earth or, for that matter, of those of the other planets in our Solar System. In other words, it is the orbit of the missing planet. It had to be a surface force, applied laterally, that caused the destruction of Phaeton."

The tektites found in the Karakum Desert, Zigel explained, have provided a precious clue by reminding us of the glasslike slag found at the source of our own nuclear explosions conducted on the ground. Tektites have been created in laboratory tests. More recently, tektites were found after firings of the Soviet Tokomak-10, a thermonuclear furnace which, while still experimental, is the largest in the world. The temperatures under which these earth-originated tektites were produced were well above 100 million degrees. The comparison with tektites of space origin left no doubt whatsoever as to their thermonuclear origin.

"It was important for us to prove this, since our opponents have theorized that tektites are a by-product of meteorites slicing their way through our atmosphere and coming down to earth with such velocity as to generate such temperatures on impact. We now know that at no time has the temperature at impact of a meteorite exceeded 200,000 degrees Centigrade."

He paused for emphasis. "We have tried to create tektites artificially using this temperature. The resulting tektites are completely different from those occurring naturally.

"What appears probable, then, is that it was a thermonuclear explosion, because nothing short of that could have produced so disastrous an effect. And if we accept this as what actually happened, we can also logically assume the entire course of events. First, the original thermonuclear explosion. Second: a thermonuclear chain reaction involving other sources of thermonuclear power. Third: the oceans exploding and with that, the crust of the planet cracks wide open."

The possibility that oceans may explode has long ceased to be a fantasy of science fiction writers. Atomic scientists have readily admitted that at a temperature of hundreds of millions of degrees, water turns into thermonuclear fuel such as powers a hydrogen bomb.

Zigel continued, "We can assume, therefore, that with its shell destroyed, the planet went on disintegrating until nothing but rubble remained.

"Conclusions: The chain reaction on Phaeton was triggered. Having been triggered, it could not be stopped from spreading. The triggering force was man—humanoid. There is no other explanation. Man of the species inhabiting Phaeton and belonging to an advanced civilization had thus caused his own destruction, probably in the course of a thermonuclear war. Even though mishaps must not be totally ruled out, I do not believe it was a technological accident."

We could imagine Zigel addressing a conclave of his peers, delivering a speech of scientific complexity, yet barely consulting his notes. He spoke with clarity and precision, each word carefully chosen. He leaned out of his chair toward us as he went on: "Some day, when our cosmonauts reach out into space, traveling to Mars and beyond, they will be able to investigate the Asteroid Belt at close quarters for traces of intelligent life on Phaeton. The larger asteroids such as Ceres, Pallas, and Vesta, whose diameters range from 380 kilometers to 700 kilometers, could become perfect jumping-off places for advanced investigations. It is quite possible that in space-archeological terms, the smaller asteroids, representing bits and pieces of the surface of Phaeton, will prove more important. At any rate, our cosmonauts—and your astronauts—will know what to look for. One day they'll come back with the first archeological finds that will tell us about a missing civilization. After that, our study of Phaeton will start in earnest.

"Obviously, we have a long way to go yet. Until that time we will have to be satisfied with a study of fragments that have landed on Earth: iron meteorites which Prof. Zavaritsky identified with the inner core of Phaeton; rock meteorites from its rock crust, iron-and-rock meteorites from its mantle; and meteorites of limestone, pumice and other substances including alloys of copper, lead, and zinc as pertaining to its surface. Not much to go on to determine the existence and death of an advanced civilization, but ample to prove the existence of some form of life."

Enthralled as we were with his account, it was now late in the afternoon and dusk was falling. Our host now produced a bottle of Georgian cognac and a box of Riga chocolates and proposed a toast: "To Phaeton. May we unravel its mystery soon." Zigel smiled a wry smile, raised his glass and politely took a sip.

We agreed that we would come back the following day to listen to Kazantsev's account. It was Zigel who said meaningfully, "Gentlemen, you had better be prepared!" As it happened, we came back not only on the following day, but twice after that. Each time, Kazantsev had something more to add to a fascinating tale—not merely of the *people* of Phaeton, but also of how unexplained phenomena in our own history—including sites and fragments discovered by our archeologists, and descriptions of what presumably were atomic wars mentioned in the ancient writings of both East and West, could be tied in with Phaeton. Kazantsev believes that the destruction of Phaeton must have been total. There could be no survivors on the face of a planet that simply broke up. When the planet exploded, a civilization vanished—but not without leaving some of its members caught in outer space.

"Since we are dealing with a civilization well into the thermonuclear stage, which we ourselves may not reach for another fifty years, we must assume that their exploration of space was at a more advanced stage than ours is today," he stressed. "Their spaceships could roam our Solar System, presumably concentrating their investigation on our system's Life Belt or temperate zone. This zone includes Venus, Earth, and Mars. They would have had the knowledge that these three inner planets were best suitable for life as known on Phaeton.

"I am sure they actually saw their own planet disintegrate before their very eyes, a ball in space that suddenly crumbled into thousands of pieces, its molten interiors pouring out, turning into solidified chunks that broke up again in an endless chain reaction. One thing was certain: they had no home to return to. Denied a return home, some of them at least landed on Earth, while the rest perished.

"This explains the origin of ancient legends about gods arriving on Earth aboard fiery chariots, legends preserved and passed on by historians of antiquity, including Plutarch. Erich von Däniken who visited me before writing his famous book *Chariots of the Gods?*, claims to have discovered traces of extraterrestrial visitors in many places on Earth, from the Andes to Easter Island to China."

Kazantsev feels that the remarkable repository of 716 inscribed stone plates discovered by the Chinese on the Sino-Tibetan border was left behind by a tribe whose forefathers had come from outer space. According to a Chinese archeologist who claims to have deciphered part of the message on the stone plates, the tribe died out. They were humanoids but failed in their attempts to assimilate.

"However fantastic this claim sounds, let us not shrug it off," Kazantsev said solemnly. "I believe that it would have been quite possible for Phaeton's spaceships to land in that area.

"Their spaceships carried tools and weapons, and we can assume that a number of the ships managed to converge on a certain area of our primitive Earth for a concerted landing. Once they had landed, this was it, of course. The survivors of these ships could have established a colony of cave dwellers in the knowledge that this was the only way.

"The main question is: How well-equipped were they to settle on an Earth that was still inhabited by the big-bodied monsters of the pre-*Homo sapiens* period? How could they survive? If Zavaritski was right, Phaeton had surface conditions very much like those of Earth today. Its air, its water, its gravity were very much like ours—thus, presumably, breeding a *Homo sapiens* again very much like ourselves. They were not little three-eyed green men, nor were they giants. They could have been no taller than twice our size— after all, we ourselves are growing taller and are at least one third taller than man was two thousand years ago. Could they fend for themselves? We can only guess that they managed somehow. But also that in the end—generations later—they perished."

Kazantsev spoke with an authority that showed this was not just idle dreaming. He had spent years researching his theory. "We still have no clue as to the exact time of Phaeton's destruction," he told us. "I tend to believe that it was closer to five hundred thousand years ago, rather than a million. This period coincided with the dawn of the Neanderthal Man, not all that many years prior to the appearance of the creative Cro-Magnon Man. Assuming that people from Phaeton lived a minimum of five hundred to one thousand years—as will we, thousands of years from today—they bridged the gap from primitive to thinking man, to perhaps help him, educate him, and leave him with the legends of gods coming down from the skies aboard fiery chariots. And the legends of atomic wars—fought, however, not on Earth but on Phaeton. Then, even as the last of the descendants of the men from outer space died, these legends lived on.

"If this was so—and I believe that it was—then the pieces of the jigsaw puzzle fall into place. Finds such as the primitive rock paintings near Fergana in Soviet Uzbekistan, depicting a figure wearing typical spaceship gear, suddenly make a lot of sense. So do the clay figures of the cosmonaut gods of Honshu.

"The Honshu figurines date back to the period when Japan was inhabited by the Ayns, a Stone Age people. Found in local graves, they feature a being very human in shape, but wearing unmistakable cosmonaut garb: helmet, space suit, space footwear. At second glance, you discover that the slit-goggled helmet appears to be fastened to the space suit in very much the way we attach it today.

"There are 'female plugs' on the sleeves below the shoulders and in the back of the helmet, and a gadget box featuring more outlets—presumably for life-and-communication lines. And the overlong sleeves end in stubs that look like our mechanical manipulators, operated from within the sleeve, rather than gloves.

"There is no other explanation. The creatures had to be cosmonauts. But it is also evident that space suits like these could hardly sustain a trip of many light years from a planet of a different solar system. This is the gear we would use when flying to explore Mars. Hence they had to have come from Phaeton."

Some fifteen years ago, while still thinking in terms of cosmonauts from somewhere in the universe, Kazantsev wrote a paper about the figurines of Honshu. After it was reprinted in Japan, a large parcel was delivered to his door one day. It contained just such a figurine, sent to him by a Japanese archeologist, who wrote that he felt no one was more qualified to have it than Kazantsev. Subsequently, Kazantsev received four more figurines.

Before we left Moscow we visited Kazantsev at his home for the last time, by special invitation. He took us to his inner sanctum, a room we had not been allowed to enter before. There they stood on a shelf—five almost identical figurines, but varying in size from five to fifteen inches in height. He said their age of circa 8,500 years had been verified by means of a radioactive carbon-14 test. They were genuine, all right. He had another surprise for us. With him in the apartment, benevolently surveying the incredible statues, was Professor Zigel, who had come to wish us *bon voyage*. Would he agree with Kazantsev that these were cosmonauts from Phaeton, once stranded on Earth and retained in the memory of *Homo sapiens*, man, their story by now a legend, passed on from generation to generation, until man reached a stage in his artistic development where he could capture and preserve these legends in images—in clay, stone, bronze?

"Yes," Zigel said without hesitation. Then he added soberly, "These statues appear to confirm Zavaritsky's theory that life on Phaeton was indeed subject to conditions most similar to those on Earth: within our range of heat, light, water, air density, oxygen content. Hence, such life would produce humanoids that were very much the shape of man. Of course, since they were here first, man came in the shape of the Phaeton humanoid. The one thing we don't want is to end up as they did. But that's up to us, really."

"This is it," Kazantsev said, rising from his armchair. "Now you know as much as we do." We nodded. He had convinced us that the planet Phaeton had actually existed and had, indeed, died a terrible death. As we said our farewells to the two men, we caught a glint in Kazantsev's eye. He was signaling to us to speak up: this was the time to ask. We had told him about that other subject, UFOs, we were so very interested in. His reply was that he could not help us directly, but that he would tip us off when the propitious moment came.

Apparently it had. And so we said, pumping Zigel's hand in genuine gratitude as we stopped by the apartment door, "We shall not forget your kindness, Professor Zigel. It encourages us to ask you when we return to Russia again, for permission to interview you on your own research into Unidentified Flying Objects in the Soviet Union?"

We knew Zigel was their top authority on UFOs, but he had flatly refused all requests to talk on the subject. Now he paused, as if he was almost about to give a flat "*Nyet.*" But our friendship had grown during our discussions of the mystery of the missing planet.

"Do not ask me now," he said. "Ask me when you return. We will see how things are then . . . it all depends."

At least he had left us an opening. And on our next trip to Moscow, we made full use of it.

13.

PROFESSOR ZIGEL AND THE
SOVIET UFO CONTROVERSY

"Unidentified Flying Objects are a very serious subject which we must study fully. We appeal to all viewers to send us details of any observations of strange flying craft seen over the territories of the Soviet Union. This is a serious challenge to science, and we need the help of all Soviet citizens. Please write to us at the following address in Moscow."

This amazing announcement was made over Soviet television on November 10, 1967 by two men obviously acting on the highest authority—Major General P. A. Stolyarov and Prof. Felix Zigel, the man who taught Russia's cosmonauts the secrets of the universe. Staring soberly at the camera in the Spartan setting of a Moscow television studio, they patiently explained the kind of details they wanted to know about UFOs: when and where sighted, how big, how fast, in what direction they traveled. They appealed to everyone, from housewives to students, from factory workers to astronomers, to send in their experiences. Their appeal was broadcast from one end of the Soviet Union to the other, in a time slot that would be regarded as "prime" in the Western world. The Soviet citizens were left in no doubt that the Kremlin had decreed that reporting on UFOs was yet another of their duties to the state.

Within days, hundreds of letters poured in to the Moscow address given on the television program. The response was phenomenal, even in a country that prides itself on the amount of letters its citizens write on every topic imaginable. A careful screening, including the follow-up interviewing of witnesses, resulted in more than two hundred documented cases of UFOs in the skies of the Soviet Union. The scientists, headed by Zigel, began their serious studies. The newspapers were flooded with news of UFOs and the research.

Suddenly, as it happens in the Soviet Union, official attitude switched from approval to disapproval. The same newspapers that used to carry reader letters of sightings now unleashed a campaign of ridicule describing sightings as "figments of idle imagination," and "products of mass hysteria." Simultaneously, the Soviet Academy of Sciences declared there was no scientific reason to believe in UFOs. As far as the Academy was concerned, the UFO case was closed. The about-face was total. A verdict had been passed: UFOs were not scientifically valid. Zigel was advised to stop his research including his search for new eyewitness accounts.

Officially, he followed his instructions. Unofficially, Zigel continued his research strictly within the limits of Soviet law, which meant he made no announcements of new findings, wrote no more papers on UFOs, and kept a low profile. Whatever studies he undertook were personal endeavors on his own time. But while he made no attempts to seek television or radio time for appeals for reports of sightings, people knew of him as Professor Zigel, the leading UFO researcher. So, while Zigel scrupulously refrained from requesting data of sightings, he could not help it if people continued to send in unsolicited reports in the mail.

Under these circumstances, interviews with Zigel on the subject of UFOs were unthinkable. Western newspaperman who applied were turned down. Although he remained Russia's leading expert on extraterrestrial probes, he was not available to offer his expertise. As a Moscow scientist explained to us, "Professor Zigel has been called a 'dangerous dreamer' by more governmental scientific bodies in the USSR than any of his colleagues. His work is delicate, if not precarious; he is constantly walking a scientific tightrope. He deals with only the cases of UFOs that stand up under the most rigorous scientific investigation and come from people of authority and scientific background. He makes a positive rule never to cross the line of strict research while looking into the UFO phenomena. That is why he will not talk to the press. He is concerned that his remarks might be misinterpreted, that there might be a backlash from authorities."

Indeed, authorities in Moscow had always told us that they would be glad to arrange an interview with Zigel "IF he is available and IF he wants to see you." Whenever we asked for one, the answer was always that he was not available and that he did not want to see us. We became convinced that it was the authorities, not Zigel, who were stonewalling.

Only after meeting Zigel through the auspices of author and historian Aleksandr Kazantsev did we realize that, indeed, Professor Zigel *did not* want to talk. He had a lot to lose from a misinterpretation of false quotes by a newspaperman, and he was just not prepared to risk it.

Felix Zigel graduated from Moscow State University in 1942, and in 1948 became an "aspirant," or junior member of the Soviet Academy of Sciences as an astronomer. The same year, he successfully defended an astronomical thesis for a doctorate. In 1943, he began to teach mathematical analysis and astronomy at Soviet universities and after 1963, when he became a professor at the Moscow Aviation Institute, also began to teach the Russian cosmonauts.

The Institute, where he is chief lecturer, is a military institution, its personnel strictly controlled in what they can do or say.

Prof. Zigel is the author of 28 books and well over 250 articles on astronomy and cosmonautics. In 1975, in collaboration with Prof. V. P. Burdakov, he wrote and published the first Soviet textbook on cosmonautics entitled *Physical Bases of Cosmonautics.* He is also the author of *Life in the Cosmos,* dealing with the question of contact with extraterrestrial civilizations, and has written many articles and manuscripts on the subject of UFOs, which he began studying in 1955.

These credentials are very impressive. Despite the obstacles, we were determined to obtain an interview with him, on the subject of UFOs in Russia. Encouraged by his "Call me and I'll see" attitude after the Phaeton talks, we asked author Kazantsev to try to arrange it. We offered to give any guarantee that Zigel requested.

His first reaction was firmly negative; he did not have time to see us. "Remind him of our previous meeting," we urged Kazantsev. "He knows he has nothing to fear from us." Kazantsev promised he would try again.

For two days there was silence, we were unable to reach him. Then, a quick phone call to our hotel. "No questions. Meet me at my apartment at 5 P.M. tonight," Kazantsev said. We agreed, hoping it meant he had arranged for us to meet Zigel.

But when Kazantsev ushered us into his living room, he was alone. We had that sinking feeling. Kazantsev waited, staring silently at us, until we had settled in our chairs. Then, giving his statement the drama and full impact it warranted, he announced "Professor Zigel never gives interviews. You know the reasons for that. Basically, there are too many dangers. However, I have talked with him at great length. I have told him I believe that this is the right time for him to speak out again."

The "right time" he was referring to was the appearance of symptoms of a new change, a softening of the implaccable official stand against UFOs. A month earlier Zigel was suddenly advised that if he were to prepare a paper on extraterrestrial probes, there was a chance he would be allowed to present it at the next meeting of the Astronomy Institute of the Academy of Sciences. Kazantsev felt that the Academy was preparing a new line of approach directly reflecting on UFOs. A number of indications pointed at a favorable decision to resurrect UFO research. In these circumstances, Zigel would do well for himself by taking a firm stand—whatever the consequences.

"I supposed I talked him into it," Kazantsev sounded triumphant. "Anyway, consider yourself lucky. Professor Zigel has agreed to see you and discuss UFOs—on one condition. You must agree that he can approve the written version of his answers."

Our smiles of relief gave him an instant answer. Of course we would give him the right of approval! When could we see him?

It was Kazantsev's turn to smile. "Right now! Professor?" The living room door swung open, and Zigel, who had obviously been waiting and listening to the conversation, walked in. The courtesies of greeting over, he shook his head and commented, "I still do not know if I am doing the right thing. You have many friends in Moscow, and they are very convincing. At least let us try."

For the next hour he listened to our questions and carefully gave his answers. The next day, he approved our written version with minor changes. It was a fascinating interview. Because of the sensitive nature of the subject, we have decided to take the unusual approach of presenting the interview in its original approved form. We do not want to risk having some

Moscow official accuse Professor Zigel of sensationalism. These, then, are the questions and the professor's answers:

What, in your opinion, is the nature of a UFO?

Over twenty years of research of the phenomenon of UFOs have led me to the conviction that of all the offered hypotheses, the most probable is that the UFO is an extraterrestrial probe. After sorting out reports of UFO sightings and concentrating on those that cannot be explained as the fruit of someone's imagination, optical effects in the atmosphere, ball lightning, etc., one faces fact. The experienced researcher of UFOs would find it as difficult to mistake ball lightning or an optical mirage for a UFO as to mistake a hedgehog for a crocodile.

As far as I see it, the mystery of the UFO is a rather hard nut to crack, even for a scientist of highest rank. I am afraid that we are still a long way from understanding the true nature of UFOs, with the exception of one thing—that they are extraterrestrial probes. Of the latter I am convinced.

Do you have any idea where the UFOs are coming from, and what is the object of these visits?

I would rather not dwell on this at the present time. Let us not forget that we have yet to prove to the doubting Thomases of the world that UFOs are probes from outer space. This is our immediate job and our immediate objective. I do not exclude, of course, that in the course of our proving the source of UFOs, we will also be able to determine the position of the source. On the other hand, to anticipate firm conclusions in so complicated a problem as this one is not very wise.

How do you explain the fact that UFOs have been observed as being of different shapes? Why are they not all of the same type?

There are two very simple explanations. The first is that we subscribe to the existence of another dimension which would cause us, viewing UFOs within the framework of only three dimensions, to watch them taking different shapes. This explains why eyewitnesses have reported the shape of the object as mysteriously changing before their very eyes. The fourth dimension—and possibly additional dimensions—is seriously considered by our physicists and is, to my way of thinking, also one explanation of space probes being capable of bridging immense distances within a short span of time where, if they were to be moving with the speed of light, it would have taken hundreds and thousands of years.

Also, UFOs have a definite characteristic of looking very different from different vantage points, or as the angle changes between the observer and the flying UFO. Finally, one must accept the fact that UFOs can be of different shapes, just as our flying machines have different shapes, from conventional jets to helicopters, etc.

What is your opinion of the size of UFOs?

I would refer you to one particularly significant sighting in which the eyewitness, a very reputable astronomer, estimated the distance between the tips of a crescent-shaped UFO as being 600 meters. I should stress, however, that what he is referring to is the plasma enveloping the much harder core of the flying object, which can, therefore, be much smaller.

Do your findings preclude the possibility that extraterrestrial probes could be smaller than that?

No, they do not. I have accepted the measurement of 600 meters applying to the plasma caused and carried by a probe as applicable to a certain type of probe. Other dimensions may be much smaller, indeed. As I stressed earlier, we are dealing with different shapes of extraterrestrial probes. We must also think in terms that some are a probe from a probe, meaning that they are reconnaissance vehicles leaving a mother ship on limited missions.

Professor Zigel, do you believe that beings from outer space have landed on Earth?

I don't think that the word "believe" matters. It is scientific conclusions that count. These have yet to come. Until that time, we have to proceed with the help of hypotheses. Thus, my hypothesis is that indeed humanoids have landed on Earth a very long time ago, at a time when life on Earth was primitive. I further contend that there have been no landings, apart from brief reconnaissance excursions, within the span of our current civilization. We have evidence in ancient writings, including those of Plutarch, which refer to fiery chariots in the sky, obviously UFOs.

I contend that—and this is where I disagree with our own noted historian, Vyacheslav Zaitsev—no being from outer space has come to Earth since the dawn of man. At that time, creatures from outer space were interested in observing but also in establishing some attempts to communicate. Our technological progress has since made it dangerous for them to communicate with us. *They* are aware of this, but their observations are continuing.

Why are they not trying to communicate with us? My own thinking differs from that of those who believe in a certain lack of interest on their part. A comparison is drawn in the fact that we observe the life of ants but do not try to communicate with them. My theory is that *they* feel that we have reached a stage of development where their contact with us could be harmful to Earth, and that they are merely waiting for our civilization to advance to a safer level.

What is your opinion of the substance referred to as "Angel's Hair" which is sometimes observed in the atmosphere following the sightings of UFOs over other countries?

The substance referred to as "Angel's Hair" is a cobweb, slightly radioactive—a jellied mass. It emanates a bad odor and dissipates rather quickly. In some cases this substance has been noted to have the form of glassy cotton. N. V. Shebalin, the Secretary of the Committee for the

International Geophysical Year, recently received several reports of a drift of a mysterious substance through the atmosphere over the Voronezh region, as well as some other areas. Unfortunately, the people who discovered the substance failed to attempt to establish any connection with UFO sightings.

Most recently, a small amount of Angel's Hair has been received by us from New Zealand. The basic research has been carried out by the noted Russian physicist, L. V. Kirichenko, who called in a number of top experts to help him in his investigation. The samples sent us from New Zealand have been tested in several of our research institutes. It has been determined that the substance is made up of elements with an atomic weight of less than 12, and that it showed no radioactivity. The scientists were unable to recognize the substance's mineral structure as being analogous to anything known to us in the family of fibrous materials. Academician I. V. Petryanov-Sokolov has offered the conclusion that the fine fibrous substance is not of natural origin. Nor can it be identified with any fibrous material, natural or manmade, that exists on our planet. At this moment we are deeply involved in search of new samplings of Angel's Hair as the substance may descend—significantly, perhaps, immediately following UFO sightings.

Is it right to assume that the famous Tungusky meteorite was a UFO?
Without the shadow of a doubt, my answer is yes, without reservations. We have scientific data that the Tungusky Body, after crossing some several hundred kilometers through our atmosphere on June 30, 1908, exploded in the air at the altitude of 5 to 7 kilometers with the strength of a 40-megaton atomic bomb. In all its elements the explosion has shown the typical aspects of a thermonuclear blast. It caused a geomagnetic effect, the lighting of the atmosphere, an increased growth of vegetation, mutational changes in the flora, and a number of other effects, including an increased radioactivity within the rings of the Tungusky trees applying to the year 1908. Usually large amounts of carbon-14 discovered in corresponding rings in California trees by the American scientists Libby and Cohen in 1966 is one of the results of the Tungusky explosion, however far away.

The analysis of observations by eyewitnesses, which I have undertaken, has brought out beyond any doubt that shortly before the explosion, the Tungusky Body carried out a certain flight maneuver within the earth's atmosphere, in the shape of a zigzag 800 kilometers in length. The details of this maneuver are being further determined, but already there is little doubt that the atmospheric trajectory of the Tungusky Body was not of a ballistic nature. The sum total of all the evidence leads to the conclusion that the body was a probe from outer space that blew up within the Earth's atmosphere for still not quite determined reasons.

As far as I am concerned, the Tungusky Marvel, as we call it, is one of the most remarkable UFOs of the past. A total and complete investigation of its nature, however, is as important for our present as it is for our future. We do not know, for instance, that the Tungusky explosion may not be repeated. Should it be repeated in our present complex international situation, it could cause someone to press the notorious atomic bomb button. To ward off such panic reaction, we should complete our research and explain Tungusky in every detail so the world knows what it was, and not to jump to disastrous conclusions if it should happen again. Only in this way can we assure ourselves that a similar explosion in the future would not be mistaken for the dropping of a manmade 40-megaton hydrogen bomb.

What has been the attitude to the question of UFOs in the USSR since 1968?

The majority of Soviet scientists are still taking a skeptical stand on the problem of UFOs. On the other hand, those who are convinced of the scientific validity of the subject are continuing to study in the capacity of private individuals, in the form of individual scientific work.

In March 1968 our original Group for UFO Research discontinued its work and so we have not had any systematic gathering of sighting reports after that. I had to limit myself to reports that came to me unsolicited. Some of those contained sightings pertaining to the time before 1968, but the majority of them apply to the years since then. I have no doubts that in reality, there have been many more sightings. But fearing ridicule, and for other reasons, eyewitnesses prefer not to get involved. Also, eyewitnesses do not know to whom they should address their reports, especially since our press has repeatedly stated that the problem of UFOs does not exist, and that only incorrigible charlatans would continue to dwell on "flying saucers." As a result, the number of sightings I receive is relatively small. However, the continuation of the UFO phenomenon is one of the proofs of its reality.

Have there been any cases of UFO landings in the USSR, or observations of their crews—the humanoids?

Reports of this nature have not reached me to date. There are, however, two cases recorded in 1961 and 1967 entailing mysterious earth disturbances which so far one has not been able to connect definitely to UFOs. However, it is important to stress that absence of information about such facts does not mean that such facts do not exist. They simply have not yet been brought to our attention.

What, in your opinion, hinders organized scientific research of UFOs?

First of all, prejudice among the majority of scientists. To bring in extraterrestrial reasoning as an explanation of certain phenomena is considered bad taste. Curiously, the skeptics are mostly those who have never themselves gone into the study of the phenomenon of UFOs and are basing their attitude on hearsay. Time and again, I have watched the faces of top scientists change after a discussion in which they have been given concrete evidence. They start by displaying an ironical smile but end up showing an expression of deep wonderment. Basically, it is the barrier of ridicule and the fear of tainting one's name and scientific reputation, which have prevented many of them from openly coming out in favor of the UFO theory.

Secondly, what seriously impedes a full study of the problem is unhealthy sensationalism created around the subject by irresponsible people. Fantastic rumors, inventions, overactive imaginations have given the subject a bad name. To us scientists, our most difficult task is to weed out the countless fantasies—to remain with the few important scientific facts. It is my considered opinion that in as important a question as the phenomenon of UFOs, deliberate misinformation should not only be condemned, but punished in the courts. The creation of a quiet, businesslike atmosphere is absolutely essential to the success of our investigations.

What would be the best way and system for organized scientific research of UFOs?

The most important, of course, is the availability to the scientists of high-quality information. In addition to eyewitness reports, particularly valuable are photographs of UFOs in various sections of the spectrum, their spectrograms, documentary film, radio observations pinpointing locations with the help of scientific instruments. Thorough exploration of areas where UFO landings have been sighted are of highest scientific value. The same applies to thorough laboratory investigations of Angel's Hair. The securing of governmental sanction, the involvement of personnel in certain governmental branches would highly enrich our exploratory work.

The way I see it, the next phase within our research is the construction of the first theoretical models of UFOs, based on our scientific data. Very little, in my opinion, has been done in this area so far. Regrettably, one has devoted much too much time and energy to discussions of the phenomenon of UFOs, and the proof of the theory of their existence. In my opinion, the moment has already arrived when the major task force of the explorers of UFOs, to which I have the honor to belong, should concentrate instead on the theoretical explanation of UFOs as existing objects.

Let us face reality. If we were to do nothing in this area, explanations would not come to us by themselves. As I see it, the proper way right now is to turn to the building of models of UFOs, based on various types of flying machines of the future which humanity already has on its drawing boards. I have reason to believe that part of the phenomena connected with UFOs will become evident through our own experimentation on Earth.

In the course of this work we shall be able to construct the first laboratory model based on what I call the coefficient of similarity. True, one has to bear in mind that we may find ourselves in the position of the man who is trying to explain the principles of jet propulsion with the help of a teakettle. Obviously, we could be as far away in our understanding of UFO machinery as man was from the jet plane at the time of the hot-air balloon. Yet a start has to be made by someone—now.

A second approach would be, as I see it, an exploration of the more exotic problems of contemporary physics that could help to explain the physical aspects of UFOs. The phenomena whose study will help us would include the study of energy obtained from a vacuum, nonreactive (nonjet) means of propulsion, the exploration into a fourth dimension that would explain the movement of UFOs. In this connection, the most promising work so far as I am concerned has already been done by the Soviet physicist I. L. Gerlovin, who has explored the theory of the Fundamental Field.

In spite of difficulties, active experiments with UFOs by using laser beams, obtaining samples of their material substance, is not an impossibility as far as I am concerned. The immense value of such experiments requires no elaboration.

How do you appraise the study of UFOs in the United States?

I watch the work of American scientists very carefully. The report by Dr. Edward Condon on behalf of the U. S. Air Force left an unfavorable impression on me. It was superficial, and on deeper acquaintance with its contents, one gets the impression that the author was trying to shut off, rather than solve, a problem.

Do you consider it possible and desirable that American and Soviet scientists combine forces in the study of UFOs?

I consider such cooperation both possible and desirable, especially within the framework of the new scientific collaboration now in the process of development between the USA and the USSR.

Significantly, the Academy of Sciences of the USSR has most recently taken a most important step which we, the scientists concerned with the UFO problem, have accepted with great gratification. In its Program of Exploration of Possible Communications with Extraterrestrial Civilizations set down in the form of a document developed in 1974 and published a year later, there is an all-important observation on Page 19. Concerned with extraterrestrial probes it says, and I quote:

> Especial attention should be given to the possibility of discovery of probes sent out by extraterrestrial civilizations which may be at present within our Solar System and possibly even in orbit around Earth. To find such rapidly-moving objects, a system of continuous observation of the entire heavens should be complemented with newly built special radio-pelengational systems (pinpointing objects with the help of radio scanners from several areas). Also, during the first phase it should be possible to make use, for this purpose, of existing radio-radar installations developed for cosmic communications and radio locationing.

Thus, a search of extraterrestrial probes in Earth orbits has now become an important point of the official program of our Academy of Science. Since our two nations have establish close cooperation in this area, this means that such a search has now become an important aspect in the cooperation between the

Academy of Sciences of the USSR and the National Academy of Sciences of the USA.

Significantly, there is only one step from extraterrestrial probes in passive Earth orbits to extraterrestrial spaceships that could actively penetrate the Earth's atmosphere. I am fully aware that this one step is particularly difficult for scientists, since it calls for crossing psychological barriers. This notwithstanding, they will have to take the step. We have reached a stage when sidestepping of the UFO as a practical issue has become impossible. The opponents will have to recognize it even as they back away from it.

In my opinion, collaboration between American and Soviet scientists regarding the UFOs should take place within the established framework, meaning an exchange of information and visits, as well as the creation of joint explorations. As far as I am concerned, the subject of UFOs has to be an important point of scientific discussion at all future conferences dedicated to the question of contact with extraterrestrial civilizations.

May we expect that sightings of UFOs will continue?

Not just continue, but increase. The more information that extraterrestrials obtain about us, the more curious they must become. That means more probes for information, more Unidentified Flying Objects. Despite what some scientists would like, they will not go away if you just ignore them. They are a scientific reality that must be fully explored. UFOs could be the most important area of research that exists today, because uncovering their secrets could solve countless problems of our world.

Following our interview, we asked Zigel if he might give us access, even if limited, to his files on UFOs overflying the Soviet Union. He shook his head in an emphatic negative. "I have said enough. You must find other sources for that information." We did not belabor the point, and we parted the best of friends. Once back at our hotel, the Intourist, we immediately began putting out feelers on how UFO information might be obtained.

14.

THE CLUB OF FANTASTS

We had just escaped from the cold night air into the dimly-lit building at 21 Sushchevskaya Street in Moscow. "The Club of Fantasts?" the old coat-check man repeated our question. "Ah, the writers' meeting. Just join these Comrades here."

We nodded politely to the three men taking off their warm overcoats and followed them to a conference room utilized during the day by the staff of the magazine *Tekhnika Molodezhi (Technology and Youth)*, which occupies the five-story building.

We had been invited to the club meeting after we had seized on Prof. Felix Zigel's challenge to find a source other than him for UFO case histories. It took only a matter of days to let our interest be known on the unofficial grapevine that links Moscow's psychics, UFOlogists, scientists, and researchers. A phone call to our hotel room one night suggested we attend the "Club of Fantasts" meeting, particularly to hear the guest speaker, noted author and historian Aleksandr Kazantsev. We knew Kazantsev well, and were of course aware of his interest in UFO subjects.

Already seated in hard chairs in the room were approximately forty people, the men quite formal in dark business suits and ties, the women in thick woolen dresses. Officially, this was the monthly meeting of the Club of Fantasts, ostensibly a group of young Soviet scientists who get together to be advised on how to become science fiction writers.

In fact, they were there to discuss a much touchier subject, "Neopozhannye Letayushchye Obyekty"—Unidentified Flying Objects seen over Soviet territory. In America, they would have gone under the title of APRO, the Aerial Phenomena Research Organization, or NICAP, the National Investigating Committee on Aerial Phenomena, or perhaps even MUFON, the Mutual Unidentified Flying Object Network. But, when Soviet authorities officially frowned on the subject of UFOs in 1968, local enthusiasts had to form a cover organization. The Soviets love science fiction, and authorities take no exception to discussions of "sci-fi" subjects. Hence, the "Club of Fantasts" was a perfect cover for the civilian UFO researchers.

When we attended the meeting, we were not disappointed. It was wholly devoted to the topic of NLOs, Russian UFOs. First, Kazantsev spoke generally on the subject. Then, after a question-and-answer period, individual members stood up and told of new and old cases they had experienced or investigated.

Typical was the case probed by a young scientist who identified himself as Yuri Mikhailovich Medvedev. "In May of 1969, I traveled to the village of Perushkovo, about 50 kilometers west of Moscow, to check out a story that local villagers had seen a UFO," he reported. "I found the village to be rather isolated, and its people too concerned with their own problems of agriculture to show any interest in modern technology. At first, the villagers were reluctant to talk about the mysterious event, but gradually I got them around to telling me what happened. I went from house to house collecting the material. I had given them no advance warning, and so there was no possibility of their agreeing on a story to tell me. Yet they all had the same tale to tell."

Medvedev, a rather small, slightly built man in his early thirties, glanced at some notes before continuing. "During the night about two weeks prior to my visit, a group of villagers observed a silver-colored disc the size of a modern airplane, landing behind the trees. They proceeded to investigate, and so reached the edge of the clearing into which the strange object had landed. Some of the grass around the object was still burning, and so was a fir tree which was apparently touched by the object's edge. They said that the 'round plane' took off vertically within seconds of their arrival and was gone. They agreed that the object could not have been on the ground longer than half an hour.

"I asked the villagers to show me the place. Accompanied by guides, I walked into the forest outside the village and came up to the edge of the clearing. The grass of the clearing had all burned, and the ground was black. Some of the trees on the edge of the clearing also showed signs of a fire, especially one fir tree whose branches had been burnt off on one side, while the other half remained untouched.

"At the time, I was reluctant to continue the investigation, and left the village, not to return there until two months ago, when, remembering the incident, I decided to check it out again. I found my way to the clearing. It was still there, except that the grass had grown over and looked normal. However, the damaged fir tree had died, and was lying on the ground across the clearing. The size of the clearing was about 40 meters in diameter."

Medvedev did not wait to be questioned on his report; he left the hall almost immediately. But we asked author Kazantsev what he thought of the report. "I have no reason to disbelieve this man," he replied, "although it is the first report I have heard of a UFO actually being seen to land on Soviet soil."

Could the villagers have invented the story or imagined it after the fir tree was struck by lightning? Kazantsev shook his head. "I don't believe that these particular villagers have much knowledge of UFOs. They would have no reason to invent the story, nor would they have the know-how to tell it this way. As for the idea of lightning striking the tree, Comrade Medvedev checked it out very carefully. There had been no thunderstorms over that area at the time of the reported landing."

After chatting with a few more members of the "Club of Fantasts," we left with the realization that Unidentified Flying Objects were just as common—and just as apparently inexplicable—in the Soviet Union as they are in the West. The sightings, unfortunately, are no longer reported in the Soviet press, but it was obvious that UFO "buffs" scattered throughout the country are not only keeping a tally of sightings, but actively investigating such cases. They interview witnesses at length and use sophisticated equipment to take measurements, including radiation readings wherever possible. In the Soviet Union, it is felt that "charlatans" should play no part in legitimate investigations. And so, in selected cases, psychiatrists are quickly able to give an opinion of the mental stability and veracity of the witnesses.

Excited by what we had heard at the club meeting, we were still faced with the problem of obtaining documented case histories. Again, we let our interest be known unofficially. Several days later we received a call from Yuri Aleksandrovich Fomin, credited as having been the first in the Soviet Union to systematically collate reports of UFO sightings within that country. We immediately accepted his invitation to meet with him and two other researchers at his home that evening to discuss UFOs. There was nothing illegal about the meeting, but we gave our assurance we would not name the other two enthusiasts.

In 1956 Yuri Fomin, then a senior instructor at the Department of Automatic Devices of the Moscow Technological Institute, became interested in UFOs after reading about foreign cases. As an engineer who has patents for many automatic devices used in industry, he reasoned that extraterrestrial civilizations might be using automatic devices to probe the surroundings of our planet, and figured he might be able to devise an automatic probe similar to UFOs. For many years he collected every possible case history, spoke to witnesses, lectured on UFOs, tried to analyze their power source.

"I have now given up collecting evidence, because I have obtained the necessary proof that UFOs truly exist and that their flights over the Soviet Union are taking place," he stated matter-of-factly. "Having reached this conclusion, I saw no reason to continue to analyze the sighting reports. I still receive many such reports, of course, but I do not actively seek them. I have devoted myself to the next stage of the problem: why are they here and how do they get here?

"It is obvious that civilizations sending probes into our atmosphere have an advanced knowledge as well as advanced intelligence. The assignment I gave myself was on the level of attempting to explain the mystery of a television set with merely a basic knowledge of electricity. Since then I have discarded the theory that UFOs have a power source that enables them to travel faster than the speed of light."

Fomin brought out file after file of UFO reports, and showed us pages and pages of theoretical calculations on power sources. "I am now convinced that we are dealing with a fourth and fifth dimension, and have now abandoned the effort to solve this mystery by applying our conventional concepts of three-dimensional technology," he said, waving at us a sheaf of papers that apparently contained his logic. "For instance, a straight line representing a distance in our three-dimensional thinking would become a loop in a fourth dimension, thus allowing one to practically cross from one end of a distance to the other end of the same distance by merely making one small step through a fourth dimension."

We thought it was a little farfetched, and we told him so. Yuri Fomin was not upset. "It is, to the uninformed," he replied. "However, this is a definite answer to the questions that are bothering scientists. At any rate, I have totally dedicated myself to the study of the fourth dimension, and to a new technology evolving out of it. My work combines both theory and practical application. I am deep into both and have already, I feel, come a long way, within the framework of my experiments. At present I am preparing for a new series of experiments, and I am very optimistic. I think some of my findings will revolutionize technology in the USSR in the foreseeable future."

When our host tried to explain his technological approach, we had to stop him. "Very interesting, Yuri Aleksandrovich," we said, "but we are reporters, not scientists. We will return another day with someone who can discuss this with you on the proper level. Now, let us talk about something we do understand: the actual reports of sightings." He looked a little sad, a scientist who wanted to discuss academically what had become his life's work. Fortunately, his companions, who obviously also had difficulty in understanding the fourth and fifth dimensions, agreed with us. Yuri Fomin then began searching through his files of case histories.

It turned out to be one of the most fascinating evenings we spent in Moscow. At the end of it, we were able to take with us information from manuscripts, handwritten letters, and conference papers which documented case after case of sightings, many of them similar to cases reported over the years in the West. The UFOs seen over the Soviet Union come in all shapes and sizes, and are seen in different circumstances by many different kinds of people.

On the night of August 9, 1957, a field group from the Moscow Institute of Physics of the Atmosphere, doing research near the city of Tsymlyansk, had gone to bed when they were awakened by loud cries. When they looked out of their tents, they saw a disc-shaped red object crossing the sky from west to east. It left a fiery trail. "We knew it was not a comet," L. N. Babin commented on behalf of the scientists. "The disc appeared to be of a hard substance, with a silvery sheen. Above the disc there were two protrusions that could have been antennae, and which appeared to be made of the same material."

Dr. B. Muratov and his son, who was a student of engineering at Moscow University, were near the town of Chimbay, Karapalpak on June 4, 1958, returning from a day's fishing on the Aral Sea. It was 9 P.M., when suddenly they both noticed a strange object coming at them at a low altitude from the northeast. They first thought it must be a plane. "Then, as it passed about 100 meters above us," Dr. Muratov wrote, "I realized it was not a plane. It was a disc-shaped flying object that emanated a melodious chiming sound—zing-zing-zing, almost like a voice. I estimated the size of the disc as 25 meters in diameter, and it had a protrusion at the tip which looked like a short antenna. The disc moved at no more than 300 kilometers an hour. Its surface was shiny and one side of it had a red glow. It disappeared within seconds." When Dr. Muratov told local fishermen of the experience, he was told that a similar object had been seen near there two years earlier.

One of the most mysterious occurrences was what the Russians call The Lake Onega Incident. The people living around this densely forested lake are hardy, self-sufficient hunters and woodsmen. But they were very alarmed by what they saw on April 27, 1961 and sent a plea for help to forest ranger Valentin Borsky.

In an official report, of which we obtained a copy, he said, "I arrived in the area on the north shore of Lake Onega at 8 A.M. in the morning on April 28. I was able to determine a considerable destruction of the northern shoreline of the lake, which itself is a bay of the large Lake Onega. The bay, which has no name, has an area of 0.75 square kilometers. An object had hit the shoreline, destroying 27 meters of the escarpment above the waterline. Within the escarpment, it left a long scar three meters in depth. The impact broke the ice that had covered the surface of the lake. Some of the pieces of ice were thrown out onto the ground and had acquired a strange intense green coloring.

"Whatever had hit this spot had left no other traces, however. I was unable to find any remains of the object that had struck it with such force. With the exception of the long trench in the shoreline, there were no craters. With the help of the villagers, I explored the bottom of the lake near the shore and found nothing there either. According to local inhabitants, an object flying low over the area had cut into the bluff at about 10 degrees above the horizon, but after impact had continued on a trajectory still very close to the ground and disappeared. The local people who saw the event from spots at least three kilometers away reported no sound, with the exception of the noise of the impact."

Borsky sent the report to the city authorities of Povenets, a town on the northern shore of Lake Onega. A civilian and a military team were sent to the area. Fydor Denisov headed the civilian group, and Major Anton Kopeikin and Senior Technical Lieutenant Boris Lapunov headed the military team. Both groups made a very thorough investigation.

Later, Major Kopeikin wrote: "Between 8 A.M. and 10 A.M. April 27, an object hit the ground of the inlet bay on the northern extremity of Lake Onega 40 meters from the houses of Entino, an abandoned village. At this point the escarpment has an incline of 60 degrees. The object left a trench of about 15 meters in width with maximum depth of three meters. A second minor trench was found at the western extremity of the impact, the distance between the two trenches being five and a half meters. A faint additional trench, 40 centimeters in width, led to the lake itself. There were no further disturbances of the ground anywhere else. However, the ice on the lake in this area had cracked and was broken up. The underside of the ice floes was a bright green, of the type of oxidized chrome. Sample pieces of ice, on melting, left a residue of string fiber. Subsequent analysis of the fiber, carried out at the Leningrad Technological Institute, determined the presence of tiny quantities of magnesium, aluminum, calcium, barium, and silicon, as well as sodium and titanium. The uprooted ground at the bottom of the lake, removed from the smaller trench, yielded a tiny plate, one millimeter in thickness, two centimeters in length, and half a centimeter in width. It was light brown in color. A chemical and spectral analysis at the Leningrad Technological Institute determined that it consisted of iron and silicone, with additional elements of sodium, lithium, titanium, and aluminum.

"Additionally, the ground yielded minute black grains of exact geometrical form that were found to have the same contents as the tiny plate. The grains were half a millimeter in diameter, and proved resistant to acid and high temperatures. They were not radioactive."

Denisov, the civilian group chief, interrogated twenty-five people and all gave the same description of what they saw—an oval-shaped object crossing east to west at tremendous speed and moving without sound. They estimated its size as that of a large passenger airplane. It was blueish-green in color.

"According to the eyewitnesses, the low-flying object scraped the ground, but continued in the same direction without slackening speed. Some of the eyewitnesses reported a wobbling movement. Some thought that it could have been a plane that hit the ground, but mysteriously continued on its course undamaged," Denisov stated in his report to authorities.

Major Kopeikin's report attracted the attention of noted Soviet geophysicist Prof. Vladimir Sharonov, a member of the Leningrad Technological Institute. He traveled to the site to determine whether the object could have been a meteorite. Subsequently he issued a statement saying, "The destruction and disturbance of the ground caused by falling meteorites was absent in this case. Specifically, a falling meteorite leaves a crater two to five times its size. In this case, no craters could be found. Additionally, the descent of a meteorite is accompanied by clearly identifiable audible and visual effects. There were none in this case. Finally, the chemical substance left by meteorites in the ground was not present in this case. The grains found on the lake bottom, while unexplainable at the present time, were clearly of artificial origin. I am convinced the object was not a meteorite."

Scientists at the Leningrad Institute discussed the possibility that the object could have been an American spy plane, reconnoitering at a very low altitude. However, technical experts ruled out this possibility, because no plane in the world could have scraped the hard frozen ground without losing some of its parts. None were found in the area.

Included in the documents we saw was a note from Prof. Zigel, who had also examined the reports. "I am tempted to assume that a space probe, coming from another planet, scraped the ground but managed to continue despite, presumably, superficial damage," he wrote. "It is to my knowledge the only such case on record within the territory of the USSR."

We were told that the Lake Onega Incident file has never been closed. No new evidence has been found to solve the mystery, and scientists and UFOlogists alike have more or less accepted Zigel's assumption that this was a probe from space.

A veritable UFO "flap" occurred in 1968, typified by a dramatic report from engineer V. P. Mikhailov, of the city of Nevyansk, in the Sverdlovsk region. Returning home at about 10:30 P.M. on the evening of June 21, 1968, he noticed a dark cloud in the northwest portion of the sky. It had a perfect oval shape, and seemed to blend with the clouds above. But Mikhailov realized it was of much greater density than normal clouds. The oval shape remained motionless while the other clouds drifted slowly across the sky.

"Suddenly, a luminous streak tore it into three parts. Two parts, now looking like parts of a spindle, remained hanging horizontally, while the third section darted away to one side. As it moved, it turned into a perfect circle. Around its edges appeared a red line that seemed to girdle the circle with a fiery strap. Then another flash in the middle of the circle, and a beam of luminous red shot out from the strap, crossed the sky like a streak of lightning traveling parallel to the ground, and disappeared behind the horizon. All this took place in a matter of seconds. It was as if life had left the circle when the ray of light departed," Mikhailov continued. "The round circle began to darken and gradually disappeared. The other two sections which had remained stationary not far away then began to move, headed in a westerly direction.

"At 12:05 A.M. three more spindle-shaped objects were observed by others moving slowly across the sky. A fourth object remained motionless until 1 A.M., then sailed away in a westerly direction. Watching the occurrence, I gained the impression I had seen space vehicles that appeared to send information via this ray I so clearly observed in the sky. It reminded me of a laser beam," Mikhailov concluded.

While flying at 16,500 feet over Adler, near Sochi, the crew of a Sverdlovsk-based military plane noticed a luminous object in the sky at 8:22 P.M. on August 20, 1968. It was red in color and seemed to be flying at the same altitude, between five and six miles from their plane. From time to time, smaller luminous objects of the same color appeared to approach the larger object, then wheeled around and darted away on a trajectory toward the Black Sea. In all, they observed four such satellites, each of which carried out exactly the same maneuver. The display lasted five minutes, then the objects disappeared.

"It was as if they had been erased from the sky," said the plane's pilot, Commander Bolchakov, in a signed statement. "Yet the sky was clear, with visibility at 500 kilometers. The event was observed by the entire crew of our aircraft."

Moscow Planetarium astronomer and lecturer L. S. Tsekhanovich, also reported a UFO experience while on vacation at Gagry, a Black Sea resort, on September 19, 1968. We were particularly interested in his report because of his obvious expertise in discounting natural phenomena in the skies.

"At 7:55 P.M. a bright, luminous orange-colored ball appeared suddenly in the sky and began an abrupt descent. It left a very slight inversion trail behind. When the object reached a spot about 25 degrees above the horizon, almost exactly due South, it suddenly stopped and remained suspended, motionless. The brightness of the object was about four times that of Venus during its most brilliant period. The light it radiated pulsated up and down with periods of about one second between pulsations.

"About half a minute after the ball had stopped its descent, to the left of it, at a distance of about four degrees, appeared a brilliant small star of a dense orange color. The tiny star made a complete circle around the ball, then continued in a south-southwesterly direction, descending rapidly toward the horizon. At the height of about two degrees, its light went out. Half a minute later, a similar tiny star was born again to the left of the suspended ball and went through the same motions. Two more tiny stars followed, exercising the same maneuvers.

"All this time the luminous object remained suspended in the sky. Gradually, its roundness turned oval-shaped. Then it began to narrow and finally it turned into a line, as if the object had made a half turn around a horizontal axis. Suddenly it was gone. About one minute later, there was a flash of light in the same spot which went out half a minute after that. The entire observation lasted five to six minutes."

Two days later, on September 21, at about 6 A.M. while astronomer Tsekhanovich was walking along the road toward the sea, he was suddenly attracted by a brilliant object hanging in the northern sky at about 45 degrees above the horizon. Studying it closely, he realized it was a crescent, its size about five to six minutes in geographical measure. Its edges were strongly defined. The center of the crescent, he noticed, had a domelike protrusion. The crescent's curvature was directed toward the Earth. The object was swaying around a vertical axis. "It was still there twenty minutes later. The sun was rising, but despite this the object remained very brilliant. A while later I realized it was slowly moving toward the north-northeast," Tsekhanovich reported.

"Forty to forty-five minutes after I began my observations I noticed that the object was now moving with its curvature pointed upward. This continued for about ten minutes. By then the sun was sufficiently high for the object to begin to change its coloring. It appeared that it was now reflecting the sunlight rather than emanating its own light. The crescent shape remained very clear. A dark oval shape now became visible on its body. For the one and a half hours of this observation the slow-moving object had crossed only 15 degrees. It then disappeared behind a high mountain peak. Both occurrences were observed by a number of other people who were watching the phenomenon with utter amazement."

When astronomer Tsekhanovich researched further, he found that similar phenomena had been observed in the area earlier in the summer. He documented eyewitness accounts from local people who did not know each other, so that there could have been no collusion.

As in America, people who have been involved in close encounters with UFOs in Russia reported that while the object was close by, or overhead, their car engines mysteriously failed, only to restart when the object disappeared. L. I. Kuprinov, a doctor of technical sciences and a contributor to the Academy of Sciences, was one who had this experience. On July 31, 1969, he and several friends were in a car traveling west from Moscow on the main highway. The weather was good, and there were only a few scattered clouds in the sky. Just outside the small town of Usovo, they had to stop at a railway crossing to allow a train to pass. The group got out of the car, and walked up to the railway barrier to watch the train. Six other cars drew up behind them, and their drivers and passengers also disembarked.

"Suddenly," Kuprinov later reported to authorities, "we all saw two silver-colored disc-shaped objects appear in the sky to the south of us. Their edges were clearly defined. They streaked over our heads at incredible speed. Although it was a very strange sight, none of us felt afraid. As the objects disappeared, the train passed, and we returned to our cars."

When he turned the key to activate the engine, nothing happened. He tried again. The engine was still dead. He got out and looked at the six other cars. Every driver was having the same problem—not one engine would start.

"I let my engine rest, and about two minutes later tried again," Kuprinov wrote. "To my surprise, the motor caught without any problem. Through the window, I could hear other motors starting up at the very same time. We exchanged no observations with the others, simply went on. What the nature of the objects was, and why our engines went dead following their crossing above us, remains a total mystery."

A similar incident happened on the road near Volgograd in May 1972. It was investigated by Dr. N. S. Volkova, who heard about it in a casual conversation with a person from the area. She subsequently went to Volgograd, and met the people involved. Afraid that they were involved in something unlawful, they would give her only very basic details.

They had been traveling along the road when suddenly at a spot 12 miles west of Volgograd their automobile engine went dead. They got out of the car and saw, almost immediately overhead, a huge metallic mass. Strangely, they felt no fear. In their minds, a voice seemed to be saying, "We come in peace. Do not fear us." The metallic object, which appeared to be at a very low altitude, moved closer to them. It began to move faster, and for a moment they thought it was going to hit them. They all ducked instinctively. But the metallic mass continued over their heads and sped off into the sky. As soon as it was out of their sight, the car engine started up again.

"These people were most definite about what they saw," Dr. Volkova stated, "but they were afraid that in revealing the details, they might be contravening some secrecy code. The object was so unusual, it would have been a natural reaction to be afraid. But all felt this sense of peace because of the 'inner voice.' There is little doubt that they received some type of telepathic message to allay their fears—and all five of them reported the same sensation."

Another report we were shown stated that cars in a large area of the city of Zagreb, Yugoslavia, also stalled after unidentified objects were seen hovering over the town. Electric power was cut. When the objects disappeared six hours afterwards, the power returned and the cars functioned normally. Engineers could find no explanation for the power failure. Even though this took place outside Russia, it was included in the reports we saw because, obviously, the elements of the incident were the same.

Most of the sightings shown us by Fomin pertained to the period before 1968, when open discussion of UFOs was permitted. After the Soviet Government clamped down on public UFO research, however, important sightings continued to be documented clandestinely. A noted Soviet journalist, Nikolai N. Pronin is the editor-in-chief of the magazine *Thought* and secretary of the editorial commission of the technical annual *On Land and On Sea*. He told of his experience while spending a vacation in the city of Berdyansk, in the Zaporozhye region, in 1970. "On the evening of August 10, while taking a walk, I was watching some falling stars. This was the maximum period of the Perseid Meteor Shower, a group of meteors that appear annually about August 11. Suddenly, I caught sight of an unusual crescent-shaped source of light crossing the skies with incredible speed from east to west. It passed a little to the south of the Pole Star, at a distance equal to that between the stars Zeta and Epsilon of the Great Bear Constellation, which includes The Big Dipper. I consulted my watch. It was exactly 10:36 P.M. The highest point of the object in the sky I estimated at 75 to 80 degrees. I was astounded by the huge size of the flying object. The distance between the two tips of the crescent visually equalled the distance between Zeta and Epsilon.

"The color of the crescent-shaped object was grayish, with blurred edges, and appeared gaseous in nature. As it flew over the stars, I thought that they shone through it. The object, moving with unbelievable speed, was flying, curvature first. It crossed the section of the sky my eyes could encompass, some 100 to 110 degrees, in not more than four or five seconds. There were no other effects visible in the sky. There was no moon and the sky was clear."

Famous polar flier and navigator Valentin Akkuratov reported: "On April 10, 1973, during the period of the polar day, at a distance of 700 kilometers south-southeast from the North Pole, I, along with five other crew members of our aircraft, observed the flight of a disc-shaped object of unknown origin. We were flying at an altitude of 2,600 meters. The temperature of the air was minus 38 degrees Centigrade. The weather was clear—visibility very good.

"The disc had a metallic sheen. It was flying in the direction of the Pole, extremely fast, and we were able to observe it only for a period of one and a half to two minutes. It left no trail of inversion and did not resemble any flying machine known to us."

On July 5, 1973, A. L. Klimenko, of Novo-Amvrosievski in the Donets region, was on the bank of the River Krinka outside the village of

Karpovo in the Ukraine when he noticed a bright yellow light in the sky. He estimated its speed as being that of a jet plane. It was traveling at an altitude of 3,300 feet. Almost instantly he noticed a second object moving parallel to the first on a course slightly to the south. Then the first object stopped, moved downward, and disappeared into the haze above the ground. What was so remarkable was that the second object repeated the same maneuver in the same spot about 45 seconds later. Ten minutes after that, a third object, with similar characteristics and emanating the same bright yellow light, followed almost exactly the same pattern. It appeared that all three seemed to be traveling as a group.

At 10 A.M. on November 3, 1974, members of the morning shift at the Machine Works of Dnyepropetrovsk saw four white objects moving high in the sky, single file. The visual diameter of each object equaled about half of the visual diameter of the moon. Two objects were oval-shaped, transparent on the outside, with a dark core in the middle. The second two objects were irregular rectangles, with two horizontal parallel lines on which the rectangle seemed to rest. The four objects could be clearly observed for about two minutes. Then they began to pale and dissolve.

As might be expected, however, most dramatic reports involving tangible evidence date from before the 1968 "freeze." V. D. Mishlakov, an oil rig foreman at the Cherdin drilling site in the Perm Region, was on the night shift in the oil fields on December 19, 1966. The night was clear and moonless. A strong north wind had been blowing for the previous three days, and the temperature was about 35 degrees below zero Centigrade.

"The drill site I was on was at the edge of a small forest. I was looking over the trees when I suddenly saw a strange moon rapidly rising from behind the treetops," Mishlakov reported. "Suddenly I realized that this was not the moon, but a strange luminous object, made of two elliptical shapes, sitting one on top of the other, like two eggs flattened out. It appeared to me that the object was headed directly for our derrick. Then suddenly it stopped, as if hitting an invisible barrier. It was not more than about the height of half a tree above the forest. At this point it began to change its form. The two elliptical shapes turned into a single ball, and then on both sides of the ball appeared two tiny curvatures which promptly assumed the shape of two smaller balls, attached to both sides of the large one.

"There was a flash of light in the middle of the large ball, then the object began to move again, taking a northerly direction and thereby missing our derricks. By now the three balls had evened out in size and appeared to be connected by an axis that ran through all three of them. At this point I estimated the height of the object at about 30 to 40 meters above ground, and the distance from our derrick at about 100 meters. The length of the triple ball I estimated at 10 to 15 meters."

Mishlakov thought quickly: he must have witnesses! He dashed inside the shack to summon others. The men were asleep, but it took them only about five seconds to answer his alarmed calls. Mishlakov estimated that he took his eyes off the triple ball for a total of 15 seconds while rousing the men. By that time, the object had gone another 70 meters. He figured its average speed against the strong wind was no more than 15 to 20 kilometers per hour.

"My comrades were able to witness the triple shape" he recounted, "just as it changed again, now from three balls into a single ball of diminishing rigidity. It seemed to be softening around a hard core that looked like a disc. Within the next minute the disc disappeared completely, and all we could see was a formless mass, a giant snowball slowly disappearing from sight behind the treetops. I was told later that the same object had been noticed above the village of Lysovo at about 7 o'clock in the morning and the village of Lekmartovo at 9 A.M. The distance from our drill site to Lysovo is about 3 kilometers; to Lekmartovo, 45 kilometers.

"In Lysovo, the object caused quite a panic among the villagers. Some of them ran into the forest to hide. In Lekmartovo the villagers thought the object was a plane with lights on, flying sideways. In all these three sightings, no sound was heard, and no trace was left when the object disappeared." But it did not end there. Another oil rig foreman and his crew members reported a similar incident in the oil fields outside the City of Oktyabrsky in the Bashkir Region—and this time, the UFO left holes in the ground.

This incident took place on April 19, 1967, five kilometers from the city of Oktyabrsky, and within one kilometer from a small village. Two night foremen at the oil fields simultaneously noted hovering objects in the night sky, at about 11 P.M. Both had crews working. In each case, they prepared a statement reporting the sightings, and all crew members—six in the first case and eight in the second—signed as witnesses of the strange phenomenon. The first crew stated that the white object visibly expanded to about 400 meters in diameter, taking the shape of a globe compressed at its poles. It remained hovering over that area for about one hour. The people on the night watch estimated the distance between themselves and the spot was about one kilometer. The men were too afraid to go closer to the object. It looked eerie and forbidding. The next morning, in the early daylight, they searched the area and found the holes.

Exactly the same thing happened with the second crew, who saw a slightly different object, about three kilometers from the object seen by the other crew. This object was dark red in color, with quivering edges. It reminded them of a full moon, except for the color. Both globes, according to the observers, were practically touching the ground.

Nobody did anything for several weeks. Then the administration of the oil fields received the reports from the two foremen. The time coincided with Prof. Aleksei Zolotov, head of the Kalinin Geophysical Expedition probing the Tungusky mystery, getting a lot of local publicity. As a result, the director of the oil fields called Zolotov in Kalinin. Zolotov requested a written report, and after he had read it, decided it was an interesting enough case for him to travel to the Oktyabrsky site. He spent the whole month of August there with a digging crew at his disposal. We subsequently met Zolotov at the Novosti offices in Moscow. "My investigations of the two holes were very thorough," he recalled. "The ground in this area is sandy clay. The sand mixed with the clay was five meters deep, while below that was clay." Using special digging equipment, Zolotov was able to slice the ground in such a fashion that the contours of the two holes were preserved. He dug out an enormous amount of clay, shoring up the area as he went. "I came to the conclusion that they were artificial and created with the help of some very exact mechanical equipment of a nature not available anywhere in that region, neither at that time or any other time. This applied especially to the hole one meter wide. A vertical tunnel, it looked like an exact engineering accomplishment."

Eventually he cut across the two holes in their entire depth. This was how he was able to discover the underground chamber. "We found a round, spherical chamber at the bottom of the 10-meter hole. Its diameter was two and a half meters. Again, it was perfectly shaped. I discovered something very unusual about the chamber. Its bottom and walls were covered with a layer of pure carbon content ashes, two-tenths of a millimeter thick. These ashes had two to three times the normal radioactivity of surrounding soil," he reported.

While he was digging at the strange holes, he uncovered a bone of a mastodon of the rhinoceros family. It was also highly radioactive, about ten times above normal. It is now undergoing laboratory testing. He added, "Under no circumstances have either of these holes been made by men drilling for oil. There are many possibilities, including that an attempt was made by an extraterrestrial probe to sample the earth's surface. We assume that UFOs use a downward thrust of energy as they come to a landing," he said.

"Could this have been the cause of the hole?" we asked.

"It is a valid hypothesis," he replied.

"Is it possible that one of the red-hot legs of a UFO had caused the hole by sinking into the ground?"

"Yes. I assume that the ashes are the result of an underground fire, but how it was brought about has yet to be discovered."

Was he able to ascertain from investigating the walls of this chamber how it could have been dug?

"No. It is still a mystery to me. I am inclined to believe that although it was made with the help of machinery, it was not any machinery that we know about."

Zolotov emphasized that the walls of the chamber were a precise, geometrical spherical shape. "We have no equipment that could bore a hole of one meter in diameter, then swing out at the depth of 10 meters to build a two and a half-meter chamber underneath it," he repeated. "On top of everything else, no traces of the missing earth were found in the surrounding area."

"Could this be in any way linked with the Tungusky mystery?" we asked Zolotov.

"Only if both incidents involved probes from outer space," he answered. "Tungusky was an entirely different case altogether. There was nothing subtle or furtive about that. I believe that it was a nuclear armed probe deliberately set to detonate just above the surface of Earth to attract our attention."

The way we had planned it, our meeting with Zolotov would wrap up the research of UFO sightings in the Soviet Union. We were delighted with the results. In all, we had obtained over 250 reports, all scientifically documented. Many cases added important new evidence vital to UFO research everywhere in the world. For instance, some sightings pinpointed the exact trajectory of a UFO over a string of cities hundreds of miles apart, enabling scientists to learn a great deal about these objects' speed and behavior.

Somehow, though, it didn't end there. The postscript came in the shape of that blockbuster science-fiction movie, *Close Encounters of the Third Kind,* that made "experts" out of millions who had never given UFOs a thought. Among the first to see the film in November 1977, we were amused and amazed by how closely fiction paralleled fact.

To the audience the movie was an event: darting UFO reconnaissance ships; stalled earthling cars; blacked-out cities; telepathic communications from out in space; repetitive musical motifs as a common language denominator. At the climactic arrival of the mammoth alien mother ship, the audience was stunned into awed silence. But we were the only ones in the audience who knew that the Russians had documented most of this, short of the landing of an extraterrestrial mother ship. Astronomer Z. Kadikov, for instance, described one UFO seen over Pyatigorsk in the Caucasus in October 1967 as being 600 meters (1980 feet) in width—several times larger than the spaceship in the movie. A few weeks earlier, another UFO, 150 meters (500 feet) in diameter was seen over the city of Yevpatoriya in the Crimea; and another, 100 meters (330 feet) in diameter, over the village of Sensava in Lithuania.

Ironically, the movie subsequently served a purpose that down-to-earth scientists like Zigel and Fomin have fought so hard to achieve. Skeptical scholars, amazed by the reaction of people who saw the film, declared UFO research a worthwhile subject. In every country where the film was shown, more and better UFO sightings were reported by eager citizens and were investigated by suddenly more receptive scientists. A new era in UFO research has begun, not because of the persistence and logic of pioneer explorers, but because the movie-makers' fantasy struck a responsive cord.

Obviously we didn't know any of this when we talked to Zolotov that day in Moscow. His mind was far removed from movies as he went on to tell us that "close encounter" he was still investigating—the death of an extraterrestrial probe at Tungusky, Siberia.

15.
THE TUNGUSKY "DIVO"—
A WARNING SHOT FROM SPACE?

An explosion that rocked Siberia, yet killed no one because an extraterrestrial force apparently wanted it that way, would make front page headlines all over the world today. Television crews would converge on the spot of the impact to let millions have a close look at the mystery of Tungusky. But seventy years ago when it happened, Prof. Aleksei Zolotov said pensively, stroking his beard, we were simply not ready for a signal from outer space.

Tungusky, which is on the same latitude as Leningrad, Stockholm, and Oslo, is the geometrical center of Siberia, really the middle of nowhere. It is halfway between the Ural Mountains and the Pacific, the Arctic and the Gobi Desert. Irkutsk, the largest city in Siberia, is about 650 kilometers to the south of Tungusky.

The Siberian tundra is mostly marshland with islands of forests interspersing the treacherous swamps. In the summer, with temperatures in the seventies, the swamps produce the largest and most vicious mosquitoes in the world.

The many rivers big and small are the means of communication. The Tunguska flows east to west to meet up with Siberia's Mississippi, the broad Yenisey River, which flows north to the Arctic. The ground along the rivers yields enough vegetation for wildlife to sustain itself, and it is the wildlife that attracts men into the area, mainly hunters. Along the waterways, a few small groups of hardy people built permanent villages as bases for deer hunting, and operated some backyard industries, primarily tanneries. But over all, it is one great inhospitable void. Winters set in early, last six months, and are so severe that the swamps freeze solid to a depth of several feet. Only in winter can the area be crossed by Soviet four-wheeled drive equipment.

"If you were an extraterrestrial civilization intent on not harming life and civilization on our planet," Zolotov said as he faced us across the table in the Novosti conference room, "you could hardly have chosen a better place—so far away from our cities, and so empty of life—to explode a nuclear device. Particularly when the cosmic body which shattered the calm of that morning exploded with a force that would be difficult to duplicate even with our present technology."

In scientific circles, the object is known as "The Tungusky Meteorite." But in Russian folklore, it has a different, much more romantic definition, the Tungusky "Divo"—meaning the magic miracle, or the marvel, of Tungusky.

"This was not a meteorite or any other type of natural phenomenon" he went on. Zolotov leaned over the table toward us so we wouldn't miss a single word. "It made no crater in the ground. This was a compact nuclear device, sent with great precision, deliberately exploded over a relatively uninhabited area to let us know we are not alone in space."

His bushy black beard, so long it almost touched his waist, gave him the appearance of being straight from the pages of history. Ironically, the top of his head was almost bald, but it was difficult to look him in the eye without having our glances stray to his magnificently groomed flow of hair. Yet Prof. Aleksei Vasilyevich Zolotov, who firmly believes a nuclear device from outer space exploded over Siberia on June 30, 1908, is a well-educated man of today, a leading scientist who is using modern technology to look into the past—and uncover a significant warning of what is to come.

At our request, Zolotov made the three-hour, 125-mile electric train journey from Kalinin to Moscow to meet with us at the Novosti Agency in Pushkin Square. His interview with us was cleared at a high level, indicating that he had been approved as a responsible member of Soviet scientific society. Despite his unusual and controversial findings, the authorities were prepared to allow him to speak his mind. He took a full day off from work and paid his own way, so anxious was he to seize the opportunity to talk without inhibition to the Western press about his favorite subject. It was an opportunity that Zolotov, who officially heads a five man group known as the Tungusky Meteorite Geological Expedition of Kalinin, could not miss.

Zolotov carefully opened a battered brown cardboard file and pulled out half a dozen file folders. "Would you like to know what happened these many years ago?" he asked with a smile. He did not even wait for an answer.

It had seemed like just another normal day as the dawn broke over the tundra in the area of the Podkamennaya Tungusky River about 40 miles from the tannery of Vanovara, an isolated outpost. The area had no roads—in fact, it still doesn't. In this village, S. B. Semyonov was sitting on the steps of his house constructing a barrel. He was about to swing his axe to shave a length of wood when it seemed the whole northern sky became a sea of fire. The heat hit him immediately, and he felt as if his whole body was on fire. He tried to tear his shirt off, because he thought it was in flames, although later he discovered it was not even singed. Then he heard a tremendous noise.

It was too much for Semyonov. He fainted, falling from the steps to the ground. His wife dashed from the house and tried to get him inside, but he was too heavy for her to lift. As he was coming to, he later told scientists, he felt as if artillery was firing all around him, and thought huge rocks were falling from the sky. Semyonov lay on the ground for several hours afterward, too shaken to move. A neighbor, P. P. Porsolopov, reported that he thought his ears had caught fire. He clapped his hands over them and sat down on the ground, too shocked to do anything else.

Tremendous devastation was created in the Tungusky area. Millions of centuries-old Siberian trees were destroyed. The explosion was heard 750 miles away. G ound tremors were recorded at the distance of 600 miles. Glass windows were broken, and lamps and other hanging objects torn from their mountings up to 200 miles away. Animals were killed, but mainly by the forest fire that followed the blast. Many domesticated animals fled their villages and were never found again. But other than the vegetation, they were the only real casualties.

Not one person was seriously injured. The only recorded human injury was a man who had his arm broken when hit by a falling tree.

Every meteorological station in the world registered the aerial shock wave of the explosion. Seismic waves were recorded at Irkutsk and Tashkent. The Irkutsk magnetic measurement station also recorded that the earth's magnetic field was upset. The following day, from Yeniseisk to London, a distance of some 3,700 miles, there was a strange bright light in the atmosphere. It was observed all over Europe, in Russia, England, Ireland, Belgium, Holland, Switzerland, France, Austro-Hungary, Serbia. The light was so strong that people could take photographs and read newspapers at midnight. Astronomers all over Europe could not make observations of the stars because the unusual night light was so bright.

Brief reports of the strange phenomenon were carried in newspapers around the world. In Russia, the newspaper *Siberia,* published in Irkutsk on July 2, 1908, carried the fullest description of the strange event. Editor S. Kulesh wrote that a "strange natural phenomenon" was observed in the area of Kirensk. In the northwest section of the sky, above the horizon, peasants saw a body emanating a blueish-white glow, gradually and steadily descending toward the earth.

"It looked as if it were a chimney, lying on its side, and flying through the air," the peasants told Kulesh. The sky was clear, except that not far from the flying object the peasants could see one small dark cloud. The glowing object seemed to get larger as it descended, and the peasants suddenly saw a huge black cloud of smoke. There was a loud rumble and a sound as if rocks were falling or artillery was being fired. Buildings trembled."

Kulesh noted: "At about the same time, a strange flame of uncertain shape was seen to emanate from the little black cloud that had accompanied the flying object. the villagers fled in all directions, thinking the end of the world had come. Women and children broke down crying." He added that at the time of the explosion, he himself had heard what he thought was artillery fire—ten bursts over a period of ten to fifteen minutes.

Despite the reports, scientists paid little heed to the event because the area was so inaccessible. But in 1921, even though civil war was still raging through Russia, Lenin ordered that scientific funds be used to find "the Siberian meteorite."

The man chosen to head the first expedition to Tungusky was Moscow physicist Prof. Leonid Alekseyevitch Kulik. There was a decided tone of reverence in Zolotov's voice as he spoke about Kulik. Zolotov considers him a hero. Kulik, a brilliant scientist, devoted his life to the exploration of the Tungusky mystery. He collected all known data about the event, including eyewitness reports, and was convinced that what had happened was so unusual that a complete investigation would be of tremendous importance to science.

One important item that convinced him this was an event unparalleled in known history was a report from A. V. Voznesensky, director of the Irkutsk Meteorological Observatory, who had personally conducted a great deal of research into the explosion. "I have reached the conclusion," Voznesensky reported, "that the first explosion of this body took place not on the surface of the Earth, but 20 kilometers above ground, which is a very unusual occurrence."

"Do you realize," Zolotov said slowly, shaking his head in wonderment, "that after setting out from Moscow, it took Professor Kulik two tedious months just to reach the site? His expeditions had to go by train and then strike out by boat and on foot. They almost perished in the marshes and lost half their equipment. The same journey now takes nine hours by plane and helicopter—and without the hazards and discomfort that Professor Kulik had to face."

When Kulik's expedition reached the Tungusky basin in 1927, he was astonished to find that the trees in an area of 12 to 15 miles around the epicenter of the explosion had fallen in a radial position, while a three-mile area of trees right at the center of the explosion remained standing. Kulik named this the "telegraph forest," because the trees looked like bare telegraph poles. Either by the force of the explosion or by the fire, they had been stripped of their branches, but the trunks remained erect.

Kulik sent his team out to collect eyewitness accounts. Just about everyone they came across as far away as 500 miles, had seen "something" in the sky shortly before the great explosion. It was nineteen years later, but so incredible was the happening of June 30, 1908, that to many it was like something that had happened only the day before.

"You must listen to some of these eyewitness accounts," Zolotov said in wonderment. He paused dramatically to shuffle some files, but we could sense that he knew exactly the one he was looking for. Finally he slapped the folder on the table, stabbed with his finger at the documents inside it, and exclaimed, "Listen to this. A direct quote from someone who was there, Vasily Okhchen."

Okhchen, the witness, was with a band of hunters only 25 miles south-southeast from the epicenter of the explosion, near the River Avarkit. They were living in two large reindeer-hide huts. They were awakened by a tremendous rumbling noise, and the ground shook violently. One hut flew into the air, with six people in it. They were then dashed to the ground, suffering slight injuries.

"There was noise everywhere," Okhchen recalled. "Trees were being torn from their roots and thrown down as if a giant storm was passing over us. Seconds before they fell, their tops caught fire. We could see a huge black mushroomlike cloud to the north, covering the entire northern horizon." A woman, Akulina Petrova and her husband Ivan, were found unconscious, but it appeared afterward that this was as much from fright at the horrifying awakening as anything else. The group of hunters, suffering only cuts and bruises, managed to flee the ensuing forest fire and escape without further injury.

Zolotov arched his bushy eyebrows quizically. "If you saw a black mushroom cloud now, you would have no doubt. It is the infamous insignia of an atomic explosion!" Zolotov believes that the instantaneous burst of flame from the topmost branches of the trees indicated a tremendous flash from the air—typical of what would happen in an aboveground nuclear explosion.

There were many more eyewitness accounts. In the village of Kamensky, on the River Yenisey, about 370 miles west-southwest of the Tungusky basin, A. Goloshchekin was up early to tend his animals. He later told the scientific investigators, "I saw a strange flying body in the air. It was long and was wider in front than at the rear. The front part seemed to be very light, and the rest of the body darker, not as clearly defined. It flew horizontally towards the northwest, then seemed to fall to the northeast. Then all the inhabitants of the village heard three tremendous underground rumbles, one after the other in quick succession." Kamensky was the most western area from which the object was observed.

E. E. Sarychev, from the town of Kansk, was working in a tannery on the bank of the River Kama, cleaning wool with some companions, when they saw a tremendous wave coming up the river. When questioned in 1921, he said that almost at the same time he and his fellow workers heard a tremendous thunderclap. It was so loud that one of the workmen, E. S. Ulasov, jumped into the river to save himself from the menace in the skies. A series of underground rumblings were heard seconds later. "When we looked into the sky, we could see a round glowing ring, tinged blue, with what appeared to be a half-moon in the middle," Sarychev recalled. "The object then flew towards Irkutsk, before disappearing behind the mountains."

Engineer V. P. Gundobin was in a boat on the River Angara that morning when he noticed a blue light in the northern sky. "Then I saw coming from the south, a flaming body, larger than the sun, and leaving a light stripe behind it. This was followed by a chain reaction of very loud noises, as if batteries of artillery were opening fire," he wrote.

The boatmen became so scared that they ran and hid in the cabin. The boat was out of control, a few minutes away from a series of rapids that could easily sink it. But the thunderclaps of noise were so overpowering that the boatmen would not man their positions. "It was only with great effort," Gundobin noted, "that I managed to get them back to work just in time to save us from hitting the rocks."

An inhabitant of the village of Kova, S. I. Privalikhin, remembered that he was about to plough a field with two horses. He had just put one horse into harness, and was about to do the same to the other when "I heard a loud shot from a cannon to my right. I suddenly saw a long flying object, the front wider, and the tail narrowing down. A bright white light shone at the front, and the body seemed to pulsate red, then black. It was many times larger than the sun, but its light was not as bright, for I could look right at it.

Behind the tail was what appeared to be a cloud of dust whirling in the air. Blue streaks of light appeared to be also left behind by the object, which was flying very fast, and horizontally."

Zolotov stared at us. "Does that sound like a natural phenomenon— all these honest, detailed reports of a wedge-shaped object, rather like a chimney lying on its side, flying horizontally above the ground, exploding in midair? These are reports by totally unsophisticated people who knew nothing, and thought nothing, about objects from outer space. Unidentified Flying Objects were just not known. Yet when you hear their descriptions, you cannot help but form the opinion that this was no meteorite, but a giant UFO. The explosion they saw is a perfect duplicate of what a nuclear blast looks like—almost as if they had seen the photographs we see on television."

Kulik was killed in the war in 1942 before his work was complete. Sixteen years later, in 1958, Aleksei Zolotov, was picked to succeed him as chief of the Tungusky exploration. His qualifications were degrees in geology, mathematics and physics, and his reputation as leading physicist of the All-Union Geophysical Institute. Between 1958 and the present, Zolotov headed four expeditions to Tungusky. Each, consisting of physicists and biologists, spent several weeks at the site living in the tiny "science village" built at the very epicenter of the explosion. On all four occasions, sophisticated equipment to examine soil, rock and plant samples was hauled in by helicopter, then carted back out again, since it could not be left behind. The extreme frost of the next winter would have destroyed the sensitive machines.

"Each time we went there gave us additional proof to support the nuclear explosion hypothesis," Zolotov said. "The eyewitness accounts were dramatic, but not sufficient for a proper scientific explanation. As a scientist I had to seek additional proof. I believe I now know the answer even if not all the evidence is in my hands. Some pieces of the jigsaw puzzle are still missing." He noticed the uneasiness in our eyes. "I'll keep it simple," he smiled. "Here is my basic reasoning.

"Obviously the object did not explode on touching the ground. The telegraph forest right in the epicenter of the explosion testifies to this. It is obvious that a force from above, blasting directly downwards, stripped these trees of their branches, but left the trunks intact. The shock wave, as it spread out, then knocked the outlying trees down in a radial fashion.

"How can you explain a flying object that travels horizontally, then blows up before hitting the ground? It cannot be a meteorite. They do not behave in such a fashion. Small meteors burn up in our atmosphere. Big meteors hit the ground and create a crater. And the Tungusky site has no crater," he said dramatically. "None whatsoever!"

The Kulik expedition tried unsuccessfully to find a meteorite crater or pieces of meteorite. It noted that the absence of these, found in all other instances of meteorites crashing in the Earth, was very strange. The light effect on the atmosphere also indicated that the Tungusky body was of greater mass than merely a cloud of cosmic dust, which some scientists had suggested. "The principal question facing us, then," Zolotov went on, "is the source of the explosion. Was it caused by the kinetic energy of a meteorite passing through our atmosphere, or was it internal energy from the body, chemical or nuclear?

"The decision on this question hinges on the speed of the object through the air. If the speed was more than 20 kilometers per second, then the explosion of the body in air could quite possibly be due to kinetic energy. But according to our examination of all available data, including the eyewitness accounts, the speed was less than 5 kilometers per second. If the speed of the object was less than 5 kilometers per second, then an explosion by kinetic energy is impossible. In this case, a meteorite must hit the ground and make a crater. This is why we have concluded that the explosion was caused by internal energy."

He was now warming up to his subject. "That raises the second fundamental question: Was this explosion chemical or nuclear? The descriptions—including the sighting of a mushroom cloud, the light burns, increased radioactivity, magnetic upheavals, shock waves—everything points to a nuclear origin.

"Damage from the light burns, the flash at the time of the explosion, extended for 18 kilometers. There are scientific measurements pertaining to the ratio of light energy to total energy. In the case of atomic explosions, light energy is about 30 percent of the total. In the case of the Tungusky explosion, the ratio was the same. This high percentage of light energy of the explosion leads us to the conclusion that the Tungusky explosion was produced with a tremendous concentration of energy within a very small space, with a resulting heat effect reaction identical with the heat effect of a nuclear reaction. The tremendous light energy and strong concentration in a small area comparable to the concentration of energy in a nuclear explosion lead to the estimate that the original temperature at the moment of explosion at Tungusky had to be 30 million degrees, or more. No chemical explosion can produce such heat."

Zolotov leaned back, seemingly drained of energy. He paused for a brief moment then continued: "It will take several more years of investigation before we can make a definite scientific conclusion. Because of contamination from known atomic explosions, it is now difficult to check radiation levels going back to 1908. However, even in California, cross-cuts of trees showing their rings, one per year, indicate increased levels of radioactive carbon for the years 1908 and 1909. This could well have been caused by a radioactive dust cloud from the Tungusky explosion circling the globe."

The measurements of radioactivity made on the Tungusky trees preserved after the explosion showed that in most of them there was an immediate increase of radioactivity in the rings for 1908. The following ten to fifteen rings showed a second leap of radioactivity that could be explained by radioactive sediments. The increase of radioactivity in the layers immediately following 1908 was brought on through the presence of radioactive isotopes of elements.

Trees in the area also apparently grew more quickly after the explo-

explosion. Zolotov speculated that there is in existence a mysterious stimulant that has not yet been identified: "Importantly, the stimulant proved most effective at the epicenter, and diminished rapidly in the outlying area. The stimulant, which is not part of the radioactivity, had to come from the disintegration of the cosmic object, as well as possibly a disintegration of gases that accompanied the moving object and enveloped it."

The ground in the area has now been very carefully explored and samples measured, but nothing very unusual has been found. "We believe, however," Zolotov shook his head vigorously, "that these samples we bring back hold the secrets of Tungusky."

In layers of peat, dating back to 1908, there is a more than average amount of spherical particles he revealed. There is no proof that these are of cosmic origin. His group believes that during the immense explosion, dust from the ground was lifted up into the high temperatures of the air above, where it fused into tiny spheres and fell back to Earth.

Typical of the methods used by Soviet scientists, the Academy of Sciences, while supporting Zolotov's investigation, has also formed another group which is trying to prove that the explosion was a natural phenomenon. This counter group has stated it is inclined to believe the object was a huge mass of snow and ice. Zolotov disagrees vehemently: "If it was a monolithic structure traveling at the speed of sound, it would have had to hit the ground, causing a crater. If it were a gaseous substance, it would have dispersed as it reached our atmosphere. If it were something formed by widely dispersed particles, the same would have happened. There would have been no shock wave. All these variations—a substantial mass of iron, stone, cosmic dust, or cloud of small particles—can be excluded.

"There is another theory, which is that this explosion was caused by antimatter. There is experimental proof that antisubstances do exist in nature, and that contact between matter and antimatter might lead to a vast explosion. But this does not fit in with eyewitness descriptions."

He leaned back, wiping perspiration off his brow. The strange man with the black beard was quite different from other scientists we had met in the Soviet Union—it was his almost childish enthusiasm, a seemingly passionate love affair with his project. He was determined to make us understand him, his motives, his objectives. By contrast, the others were cool and composed.

This was the first time we used the patronym "Aleksei Vasilievich" and he sat up, pleased with our expression of respect. "Would you agree that the body exploding over Tungusky could have been a giant 'calling card' from another civilization?" we asked.

He stroked his magnificent beard, and we couldn't help thinking of the long hours he must spend to maintain its magnificent lustre. "Yes," he answered without hesitation. "I have no doubt it was sent by inhabitants of outer space to attract our attention. Even our most serious scientists openly state that there must be other civilizations in space. It is a philosophical dialogue, because we have not yet been contacted or made contact with such civilizations. Unless, of course, the Tungusky object was that first contact."

From these original eyewitness descriptions, taking the distance into account, he estimated that the object was "a cylinder, 50 to 60 meters in width—enormous even by today's giant rocket standards.

"I am aware of the theory that this was a nuclear-powered spaceship that, out of control, exploded in the air," Zolotov reflected. "It is a possibility, yet I cannot see that a civilization capable of constructing such a ship, piloting it through space to Earth, would not have sufficient safety factors built in to prevent this happening. Even if all these systems had gone wrong, and an explosion was inevitable, I would be inclined to believe that some method of 'abandoning ship' would have been used, and the extraterrestrials would not have been destroyed with their spacecraft.

"Instead, think what happened in our own history. Advanced civilizations on Earth used a similar technique to impress uncivilized natives—a cannon shot, for instance, that made the natives, who did not know about gunpowder, understand that they had met a superior race. The Tungusky explosion was an amazing demonstration of pinpoint precision and humanitarianism. You can only conclude that the site was deliberately chosen and the device, unquestionably nuclear, exploded above the Earth's surface to cause only superficial damage."

We thought back briefly to our earlier interview with Felix Zigel. In discussing the Tungusky meteorite, he warned that World War III could be caused by a misunderstanding between the major powers following a mysterious nuclear explosion. Did Zolotov agree?

"Yes," he replied emphatically. Pausing for a moment while stroking his beard thoughtfully, he added, "It is logical to expect at any time a second demonstration of the power and the precision shown in the 1908 Siberian explosion. A delay of years in our time scale could be only hours to an outer space civilization. But we have nothing to fear. They do not want to kill us. If they had evil intentions, they would have wiped out one of our large cities. But they didn't.

"Still we must be on the alert. The next great explosion directed from outer space may well be in the Arctic or the Antarctic, but nations could interpret it as having been initiated by somebody on Earth, and respond accordingly. It would be terribly sad if, by a simple demonstration to attract our attention, a peaceloving, advanced civilization signaled the end of our world in a nuclear holocaust! We have only ourselves to fear. Hopefully, instead of lashing out at each other, we will check our computers and other equipment to find out the origin of the device."

Zolotov obviously enjoyed meeting people from the "outside" world so much, in fact, that following our long discourse he insisted that we be his guests for dinner that evening. It was a very pleasant experience, typically Russian, with Zolotov the perfect host. Somehow, he had convinced the staff to reserve a booth on the second-floor restaurant of the Intourist Hotel. When we had finished wining, dining, and talking, Zolotov picked up a bill for 70 rubles—over $100, a lot of money in Russia.

It was his pleasure to spend it, he told us. He had enjoyed it as much as we had. When he left us to catch the 12:30 A.M. electric train back to Kalinin, the cognac bottles empty, it was like saying goodbye to an old and dear friend.

The caution of the scientist's mind was very much in evidence as he told us in parting. "As scientists, we must not act too hastily. That is why, while we are at this moment of the strong opinion that this was a nuclear explosion, we are not yet prepared to publish a paper stating it irrevocably. Not all scientists will agree with our point of view, and the problem is not yet solved."

We walked out with him into Gorkey Street, by now empty and lifeless. Suddenly he blurted out: "You know, friends, that will be the day when this beard comes off—when I finally solve the mystery of Tungusky." So *that* was the story behind that beard of his, going back to the late 1950's when he got the job of heading the Geophysical Expedition, taking over where Kulik left off. With the impetuousness of a young scientist thrilled with his assignment, he swore he would not shave until the job was done. The next time he goes down there, the permanent base camp at the very epicenter of the Tungusky explosion will have grown to encompass more blockhouses where scientists can live and work for weeks, probing through the forest under the protection of special mosquito nets. The camp is already fully equipped to be self-sustaining in the Siberian wilderness and there is a shortwave radio station, as well as a permanent helicopter landing site.

His eyes flashed as he reemphasized his stand, "I do not waste any time hoping that we will soon prove my theory that this was an unmanned probe, an automatic spaceship, deliberately sent to explode in an uninhabited region. One has to be patient and persevere. But I am 49. I hope my beard won't be reaching to my knees or be all white by the time this happens." He gave a good-natured chuckle. "It is already bothering my wife."

Still, he may be provoked into keeping it, he added with mock disdain, if challenged by colleagues to probe into the origin of the extraterrestrial craft. Where did it come from? He shook his head. "That will be the next stage after I prove it was a nuclear explosion. We are now convinced there is no intelligent life in our own solar system except on Earth. The probe had to come from another planetary system. But we don't know from how far away."

He would not get home till 3:30 A.M., and he had to get up at 7 A.M. But he was not worried. He would sleep on the sofa, he said, in the large living room of his apartment, so as not to disturb his wife, who also works at the Institute. Since she started work at the same time, he had no fears of over-sleeping. "Good night, my friends."

We laughed and told him we also hoped the beard would come off soon, then watched as the squat figure of the man from Kalinin strode purposefully toward the entrance of the Moscow subway.

Back at the Hotel, we had to push our way into the self service, Prague-made elevator. A crowd of tourists had just arrived, one of the many travel groups from Britain, but wearing kilts for a change. Sandwiched in between the Scots and their freckled, blue-eyed lasses, we thought of the next item on our agenda. Extraterrestrials had been covered. Tomorrow we planned to zero in on where all of this—including the Scots—had begun. We had arranged to talk to investigators who believed that the Neanderthal Man was still around, virtually unchanged in 50,000 years, the subject of tales about the Abominable Snowman, alias Yeti, Big Foot, Sasquatch. . . .

The Russians had added their own version: The *Almasty.*

16.
ON THE TRAIL OF THE ALMASTY—
THE CAUCASUS' ABOMINABLE SNOWMAN

It is not Lt. Col. Vargen Karapetyan's long and distinguished career in the Red Army medical corps—which included service in some of the toughest campaigns against the Nazi invaders in World War II—that makes him so unusual. Rather, it is the incredible fact that he is the only medical man in the world ever to have conducted a close physical examination of an *"Almasty,"* as the Abominable Snowman is referred to in Russia's backwoods. Several days later, after a field court-martial for "desertion," the Abominable Snowman was executed! The bizarre incident happened in December, 1941, at the height of the defense of the snow-covered mountains of the Caucasus. Subsequently, with the other principals of the drama having vanished into thin air, Karapetyan was left, the only witness to tell the tale.

The Army doctor kept the story of his encounter to himself until one day in November, 1958, when, on a visit to Moscow, he came across an article in the newspaper *Evening Moscow* by Prof. Boris Porshnev, Scientist Laureate. The article contained a request for anyone who had information about encountering wild, primitive people to get in touch with him.

Karapetyan had harbored his knowledge too long. He had to share his secret with someone, and the article pinpointed the man. He inquired and was told that Porshnev was the country's leading anthropologist who had made the study of the Abominable Snowman his mission in life. On November 20th Karapetyan phoned Porshnev and was told to come over. Once in Porshnev's office he found himself facing three men. They introduced themselves as Prof. Porshnev, Prof. S. E. Kleinberg, and Prof. A. A. Shmakov.

The three men sat silently through his narrative, then for a solid hour fired questions at him. He realized they were not prepared to believe him. Would he come back the following day? they asked.

He did. The second interrogation lasted three more hours. He was asked to repeat his story. He told it again, in minutest detail, and his two reports tallied. Eventually they asked him to leave the room, and after a long discussion, called him back to ask, "Who do you think this creature was?"

Karapetyan expounded his theory that it must have been a man who, abandoned in the mountains as a child, grew up in the wilderness fending for himself and protected by wild animals, who sort of adopted him. "Romantic, but not true," Porshnev said. "You met a real-life *Almasty*. Do you know what *Almasty* are?"

Porshnev then handed him a volume he had written on the evolution of higher primates and said benevolently, "You'll find your man in there." He did. Interspersed between the text, were sketches of a hairy creature that looked identical to the "wild man" seen by Karapetyan. The sketches were by Goppius, an eighteenth-century traveler and explorer. Additional sketches in the book depicted the *Almasty* as described by eyewitness accounts in the early twentieth century, and they too looked strikingly familiar to him.

Two months later, in an article titled, "I Believe in the Abominable Snowman," published in a prestigious Soviet scientific journal, Porshnev described his meeting with Karapetyan and confirmed his conclusion.

Ironically, Lt. Col. Karapetyan was nearly as elusive as the creature he had examined. We heard his name mentioned for the first time in the office of Vasili Zakharchenko, editor in chief of the Soviet monthly magazine, *Tekhnika Molodezhi.* Zakharchenko had just returned from Scotland, where he had gone to collect data on the Loch Ness monster. As we discussed other mysteries of the world, like the Bermuda Triangle and Big Foot, the wiry, mercurial man, so Western in his approach to what we call "human interest" features, revealed the story of how Karapetyan met and examined the Abominable Snowman.

Could we locate Karapetyan, we asked? He shook his head negatively. We persisted, "Why is it so impossible?"

Zakharchenko stared at us silently for several moments. Then, grinning almost benevolently, he said, "Nothing is impossible" in the imperious manner of a James Gordon Bennett deciding to dispatch Stanley to find Dr. Livingstone. "Give me time, and wherever Colonel Karapetyan may be, my men will find him and bring him here. You will hear from me."

We did not hear from him. And, on good advice, we refrained from trying to locate Karapetyan on our own. Though eager to find him, we had been warned not to attempt anything foolish, and we knew all too well that the warning was valid. The most innocent inquiry about the whereabouts of a Red Army officer smacked of seeking out military intelligence. It was one of those encounters one wishes for adamantly, while fully aware that the chances are one in a thousand. Instead, we left for home.

A year went by, and we returned to Moscow to investigate parapsychology. It was two weeks later that Aleksandr Kazantsev, the noted Russian author and historian, called to say, "I have some interesting news for you." He paused for dramatic effect.

"What's the word, Aleksandr Petrovich?"

"Zakharchenko wants you to know that he has located Colonel Karapetyan. This is his message: Colonel Karapetyan has arrived in Moscow and will be at Zakharchenko's office tomorrow, at three o'clock." He was savoring every word. "I took the liberty of telling him you'll be there, promptly at three."

And so, precisely at 3 P.M. the next day, we entered Zakharchenko's office—a well-appointed, friendly room with a huge desk and bookshelves on the left, a wide sofa, armchairs, and low coffee table on the right. Outside the windows was old Moscow, winding shallow canyons of flat-fronted beige and pink two- and three-story buildings with tin roofs. The snow, gone from the rooftops, was piled in gray heaps alongside the sidewalks. A friendly sun hanging in a pale blue sky was filling the room with little pools of light. There was quite a group gathered around a snack-laden coffee table. Standing in the middle of the room, Zakharchenko made the introductions: his editors, Yuri Filatov and Grigori Reznichenko, Kazantsev, Prof. Igor Bourtsev, curator of the Darwin Museum in Moscow, and his guest of honor, Lt. Col. Karapetyan.

We had gone full circle, there he was, in the very office where we had first heard of him almost a year earlier. As he rose to his feet to shake hands, he looked every inch a Red Army officer. He was stocky, round-faced, and bull-necked, a well-fed, pink-cheeked, barrel-chested man from the foothills of Mt. Ararat in Soviet Armenia. His neatly-pressed khaki uniform carried an impressive array of campaign ribbons on the left side of his chest, and on the right side a lone medal of merit.

There was a knock on the door, and parapsychologist Viktor Adamenko slipped in, muttering apologies. "You know Viktor, of course," Zakharchenko said, nodding a greeting. "I've asked him to join us because parapsychology has a special interest in the *Almasty*. Isn't that so, Viktor?"

Dark-haired Adamenko smiled rather uneasily: "We believe that a close look at a live Snowman of the species existing in the Caucasus, using Kirlian photography and acupuncture, will give us a unique opportunity to study evolution. In fact, parapsychologists would give anything for a confrontation such as that of Colonel Karapetyan."

"I quite see your point," Zakharchenko said, impatiently waving his hand. "All right, gentlemen, this is it. Why don't we all settle down?" With that he withdrew behind his desk. "Colonel Karapetyan, the floor is yours," he ordered. "We'll ask you questions after you finish."

It was early December, 1941, the Red Army colonel recalled. His unit, a motorized fusilier battalion, had just taken up a position alongside a mountain ridge commanding the approaches to the town of Buinaksk in the valley below. This particular area of Daghestan on the eastern flank of the Caucasus was of particular strategical importance. A German breakthrough here would open the door to an invasion of the Caspian shore, could bring about the loss of the city and oilfields of Baku some 220 miles to the south, and, in a pincer movement, could lead to a Nazi conquest of the entire Transcaucasus.

It was up there, then, on the ridges blanketed in deep snow, that an enemy would have to be held at all cost. The Russian defense lines were thin, their armament poor. Every man counted; every sharpshooting mountaineer was mustered to help block the narrow passes. The Red Army had called on every Daghestani and Ingush, Kabardine and Balkar, of the mountains and of the lowland, to augment the regulars with partisan units. The units spread out across the mountain ridges, manning every crevice that had a commanding view of the valley the enemy had to come through. Red Army and partisans from other areas, such as the Ossets and the Chechens, moved around as best they could, guided by local mountaineers who had left their *aouls,* native villages.

All these many years later, Karapetyan could still see it all in sharp focus. "We had been in the area for a few days, getting ready to fight off any penetration of Nazi troops when suddenly I received word by field telephone that I was wanted. A group of partisans who had dug in above an abandoned *aoul* requested that I go over to examine a strange man who had been taken prisoner. Their objective was to determine whether he was a Nazi saboteur who had infiltrated the area, a Red Army deserter, or a common criminal."

When Karapetyan asked why he, a military doctor, was wanted for the questioning of a prisoner, the answer was that the captive's behavior was strange. He was a weird apparition, a man covered with long hair. The partisans believed he was using this particular disguise to deceive them. The opinion of a medical man was imperative.

"Very well," Karapetyan said. "I'll have a look at him. Can you bring him over to our headquarters?"

The reply was, "No, he can not be taken out for a variety of reasons." It was essential that Karapetyan go to the prisoner.

The outpost base near the *aoul* was not very far away. When Karapetyan arrived at the mountain village, he was led into an isolated house where the outpost had established its headquarters. Once inside, Karapetyan took off his fur coat and said, "Bring in the prisoner!"

The partisans glanced at each other, then their leader said, "Sorry, doctor, you will have to put on your heavy clothes again and come with us. We can't bring him in here."

"Why?"

The answer, almost spit out in contempt was, "When brought into a heated room, he sweats. Sweat just pours off him. He stinks and is covered with lice. We have him under guard in a barn nearby."

The barn was old and decrepit, barely standing up against the howling wind and heavy snow that had started coming down. The temperature inside was that of the outside: below freezing. A guard flung open the wooden door and Karapetyan was led into the dark interior. A storm lantern was brought in and in its flickering light, Karapetyan caught sight of a man standing in the middle of the barn.

The first question that crossed his mind was: man or beast? A bear standing on his hind legs or a human being? He gave the captive a second, closer look. A partisan held up the lantern. "Looks like a man," Karapetyan said to himself, "naked, barefoot, hairy, but a man."

We glanced at Zakharchenko, who nodded silently: Every word was true. "He was standing erect," Karapetyan went on. "His legs were spread out, his arms hanging by his side, his head thrust forward, in a stance of strength. He was covered with dark brown hair, yet his proportions were definitely those of a man. His height was a little above medium—I would say about 175 centimeters—very powerful, wide-chested and broad-shouldered. I estimated his age, in human terms, at being between 45 and 50.

"The hair covering his back, chest and most of the abdomen was thick and long. Other parts of his body were covered with thinner hair. The backs of his hands were covered with long hair, his fingers had less, his palms had none. On the average the hair was about two centimeters in length.

"He was bearlike in some respects but definitely not apelike. I noticed that his hands were very big and his fingers unusually strong. At first his face confused me because of the absence of beard or moustache. His nose was not broad, squashed-looking, or protruding; in fact, it also looked human. The face was oval-shaped, the hair on the head wavy but not long. His face was covered with a light fluff—like that of a calf. His genitals appeared human. His eyes focused on something that wasn't there; his look was dull and vacant. He blinked occasionally.

"His captors had told the truth—he was crawling with lice. They even crawled around his mouth, through his bushy eyebrows, and all around his neck. They were larger than the lice we know. Yet he paid no attention to them.

"I was so shocked at what I saw I turned around to the three guards who had come into the barn with me and said, 'Hell, Comrades, you could at least have disinfected him before bringing him out for a medical inspection.' One of the guards replied, 'We didn't think he would survive it.' I said, 'You are right. Let me have a closer look at him.'

"I walked up to the man—to me he was a man—and stretched out my hand for a handshake. His arms didn't move. I screamed a command, 'Attention!' Nothing. He didn't even blink."

Karapetyan had been talking in a strong, military monotone. His repeated command, "Atten-shon," was truly a professional soldier's command. He shrugged at the recollection, then went on, not looking at anyone of us in particular.

"There was a bucket of water on a stool in a corner, and a piece of bread on a newspaper. The water was iced over. Neither, obviously, had been touched. 'How long have you kept him here?' I asked. They said, 'Since he was caught two days ago. He was brought in by our patrol.' Had he eaten at all? The answer was no."

At this point, Karapetyan remembered with a slight shudder how he took a medical tweezer out of his bag, went up to the prisoner and proceeded to pull hair from various parts of his body. The creature flinched but made no sound. This proved that Karapetyan was pulling it from the man's own skin and not from an animal pelt that an enemy saboteur might possibly be wearing. The skin was taut and fleshy. Not satisfied, Karapetyan pulled at a hair in the man's nostril. He growled in obvious pain but did not raise his arms in self-defense. He blinked several times and Karapetyan read a plea for mercy in the man's eyes.

"I truly felt sorry for him at this point, but I had a job to do. The guards stood by my side with their revolvers at the ready should the strange beast attack. It appeared he had submitted to me in a situation he could not understand. I stepped back and called out, 'Come over here.' I beckoned with my hand. Still nothing. Obviously he did not understand me. Two of the guards then pushed him in my direction. He raised one leg, made one step toward me. The movement was half-man, half-bear. He groaned, seemingly in protest. The sound came from deep within his throat. I could tell he could not speak.

"I looked at my watch. Exactly eight minutes had passed since I had entered the barn, and I had reached my conclusion. 'He is not a spy, a saboteur, or deserter,' I told the men. 'I would say that this is a harmless creature, a man who has chosen to live in the wilderness.' Catching a frown on their faces, I added, 'Obviously he is your prisoner, not mine. The decision as to what to do with him rests with you.' At that I turned around and left, followed by two of the guards. They took me to the command post and there I repeated my statement. I could see on their faces that they would have preferred that I decreed the creature a spy or deserter. As I was leaving, escorted by one of their commanders to the rim of the *aoul*, I asked, 'What do you plan to do with him?'

"He shrugged: 'What can we do? Get rid of him.' He didn't specify. It could have meant setting him free or shooting him. My impression was that they would set him free. I don't know why I thought so. Maybe I was hoping they would.

"I returned to my unit, and a couple of days later I was told by a soldier that the creature the partisans had caught had escaped. This absolved me of any responsibility—or additional action. I breathed a sigh of relief. Mind you, we were involved in a desperate rear guard action and were ourselves cut off from our cities. We were fighting for our lives, the survival of our country. The Nazis were at the gates of Moscow and were threatening to slice across the Caucasus into Iran. There was no time for me, as a medical man, to think of carrying out an additional investigation, to check out whether the man had really escaped, and if not, to get another close look at him, take pictures. Even if the thought had occurred to me to get him away from the partisans and to preserve him for science, my mind was on the war." His voice faded, and he was obviously feeling ill at ease. "Anyway, this is my story."

Zakharchenko spoke without hesitation, sounding compassionate and warm. "Colonel, you were a soldier. You did the right thing. It couldn't be helped. And you have rendered a service of inestimable value to science by preserving the details of your encounter. On behalf of all of us here, thank you for this remarkable account. I know that Professor Bourtsev has something to add to your report."

"Correct," Bourtsev replied. "The execution was officially confirmed!"

We turned in the direction of the sofa. Wedged in between Kazantsev and Adamenko, Igor Bourtsev was young, lean and handsome, in every way the exact opposite of a Hollywood typecasting of a curator of an anthropological museum in Moscow. Impeccably dressed, business suit, tie and all, he was pulling at a bulging briefcase sitting by his feet. Nearby, leaning against the leg of the coffee table, was the plaster cast of a huge foot, evidence of the *Almasty* that he had brought with him. A lock clicked open.

He pulled out a folder, produced a document, sat forward and read aloud:
"'Report on an inquiry at the Ministry of Interior of the Autonomous Soviet Socialist Republic of Daghestan in Makhachkala. In response to an official inquiry as to the fate of one unnamed person allegedly executed following a court-martial by partisan forces near the town of Buinaksk in Daghestan, circa mid-December 1941, it was ascertained that a prisoner fitting the supplied description was dealt with in accordance with the laws of war applying to deserters. The reply was signed by Comrade Aliev, Minister of Interior.''

He put the sheet of paper back into the folder and clutching it in one hand went on, looking straight at Zakharchenko: "This means the prisoner was executed by a firing squad. I should explain that this came to light many years later, after Colonel Karapetyan came forward and told scientists of his experience. We immediately went into action. By then it was 1960, and Aliev had retired, but we were able to secure the information from him, as he was very interested in helping us find out the truth. At the same time, we sent out our first team to the area to interrogate local people and to look for a body. I am sorry to say that nothing was found, even though we went back several times. We found the local people very secretive, as though resolved to deny us information. This puzzled us, until our esteemed colleague Dr. Kofman succeeded in solving the riddle. It's quite a story."

We had hoped to meet Dr. Jeanna Kofman, a living legend among Russia's anthropologists. Born in France, she had chosen to live in the Soviet Union, and later devoted her life to seeking the Abominable Snowman of the Caucasus. Zakharchenko anticipated our question. "Dr. Kofman," he reflected pleasantly, "got stuck in a detour on the road from Leningrad to Moscow. She will be late in arriving. She phoned in her apologies. You should be able to catch up with her tomorrow. Fascinating woman." Zakharchenko rose from behind his desk and was coming toward us, tall, gaunt, mercurial, a picture of perpetual motion, Soviet style.

"I suggest that before we put some more questions to the Colonel, and I know I have some, why don't we have a bite? But I suggest that we first raise a glass in his honor—Lieutenant Colonel Vargen Karapetyan."

It was evening when we left the *Tekhnika Molodezhi* building on Sushchevskaya Street. Bourtsev had offered to walk us to the hotel and we wandered off, our footsteps echoing through the poorly-lit, winding side streets, empty of people. Occasionally a car, a Moskvitch or a Volga, rumbled by. The buildings on both sides appeared dark and lifeless, shut off from the street by the absence of shop windows. A huge communist metropolis was settling down for the night.

To Bourtsev, the emptiness and quiet of a Moscow back street was home. It helped him concentrate on his subject, which was the *Almasty*, first and last. As he spoke, we realized he was totally dedicated to the Abominable Snowman. Like Russia's parapsychologists, he was battling skepticism and disbelief while still only expounding hypotheses in the absence of conclusive evidence. "People just won't believe," he was saying, "that the Neanderthal

Man who lived some 40,000 to 70,000 years ago could have survived man's evolution. That's why Colonel Karapetyan's contribution—whether he, as a soldier, realizes it or not—is so valuable to us anthropologists. Today was the fourth time in fifteen years that I met the man and listened to his story. It fascinates and inspires me each time he tells it. His meeting the snowman face to face is a valid reminder that many more of them roam the wildernesses of the world."

"The Darwin Museum in Moscow," Bourtsev observed proudly, "is a home base for Soviet expeditions into areas where the *Almasty* have been reported. Several teams organized by the museum have swept the mountain ranges of the Caucasus in search of the wild man of the mountains. But the Museum is also unique in the world as an internationally known depository of evidence collected everywhere. Some fascinating eyewitness reports from the Caucasus are on file at this museum, but just as importantly, he had reports from elsewhere in the Soviet Union as far as Yakut country in Eastern Siberia, Tadjikstan and the Kirghiz republics, both bordering Afghanistan and China's Sinkiang. There too, in the vast emptiness of mountain plateaus, the Abominable Snowman has survived, occasionally to show himself to man.

"The *Almasty*, of course, has been observed in other countries, he reflected, where it is known by different names: the Yeti of the Himalayas, Big Foot of Northern California, Sasquatch of British Columbia, Zhen-Su of China. They are part and parcel of the legend of the Abominable Snowman spun down through the ages."

He paused briefly. "I wish we had something more substantial than just reports. The best evidence we have are footprints preserved in plaster, and a copy of the film taken at Bluff Creek in Northern California in 1967, showing a creature that Karapetyan told us was like the beast he examined. One thing is certain, though. Everywhere in the world the *Almasty* is an object of hunters, and he knows it. We have verified several incidents, particularly in Tadjikstan, where *Almasty* have been shot and wounded, but never captured. These were cases where native hunters deliberately stalked the creatures through the snow with the sole intention of killing them.

"The *Almasty* is determined to elude us to the point of even hiding his dead—very much like the apes of Ceylon. But he is relatively safe in the Caucasus, thanks to the local people, and he knows that, too. That's why we are concentrating on these mountains, and Dr. Kofman is gradually closing in on them. She knows exactly where to look!

"I am sure Dr. Kofman will have much to add to this when you see her. You'll enjoy meeting her," he concluded as we parted company in front of the Intourist Hotel on busy Gorky Street. We couldn't wait to hear from her.

The next day she strode into the room, a powerfully built woman with cropped hair and keen eyes.

"Dr. Kofman?" we said hopefully.

"Please," she raised her hand, "call me Jeanna." She was en route to the Caucasus, she said, stopping over in Moscow for one day only. She apologized for the delay: a bridge was out, forcing her to make a long detour. She got lost and it cost her an entire day.

"I am so sorry I missed Colonel Karapetyan. I never pass up an opportunity to meet with him. Each time it encourages me to go on." She paused, then with a pretended sigh, "Do you know that I have agreed to give ten years of my life for an experience like his? Nobody's taken me up on my offer so far."

She grinned. We assumed that she had read Goethe's Faust.

Without waiting for our reaction, she went on at top speed. Was it true that we were in Moscow interviewing parapsychologists? "Good, good, good . . . ESP! Very useful in a case like mine when there's no telephone at the field station and you need to get in touch with someone." She had studied ESP, and thinks she can use it effectively. She is also an amateur UFOlogist. "My group and I have reported several sightings to Dr. Zigel. I also have a pact with Viktor Adamenko that the moment we catch an *Almasty*, we send him a telegram to come down and bring his Kirlian gear and his acupuncture equipment along."

Her accent was so slight that one had to be reminded she was not Russian. That a real Parisienne would end up in the wilderness of the Caucasus hoping to catch the Abominable Snowman is another paradox of our times. Born in Paris some sixty years ago, of pure French origin, she came to Russia with her parents in the 1930's and stayed. During World War II, she led a unit of Red Army skiiers who fought the Nazis on the northern slopes of the Caucasus. Later she took up medical science and became a surgeon, only to give it up in favor of anthropology and the quest for the Abominable Snowman.

"Actually I've been studying the subject since 1955. I was not a novice when I read Porshnev's report on Karapetyan. I managed to meet the Colonel, and interviewed him at length. Like Porshnev, whom I knew well, I realized he was telling the truth. I was so envious I could die."

Two weeks later she was off, headed for the Caucasus with skis, snowshoes, and all. There were three in her hastily organized expedition. They set out for Buinaksk and from there went by truck as far up as it would take them, then continued on snowshoes. Karapetyan had given her exact instructions. When Porshnev's article on the *Almasty* appeared it caused a sensation in Soviet anthropological circles and touched off a chain reaction. "Find the *Almasty*!" was the cry. Before long several teams were en route to Daghestan and the mountain ranges skirting the town of Buinaksk to the west. But the first to get to the *aoul* overlooking the town from a peak some 20 miles away in a countryside covered with snow six feet deep was no one else but Dr. Kofman.

"We reached the *aoul* where it all took place, but the local people just shook their heads. They didn't remember, they said. We stayed as their guests for a week, looking for footprints in the snow or any other sign of the *Almasty*. Nothing. I wasn't discouraged. In this business, you cannot afford to become discouraged."

She waited until spring, then roamed the mountains until she discovered the town of Nalchik, a junction of several important mountain roads. She figured it to be a perfect base for sorties in search of the Abominable Snowman. She found a little house that could serve as a field station, posted a sign on the door saying, "I'll be right back," and left for Moscow to recruit an anthropological group that would be permanently stationed in the Caucasus. One month later, she was back with a dozen young students, all eager to participate in her search. "This is how it all began," she said grinning amiably. After all these years, she has yet to meet an *Almasty*, but she's not discouraged. "I can wait a little longer," she winked. "I get satisfaction from the fact that I have plenty of eyewitness reports. On record. Verified. Would you like to hear a few stories?" She rattled them off, one by one, in rapid succession.

Mukhamed Tomakov, 39-year-old manager of a state farm in Kabardin, saw an *Almasty* at Getmish, a gorge between Zayukovo and Kurkuzin, in 1946. "There was movement in the high, wild grass, and when I rode over to have a closer look there was this ape—an animal I had never seen in my life before.

"I chased him to a mountain cabin and trapped him inside. There I had a good look at him. His body was just like a man's, but covered with pelt, his face was also like a man's, but much flatter. His forehead was high and curving, his eyebrows sticking out, eyes squinting. The nose was small and flat, the chin round. He had eye teeth like fangs, sharp and yellow.

"His hands were small, their palms flat and narrow, long nails on the fingers but not sharp, and black callouses. His ears were flat and set higher on the head than a man's. And the creature had no tail. I noticed it all so well because I made a special point of looking him over carefully. While I was chasing him, he was running on all fours, but whenever he stopped he rose up on his hind legs. The creature did not speak or scream, but was merely moving his lips and hissing like a cat.

"I closed the door behind me—it had a latch—and left to get a rope, thinking that the creature would never be able to open it. I was wrong. When I came back the door was wide open. The creature was gone."

Her most interesting and tantalizing notes concerned Shagir Boyev, a student of the Agricultural Technical College in Kabardin. Intelligent, well-traveled, he had met the *Almasty* several times. Boyev told her, "The first time was in September, 1956. It was 11 P.M., with a full moon. I was riding my horse along the main highway. At one point my horse, frightened by something, switched from a trot to a gallop. Suddenly the horse neighed and stopped, its ears pricked up. . . .

"There was a man by the side of a fence leaning against it with his left arm. Suddenly, he jumped. It was as though he flew over the fence, he did it so lightly. Then, after glancing in both directions he started crossing the highway—not more than eight meters away from me. At this point I could see him more clearly. He was rather tall, hunched over, his knees slightly bent. His arms, unusually long for a man, hung limply by his sides. His head was covered with long hair. He had no clothes on, but I could see a sort of hairy pelt covering his entire body. It was glistening in the moonlight.

"I turned around, gave the horse the spur and galloped for home. My father screamed at me that I was stupid and a coward, that there is no such thing as an *Almasty*. Except that I again saw the *Almasty,* just the other day."

This was in November, 1959, two days before he came to her station to report. What made her angry was that the Abominable Snowman had been practically outside her house! She went on, "Boyev was walking down the road late in the evening when he noticed a dark human shape at the corner. He reached the figure, then walked on past him. The man started following him. Boyev decided it was a drunk. 'Who are you?' he asked. No reply. Boyev then turned around and stopped about two meters from him, took matches out of his pocket and struck one. Then Boyev knew it was an *Almasty*—he recognized the bent fur-covered knees and the huge bare feet. He turned around and ran.

"I asked him why he didn't come at once. We could have looked for the creature together and at least secured his footprints. Boyev apologized and said, displaying typical Caucasian courtesy, that men didn't come knocking on the doors of ladies whom they did not know. He had found out about me and my work only when he told his mother about the man, and she convinced him to come over and talk to me. By which time it was too late."

Khazhisuv Khutov, 33 year-old electrical mechanic in Kabardin, saw an *Almasty* twice, both times in 1964. "The first time was on May 25. Father sent me and my younger brother to cut wood by the Chegem River. Suddenly, my brother called out, 'Look!' He sounded scared. Not more than 20 meters from us was the creature, the height of an average man, all covered with dark fur. He had long hair on his head, the shoulders were heavy, but the arms were thin, especially at the wrists. His hands were long, with long fingers and long nails. There was no hair on his palms. Their skin was brown. He had heavy hips, but very thin ankles. The forehead overhung his eyes like a peaked cap. The eyes were slanted, the nose aquiline. I could see his palms so well because he was raising both hands up in the air with the palms towards me. He stood there for a few moments, then turned around and left. All this happened in daylight.

"The second time I saw the *Almasty* he was in the same spot. It was on a September day, around noontime. He was no more than ten meters away. He was lying in the grass on his right side. I recognized his back. It was all covered with hair, but the buttocks had no hair and the skin was brown. As I started walking in his direction, he sat up, turned, and ran."

By Spring 1979, Dr. Kofman will have been searching the Caucasus for 20 years. "I come and go, but there's always somebody at our field station to take an eyewitness deposition," she explained. In that time Dr. Kofman has personally interviewed close to four thousand people, whose tales of the *Almasty* fill a long row of volumes at the field station in Nalchik. Her research has made her an expert without peer, not only on the *Almasty* of the Caucasus but also on local folklore. She is known as the "Shaytan Lady," the lady protected by good spirits, in the mountain villages and hamlets from the slopes of Mt. Elbrus to Mt. Dikh-Tau, to Mt. Kazbek, to the Talysh mountain range. The only mountain she has not scaled in her search of the *Almasty* is Mt. Ararat, and this only because the "prisoner mountain," as the locals call it, is across the border in Turkey.

In all these years she's come across the footprints of an *Almasty* only once, on the slopes of Mt. Elbrus. "He had been wandering in the snow in a straight direction and when he came to a ledge obstructing him, he jumped, without going back to gather momentum. He landed on the ledge three meters above and continued walking. Incredible! We didn't follow the trail. It was late and we were heading for a place to spend the night. We came back in the morning and by then new snow obliterated the footprints. We swore at the *Almasty,* and we turned back." Every so often when the researchers get discouraged, they tell one another, "Remember Karapetyan!"

Prof. Yuri Efremov, the noted Russian physiographer, told Igor Bourtsev how, back in 1966, he chanced on a meeting of the Geographical Institute of the Soviet Academy of Sciences and heard Dr. Kofman report on what she had learned of the primitive man of the Caucasus. She was, Efremov remembered, loaded down with eyewitness accounts she had collected throughout Kabardino-Balkaria, Daghestan, the Lenkor region of southern Azerbaijan—really remote places.

As a geographer, Efremov's first doubts were concerned with the question of how an unusually big man could hide out in the area. The creature had been reported in the valleys of Kabardy, Malka, Gundelen, Baksan. Yet these were only several dozen miles from the city of Kislovodsk, with a population of 80,000. What would he eat? Where would he winter? How could he escape detection by huntsmen and by pursuing dogs, and how, for that matter, could he escape disease?

Dr. Kofman answered each and every question. The area abounded in deep caves, tunnels, and nooks and crannies carved by nature into the limestone. Even though the main valleys nowadays feature automobile roads, the canyons of the mountain streams still are impassable to machines, and accessible only to the best mountain climbers.

A "wild man" could move around freely, could live off the land, but more importantly, off the simple local villagers, who had developed a boundless loyalty to the *Almasty*, the man of the mountains who would harm no one. Down through time he had become part of local legend: He was the man in whom lived the good spirit called *Shaytan.* Moslem beliefs made him holy and untouchable. Anyone who destroyed an *Almasty* was himself subject to severe punishment. In fact, about a century ago, the *Almasty* stayed with the villagers, helping with domestic chores and in the field. But as their villages, or *aouls,* became more and more accessible to strangers, the *Almasty* were let go by their mountaineer friends. However, they would leave out food for them to snatch during the night. And while the *Almasty* lives in areas not contaminated by man, they come down to forage for themselves, to pick up the food—sour milk, cheese, cabbage heads—that people leave for them outside their houses. It was considered a good omen when they came back at night for food.

So they can easily live off what the villagers let them have, while being protected from strangers. Their fur keeps them warm in wintertime. Their animal ruggedness is their shield against disease, their strong hands are their protection against wolves and mountain lions. Incredibly strong, they have no fear of the beasts of the mountain and they can cope with all of them, including the bear. They have adapted themselves to night living—they can see at night as well as any other animal. They are lonely creatures, wandering through the mountains and maybe dreaming of the time they didn't have to hide from their cousins, the creature called man.

By now Dr. Kofman had told us everything, it seemed, except for one thing—how she had solved the riddle of Karapetyan's *Almasty*. She was at first reluctant to discuss it, then finally gave in. It was her female instinct, she said, that told her something was wrong with those partisans in Karapetyan's account. Karapetyan's story had no ending. It was provided by others, confirming that the *Almasty* was executed. But why would those fine, upstanding mountain people execute a friend? They knew better. He was not a spy, nor was he a saboteur or deserter.

"I had to learn the truth. It would be my contribution to history, if you will." That summer of 1959, she crisscrossed the area again and concluded that the local people were definitely hiding something. She decided to look elsewhere for the answer. The elsewhere would have to be the low country, the narrow strip of flatland that stretches alongside the Caspian Sea not 30 miles away. She went from village to village and then, through sheer luck, chanced upon some folk who had heard about an *Almasty* who was shot as a deserter in World War II. It had been passed down to them from the mountains, a strange tale.

How had it come down? Somebody had to tell it, somebody who knew. It was thus Dr. Jeanna Kofman pointed an accusing finger at an old villager bearing healed scars of war. She accused him of having been one of the executioners of the *Almasty*. He fell for her bluff, admitted it, and told the story of what had happened.

The man, whom she refused to identify, had been a member of a patrol of local Ossets who had been guarding the railroad that runs north from Baku along the Caspian Sea into Russia proper. The railroad was an ideal escape route for possible deserters. And there were deserters there among the local tribesman, not all of whom were willing to fight an enemy they'd never even heard of before.

One morning in December, 1941, the patrol checking the railroad tracks came across footprints left in the freshly fallen snow. The footprints led away from the railroad into the mountains. Who, the men asked themselves, would want to run through the snow on bare feet in wintertime? It had to be someone trying to escape—a deserter who knew of a hiding place in the mountains.

"The men set out in pursuit," Dr. Kofman recounted, "determined not only to catch the man but possibly come upon a nest of deserters hiding out in the mountains. As night fell they reached an abandoned *aoul* and stayed for a brief rest, continuing the pursuit in the early morning. They were following the same footprints. They were fresh and they were obvious. A man was walking into the mountains to hide.

"The Osset partisans had enough provisions with them to keep going, higher and higher into the mountains. They spent the second night in a cave. By the evening of the third day they caught up with their quarry.

"When they first caught sight of their man, they thought he was wearing a suit of fur. Under one arm he was carrying a large head of cabbage. They demanded that he present his documents. There was no reply. According to the old man who came back, the 'deserter' didn't even try to resist. I assume that the poor *Almasty*, who had gone down into the lowlands looking for food because all his benefactors had gone, was in a state of shock.

"They tied his hands, attached a rope to his neck, and with their prisoner in tow, pushed on looking for another *aoul* to spend the night. They came across the partisan outpost, identified themselves as partisans from another area, and said they had brought a prisoner, a deserter.

"The rest I surmise. The old man didn't quite remember the details or the order of events. The Ossets took it upon themselves to guard their prisoner, planning to take him back. A heavy blizzard that set in, which Karapetyan clearly remembers, upset their plans. It would be simpler to get rid of the man by shooting him on the spot. After all, he was their captive, he belonged to them. I like to assume that whatever local people there were among the partisans at this outpost knew or realized that the prisoner was an *Almasty*. I would say that only a few of the men up there knew about the prisoner, anyway. By the same token, the Ossets of the patrol, being lowland people, had never dealt with an *Almasty*. A warlike tribe and heathens who became Christians a mere hundred years ago, they would have no knowledge of Moslem legends about the man of the mountains. Anyway, they obviously decided not to bother taking the weird deserter back, shot him, then made out a report about a court-martial and firing-squad execution.

"I believe this is how it really happened, because it explains so many incongruities, especially why the local people subsequently questioned by me and by Bourtsev clammed up. They pretended they knew nothing, and never heard anything. I think they were ashamed of their failing to protect a friend. I also think that they buried him, making sure the grave would never be found. I also have a theory about the reason the Osset patrol subsequently disappeared—totally, fully, as though they never existed, with the exception of this one badly scarred man. I think the mountain folk caught up with them and avenged the death of their *Almasty* the only way they knew: eye for eye, tooth for tooth. And only one man escaped them. But we'll never know for sure, because this man is now dead, too. He took the secret of another execution—if there was one—to his grave."

Dr. Kofman was not in a hurry, staying the night with some friends and taking off in the morning for the Caucasus in her beat-up Volga. So she let herself be persuaded to have dinner with us in the foreign currency dining room of the Metropole Hotel across the square from the Bolshoi Theater. We thought she would enjoy it—before submerging in the snows of the Caucasus.

The evening proved an unusual experience for her. No queue, no waiting at the door of the Boyar Tearoom fashioned in sixteenth-century peasant style and tucked away in a corner of an upper floor—an attraction for foreigners. The service was fast and courteous. As the waiter poured the wine, then stepped back to have her taste it before filling up her glass, Dr. Kofman looked at us.

For a brief moment her lower lip quivered, betraying the woman, the Parisienne in her. "Do you miss Paris?" we asked.

"I visit there when I feel like it," she answered proudly. We didn't argue. "But I don't even miss Moscow. My world is down in the Caucasus, with the Abominable Snowman.

"I intend to spend the rest of my days down there, working on my monography. It isn't published yet because, obviously, the key chapter is still missing." She thought she knew where the *Almasty*'s favorite areas were, but she would not identify them because after all these years, the last thing she wants to see happen is someone else beating her to the wild man of the mountains.

We told her that Bourtsev, the curator of the Darwin Museum estimated the total *Almasty* left in the Caucasus at less than two hundred. "Bourtsev is right," she said. "Unfortunately, civilization is catching up with them. They are dying out. There used to be a time when they moved around in groups. Ten or twelve of them. They're nomads, you know; never stay in any one place. But of late, the most anyone has seen together was three, a mother and her two young. The males move around singly and get together with the females only briefly, to mate. Then they push on." Then, a last thought:

"You have no idea how I envy Lt. Col. Karapetyan. You want to know what I'd like to do before I die? It's to get them together—the *Almasty* and our parapsychologists. A living specimen of man's past, and the explorers of man's future. It would be a crowning event for our young scientists who, God knows, need such a breakthrough: to be able, putting to use all this new parapsychology research, to explore the recesses of the human mind as it was when we were coming into being. To pinpoint man's evolution, but also possibly to bring out and record all those atavistic memories now dormant in the primitive mind of the Abominable Snowman.

"What a task," she said, her face brightening up at the thought of expeditions—perhaps successful—that lay ahead. "What a task!"

Part Three

THE
SCIENTIFIC INVESTIGATIONS

17.
DR. VASILI KASATKIN,
COLLECTOR OF DREAMS

On January 27, 1942, the siege of Leningrad was in its 170th day. "I doubt that I will survive it all," Vasili Kasatkin, aged 23, wrote in his diary.

Outside the badly damaged hospital, a howling blizzard had combined with a deafening artillery barrage. The room in which young Kasatkin was billeted was cluttered with debris and pieces of plaster from the ceiling. The windowpane had been pasted over with strips of paper to prevent it from falling out into the snow-covered courtyard below, but it was cracked anyway and the icy wind reached inside.

Kasatkin was so numbed by the cold that he could hardly hold the pencil. In another half-hour, his so-called rest period over, he would report to the wards to help the wounded, frozen, and sick in their beds, on cots, on the floor, wherever there was room for suffering. He had not eaten all day, even though as a doctor tending to the victims of the siege he was entitled to a special food ration: lentil soup and a piece of black bread twice a day. Out there in the martyred city, people were on their own rations, such as perhaps a small bowl of thin soup made of coarse bran once a day, diluted jellied carpenter glue, minced meatless bones cooked in machine oil.

"If I do survive," young Kasatkin wrote on, "I will continue looking into the substance of dreams for purposes of diagnosis. I have stumbled onto something new and very strange. Even though everybody in Leningrad dreams of food—none of us seem to dream of anything else—some of my patients do have repeated additional, different dreams. I make them tell me about them. And they point to symptoms of an illness they don't actually show until a few days later. I feel I am on the verge of an important discovery."

One year later, on January 27, 1943, the siege was in its 535th day. The hospital had been evacuated to a different building, which had somehow escaped the merciless pounding by the Nazis' long-range guns, bombers, and dive bombers. Young Kasatkin was still on the staff. Working all day and most of the night, he was tending to the wounded brought in from the bloodied snow of the ravines and gullies where Russian soldiers were making their last stand behind jagged pieces of concrete—improvised tank traps.

Every night, young Kasatkin closed the eyes of soldiers and civilians who had died, the latter mainly of starvation. There were more civilians dying than soldiers. The siege was taking a terrible toll. A large city was being starved to death despite the lifeline that had been opened across the ice of the

Lagoda Lake, with trucks under Nazi fire groping their way across the ice in total darkness. There were now more medical supplies at the hospital, and a little more food in the beleaguered city—canned and frozen meat, flour—dispensed in minute rations to people standing in line under signs reading, "During shelling, this side of the street is safer." In too many cases, it was too late.

"They are now dying like flies," Kasatkin wrote in his diary in the dim light of a flickering electric bulb. "I have recorded 485 different hunger dreams related to me by 102 people. I was told many more, but I have no time or strength to make that many entries. I can now determine by the intensity of the dream whether the person can survive or is doomed.

"Yesterday a 32-year-old munition worker died in my ward—as I expected. He was dreaming of food every time he fell asleep. It was always the same dream. He was back home in Kazakhstan visiting his family. To celebrate his return, they were holding a feast—boiled lamb, incredibly white bread, fat cabbage soup with pieces of meat floating in it, roast chicken.

"He was eating, eagerly gobbling up the food, actually feeling it going down his digestive tract. Yet as much as he ate, he could not satisfy his hunger. Suddenly, out of nowhere, Nazi bombers were overhead and everybody was running, but he was telling them not to worry. 'It's not that bad, let's go on with the feast.' Then the planes were gone. He was left alone with the food, and he resumed gorging himself on it, only he still was not able to satisfy his hunger. Tired out, he tried to get up from behind the table, but he was too weak, and his legs were heavy. With that, then, he woke up. Feeling terribly weak and cold, and hungrier than ever. . . .

"He died yesterday of the effects of malnutrition. I know the death symptoms now. Their dreams are telling me more and more."

During the night of January 27, 1944, the 900th day of the siege, all hell broke loose for the Nazis. Attacked from everywhere including the rear, they were put on the run, their tanks rolling over their own dead and wounded. The vise around the city broke; Leningrad was free. Eventually, the city would honor its five hundred thousand dead men, women and children by burying them in common graves under the huge granite plates of the magnificent Piskarevskoye War Memorial Cemetery.

Kasatkin stayed on in Leningrad, and when we met him the horrors of those nine hundred days were some thirty years behind him. Now in his late fifties, an agile, graying man with intense blue eyes and a kind smile, he is a celebrated Soviet scientist and author of a famous book, *Theory of Dreams*, which has had quite a few printings in Russia since it was first published in the late 1960's. It has become a popular textbook in Soviet medical institutes concerned with psychiatry and neuropathology, and is included in university courses on psychology and physiology.

We had come to Vasili Nikolayevich Kasatkin, M.D. by a devious route, having first asked ourselves whether he should be part of our probe of psychic phenomena. What eventually made us ask to meet him was a realization that a world authority on dreams, like Kasatkin, might throw light on something in his own field that is also related to psychic phenomena—namely, premonitions. Who hasn't had premonitions of this or that? A visit from someone dear to you, a visit totally unexpected, without a hint it was forthcoming except you had that dreamlike feeling. And then, on the day it is forecast in the dream, the visitor arrives. Among the people you know, hasn't at least someone told you about a "terrible dream" of a person far away dying, which came true?

To be sure, both ancient and very recent history is full of tales of premonition that have added a touch of mystery to lives of the great and near great. Indeed, premonitions are part and parcel of superstition, a power that used to rule destinies in older times. If there was any truth to it, what was it, and how did premonition fit into psychic occurrences?

We were still in Moscow when we requested that a meeting in Leningrad with Kasatkin become part of our official itinerary. We told the Novosti Press Agency that we had heard back home of a man who collected dreams. Others collected stamps, coins, ashtrays, we told our hosts glibly, but this Kasatkin was a dream collector, who saved lives by interpreting the meaning of the dreams.

Yuri, our methodical guide who was sitting in on the meeting at the Novosti Press Agency, nodded and glanced at his boss, Vladimir Makhotin, as if saying, "May I speak up, please?" Makhotin nodded approval, and Yuri cleared his throat. "This is true, Vladimir Aleksandrovich," he said cautiously. "There have been articles about Kasatkin. A quite remarkable man."

Yuri was told to look into the matter and to determine whether a meeting with Dr. Kasatkin could be arranged during our Leningrad stay. As in all other cases, there was no promise of success. In all fairness to our hosts, they never took advantage of us. But they'd leave themselves an out and use it when necessary. When they could produce, however—following all sorts of secret manipulations on certain occasions—they usually did. When they failed, we took over and tried to accomplish it on our own, but we never rubbed it in. In fact, we made a point of thanking them for their help on each and every occasion, even when they had nothing to do with our getting to a subject.

"Dr. Kasatkin," Yuri said when we left the meeting, "operates a kind of dream laboratory based on the premise that people who have certain dreams appear to be susceptible to certain illnesses. Trust me, I'll do my best to arrange the meeting."

We had been in Leningrad several days when one morning Yuri knocked on the door. "Good news," he said with that meek smile of his. "Dr. Kasatkin is coming over today to see you. May I use your car to pick him up?"

He never took our chauffeur-driven car—the one we had ordered via Intourist to be at our disposal every day of our stay in the Soviet Union—unless we gave special permission.

"It's *your* car as much as ours," we kept telling him. Yet the next day he'd still ask permission. He could never get used to a chauffeur-driven automobile that could be his for the asking.

"You are picking him up at his home, and what then?"

"I'll bring him back to the hotel. You'll join us and we'll go on to the Novosti office."

As planned, we were back later that day in the familiar surroundings of the huge, ground-floor Novosti office in a quayside former palazzo facing the broad majestic Neva River. The office was again empty save for a woman secretary who guided us through lifeless, ornate, high-ceilinged rooms to the big conference room with the blue-and-gold ornamental window drapes.

"We might as well make ourselves comfortable," Kasatkin said, settling into what could have been a geniune early nineteenth century armchair. He grinned, a bit self-consciously. He was a stocky man with the broad shoulders of a football player. His light blue eyes and sand-colored hair over a low, furrowed forehead seemed to indicate a north Russian origin. We hit it off the moment we met in the lobby of the Astoria Hotel, and we kept up an animated conversation in the car all the way down to the Novosti office.

"Isn't my city beautiful?" he said at one point as we rolled along the quayside. Pastel-colored palazzos—pink, light blue, light green, yellow—clearly outlined against the pale sky, dotted the opposite side of the Neva. "It is," we agreed. Then as we passed a broad, gray stone baroque bridge that reminded us of the Seine and Paris, he said proudly, "Did you know that Leningrad sits on 101 islands and has no less than 350 bridges, one more beautiful than the other?

We continued to chat as we set up our tape recorders in the Novosti office. One of us, Henry Gris, brought up the subject of the Leningrad siege and told him that while Kasatkin was attending to the wounded and sick, Gris was picking up the voice of the beleaguered city on radio monitors in High Barnet outside London.

With the London Bureau of UPI at the time, Gris was head of a radio monitoring service and managed to pick up the only and ostensibly secret link left open between Moscow and Leningrad, a radio telephone. He eavesdropped on conversations—as did, presumably, the enemy—but concentrated on the war news and communiqués dictated by Moscow to the only Leningrad newspaper still functioning. Minus power, the presses practically hand-cranked, its editors needed the news much earlier than their Moscow counterparts to be able to have the paper out in the shelled streets by morning.

"I never knew you could hear us in London," Kasatkin said. "I got to use this line once—for a coded message allegedly talking to my grandmother."

"You *all* talked to grandmother," Gris recalled. "I wonder if the Nazis ever got wise to it."

"Probably not," Kasatkin said good-naturedly. The horrors of war were far back in the dim past.

"Now," he said, his bulging briefcase on a chair by his side, "we will talk about dreams, all right? You see," sounding just a shade apologetic, "I have devoted my entire life to dreams. I first became interested in dreams while still a student in medical school but it was during the blockade, under

Nazi fire, that I became so totally involved. I think dreams, I eat dreams, I sleep dreams, I live dreams. But above anything else I interpret dreams. I now have no doubt in my mind that this new method of diagnosis, dream interpretation, will revolutionize medicine."

There was a remarkable calm about him, a feeling of scientific conviction that gave him self-assurance, as he went on: "I have now recorded and analyzed 17,300 dreams after interviewing 1,360 people. This total breaks down into 1,150 sick, 148 people in good health, 49 blind, and 13 deaf mutes. The sick included 391 suffering from various psychoses, 365 with tumors or other problems of the brain, 80 suffering from neuroses, and 314 with illnesses of somatic and other origin. I have also completed a study of 260 basic cases, each presented in drawings depicting the actual dream.

"We have found that patients who are unable to describe their dreams to us find that they can identify with the drawings, relate to the one that is like the dream they had, point to it. Forgotten after awakening, it now returns to their conscious mind and offers us invaluable clues. It's almost like those books of photos of criminals at the police station. You call them mug shots, you say? Whatever you call them, the truth of the matter is that a dream, especially a nightmare, is like one of them—a criminal caught just in time. So, looking back, I may say that I have done what I set out to do during those grim days of the blockade, promising that I would keep searching for the answer if I was spared. I have kept my promise—to God."

A gentle smile crossed his quiet, craggy face. Yes, he was a religious man all right, he seemed to say, and he had no intention of keeping it a secret. Among the many Soviet scientists we interviewed, Kasatkin was not the only man displaying for the record his belief in a Superior Being. It almost seemed that believing in God and probing into the mysteries of the universe by high intellectual minds went hand in hand: religion based on science, rather than superstition. Kasatkin is now head of a scientific group conducting dream interpretation research at the Neurological Surgical Institute in Leningrad. A professor of medical sciences, he also regularly visits clinics, hospitals, and medical institutes throughout the USSR to analyze the dreams of sick people. "It is very clear," he continued, "that dreams are sentries watching over our health while we sleep. They play a very important defensive role. Different illnesses show clearly defined brain patterns."

He started to undo the binders of the bundle of manila files he carried with him. "Brain tumors, mental illness, diseases of the heart, lung, and stomach, are commonly depicted in dreams, from two weeks to a year before the person knows he is ill!

"We in this country have already saved many lives by using this method of dream interpretation. It can result in the diagnosis and treatment of serious illnesses long before they would be diagnosed in any other manner."

Individual dreams can give short-term warnings of minor illnesses, such as stomach upsets or headaches which anyone can self-diagnose. But the intensely serious Kasatkin urged: "See your doctor and give him full details of any dream that keeps recurring. Dreams that repeat themselves are the early warning signals of serious illnesses. Although the doctor may not be skilled at interpreting dreams, in many instances an explanation of a recurring dream will draw his attention to a particular area of the body that should be investigated medically."

Dreams of difficulty in breathing are a warning of TB or lung cancer. As evidence, Kasatkin showed us file after file containing the actual case histories of people he had personally examined. There was, for instance, the woman student at the Medical Institute who told him of the recurring dream in which she saw herself lying down naked on the raw earth. Suddenly, the earth underneath her settled down, forming a wide crack. This woman described how she sank into the crack in the slow motion we all see in our own dreams. Then the earth started coming back in on her body, pressing her rib cage so that she had difficulty breathing. Night after night she had the same dream, invariably waking up in a cold sweat. And day after day, she became weaker, sicker. Finally, she went to a medical center.

Two months after the dreams began, doctors diagnosed that she had contracted tuberculosis. Her dreams of the earth pressing in on her rib cage and constricting her breathing had been warning of tuberculosis crippling her lungs!

Another woman tuberculosis patient got the same warning in a slightly different way. Repeatedly, she dreamed that she was crawling through a narrow passage. It would gradually close in on her, until she was completely stuck, her chest area pressured beyond all endurance. At this point she would wake up sweating, and feeling very uneasy.

Such dream "early warning" signals can occur as early as two weeks before a heart attack, up to a year or more before mental illness. Kasatkin has found that most "repeat dreams" start a month or more before the patient begins to feel symptoms.

In doctors' lexicons all over the world, hypertension is a serious illness that is very hard to diagnose in its early stages. But in our dreams, Kasatkin found that we have early warning signals, with images related to fear and anxiety forecasting serious hypertension: "I had as a patient an engineer, quite a famous man who had been in charge of constructing many buildings in Leningrad. He was already in a hospital, immobilized by hypertension. But in my research, he told me an amazing story.

"Three months before he was hospitalized, he started having very unpleasant dreams connected with building. One recurring dream showed that he was on the site of a tall building that was constructed according to his plan. As the engineer watched in his dream, the building started to sway. He could see cracks in the walls. Suddenly, while still asleep, he was overcome with a terrible feeling of anxiety. He was going to be made responsible for the bad structure! Then suddenly the building collapsed and he was buried underneath. His head and chest were covered with the earth and rubble that he had ordered to be made into a building. There was no escape.

"At this point, he would waken and lie in bed, overcome with a terrible feeling of fear, still feeling as if there was a terrible weight on his heart. Night after night the same dream disturbed his sleep, although he was not consciously worrying about his work. None of his buildings ever did collapse. But *he* did! We had to send him to a hospital with an acute case of hypertension." Kasatkin looked at us sternly. "Three months before he collapsed, this man was warned that he was going to be seriously ill! How much better for him if he had recognized the symptoms then."

It was obvious that Dr. Kasatkin really believed in all this, with all his heart and mind. He was devoted to his research, convinced he could help people—like the 19-year-old student who started dreaming of flunking his exams at the University. In his dreams his fellow students passed, and he was left behind. He had a terrible feeling of despair, believing he was unable to do the most simple assignments, even though he knew that his previous record proved him an above-average student. He would waken in the middle of the night, alarmed and concerned about the coming day's university work. Gradually, this dream changed to yet another: He had never been a sailor, yet he began to dream that he was aboard a ship in a stormy sea. When the ship foundered on a rock, he was thrown into the waves—and he could feel himself drowning. At this point, he always woke up.

This sequence of dreams began in December. By April of the following year, doctors and psychiatrists were treating him for extreme neuroses. Yet dream doctors, told of the symptoms when they occurred, could have made an instant diagnosis.

Dreams can even forecast when you will commit murder. Kasatkin's casebook contains two incredibly documented cases of convicted killers.

A Leningrad chauffeur started dreaming that a girl friend of his wife was trying to poison him. Night after night, he saw himself nearly die from the poison—then go out, take a metal pipe, and beat the woman to death.

One year after he started having this dream, without really knowing why, he set out to do just that. As the woman approached his home to visit his wife, he walked out to the street and struck her repeatedly on the head with a metal pipe. She was dead before anyone could intervene.

"The dream didn't make him do it," Kasatkin stressed. "It was only warning him of what lay ahead. Nor was anyone trying to poison him. The man was diagnosed as a paranoid schizophrenic, and he is now in a mental hospital where he'll probably remain for the rest of his life. But the murder could have been prevented if he had reported the dream to a properly trained doctor."

Two years before Andrei Krylov carried out three burglaries and killed two people, he started dreaming about World War II. He was taken prisoner and his life was threatened. Voices in the dream told him he must kill to save himself. He followed his orders. He dreamed he killed one person, then while fleeing he ran into a huge bog in which there were more people. Thinking the bog would draw him in, he felt panic-stricken and struck out in all directions. He ran and ran, but always behind him there was a huge dog trying to catch him and kill him. He always woke up before the dog caught him.

Then in real life, Krylov started to drink, so that he would not have the recurring dream when he went to sleep. To get the money that would allow him to drink, he committed two burglaries. During his third break-in, two years after he had first dreamed of killing to escape, he was caught in the act. As he fled the home, he killed a young girl, then her father. Just as in his dream, neighbors' dogs followed him over fields, and one huge wolfhound eventually cornered him against a high stone wall. He was not touched by the dog, but with the terrible dream now so fresh in his mind, he lay helplessly crying. The villagers arrested him. Krylov is now in a mental institution.

Falling over a precipice usually indicates arteriosclerosis. However, a 43-year-old patient of Kasatkin's began dreaming that he was falling over a precipice, only to float down onto a surgical table. Within seconds, he was surrounded by gowned surgeons who started cutting open his head. Two months after he started having the dreams, he was on a real surgical table— with surgeons fighting to save him from a blood clot on the brain. The patient survived his ordeal, but had he gone to doctors when he first started having the dream, his life might never have been in danger.

There are literally thousands of other incredible cases in Kasatkin's files. A blond man started dreaming he had five heads, all covered with black hair. As he watched in his dream, the five heads shook as if in sorrow for him. Five months later the man was being treated for brain damage suffered in a minor sports accident he had dismissed as being of no importance.

For a long period of time, a university student dreamed that a python had wrapped itself around his body. He could not move his chest nor his arms or legs. The student felt he was ill, and went to his doctor. But he never told the doctor of his dreams, and the physician could find nothing wrong. One year after his dreams began, he was in the hospital. Surgeons found a tumor on his spine that threatened him with paralysis and possible death.

Some other repeated dreams commonly indicate serious illness ahead. Being wounded in the chest indicates an approaching heart attack. A stomach wound tells of stomach cancer or kidney trouble developing. Difficulty in walking warns of a spinal tumor. Difficulty in talking tells of danger from Parkinson's disease. But being *unable* to talk indicates a growing brain tumor—as do dreams that show facial distortions or tight or unusual head gear. There was the case of the man who kept dreaming that his wife was wearing a tight headband. Although his wife never wore headbands and he tried to reject the thought, he dreamed the same thing night after night. The warning was for him, not for her. Within months, he was under psychiatric care for a serious brain disorder.

Although dreams may be about someone else, they invariably are related to *your* own health. A doctor started dreaming about a patient who came to him for eye treatment. In the dream, the patient's eyelids and eyeballs were red, and the eyeballs protruded. Eventually the patient's left eye closed completely, and started to weep. As the dreams progressed, the doctor could see tears dripping from the affected eye. But it was the doctor himself who, weeks later, found that day by day he was going blind and ended up under an eye surgeon's knife.

Kasatkin showed us the documented case of a 56-year-old medical doctor who, night after night, dreamed that he was watching out of the medical center window when he saw one of his young patients being attacked by robbers. He rushed out into the street to help, but there was nothing he could do. The patient was lying on the street, his head covered with blood. He had a long wound across his stomach, and next to him, detached from his body, was his right kidney.

Alarmed by his dreams, the doctor began to watch over his patients as they left the medical center in the evening. He was concerned for their safety. Although his dreams recurred, none of his patients were attacked. Instead, one day he collapsed in his office. His life was saved only after surgeons removed a badly infected right kidney!

Nowadays Kasatkin's expertise in dreams is also used in the Leningrad court system, where suspects facing serious charges often feign mental illness and blame their crimes on dream voices or visions. By questioning them on what they saw or heard, he can easily determine whether they are lying—and his evidence is accepted by the courts.

Kasatkin's research has also turned up some very interesting facts for the law-abiding population. Only three percent of dreams have voices in them. Women have two percent more dreams than men. People who are blind from birth do not dream, but people who become blind still "see" dreams. Dreams become less colorful the older you get, and people with low intelligence sleep better and have fewer dreams. Although the research Dr. Kasatkin is conducting is obviously yet another Soviet effort to probe the limitless boundaries of the human mind, he himself believes there is nothing mysterious about it. "One has to remember that the sensitivity of the outer layer of the brain is very high, much higher than that of any other part of the brain," he postulates. "I call it the dream band. It is a thick skin around the brain, with about sixteen million nerve cells.

"We have found that the pain centers inside the brain do not pick up deviations as quickly as the cells on the outer layer. During sleep, when other abrasive elements are dormant—tight shoes are not causing pain in your feet, bright sunlight is not causing headaches or pain in your eyes—the outer layer takes over. Its more sensitive cells monitor what is happening in your mind and body and react to the minutest deviation from normal conditions. The danger, then, is registered in these outer layers. It becomes a vivid dream as you sleep, indirectly issuing an early warning of coming illness. Different areas of the 'dream band' handle specific illnesses."

Single dreams which warn of stomach trouble or headaches are usually the result of environmental conditions, such as a stuffy room, too much to eat or drink, or too much noise. Even happy dreams can warn of oncoming illness. For instance, alcoholics often dream of parties and happy meetings with friends. Once they are cured of alcoholism, these dreams stop. But most pleasant dreams that repeat themselves are invariably indications that your body and mind are in good health. Kasatkin, a healthy man, said he always has pleasant dreams, unless he is overtired, has had a few drinks, or becomes overexcited before going to bed.

"The dream reports of wounds in the body are among the most serious, for they invariably indicate a very dangerous illness, such as cancer, liver or kidney trouble, or heart disease. Repeatedly dreaming about being forced to eat bad food can also indicate serious stomach ailments, such as intestinal cancer."

However, your occupation or upbringing is reflected in the dream warning. For example, a military man might dream he had been shot in the head. A housewife might dream of a very tight-fitting hat. And a sportsman might dream of being hit on the head with a bat or ball. But all three would be getting the same warning—in this instance a developing brain tumor.

"The frequently reported dream of a wound in the chest area, which indicates heart trouble and a heart attack in the not-so-distant future, is often described by military men as a sword wound or a bullet wound," Kasatkin told us, "while a housewife will say it was caused by a kitchen knife." Partly for this reason, he warned that ordinary people should not try to diagnose their ailment from their dreams. "Dreams do clearly indicate ahead of time that you are about to become ill, and pinpoint the particular part of the body that is affected. But it is then up to the doctor to examine you with all the means at his disposal and make a proper diagnosis."

Repeat dreams continue through the illness, but disappear or change to pleasant dreams when the patient is treated and cured. For example, people who have unwittingly become addicted to drugs through medicines prescribed by their doctors frequently report recurring dreams of searching all over town for something—they rarely know quite what—but not being able to find it. When they are cured of their addiction, these dreams disappear. At present, Kasatkin is working with other doctors throughout the Soviet Union to categorize dreams more thoroughly, with the ultimate aim of formulating a dream warning system that all doctors can use. They are currently consolidating and coordinating the information they get on dreams from other doctors. There are many variations of dreams, and they want to tabulate and index all of them before the system goes into general use.

It means a lot of work, because every reported dream must be carefully compared to the patient's medical history. But Kasatkin already uses the dream method to predict and diagnose illness in patients in his visits to hospitals, clinics, or patient's homes. When a doctor tells him that a patient is reporting a recurrent dream, Kasatkin elicits the full dream information and diagnoses from that alone. During lectures, many people have told him of repeat dreams, and he has been able to diagnose ailments for which they had no physical symptoms.

"We have saved many lives by our dream interpretation," he said. He didn't even try to drive home his point. His facts spoke for themselves. He collected his folders and was up on his feet when we suddenly remembered.

"Dr. Kasatkin, you haven't mentioned premonitions. Yet this interests us very much indeed."

He smiled. "Premonitions interest me very much, too." He sat down again. "You mean dreams that come true. '*Veshchye sny*,' we call them. Russian mythology, Russian history, and Russian literature are chock-full of such incidents.

"Our famous Dr. Ivan Petrovich Pavlov once told students of a dream he experienced. He saw his son coming home from the war, although they had not heard from him for many months. When he awoke, he said to his wife, 'My dear, you had better set a samovar up, because our Volodya is coming home.' And sure enough, his soldier son arrived, exactly as in the dream.

" 'What is your conclusion, students?' he asked us. There was silence in the lecture hall. 'Well, I guess we've yet to find out,' he said with a big smile. 'And seeing that *veshchye sny* have been guiding us for thousands of years, a few more years won't hurt.'

"I suppose I'll reply to you in the words of Dr. Pavlov. I have looked into the subject. I'm fascinated by it. I've considered the odds of coincidence—which are not that great—as well as its being a psychic phenomenon of sorts. Perhaps when we are asleep, a telepathic communication reaches our subconscious, rather than our conscious mind.

"I consider subconscious telepathy quite a possibility, but we have no facts at this time to prove it. On the other hand, I admit I've turned it over in my mind many times. Except that at this point I am more concerned with dreams that save lives than with dreams that carry news. Remember to ask me about it again on your next trip."

18.
POLIKLINIKA NO. 26
Hypnotherapy for Children

We had already spent a week in Leningrad, a city of melancholy and faded grandeur that once made it the Venice of the North. We were rather pleased with our stay because things seemed to be moving faster here for us. The interviews were coming more or less on schedule, which in itself was quite an accomplishment.

Yuri Shevyakov of Novosti was hard at work making calls, shuttling our subjects back and forth, and making sure we kept busy—in line with our claim that in America we interview at least two important people a day. He didn't believe us, but was determined to prove that if you try hard enough, you can have the same efficiency in the Soviet Union. He kept in touch with his Moscow office to brief his bosses on our progress. Out of sight, we were not out of their minds.

It was morning when we set out across the Neva River, its black water edged in a lace of ice. Poliklinika No. 26, Zhdanov Region, Russia's famous "hypnosis haven" for children, was all the way up the Kirovsky Prospekt, a straight, busy thoroughfare in the less attractive section of an island city. The Zhdanov Region, the workers' Leningrad, was devoid of frills, its prevailing color gray.

On our previous visits to Russia we had toured various hospitals, especially cancer treatment facilities. Some, like the giant Blokhin Institute outside Poliklinika No. 26 did not stand out among the monotone of the many others, with their crowded corridors, their walls peeling, the uneven floors, covered with cracked linoleum, were distinctly oppressive. On the outside, Poliklinika Number 26 did not stand out among the monotone of the bland fronts along Engels Street. Yet the world inside the gray shell was distinctly friendly and cheerful. Even as we stepped inside the door, the old lady outside the cloakroom smiled at us. A passing orderly in white grinned at us. Even the women standing around the lobby faced with pretty ceramic tile—obviously mothers who had delivered their children and were settling down to wait for them—smiled at us.

The tall man who greeted us at the entrance must have stood there quite a while to be at the door when we arrived. He too smiled and thrust out his hand. "Welcome," he said in Russian. Yuri stepped in to make the introductions. The man was Dr. Vilen Garbuzov, head of the Department of Treatment of Neuroses in Children.

Would we follow him, he said, looking somewhat uneasy. He was getting straight down to business, without the niceties which might be misunderstood by a visitor from a non-communist world. He had his instructions: give the best impression—good, solid Soviet efficiency.

Garbuzov was no different from other Soviet scientists who on earlier occasions had similarly met us at the door of their special work domain, be it a hospital or laboratory, and we had long developed a foolproof way of how to handle them: the old, time-tested "kill'em with kindness" technique, tinged with a little helplessness and translated into simple, colloquial Russian. "We'd rather not rush, Vilen Isakovich," we told Garbuzov, "seeing that we're a bit tired . . ." The patronym always worked; as did the appeal for sympathy with two overworked newspapermen. "We'll just make it a pleasant little visit if this is all right with you, and you tell us as much as you can." He grinned, relieved. In another ten minutes, we knew, the information we sought would freely flow.

As he led us down a hallway, its light-blue walls hung with colorful pictures denoting Russian fairy tales, he said proudly: "We're a bit unusual, you know." He was referring to the work done at his Poliklinika, but also, obviously, to the framed pictures on the walls. "*Very* unusual," Yuri said approvingly. He recognized scenes from what must have been favorite stories of his childhood and he beamed with delight. We didn't have the heart to tell him that such pictures were nothing new in American children's hospitals. But then, in Yuri's austere world they stood out like a breath of fresh air.

Garbuzov swung open a typical wide hospital door. Behind it was his office. A group of men and women in white rose from their chairs. "Meet my staff," Garbuzov said cheerfully. "There are seven of us. Seven doctors." We shook hands, polite to the extreme—which, too, is a feature of a first Soviet encounter. Names were exchanged, to pass by our ears. As they stood around us, Garbuzov, who unlike the others wore a business suit, explained their functions. He was very much at ease now and beginning to enjoy his role. Each of his doctors, he said, handled from 40 to 50 children at one time. This was the regular quota. They did not go beyond that. Each saw up to 20 children on any day. The treatments prescribed after the initial examination called for children to report once, twice, or three times a week depending on the case. Hypnosis cases—and the bulk of them were just that—called for trances lasting from 15 to 30 minutes. The children mainly came from schools all over Leningrad, but some were from other parts of the Soviet Union. Only the out-of-towners were kept overnight, in a special ward. The others were outpatients—hence the definition policlinic.

We now had time to check on the number of doctors he had introduced—six. No matter how we counted, we could not make seven. "You must wonder who is missing," Garbuzov said, ending the suspense. "Let me take you to her. I want you to meet our 'miracle woman' and her star pupil." Thrusting open the door, nodding at the others as if saying, "You may now continue as you were," he hurried us up a stairway and down a long corridor.

Behind a desk in a practically bare office sat a woman in white, her pleasant pensive face framed with black hair. Her desk was in a far corner. She winked at us as if to say, "Come on in, but watch this." By the side of the desk sat a little boy wearing dark sweater and pants, his neatly trimmed hair carefully combed onto his forehead. His eyes, big and round, glowed with excitement. They had been waiting for us, this was quite evident. The woman nodded, and the boy jumped up, and stood rigidly to attention. Then, with obvious effort, but also with just as obvious pride of accomplishment, he intoned: "I am Vasya Vasilevich." Joyfully, he enunciated every syllable.

For most 11-year-old boys, this would have been a simple enough statement, but for Vasya it was a giant step forward. And for a moment after he said it, his face broke into a shy little smile. His reward was a motherly hug from the woman beside him, Dr. Aleksandra Chernopolskaya. Vasya had just passed an important test. For five years, before being treated by Dr. Cherno-polskaya, Vasya had not uttered a word—not even to his two brothers, or his anxious parents in his home town of Alma-Ata, in Central Asia. He *had* talked, although with a slight stammer, until he was six years old. Suddenly, one day, it seemed he had been stricken dumb.

His parents took him to doctors: there was no reason the boy should not talk. His vocal chords were perfectly normal. A battery of psychiatrists examined him, but could find no mental problems and, hampered by his refusal to speak, could not find the cause of his silence.

His mother, a teacher, tried everything from threats to rewards to get him to speak. All her efforts met failure. His father, a medical researcher, phoned and wrote friends in various medical disciplines all over the Soviet Union. But their well-meaning suggestions proved worthless. Vasya, who was physically strong and healthy, continued to turn inwards, shunning people as much as possible, refusing to play with other children, acknowledging his parents' attention with only a slight nod of his head. At school he fell far behind the learning standards of children his age because he would not speak to them or the teacher. His future looked very grim.

Then one day, his father received a letter from a friend in Moscow. "I hear great things about the policlinic in Leningrad which is helping children overcome such problems through hypnosis. You should try them." Boris Vasilevich placed a call to Polyklinica No. 26 in Leningrad, spoke to the director, Dr. Garbuzov, and explained the problem. He was told to send the clinic all medical records and information. Within three months, the answer came back: "Yes—we think we can help. Send Vasya to us."

The 2,400-mile trip from Alma-Ata to Leningrad was no obstacle. Within days, the boy and his mother reported to Garbuzov. After a battery of medical and psychiatric tests that confirmed previous examinations—showing the boy was physically well and mentally fit—Vasya was placed in the hands of Dr. Chernopolskaya. She put Vasya into a hypnotic trance and with careful questioning unlocked the secrets of his mind.

We settled into a sofa. Vasya sat erect beside the doctor's desk, as she told us the story behind his inability to speak. "When Vasya was six, he was very conscious of his speech impediment. It caused him to stammer whenever he got excited. One day, a group of bigger boys, hearing his talk, surrounded him and taunted him unmercifully. Vasya broke down in tears. Something snapped in his mind. Then and there, he resolved he would never risk talking again. And he didn't, until he was brought here."

After three sessions, in which he was induced to wipe the memory of the taunting from his mind, Vasya made a first attempt at issuing the sound of speech. Two more sessions, and help from speech therapists in the logopedics class of the policlinic, brought him to the point where he would say short phrases to Dr. Chernopolskaya—but only to her. She had won his confidence. During the next two hypnotic sessions, he was prompted to have confidence in himself and in the clarity of his speech. Only four weeks of treatment from Dr. Chernopolskaya brought him to the proud moment when he was willing to talk to us. This was a big test for the new Vasya. If he could meet and talk to two total strangers, he could meet and talk to anyone.

"He is an intelligent boy, but his reaction to the taunting could have ruined his whole life. If it were not for hypnosis, we could never have found out," Dr. Chernopolskaya confided, clasping her hands together on top of the desk almost as if in thanks. A plump, likable woman, her hair carefully coiffured, she was not at all formal-looking, even in her spotlessly clean white hospital smock. It was easy to see how her warmth and frequent smile could win the hearts and confidences of troubled little children like Vasya.

She rumpled his hair in a gesture of love. "Vasya will stay with us for two more months. By then, his future will be secure. We will give him further hypnotic treatments and ensure that his mind has the strength to ignore any taunts he may face in the future. By that time, of course, we hope that we will be able to have him talking without a stammer. We still have not found the cause of the stammer, which unquestionably dates back to another mentally troubling incident in his early childhood. But we will. Perhaps one day Vasya, grown into a handsome man, will come to pay us a visit. That is something to look forward to."

The little boy nodded and flashed a self-conscious grin. As we stood up, Vasya jumped to his feet, thrust out his hand, and said firmly, "Goodbye." It was only the fifth word he had spoken in the half-hour we had spent in the room. But again, it was a major accomplishment for him—and for Dr. Chernopolskaya. "Had you met him only a few weeks ago," she shook her head, "you would not think he was the same child. The knowledge that he can again talk, to anyone, has made him ten feet tall."

We were walking unhurriedly down a corridor with more pictures from Russian fairy tales on the walls.

"Stammering is a problem we have to deal with frequently," Dr. Chernopolskaya said. "We usually put the child under hypnosis for fifteen minutes. Sometimes we will also discover that a stammer is brought on by a certain situation—like asking for something in a shop, or talking to a teacher. Usually, there is something in the past that has caused this. We will also put in his mind that he must forget that incident. Then we try to convince the child of a certain idea we want him to accept as his own. For instance, we place in his subconscious that he must not be afraid to speak any more. That he should speak slowly and freely. That his speech is not different from that of any other child. The message that gets through to him is simple. 'You are absolutely normal. You have clear speech. You will sound just like any other child.' When the child comes out of the trance, these thoughts are left in his subconscious.

"When you say you have cured a person of stammering, most people dismiss it lightly. But most people don't realize what havoc stuttering or stammering can wreak in a child's mind. Children growing to adulthood may be effected forever, often becoming introverted. Their relationships with other people will suffer, and their brooding may directly cause physical illnesses. Their subsequent suitability for jobs for which they would have otherwise been qualified is seriously affected. It is an illness of great importance.

"Let me tell you the story of Anna, a 19-year-old girl who recently came back to us because her stammer had recurred. Anna first came to us when she was fifteen. She had been stammering for years, but it had reached such a peak that she could hardly make herself understood. In a hypnotic trance, she told us that it had been caused by seeing her parents have a bitter fight, in which her father beat up her mother. The parents subsequently made up their differences, but they had harmed a very sensitive child—apparently irrevocably.

"We managed to remove her stammer under hypnosis, and returned the girl to her home speaking perfectly normally. Anna went on to become a top student and was doing well at college, when suddenly we got a letter asking if we could help her again—her stammer was worse than ever. Waiving the rule that we don't treat anyone over seventeen, we said we would try. Anna was like a daughter to all of us here. When she arrived, we put her into a trance and quickly found out what had happened.

"She had grown into a very beautiful girl, and at college found herself vying with her roommate for the favors of the school's handsome young track star. Anna had won his heart when it happened. Her roommate, who had known her for many years, was upset over the loss of an admirer, and when she ran into Anna and the boy strolling arm-in-arm together, she screamed, 'You are nothing but an old stutterer,' and struck out, tearing at Anna's dress. The shock of hearing this, and the embarrassment over an old secret coming out into the open in front of her boyfriend, were too much for Anna. Back in her room, sobbing, she found herself stammering helplessly every bit as badly as before. Her boyfriend assured her it didn't matter to him; he still loved her. But the mind had reacted and the girl needed our help. Isn't the mind a strange machine!"

It took six intensive hypnotic sessions to restore Anna's confidence in her speech, and to build within her a defense that would nullify the effect of ever again being called an "old stutterer."

"Anna has just written me to say she has now become engaged to the boy," Dr. Chernopolskaya concluded. "Isn't that wonderful?"

A familiar figure met us as we turned a corner. It was Dr. Garbuzov, eager to show us more. We wandered on, the four of us, Garbuzov elaborating en route on the cases treated at the Poliklinika.

Children suffering from neurotic diseases, such as bed-wetting, asthma, and phobias, he said, were sent to Poliklinika 26 only after all else had failed. "This is the only such center in the Soviet Union," Dr. Garbuzov stressed. "Our job is to succeed, to give children a normal life, when there seems no hope. Hypnosis is a powerful tool in accomplishing this. However, it is only part of the treatment. We also use advanced medical treatment, psychology, and good common sense."

Dr. Chernopolskaya nodded. "We always study the children's personalities, intellectual capacities, aspirations and general outlook. We study the history of the person, the history of the family, the history of the illness. How do the children relate to other people? Are they extroverted or introverted? Who is the dominant parent? The answers can give important clues as to what is troubling the child. We do a very complicated series of analyses before starting treatments."

"There is always a reason for the neurosis," Garbuzov nodded in agreement, "and in most cases it lies at home. When a child is brought to us, we have a staff here who do nothing but examine the home conditions. Has the child been mistreated by the parents, or older brothers or sisters? Do the parents fight? Do they drink? Do they neglect the child or, like so many ambitious parents, exert undue pressures, particularly to do better at school or in sports?

"There is no point in our trying to effect a cure if these conditions continue to exist. So, first we must deal with them. It may be that the parents themselves need to undergo psychiatric treatment. In some extreme cases, we place the child in a residential school so that he is not influenced by a bad family environment and can be treated by skilled sociologists.

"We check to see if the child is suffering from 'growing pains'— actual deficiencies caused by his growing up. These can bring about complicating factors, such as susceptibility to colds and headaches. We look for actual physical deficiencies that might worry the child, and try to put them right. The child may have a blemish, or a badly shaped finger or toenail, which in his mind becomes a serious matter. We try to put that right."

It might be any combination of these causes, or just one, that results in the child's problems. They use hypnotic therapy only after they have examined all these areas and found no reason for the neurosis—or if the neurosis continued when the problem had ostensibly been removed.

"By using hypnosis, we are not dealing with the disease itself, but with the symptoms. Our cases mainly involve bronchial asthma, skin deficiencies, certain forms of eye tic or speech impediments. We can start with children as young as two and a half, but the average beginning age is normally seven years. What is important is that the children can follow instructions. They must understand what you are saying, the directions you are giving while they are in a trance, and be able to retain these instructions in their memories and carry them out once they are brought back to a normal state."

We were passing the open door of what seemed to be an empty room, when Garbuzov stopped us. "You have to see this place. Austere, yet effective. This, in fact, is where it all happens; our hypnosis room."

Lining the walls of the room, which were painted in a muted off-white, were seven neat single beds. Each had a light blanket folded on top of the boxed white sheet and an inclined top end to make a comfortable head-rest. Garbuzov said, looking rather proud, that the room was deliberately quite small to give it the cozy, relaxed atmosphere needed to get the best results in hypnosis. The beds were close together so that younger children particularly could have a brother, sister, or little friend lie beside them to help allay their nervousness when they are treated.

"Say, for instance, a very young child is suffering from an eye tic. We can find no reason for it. It is something in the child's mind. For the first time, certainly, we would try to get the child to be accompanied by an older brother or sister so that he would have confidence, or we would put him in a group with children the same age."

Dimmer switches control the lights so that the room can be darkened at will. In one corner, a record player stands ready. "Older children can be put into a trance through the eyes, by staring at them while swinging an interesting object. But younger children must be put to sleep by talking to them, while playing soothing music in the background.

"The idea is to get a feeling of isolation, peace, and quiet without frightening the child," Garbuzov explained. "We lower the lights, transmit to the children the feeling that they must rest. We must get them into the condition where we can still reach their minds, where they can still listen to us so that the suggestion will penetrate and be retained. That allows us to put in their minds a great deal of new information."

In other cases, the children are put into deeper hypnosis. "It enables us to obtain greater isolation, a greater degree of receptiveness in the children," Chernopolskaya said. "There is a much greater rapport between the children and the doctor, and we can reach into their subconscious."

In this condition, the children may tell the doctor what they may have been afraid to say when they were awake. This can give the doctors clues to problems that even their most exhaustive probes have overlooked, such as troublesome dreams—or incidents that happened years before, too insignificant to be recalled by anyone except the children, and yet over the years, distorted into memories which are so dreadfully frightening that lives can be ruined.

"For example, we had one boy who, although he had no impediment, no stammer, was absolutely afraid to speak. When he saw a group of people together, something seemed to steal his voice away. Under hypnosis, we found that this was caused by fear, stemming from an incident when he was three. His mother was walking him along the street, when a car crashed into another right in front of them, catching fire. Immediately, people rushed from all over to try to free the people inside. There was shouting, confusion, bursting flames. The little boy was shocked and frightened. He then connected this disaster with *any* group of people he saw after that, and the fear completely took his voice away. While some of us smoothed out his memory with hypnosis, and implanted new confidence in him, other members of our staff took him to events where there were happy crowds—soccer games, the circus—all the time inducing him to talk more and more."

By now, we had returned to Garbuzov's office. An orderly brought refreshments, and tea was poured.

What was their most memorable case? Garbuzov was asked. He did not hesitate. "A 16-year-old girl was brought to us with a terrible case of eczema that particularly affected her legs and arms. She was very conscious of it and had become very emotional, sobbing at the slightest, often imagined, setback. She was tormented by the itching skin, which made her very bad-tempered. She lost all her friends. In fact, she reached the stage where she did not want anyone around her. She even talked about killing herself. No medical treatment could help.

"I placed her under hypnosis. It took several sessions to discover that the cause of her illness dated back to an experience when she was ten years old in which an old man, horribly scarred by the war or an accident, had attacked her. She escaped unharmed and told no one about the incident, but under hypnosis, she vividly recalled the scaly scars on the man's face and arms—it seemed that at some time the man must have been badly burned. The horrible memory was tucked away in the dark recesses of her mind, gradually surfacing over the years in the shape of the disfiguring eczema."

The way he spoke, Garbuzov obviously had a well-organized mind. Words flowed from him in logical sequence, a newspaperman's dream. "During the hypnosis," he went on, "she also revealed her secret dream—that one day she would join the other teenagers at the beach on the Gulf of Finland, her skin clear of the ugly disease. She had refused all offers to go to the beach because she felt people would be repelled by her. But she desperately wanted to go—it was the most important desire in her life, linked as it was with getting rid of the eczema.

"So first, I induced her to wipe out the memory of the scaly old man. Next, I instilled the confidence that soon her skin would be normal. Lastly I placed in her mind: 'The second Sunday in July this year, you will go to the beach with your friends. You will get a wonderful suntan, because you will be wearing the very latest style of bathing suit. You'll be a very big hit with the boys. Your skin will be absolutely clean. Remember, this will happen on the second Sunday in July.'

"When she awoke from the trance, she of course had no recollection of what I had said. I repeated the treatment and suggestions over several other hypnotic sessions, and gradually her skin did start to clear up.

"I lost track of her for a while, but I was amazed that on the second Monday in July, I received a call from her. 'Dr. Garbuzov, you won't believe this, but yesterday I went to the beach for the very first time—and no one laughed. My skin was as good as anyone's. I lay in the sun for hours. Now I am tanned, instead of being covered by those ugly red sores.'

"Somehow, the mind had retained the suggestion I had implanted a full three months earlier. It got rid of the eczema and even induced her to go to the beach on the exact day I forecast! I am very proud of that achievement."

With bed-wetting, after finding the mental cause, he and the other doctors will often just tell the child under hypnosis: "You will not do this. You will come back to me in seven days' time, and you will not have wet your bed. It is easy." It is surprising how often this approach works—particularly if the causative problem has first been resolved.

Learning disorders, such as difficulty in reading or writing, usually are caused by a hidden subconscious fear, and these too can be readily cured under hypnosis. The children are told how they can improve their memory, and the benefits they can achieve by being able to read and write. Another typical situation dealt with successfully is children whose fear of school causes them to get sick in the morning, subconsciously hoping they will not have to attend classes. Hypnosis is used to tell them how much fun they can have at school, and how much they really like it.

A logopedics class was in session across the hallway. "It's important that you see it," Garbuzov said. It was a typical classroom, its walls hung with charts, rows of school benches facing away from the door toward a blackboard where a young teacher was enunciating the vowels of the Russian alphabet. A group speech-defect-elimination session was in progress.

The youngsters, who aged from nine to sixteen, seemed slightly embarrassed as we were introduced. But they could talk, and they did not hesitate to chorus a welcome. We asked them if they liked the hypnosis room we had just visited. A tall 15-year-old boy, acting as spokesman, answered, "That is our favorite class."

We had no time to question them further. Dr. Garbuzov glanced at his watch and announced, "You have already met Dr. Zakharov, but I want you to see him in his natural environment. His is different again."

Indeed it was! "As you can see," the young doctor said, expressively waving his hands at the toys scattered all around his office, "I like the children to feel at home when they're here. I don't want them to think of it as a doctor's office, because it is difficult for them to relax in that atmosphere. I want them to think of this as more of a playground, where they have met a new friend—me."

Dr. Aleksandr Zakharov, a slight, mod-dressed doctor with a small, neatly trimmed beard and moustache, is known at Poliklinika No. 26 as the "puppet man." Although a skilled hypnotist whose expressive face and piercing eyes appeared to go well with his profession he generally deals with younger children who are often not as receptive to hypnotic suggestions.

"Younger children are difficult to deal with, but the challenge is even greater," he said, dashing from behind his desk to remove some toys from chairs to allow us to sit down. "I have successfully treated children as young as two years with hypnosis, but most children of that age cannot follow your instructions or tell you what is troubling them." Zakharov likes to get to the bottom of their troubles by acting out scenarios with hand puppets, which are piled in one corner of his playroom/office, or by analyzing their drawings and paintings, examples of which decorate the walls. "I let the child just play for a while with the toys and the puppets, while I talk to the parents. All the time, I am carefully watching the child's reactions to certain features of the toys, for often that can be a clue to something that is troubling him."

Zakharov moved to the corner, selected a couple of puppets, and put them on his hands. "I suggest a little game. Everyone takes a hand puppet, but for the fun of it, we'll change roles. The child plays the father; the father the mother; the mother the child. Then I tell the child to enact what he sees when father arrives home from work, and I tell the others to act out their respective roles."

Sometimes, to find out even more, Zakharov will join in the role-playing. He may pretend to be an older brother or a grandparent living with the family. "With careful observation, particularly of the child's actions, I can usually tell what is wrong within three to four sessions." By cleverly throwing out questions, constructing certain situations, playing out a carefully planned role, he can find minute cracks in the family structure—a fact of life, perhaps, to adults, but incredibly devastating to young children. "I see the husband beating the wife or the wife scolding the husband, with the child, at the center of everything, suffering great mental trauma. Often, this 'play' reveals to the parents conflicts that they did not even realize. It shows emotional conduct, the secrets and fears of not only the child, but the whole family. In particular, it can tell me how the child fits into the family; sometimes, it can be even as innocent and simple as the child being overprotected and pampered—a 'mother's boy,' for example. Or it can be that the child is being pushed ahead too far and fast; or that he resents the father being so close to his mother.

"Every one of these things can cause emotional stress and scars that are reflected in the child by bed-wetting, eye tics, stuttering, and medically inexplicable illnesses. The hand puppet acts can tell us all."

The toys and puppets are particularly useful in detecting hidden phobias. "Although we don't realize it, many young children are very afraid of simple things—toy mice, horses, cows, bears, wolves, engines, cars, or people in different uniforms—because of something they have seen, over-heard, been told about, or dreamed. Fear builds up in their minds until it shows itself physically," Zakharov explained.

He flicked open a folder. "Here is an example I dealt with earlier this year. A 4-year-old girl, Nadya, was brought to me with a most unusual complaint. Every night for weeks, the little girl, although still asleep, would let out the most ear-piercing, terrified shrieks. I heard tape recordings of the sounds, and they were really frightening. Often she was so deeply in sleep that her mother could not waken her to stop the screaming, which could go on for as long as half an hour. Although this did not seem to have any affect on the child's health, it was badly affecting the parents, who lived in a small apartment.

"It was a very puzzling case. There was absolutely no medical reason for the child's screaming, and her home environment was excellent. But when the child was brought to my room, I quickly got a clue. As little Nadya played with the toys, I noticed that she had a great aversion to a wolf doll. Although it was dressed in human clothes and didn't look fearsome, the child kept away from it, kept glancing at it fearfully. At one point when another toy she'd thrown knocked the wolf doll forward, she cringed backward."

As he spoke, Zakharov, with facial expressions and hand gestures, colorfully re-enacted the drama. It was easy to see why children would find him friendly and amusing. But his face grew serious as he continued: "With the parents' permission, I put the little girl into a hypnotic trance. I questioned her simply and carefully. It turned out that she had once dreamed of running through deep snow pursued by a pack of snarling wolves. She fell, and she saw the pack leader, a huge wolf with blood dripping from his teeth, begin to tear her apart. The dream probably was the result of seeing an oversensationalized drawing of a wolf attacking a person. Anyway, although Nadya did not remember the dream while awake and told no one about it, the haunting memory that she was being eaten by the wolf came back when she fell asleep. Night after night, the full terror flooded her mind, and she screamed uncontrollably.

"It was a question of building great confidence in the child's mind. But I felt it would be very difficult to erase such a strong memory. Since it *was* so firmly implanted in her mind, much better, I thought, to take it and devise a happier ending. I did so, inducing Nadya to believe that when she fell down, her hand grasped a big stick. She got to her feet, and beat the wolf so badly, he ran off, leaving her untouched and taking the rest of the pack with him.

"The treatment worked. After five hypnotic sessions, the little girl stopped screaming in the night, and I noticed that when she came into my room after the third treatment, she beat the living daylights out of the toy wolf in the corner!"

Zakharov has found that getting a child to draw in color what is in his or her mind is another invaluable way to see the conflict affecting the child, a great aid to later hypnotic treatment.

If the child draws a house on fire, for instance, Zakharov invariably knows there is trouble at home. If the child draws a house in serene surroundings, with smiling people, he knows he must look elsewhere for the trouble. When a child paints his mother red, Zakharov takes it as an indication that the child knows the mother is filled with anxieties, and this may be causing his emotional problem.

Back in his office Garbuzov summed it all up for us: the overall results were excellent. In 50 percent of the cases, the cure was swift and complete. In another 25 percent of cases, there was marked improvement. In

15 percent, there was moderate improvement. In only 10 percent was there complete failure.

"The ratio of failure is gradually diminishing," he said simply. "I can't determine how soon—if ever—we'll have reached a point of complete success, but let me say we are working on it. We like to think that the children's troubles are over when they discover faith in themselves, but it isn't all that simple. It is still up to us to guide them out of the darkness and into the light.

"What you have seen today is an experimental center where new theories, new philosophies, new methods are tested and formulated, not just for ourselves but for the benefit of similar clinics throughout the Soviet Union. This way, then, our cases become textbook cases. And with a vast network of clinics from here to as far as Vladivostok on the Pacific beginning to emulate our work, our responsibility is obvious: we cannot afford to be wrong. A Vasya Vasilevich is multiplied a thousandfold, as is an Anna, little Nadya; all the children you saw today.

"As for us seven," he grinned, "think of us as multiplied also, into a vast army of psychotherapists who have specialized in redirecting and readjusting the mind of a troubled child. It may be a limited segment of human life that has come under our study, but it's the beginning stage of *Homo sapiens*. And to understand him, you do have to start from Square One."

19.

HYPNOTHERAPY FOR ADULTS:
The Leningrad Hypnotarium

The following day, our meeting with Professor Pavel Bul was a lucky break. We had arrived in Leningrad with other subjects on our list, but Dr. Nikolai Kozyrev, the astrophysicist, our scheduled interview, was sick with the flu and sent his regrets. Yuri felt he would be letting us down if he didn't promptly find a replacement. Joining in our enthusiasm over the visit to the Poliklinika he mentioned that he had heard of the famous Leningrad hypnotist, Bul.

"I am told he has cured victims of serious illnesses, drug addicts and chronic alcoholics, all by simply healing their minds under hypnosis. Bul is incredible. Yet he is not a touch-by-hand healer, a faith healer, or any other miracle man, but a scientist whose methods are copied by other hypnologists all over the Soviet Union."

Because of our newfound interest in hypnosis, he would be the perfect substitute. We went along with Yuri. He said he'd see what he could do. Although we knew he had our interests at heart and we had learned from experience to respect his judgment, we double-checked anyway. We called Dr. Kasatkin, the dream man who had made such an impression on us. Kasatkin was at home.

"By all means talk to Dr. Bul," he said approvingly. "But make sure he doesn't put you under a hypnotic spell. He's certainly better at it than your Mesmer was in his day, or Braid in his." He obviously meant Franz Mesmer, who "mesmerized" Paris society in the 1770's, and James Braid, the Scottish physician who coined the name "hypnosis" half a century later.

The next morning, Yuri told us a meeting had been arranged for that evening. At 6:30 P.M. he appeared at the bedroom doorway and reminded us of our appointment.

We had expected the image of a Soviet Svengali—a pair of penetrating, magnetic eyes in a dark, compelling face commanding one to sleep at the count of three. However, as we shook hands in the lobby of the Astoria Hotel, Professor Pavel Ignatyevich Bul turned out to be nothing like that. On the short side and roly-poly, he looked scholarly and at first a bit withdrawn. He was wearing a good-looking if old-fashioned business suit that seemed to point up his professional status. His voice was soft, friendly, his manner delightfully polite. We walked together to the restaurant.

The maître d'hôtel was waiting for us at the door to direct us to our table. On an elevated tier, protected by a railing, it had a commanding view of the restaurant.

"The best in the house!" the maître d'hôtel announced proudly, skillfully picking up our folded five-ruble bill and making it disappear in thin air. The dining room of the Astoria Hotel was literally rocking under the feet of couples stomping to the music of a blaring Russian dance band. The women, most of them heavy-boned and big-bosomed, were latching onto their men, who ranged from burly to spindly, all wearing the same stoic expression and ill-fitting square-shouldered suits. There were many rich Georgian profiteers from the Caucasus out on the town with their women. Who could mistake their swarthy faces and bedroom eyes? And the young Finns, out on a weekend of boozing across the border, were easily spotted by their long blond hair, light blue eyes, and craggy faces. The band was playing old Russian folk songs and ballads transposed to a rock beat.

"Why don't you sit here?" We pointed at a chair facing the audience, and Bul sat down, slightly bewildered by the unfamiliar scenery. He looked around, enthralled by what he saw. His eyes, under a high, receding forehead, had a warm glow. He looked even more professorial now. With him he had brought a bulging briefcase that he placed under his chair. Bul shook his head and said something, but the noise drowned him out. He tried again, louder, "I don't get to see much of this! Fascinating!" As we struggled to speak, getting nowhere, he seemed to enjoy the adventure.

Still, in these circumstances our interview was doomed, and after a while we gave up struggling, to concentrate on Hotel Astoria's *pièce de résistance*, chicken à la Kiev and *petit pois* in miniature baskets of baked dough. Bul was enjoying his meal and the white Abkhazian wine, and we even managed to exchange a few thoughts with the help of lip-reading and animated guessing. He had brought a book for us to take home, a relatively new monography on hypnosis he had written.

Just then the band stopped abruptly, and the musicians left their instruments and marched out for a long-overdue recess. The crowd on the dance floor wandered off in all directions, and suddenly the place was ridiculously quiet. We looked at the Professor, his mouth still open after an unfinished sentence. He smacked his lips shut, registered mock surprise, then said, "At last we can talk!" obviously enjoying being able to hear the sound of his own voice again.

As he laughed, we became aware of a gold tooth that made him even less like Svengali. "We'll have to meet again, though," he added, "maybe tomorrow, and not here."

We looked at Yuri, who nodded: "No problem." He turned to the Professor: "Leave it to me, Pavel Ignatyevich."

So this is how we met Professor Bul of the Pavlov Medical Institute, the Leningrad hypnologist and noted neurologist. What we report is based on the half-hour the Astoria dance band so generously let us have and the quiet meeting with Bul upstairs the following day.

If Russian scientists dedicated to psychiatry and psychotherapy have wandered off into areas foreign to us in the West, it's probably because of a rift that took place as far back as the late nineteenth century when Sigmund

Freud created a method for treating mental disorders which he named psychoanalysis—and which Russian scientists of the time refused to accept as gospel. The break came then and there, long before Imperial Russia became Soviet Russia, all because of Freud. What is now the Western world sided with him and set up a vast network of psychiatrists trained in psychoanalysis. The Russians categorically rejected Freud's concept of the existence of infantile sexuality and the role of sexuality as the origin of neuroses. At the turn of the century, Russian neurologists and psychologists, including the world-famous Ivan Pavlov and Vladimir Bekhterev, stated that Freud's theory of infantile sexual complexes was nothing but that—a theory.

"Down through thirty years of work with hypnosis, in all those thousands of cases I have helped by getting to the root of the problem, sexual childhood memories or guilt complexes took up no more than 15 percent, if that," said Bul.

For the record, the brilliantly pragmatic Pavlov was able to determine the speed thoughts travel within the human brain—100 to 150 meters per second, depending on the person measured. As Pavlov, the theoretician of the "conditional reflex," put it, "When I think of Freud and myself, I see two teams of workmen cutting a tunnel through the base of a mountain —the mountain of human psyche. The difference between us is that Freud struck out in a downward direction and got lost in a maze of the subconscious, while we came out into the daylight. By studying irradiation and ascertaining how brakes work within the human brain, we were able accurately to follow a nerve impulse to the section of the brain it has to trigger, to see how long it stays there and when exactly it returns to its starting point, while Freud is still brilliantly guessing about the inner condition of man."

His contemporary, Bekhterev, preached the need to apply pure and uncluttered hypnosis to medicine in Russia until the day he died in 1927, leaving a son and subsequently a granddaughter to head the world-famous Leningrad Brain Center. When Pavlov died in 1936, their pupils, A. G. Ivanov-Smolensky, V. E. Rozhnov, K. I. Platonov, and I. V. Strelchuk, all brilliant scholars, took up where the two giants had left off.

Whether the original root of the split was a personal feud or a genuine and deep divergence of concept, now, seventy years after the first international congress of psychoanalysis presided over by Freud, Russia still rejects psychoanalysis. In its place, Russian scientists have concentrated on what they call rational therapy—the psychotherapist rationalizing with his patient—and "suggestive psychotherapy" which covers every type of hypnosis from auto-suggestion to collective deep-sleep, or mass hypnosis.

They have carried research of hypnotherapy through many stages, working on new methods, widening the scope of its application from psychiatric problems to cardiovascular disturbances to pulmonary diseases to obstetrics and gynecological problems. It is even used as a substitute for anaesthetics—the list seems inexhaustible. Hypnosis is currently widely used by thousands of trained psychotherapists throughout the country. A children's clinic using hypnosis as its main tool such as Poliklinika 26, is, however outstanding, the forerunner of many. The work is done in general hospitals and neurological institutes throughout the country where "hypnotariums"—hypnotherapy treatment rooms—are a latest addition. Moscow was first, followed by Leningrad, Kiev, and Minsk. But Moscow is still the only city with a training center for doctors specializing in hypnotherapy. They, then, are hypnologists of the highest order, an elite that knows the secrets of making the human mind obey. When the Leningrad center opens next, the man who will head it will undoubtedly be Professor Pavel Bul.

Until this happens, though, Bul remains the master of the Pavlov Medical Institute, Leningrad's "hypnotarium" where hundreds of patients are treated using Bul's methods. Among *his* case histories were the following:

A young woman was dying of malnutrition, her esophagus blocked, not by an obstruction—there was none—but by her having convinced herself that she, like her mother, was suffering from stomach cancer. She had watched her mother waste away, unable to swallow the smallest morsel of food. One year after the death of her mother, the daughter, taken to a hospital, was put on intravenous feeding. Unless she was able to swallow again, she would remain in a hospital bed, attached to a catheter for the rest of her days.

Told about the case, Bul requested that the young woman be taken off the intravenous tube and be transferred by ambulance to a ward at the Pavlov Medical Institute. Within an hour of the transfer she was in a special room, being hypnotized. At the end of the first session she was taken to a ward where she took some liquids, her first nourishment in months. She was on her way to full recovery. Hypnosis had virtually saved her life.

A diabetic man was brought to the Pavlov Medical Institute after he ceased to respond to insulin. Doctors who had treated him at a different hospital gave up on him after a special diabetic diet had similarly failed to affect the sugar in his blood. Conventional medicine, having exhausted all known means to save his life, could go no further.

Questioned under hypnosis, the man admitted a number of emotional causes that had undermined his health. Earlier his wife had left him, taking their children with her. He had recently lost a brother. The man had nothing left to live for.

He was given hypnotherapy. With each session, the overpowering thirst and hunger that had caused him physical suffering diminished and were gradually brought under control. After ten treatments, all traces of sugar in his blood and urine were gone. He was sent home proclaimed cured. Checkups as late as two years later showed no recurrence of diabetes. The man has been restored to a healthy way of life and has remarried. His wife is expecting a child.

Another diabetic, a 47-year-old actress, suffered from an acute case of sugarless diabetes expressed an unquenchable thirst and hunger. At the time she was brought in to the Institute, she was consuming twenty glasses of water and an average of eight pounds of food a day, including three pounds of bread. It was a compulsive desire she could not control, nor could conventional medicine help her.

Under hypnosis, she described a series of mishaps that caused her heavy emotional trauma. It all started when she fell backstage, suffering bad cuts on her head and face. The scars on her head healed, but her face was so deformed that the theater refused to let her resume her work on the stage. Humiliated, refusing to accept a compounded punishment for sins she had not committed, she took to eating. It didn't do anything for her. Growing despondent, because by now she was not only ugly but big and fat, she left her husband and children and attempted suicide.

It was at this point that she was brought to the Institute, a hopeless case, and placed under hypnotic treatments. After four such sessions, her thirst was satisfied by only ten glasses of water a day and she consumed half the daily amount of food she needed when brought in. After ten sessions she was declared cured of diabetes. Her food and liquid intake were normal.

Now the second stage began. After two further sessions, she approached Bul with the request to recommend to her a plastic surgeon who could restore her face to normal. She didn't realize that actually she was following a command given her under hypnosis. She told Bul she felt confident plastic surgery would bring her old beauty back. The actress was subsequently discharged and assigned to a plastic surgeon to follow up on her case. In a letter Bul received from her a year later she reported she was back happily with her family. Plastic surgery proved a success. She was called back by the theater, and resumed her acting career—even though, for the time being, in supporting roles.

A woman suffering from bronchial asthma was declared incurable by conventional methods after many years of hospital treatment. She was sent to the Pavlov Institute for a last try. Under hypnosis, the woman told what had happened. A letter telling her that her sister and all her family had died in the disasterous Ashkhabad earthquake deeply shocked her. Left alone, unable to cope, she went into severe depression. Taken to a psychiatric hospital, she was discharged two months later. But the first night at home she had an asthma attack. Waking up short of breath and feeling she was suffocating, she was forced to sit up the rest of the night. This was how her nightmare began. She was treated repeatedly, but to no avail.

Placed in a ward at the Institute alongside other asthmatic patients, the woman started hypnotic treatments. After only five sessions the attending physicians saw slight improvement—a lessening of her coughing spasms and less constriction of the chest. After twenty hypnotic treatments she was breathing quite normally and spent quiet nights. But in all, it took forty sessions before it was felt she could live comfortably away from medical supervision. Sent home, she has been returning for annual checkups, and now, six years later, has had no relapses.

Bul anticipated our question: "What did I tell her under hypnosis? What did I tell the girl with the blocked esophagus? Basically I tell all of them that they can get rid of what is troubling them—if they try hard enough. Day after day, week after week, 'You are coming along well, you are feeling better, you are winning your battle.' I told the girl her esophagus was free because she did not have stomach cancer, and just to try a little food and see what happens. I told the diabetics that they didn't have diabetes, to trust me. I told the woman with bronchial asthma that she could free herself from the constriction. She would have fewer and fewer attacks. She would not be affected by outside elements that had bothered and worried her such as smells, heat, humidity, barometric pressure; that she would not become upset by bad news. 'It's going to be better, it's going to be better.' "

His brow furrowed as he emphasized: "We attack the very source of one's trouble in the deep recesses of the human mind as it is being tortured by something, mostly subconsciously. What is this something? Bring it out into the light and examine it, and half our battle is won then and there."

Not that hypnosis is an answer to all ills, a cure-all, "It is not. Whenever illness destroys nerve tissues, hypnotherapy is as helpless as conventional medicine. However, many months after the initial damage was done, other nerve centers may substitute and take over the administration of the afflicted area. It is then that near-normal and even normal functioning may resume, as is the case with some forms of stroke. Cases where hypnotherapy has performed with 100 percent effectiveness deal with functional ailments brought on when nerve cells of the human brain failed under the weight of an overload and shut off."

What happens, according to Bul, resembles a circuit breaker in a home shutting off the electric current in a case of overloading, thereby preventing a fire or an explosion. The house is now dark and, in the case of the nerve cells shutting themselves off, will remain dark until something is done. After a period of rest and subsequent treatment, the nerve cells spring into action, in turn relieving the patient of attendant physiological problems that had been triggered by the original malfunction.

What threw the "safety switch" that shut off the "juice"? In the case of the human machine, Bul reminded us, it was the brain, an incredible instrument that had delegated a separate function to each of its 14 billion nerve cells. It applied functional brakes at the clusters of cells—called nerve centers—which were affected by an emotional upheaval. The function of the Russian hypnotherapist, then, is to make the subject recall this upheaval, the root of the problem, and then to determine the course of treatments. There is no single rule applicable to all.

As Bul described his "hypnotarium" to us, it's a separate, soundproof ward making up a series of hermetically sealable rooms of all sizes—from individual treatment rooms to group therapy rooms, where patients are put on beds lined up in single rows and subjected to hypnosis at the same time, either by man or machine.

The machine in this case is a monitor with a video cassette that "plays" Dr. Bul's admonition to sleep. It apparently works as effectively as if he were in the room, provided the patients watch the monitor closely. It is placed so that all of them can view it simultaneously from a lying down position. After the patients are asleep the tape recorder takes over. The hypnotic suggestion emanates from a loudspeaker. This method obviously applies to treatments of patients with a common denominator. But it also means that hypnosis can be packaged and sent to wherever it can be put to use, particularly hospitals lacking trained hypnological personnel.

Bul produced from his breast pocket a shining metal rod with a miniature hammerhead. His "medicine man's magic wand," he called it, the rod he used mostly to get his subjects to fall asleep. He gave it an indulgent look. "I am not sure this thing has already opened for me all the doors to the human mind I would like to see open," he said pensively. "In fact, I am certain this thing knows much more than it has told me. Hypnology is still terribly young."

Even so, Bul has most impressive figures and facts applicable to his own operation within the last year. Of 132 patients suffering from debilitating Basedow's disease—also known as an exophthalmic goiter—106 were cured totally without surgery. The rest are still being treated. Of 160 outpatients—60 men and 100 women—suffering from extreme high blood pressure, 90 have completed treatments, another 60 will have completed treatments after two years. In all cases, marked reduction of blood pressure and a slower pulse were effected within two months of once-weekly visits to Bul's hypnotarium. The bulk of the patients had a history of emotional upheaval. Only 15 could not recall any, but still responded to treatments via a hypnotic "calming down." In one case, after a single hypnotic session, the pulse was brought down from 112 to 72 beats. Of 30 patients suffering from angina pectoris—repeated spasms of the heart—20 cases obtained a stable remission that is still in effect a year later. Five patients could not be helped: they resisted hypnosis and could not be put to sleep, which is typical of some five percent of all Dr. Bul's patients. Half the angina pectoris patients were taken off all medication, the remainder received reduced medication. In all instances, two months of hypnotherapy removed the prevailing fear of a fatal heart attack. Of 200 patients suffering from bronchial asthma, 180 were inpatients undergoing treatment in a specially constructed "barochamber"—a simulated sealed gondola of an aerial balloon. Treatments consisted of placing patients in the chamber and ostensibly taking them to higher altitudes with rarified air.

Actually, the asthma patients weren't going anywhere. All the changes were merely suggested to patients through a headphone. The hypnotherapist, speaking into a microphone, put the patients to sleep, then suggested barometric changes. To compensate for the resulting lack of oxygen, patients were told they would be fed pure oxygen through an oxygen mask they were to wear during the ascent.

In reality, of course, no oxygen was fed through the mask, and the pressure inside the barochamber remained normal. The objective of these treatments has been to bring the oxygen content in a patient's blood to a normal level and to keep it there. But as the patients were being observed and the oxygen in their blood measured, the hypnotic sessions showed changes in the oxygen content in their blood as they "inhaled" it. It was as though the oxygen, too, was obeying hypnosis. Bul is particularly proud of the baro-chamber treatment of asthmatic patients. "It works without fail, even though it takes longer in difficult cases. Of the 200 cases under observation, 22 were completed—the patients cured of asthma. Eighty-four have greatly improved. Nine-four are still under full treatment."

Possibly his most dramatic cases have been the five surgery patients who had to be taken off the operating table at the last minute because of excessively fast pulse—200 to 240 beats per minute. In three cases, operations had to be canceled four times. With Bul's help, all five cases were resolved to the operating surgeon's satisfaction. Called in to assist, he hypnotized the patient just before the operation—the anaesthetic notwithstanding. With the patient in a trance he then induced him to relax and bring his pulse down to normal. In all five cases, surgery was finally carried out when the patients' pulses registered between 100 and 110 beats per minute.

"We are particularly concerned with alcoholism in our country," Bul said, "and so, of late, hypnotherapy has been paying it increased attention. Our conclusion, however, is that we are not equipped to tackle alcoholism in Russia on the scale necessary to achieve important, lasting effect. Since our hospital facilities are inadequate to handle all the chronic drunks we could collect off our streets on any given day, we are thinking in terms of equipping police-station drunk tanks with tape recorder cassettes containing hypnotic treatments for alcoholics."

This lack of space has made Bul limit admission of chronic drunk cases to only such cases where treatment is imperative—as it became, for instance, in the case of one 40-year-old man who had attempted suicide while drunk. His neck was literally taken out of the noose.

"When dumped into our ward," Bul recounted matter-of-factly, "he had sobered up and was in a state of depression. He admitted that he had been a drunk since the age of eighteen, going on drunken binges lasting two and three weeks. We kept him under observation and gave him individual hypnotic treatments. After three such sessions in three days, his urge for alcohol was considerably reduced. After five it was gone. Simultaneously, he resumed eating normally—something he had not done in years—and his will to live returned. He was discharged. Six months later he came to see me to thank us. He had not touched alcohol in all this time, he reported. The smell alone made him physically sick. Three years later, he is still sober.

"Nevertheless, our own experience at the Institute with some 60 patients is not as impressive as the experimental handling of chronic alco-holics by my colleague, Dr. Ivan Vish. He has treated 760 cases and has kept them under surveillance after that for ten years. His patients included 696 men and 64 women. Of the total, 480 were treated as outpatients. All were given the same treatment—an induced revulsion against alcohol to include nausea at the mere smell of it. Dr. Vish found his treatments most effec-tive when he first put his patients through hypnosis then gave them several hours of additional sleep induced by the so-called 'electrosleep' machine—

high-frequency, low-voltage current fed through their bodies from electrodes at the temples."

Does hypnosis have a similar effect on drug addicts? Bul claimed a lack of experience with such cases; apparently Soviet Russia has been spared the drug blight—at least so far. Still, he has handled a few cases of drug addiction, and hypnosis did the trick in each case. "I remember a woman who was brought in as a morphine addict. She had been given morphine to alleviate lingering pains following an operation. She was shown how to use the needle, and before long she was an addict. Her husband reported that she had been giving herself at least four morphine injections a day while swallowing up to 20 tablets of Nembutal to help her sleep. When she was brought in, there wasn't much life left in her tortured body. We immediately started on hypnotherapy, and following five sessions, she was able to endure without morphine, taking only 5 Nembutal tablets a day.

"After the tenth session, by then up and around with some of her strength returned, she came to see me and voluntarily surrendered a morphine syringe and a box of ampules she had managed to smuggle into the hospital. Three weeks later she was home. Another year went by and she was back on morphine. This was caused by the tragic death of her daughter. However, she came back voluntarily. We put her through her hypnotic paces, inducing revulsion for morphine, and a week later she was discharged. She is well and happy at this point, two years later."

Bul treated one additional drug case—a 40-year-old cocaine user, who had started drinking at 16 and had been on "coke" since the age of 21. Sent to a psychiatric hospital at 27 and eventually cured, he resumed sniffing cocaine, and four years later was delivered to Bul as a last resort. "He was a wreck," Bul remembered, "written off as a lost cause. But we accepted the challenge and worked out a regime of medication plus hypnotic treatment. First week: hypnotherapy daily. Second week: every other day. Four more weeks: twice a week. He was then sent home in more or less stable condition, his hypnotic command being never to touch cocaine or drink. So far, one year later, there has been no recurrence."

Bul pondered a moment, then said: "We have helped obese people to shed pounds by inducing them to eat less and to exercise more. But I feel somehow that we have not done well enough. Our pattern of hypnotic cure for obesity has not yet fully crystallized. At this point we have as many failures as we have successes. We have done better with inveterate smokers getting many of them to stop. But there, too, we should improve. To be effective it takes eight to sixteen hypnotic sessions—much too long.

"Frigidity is a problem in Russia, brought on, I think, by the fact that many Russian women are rather prim—old fashioned, I suppose, by your standards—while most of our men, as you say, are 'with it.' Recently we've carried out a study of frigidity and worked out what we consider a successful technique. Luckily, it is easy to cure, since there we have definite symptoms of subconscious fear and repugnance, a lingering abhorrence that can be removed in a couple of hypnotic sessions. What do I tell them under hypnosis? Mostly, 'If you really love your husband, you must feel free to do anything.' "

A quick, self-conscious grin—women are not the only prudes in Soviet Russia. "And if your hair is falling out, don't despair," he said, changing the subject. "Human baldness, especially when affecting the scalp in places, has a traumatic origin, usually a forgotten but subconscious fright. The incident is brought out under hypnosis. The subject is then told that it was this and nothing to do with his hair itself that made him develop those bald spots. It takes us anywhere from four to ten sessions to convince the subject. Hair resumes growing almost immediately.

"We've even been effective in removing warts, especially with youngsters suffering from warts on their hands. We simply tell them under hypnosis that each and all of the warts we circle with a tweezer will fall off within one week. 'Bandage your hand and you'll see.' As they awaken, they ask that the hand be bandaged, which we do. And a week or two later, as a rule, the warts will actually have dried up. Our hocus-pocus in this case reminds me of the old Arab tribal doctors who have used similar tricks down through the ages. But then, we are not the first hypnotherapists. The ancient Greeks used it effectively three thousand years ago, and so has the tribal witch doctor in darkest Africa. Probably the only difference is that we know what it is, and they didn't. At least, we claim we know."

It was dark now outside our window and we switched on the table lamp. Yuri had been with us all through what we later referred to as our "Bul Session," he wanted to ensure we were comfortable in the little sitting room set aside for our interview, its window opening to St. Isaac's and a huge snow-covered square, with colored Intourist buses darting across it. Yuri made certain we were fed, ordering first lunch, then tea. In between he hung on to everything Bul was saying, grasping a copy of the book he was given in memory of our meeting. Published in 1974, Bul's *The Origins of Psychotherapy* contains much of what he had been telling us. We, too, had quickly glanced at our copies earlier in the day, and while we learned a lot from it, we felt shortchanged by the absence of personal data about the author. Somehow we had managed to talk through an entire day, and even then, we had merely scratched the surface.

We of course mentioned to him the reason for our trip to the Soviet Union, only to discover that Bul, not unlike other Russian scientists we met, was himself sitting on the fringes of parapsychology. He knew personally many of the parapsychologists we had interviewed—Sergeyev, Adamenko, Inyushin. "After all," he reminded us, "we are also concerned with the secret powers of the human mind, and the mystery of the human psyche. The human brain is the most fantastic of all tools on this Earth. We try to control it, and the parapsychologists try to harness it in a different way.

"Indeed, it is a matter of record that our parapsychologists have included hypnosis in their program, convinced that it is an important tool—essential to regression, for instance—and that one day soon hypnosis may be measured in physical terms. The question is, what sort of matter is involved?

Is it what parapsychologists call bio-energy?" He shook his head. "Frankly, this is out of my depth. I leave this subject to men like Professor Sergeyev to contemplate at leisure."

After Yuri took Bul home in our car, we phoned Sergeyev to say we had just spent a day with Bul. "Incredible," he called out. "Well done. Bul is a highly respected scientist, educated in Leningrad, one of Pavlov's brilliant young pupils. I call this an accomplishment. How did you do it?"

We told him about our aborted attempt at a dinner interview the night before. He laughed: "He felt he owed you this. He could not let you down. Dr. Bul is a gentleman." He was, Sergeyev insisted, an authority on hypnology without peer in the Soviet Union, or indeed the whole world. Correction: one peer. "We have two great hypnologists in this country," he said. "Bul in Leningrad and Raikov in Moscow."

We looked at each other feeling as though we had just scored a double bull's-eye. For the man next on our list, set for an interview as soon as the Red Arrow delivered us again to Moscow was—Dr. Vladimir Leonidovich Raikov.

20.

DR. VLADIMIR RAIKOV:
Releasing Talent in the Subconscious

Unlike Professor Pavel Bul, Dr. Vladimir Raikov, the noted Moscow expert on hypnosis, had been on our list. We knew of him from reports published in the West, and from the Moscow parapsychologists who heaped praise on the Moscow Medical Institute-educated scientist as an outstanding Soviet psychologist. In contrast to Bul who uses hypnosis to tend to the sick, Raikov, we were told only dealt with subjects sound in mind and body. What he did was develop new abilities and intelligence. Having collaborated with Viktor Adamenko in a series of advanced experiments, he was considered a near-convert to parapsychology.

We were told that Raikov would meet us at the Moscow Pedagogical Institute, rather than at his office at the Psychoneurological Clinic, where he works. It was all the same to us. Our driver knew where to go. We set out across the Moskva River and before long were deep into a maze of winding, lackluster streets and weather-beaten, aged brick or ash-colored buildings. The car came to a stop in front of a drab building devoid of all signs of life. "Here we are," the driver said.

"Are you sure?"

He shrugged. We got out. "Be back in two hours," we said grandly, not at all sure we liked the idea of being left in an utter emptiness all by ourselves. He nodded.

A single wooden door squeaked open. At least it wasn't locked. We wandered into a narrow empty hallway, and we continued up a steep wooden stairway. Were we in the right place? It was then that we caught sight of a man on the landing above us. Bespectacled, broad-shouldered, wearing a rough, brightly-patterned sweater, he didn't really fit into a place of pedagogical study: five o'clock shadow stubbled his round, jutting chin, and a carelessly swept-back mop of black hair added to a decidedly unacademic look. He was eyeing us amiably. We exchanged glances, and decided he must be the building superintendent.

"Are we in the right place?" we addressed him cautiously. "We are looking for Dr. Raikov."

The man grinned from ear to ear, and thrust out his hand. "I've been waiting for you. I am Raikov. Welcome."

We muttered words of embarrassment. We should have known better. He explained that the Institute was practically empty. The doorman was away, the wardrobe woman was missing, so he was waiting for us on the landing to pilot us in. "Anyway," he said, "follow me."

Several corridors later, up and down steps, we found ourselves entering a vast, empty, cold auditorium. Its ornate ceiling revealed the era of the building's construction—late Czarist or early Stalin.

In contrast to Raikov, the man greeting us at the door—as all Russian hosts like to do, resolved to wait endlessly for a tardy visitor—was dressed in an immaculate dark business suit, tie and all. He was Dr. Artur Petrovsky, Academician, director of the Institute, and a vice-president of the Soviet Psychological Society—also a professor. "And also," Raikov said jovially, "my boss."

He spoke the English word in Russian, a modern Soviet adaptation of a meaningful term. "I hope you'll be comfortable here," Petrovsky said, waving us into the huge auditorium.

There were rows upon rows of chairs, all empty save for two chairs midway on the extreme right, occupied by two plainly-dressed women. They looked lost in the vast emptiness, waiting to hear what was going to be said up front on the podium where, under a portrait of Lenin, a long table stretched the width of the hall. It could seat at least thirty people—the whole presidium of a Soviet labor union—but the chairs facing the hall were also empty.

"Follow me, please," Petrovsky requested and marched in the direction of the table, stopping briefly to whisper something to the women. Presumably, that this was not going to be a public lecture. But the women shook their heads and settled deeper into their chairs. Evidently, they had made up their minds not to budge. We went up the podium, Petrovsky showing us courteously to our seats in the middle section of the table, Raikov following, a playful grin on his face as if to say "we'd better do as the boss says." From the wings, two men in white smocks were already advancing with trays—the traditional Soviet cookies and pastry—while at the side of the table, a man and woman busied themselves with a samovar.

Raikov looked at us and grinned, he was ready. Foremost on our minds were the questions: Was it true he successfully regressed people into previous lives? And in doing so, had he proven reincarnation, as was reported?

"I expected you to ask me that," he said pleasantly. "I know that your press in the West has given me credit for being some sort of reincarnation expert. I am flattered, but it is not true. This is not what I am doing. As you would say it, reincarnation is not my bag, nor will it ever be."

He gave out a good natured chuckle. "I am a hypnotist pure and simple, and have, with the generous help of Professor Petrovsky here, conducted some experiments which we believe are of considerable scientific value. I do hope that you have not come all this way to see me prove reincarnation. . . ."

Just then, the refreshments reached our table and were laid out in front of us. As we sipped coffee and nibbled cookies, we assured Raikov we had guessed that much anyway: reincarnation was not the reason we wanted to see him. In fact, we suspected that he could indeed send people out of one "life" into another, and was denying it because of orders from above. An hour later we were convinced that although he was telling the truth, Dr. Vladimir Raikov of Moscow was certainly unique.

"We are not trying to find out whether a person has lived before," he stressed. "We use hypnosis to induce into the subject the character of another person that he will want to retain—at least for a while. He will use the qualities of the suggested person to improve his own abilities. To someone looking on, it will appear that the subject is trying to impersonate someone he is not. However, it is not just a surface effect. A much greater change has taken place inside his mind. We really do help a person improve his talents by making him believe, under hypnosis, that he is a famous painter, singer, pianist, or intellectual. But it is not regression into another life. I tell him he is that person, and he believes me, because under hypnosis he accepts what I tell him as the truth. If he has the right mental attitude, when he comes out of the trance he can still retain some of the desire and abilities of that person."

With that, he rose, went to a table beneath the podium and unwrapped several large packages. "Come here and let me explain," he called out. "Here are good examples of what we can achieve." We followed. The items emerging from the brown paper packages were framed paintings and pencil sketches. To our untrained but relatively discriminating eyes, they were rather well done. All were portraits of young women.

"These are excellent artists," we complimented him.

"Artists?" he grinned. "Would you believe that before hypnosis the people who did these had absolutely no training as artists, and displayed no talent to be artists? They learned these skills under hypnosis."

It was, indeed, difficult to believe. The results on the canvasses appeared professional. Yet with Petrovsky at our side nodding confirmation, we had to take him seriously.

"Look at this set of four paintings of a black-haired Madonna," Raikov said, a pleased expression on his face. "It is primitive to start with, but look at Number Four. Compare it with Number One. All were done by the same person. This painter, a girl, had no artistic training at all. I told her under hypnosis that she had the talent, and to try her hand at the easel which I had standing in the room. With each session she improved, and the final painting can compare favorably with the work of professionals. So during the hypnotic sessions—it took about three to complete each painting—her skill grew. She changed the facial expressions and hairstyle, but basically retained the same image. All the time, though, she improved, making each one better."

Raikov stood back to let us examine the paintings more closely. He was right. The paintings did show progression. They were good, particularly the last two. Another of his examples was the portrait of a blonde Nordic model, resembling Liv Ullman, the Norwegian film star, which an untrained pupil had drawn under hypnosis. Then he showed us the work of a medical nurse who also learned to paint during her hypnotic sessions. Responding to some unexplained powers that evolved under hypnosis, she had developed a rather unusual technique. Soviet art critics under orders not to allow "bourgeois decadence" to creep into Soviet art would have objected to it vehemently had she been a regular artist. The hypnotic state, evidently, absolved her of all responsibility, and so Raikov was free to exhibit it. The woman was in a trance when she painted the canvas he showed us, a psychedelic rendition of a girl's face.

Eventually, he said, observing the painting with the eye of an art connoisseur—she is an accomplished artist—she continued to produce paintings, not as daring, and is now accepted as a professional painter. Another of his students, a former engineer who had undergone extensive hypnotic training, ended up giving a one-man exhibition of his work at the prestigious House of Painters. He was promptly acclaimed as one of the country's promising new painters, on merit, although in all thirty-four years of his life he had never touched a paintbrush. And then there was little Volodya. . . .

Raikov chuckled at the mention of Volodya, Professor Petrovsky's 11-year-old son. A year or so ago, having worked together with high school children, they picked Volodya as a subject because his father always felt that Volodya had talent, but the boy steadfastly refused to even try. "We put Volodya under hypnosis, told him he could draw. He promptly agreed, and two sessions later he was busy drawing terribly talented cartoons. Amusingly, they were all of his father," Raikov grinned. Since then, Volodya has kept up drawing cartoons. They are good. And he likes it.

Raikov has convinced his subjects they are Repin, Levitan, Ayvazovsky, Serov—all internationally famous Russian painters whose works are hung in galleries around the world. He makes sure that a student is always introduced to the personality of a *dead* person, because he does not want to embarrass people who are alive. Some of the students, when introduced to the works of a famous painter while under hypnotic sleep, managed to copy the master's style down to the signature. Others, while emulating the artist's style, put down a wrong date—before or after the painter's lifetime—thereby unconsciously revealing that they knew little about the artist himself. "Interesting, but not significant," Raikov says, "since all we are trying to bring out in the subject is his latent talent. He can read up on the artist later."

While the students are in a trance, and there may be a whole group of them in what amounts to an odd art class, Raikov wanders around looking over their shoulders and giving advice. The students, wide awake of course, but convinced they are someone else, readily accept his suggestions. "They learn fast and well," he explained, "because their latent talent has now been mobilized to the full. Motivation is intensified through their feeling of responsibility to the famous name they think they carry, and there is an emotional uplift that causes sensitivity within them they didn't think they had before."

Professionals have come to him for help when they felt they were losing their touch. Raikov "recharged their tired batteries," as he puts it, and they resumed, their confidence restored. But painting is only one of the areas

Raikov uses to trigger talent and improve learning ability. He also works with linguists, chess players, inventors, and musicians.

Raikov once decided to try to help a young girl pianist who was to take part in the famous Chopin Prize competition, but whose performance suffered because of stage fright. "Remember," he told her, "that Rachmaninoff himself was badly affected by stage fright, and was actually cured by hypnotism." Shortly before she was due to go to the local conservatory to audition for selection as a representative of the Soviet Union, Raikov put her in a trance, telling her that she was a better pianist than anyone she would meet, that she was capable of giving perfect performances. Then she was brought out of the trance, and sent to the audition. She won first place, and was chosen to go to the finals in Paris.

"I feel that I removed her stage fright and gave her great confidence before the auditions," Raikov recounted. But by the time of the finals, this effect had worn off. She did not undergo hypnosis before the finals, and there lacking the confidence given her by Raikov she took only third place, behind two other Russian contestants whom she had beaten in the audition.

"I induce the thinking of a master like Rachmaninoff into the student's mind." Raikov went on after a brief pause. "It works, provided he has good knowledge of Rachmaninoff. I also hypnotize subjects into thinking they are the artist, then play them records while they are in a trance. I have them sit at a piano. They usually pick up the piece as they hear it and play it, beautifully, by ear."

As he makes recordings of this, his students later hear themselves play, often in total bewilderment over their newly-acquired skill. This in turn helps them to understand they *can* be better musicians and so, Raikov says confidently, they become better musicians. Hypnosis did its job. Overzealous pupils lose out with him though. One student, at his own request, was hypnotized into believing he was Tchaikovsky. He was asked, while in a trance, how he liked *The Moonlight Sonata.* He answered that he had written it, and it was one of his favorites. Raikov, who knew all too well that it was written by Beethoven, immediately brought the student out of the trance. "It would have served no good purpose to make him *be* Tchaikovsky if he didn't know the first thing about his music," Raikov said.

Chess, of course, is a great Soviet pastime, and one student asked Raikov to help him improve his game. The hypnotist introduced the student to the former Russian Grand Master Mikhail Tal. Awed at meeting someone of Tal's fame, the student could hardly talk. Raikov suggested the student play three games with the grand master.

Ruffled and fidgety, he sat down across the chess board from Tal and was soundly thrashed. In the second game, Tal again let him make the first move, and again the student fumbled to defeat. A third time, and he still showed no improvement. Then Raikov took the student into another room and hypnotized him. He induced him to think he was the late American champion Paul Morphy, then he led him back to where Tal was still seated at the chessboard.

Tal was amazed. "Before, he looked just what he was, a young man very unsure of himself. Now, under hypnosis, he strode across the room and sat down opposite me with all the authority of a champion player! It was a complete transformation." They played three more games. "Now he was expansive, brimming with energy and imagination, daring and at times brilliant. He was immeasurably better. He acted as if he really believed he was Morphy," Tal said afterwards. The grand master still won two games, but the hypnotized student managed to stalemate the third.

"Under hypnosis," Raikov is convinced, "a person's level of aspiration increases. He is sure he is capable of doing the work achieved by anyone else, Repin, Raphael or Rachmaninoff, or any other famous person you want to name."

In other words, the person under hypnosis forfeits his own personality. It is impossible to reassure him that he is not the famous person he has been induced to think he is. Once he has taken on that identity, his mind and knowledge are totally of that man and that period in time for the rest of that day. He wakes up in the morning not remembering anything but feeling strong, confident and generally invigorated. But while it lasts, the identification with the "other" person is total. Raikov convinced the people hypnotized that they were living in a previous century, that man can fly to the moon, speak across thousands of miles, travel in horseless carriages. They shook their heads in genuine disbelief. A person in hypnotic trance does not speak the language of the famous personality, but continues to speak Russian while thinking he is speaking in that person's tongue.

It all began twelve years ago. Raikov was still working as a psychiatrist in Moscow's Psychiatric Hospital No. 3 when he first applied hypnosis while treating mentally disturbed patients. Eventually he joined forces with Prof. Petrovsky, who was already a leading member of the Soviet Psychological Society. Together, they began to explore the possibility of improving minds of healthy people, something they theorized was possible with the help of hypnosis. The two have been conducting joint experiments using the facilities of a number of Moscow institutions, from hospitals and neurological clinics to, most recently, the Moscow Pedagogical Institute. They prefer the latter, since what they are after is improving the human mind—enlarging the mental capacity of the average person so it may be filled with new knowledge.

Raikov gives many lectures in colleges, telling his audiences that anyone who'd like to take part in his experiments may report to the Institute. Then the subjects are tested for mental abilities. However, 90 percent of the applicants are eventually rejected for reasons of mental incompatibility. Raikov prefers people who can go into a very deep hypnotic state and who believe in the effectiveness of hypnosis. Nowadays he puts them into a trance in two minutes flat. He has done hypnosis over television and radio, and by taped messages, something that can usefully augment his direct experiments. He told us how on one occasion, one of his subjects missed class, later reporting over the phone that he had the flu. "Relax and listen," Raikov told him. Then, while still on the phone, he put the pupil into a hypnotic trance and told him it was important that he be well by morning. In the morning, the subject phoned to say he was well and on his way.

While Raikov prefers to work with art students—all forms of art—Petrovsky has a definite preference for technical students. Their minds are trained to think in abstract terms, he says, and as such are good material to work with. He leaves manipulation of emotions to Raikov. His own experiments as described to us that day at the Moscow Pedagogical Institute have proven that hypnosis can, without a doubt, increase a subject's mental capacity many times.

"I'll give you several examples," Petrovsky said. "One type of our tests consists of placing a sheet of paper in front of the subject. On it are typed meaningless lines, a jumble of letters. First the subject is asked to cross out two letters, say S and T. He is given twenty lines, and five minutes to do it. Normally a person makes five or six errors. But when we induce the subject to think he is Einstein, he does it with 100 percent accuracy in half the time. Obviously, identifying with someone like Einstein mobilizes the entire mental potential he would not have put to work under 'normal' circumstances." Another student learned to memorize up to 200 words of a foreign language inside a single session. After that, thanks to his hypnotic experience, the same student was able to memorize up to 150 foreign words without hypnosis during every one of his subsequent lessons.

Occasionally, experiments in teaching foreign languages have led to amusing discoveries. A student of a technological college was induced into thinking he was an Englishman and was asked to memorize English words out of an English-Russian dictionary. Before hypnosis, he remembered 28 out of 50 new words. Under hypnosis, he was given 50 more words—but afterwards he remembered none of them! The experiment was repeated, with the same results. It turned out that his mind had become so *completely* English under hypnosis that he was not able to read the Cyrillic *Russian* words. Therefore, unable to read the meaning of the English word, he could not memorize it.

What hypnosis does, both men believe, is free a person's natural abilities. "It takes off the locks," Petrovsky said, "and it opens the doors of the mind. In childhood, everyone possesses a tremendous variety of talents which, at the time, can be brought out clearly and easily. But as the mind grows, the process of development is encumbered with processes of blocking, and even suppressing this potential. Hypnosis allows these natural abilities to be freed.

"As man grows, he learns to distribute his mental abilities in such a way that he can apply himself fully in one area while putting on the brakes in another. He deliberately blocks certain functions and abilities so he may concentrate on certain self-chosen assignments. Again hypnosis redistributes man's abilities—giving him the opportunity of fast and easy learning in areas that he had deliberately shut out while his own master. Not everyone can be brought to a high degree of accomplishment, but each one will definitely benefit. It only goes to show that the ability of taking pen and paper and drawing images is an ability that may be dormant, but exists in all of us. Three hundred years ago, our forefathers were doubting that everyone could read and write. Now no one has any doubt. Our experiments show that we have abilities far beyond our known knowledge, but the capacities of individuals is different.

"We do not exclude the possibility of the existence of a definite connection between hypnosis and the creative genius," Raikov interjected, adding, "we consider that hypnosis is a form of total creativity. Under hypnosis, man can have a completely new outlook and conception of things and the world."

Students remember nothing of actually being under hypnosis, except what they have learned. In other words, once brought out of the trance, they do not still think they are famous painters or musicians. But the creative doors remain unlocked. "We give them a push into creativity," Dr. Raikov said. "After the push, they continue to develop on their own."

People who really like and are interested in the hypnosis experiments find that this enhanced ability lasts indefinitely. But those who have had only a passing conviction of its effectiveness find that it quickly wears off. In any event there are no ill effects on their lives. In fact, as well as having their abilities in a specific field, such as painting, enhanced, the people sleep better and their memories, personalities, and dispositions improve. They have more interest in the world in general, better contact with their families, better relationships with their fellow workers.

"There is a tremendous future for hypnosis," Raikov added. "We still have to perfect our methods, and in fact publish our results in scientific publications. We have yet to establish a ceiling for human potential. We are really at a reconnoitering stage at the moment. But one area we will certainly be going into is the use of psychology in the hypnotic state. We need more experiments, but this could be a new science."

"At this point in time, we monitor changes in electrical impulses coming from the brain," Petrovsky revealed: "We do notice changes, under different induced conditions, but we have not yet systematized our findings. We are also conducting experiments that change the consciousness of the subject. Altering the consciousness is a brand-new area, of which we know very little. But we do know that sooner or later hypnosis will allow us to unlock the secrets of the mind."

"What else can hypnosis accomplish?" we asked. "Even if you had not yet perfected your techniques?"

"Knowledge could be capsulated," he replied. "Because you could learn anything faster under the influence of hypnosis. I also believe that we can get, say, a highly trained rocket engineer to project himself into the future and draw plans of what he might see. He will already have the basic knowledge of rocket design. Hypnosis merely opens the subconscious doors that allow his secret thoughts to emerge and be utilized to the fullest."

Now, Petrovsky explained why he had us come here. It was in this auditorium that Raikov had performed one of his most successful mass hypnosis experiments: 200 students made to believe they were someone else. Nothing like this, Petrovsky said proudly, had ever been done before. Raikov looked away, for once a bit self-conscious. "All in the service of science," he reflected. "I simply had to know if it could be done." We knew he could do it if he wanted to. In fact, we knew if he wanted to make us see this hall actually filled with non-existent people, he could do it!

For now, the auditorium was empty, save for the two women who still, two hours later, were stubbornly hanging on to their seats. Yet as the two men spoke, each complementing the other with additional observations on their experiments, we had the strange sensation of the hall in front of us filling with their students, young men and women, a vacant look on their faces. Taking their seats in those rows of empty chairs were would-be painters, musicians, chess grand masters, space engineers. . . .

Raikov, catching our thoughts, grinned. "No, I'm not going to hypnotize you into believing this auditorium is filled with people. I would not do it to guests like you." But he *did* read our minds, meaning he got a sort of telepathic message. The near-convert, we thought, was much closer to being a *bona fide* parapsychologist than he himself realized.

At the foot of the stairs, beyond the entrance door, our car was waiting. There is a certain awesome efficiency about Soviet travel arrangements. As we headed back to the Intourist Hotel in our black Volga, its wheels crunching in the crisp freshly fallen snow, we could not help thinking that the last two days' interviews dovetailed to give us a gripping awareness of the absolute power of one mind over another mind. It left us with the disquieting question of *why* the Russians are so interested in hypnosis.

Since Raikov, Petrovsky, Bul, and Garbuzov mentioned parapsychology in passing only, one easily surmised that it never figured in their training, was never mentioned in their textbooks. To be sure, Soviet parapsychologists have long adopted hypnosis as an extremely useful tool and are ready to enter it in their equations. But if hypnosis is actually being used in Russia on as enormous a scale as our informants indicated—and we had no reason to doubt them—then not only the sanction but also the encouragement had to have come from above. In a country like the Soviet Union, approval of anything *has* to come from the state, and there is only one primary consideration: defense. Translated, this means war. We could clearly see how those truly frightening aspects of hypnosis could fit military needs. Certainly they would justify the expense, the assignment of the manpower—in this case, a corps of scientists—to a specialized task that, in times of peace, would actually help people.

Bul had told us about the boxer who, worried about the outcome of his forthcoming bout, came to ask for help. Bul put the man in a hypnotic trance and told him not to be afraid, that he would be better than he ever was. Bul then told him he would lick his opponent, knocking him out with a series of vicious, destructive blows in the sixth round. Bul related the story with unconcealed pride. "It happened exactly the way he was told it would go. He fought as he never fought before. And in the sixth round, he unleashed a series of blows that finished the other man off."

As Bul fell silent, we did not dare to ask him about what his remark brought to our minds—that combat soldiers could be given similar courage by hypnotic treatment—all too aware that even fantasizing on this subject would embarrass him. If we persisted, he would certainly refuse to talk about it—and we would be suspected of attempted espionage.

As our car emerged from the maze of dark, gloomy streets onto a light embankment with the Kremlin looming mysteriously beyond the Moskva River, we wondered aloud about what sort of master plan the Red Army High Command *may* have for Russia's corps of hypnologists. There may be many ways of putting them to use, from having them hypnotize men on daredevil missions, to having spies carry data in their minds but have it come forth only when desired, to battle-conditioning battalions, air squadrons, submarine crews. That Russia already has such a military corps of hypnologists at the ready right now—with new training centers planned for Leningrad, Kharkov, Kiev, Minsk—is a sobering fact. We could almost see Dr. Raikov mobilized to become *General* Raikov, head of a cadre of hypnotists, convincing men to think they were invincible when Mother Russia called on them to fight.

"Let's change the subject," we said. It wasn't a pleasant thought.

21.

DERMO-OPTICAL PERCEPTIONS:
The Science—and Art—of
Sight-by-Touch

The confidential report was typewritten on green legal-size paper, and was obviously intended for the eyes of the chosen few. It bore no signature, but the text indicated that it had been put out by one Larisa Vilenskaya, identified as "lecturer and instructor" of the Bio-Information Department of the Popov Group, Moscow's parapsychology center. What caught our eye was Part 1 of the Report. It read:

"Investigation of optical sensitivity of the human skin to record images, both by direct contact and at a distance.

"Experiments have demonstrated that with proper training students can be taught to

    A. Identify the color and form of images by touch or near-touch

    B. Identify hidden objects

    C. Pinpoint magnetic fields

"Courses have been conducted by Larisa Vilenskaya, chief instructor, with 60 to 90 percent accuracy. This success ratio almost equals the results of the experiments currently conducted by the Ural Group that started this work quite a few years earlier."

We had heard about Vilenskaya from several sources, including Varvara Ivanova, Russia's nomad parapsychologist and Vilenskaya's temporary roommate. We had also caught her name in print as the author of articles on parapsychology, including one on the Kirlian Effect. But somehow the name never registered properly. Now it transpired that she was also connected with a fascinating subject, sight-by-touch, in charge of experiments that were mainly successful. We looked at each other and one and the same thought crossed our minds: find Vilenskaya.

We picked up the telephone by the hotel window.

The next morning, the woman who stepped into the room of the seventeenth floor of the Intourist was thick set, of medium height with a strong face, her hair cropped rather short, her eyes clear and solemn. She was wearing wire-rimmed glasses.

"I am Engineer Larisa Vilenskaya. What can I do for you?"

In the Soviet Union, an "engineer" is equivalent to a technological institute graduate. She was offered an armchair. We exchanged a few niceties. She sounded cool, efficient, and at ease. There was no doubt that she got the message that we were okay. She need not be afraid of us, and she knew she could talk parapsychology. There was none of the fretfulness about her, no fear of microphones that had made Varvara Ivanova's visit so dramatic.

"Can we talk here?" we asked, just in case.

She shrugged: "Why not?" With that she looked us over. What she saw seemed to satisfy her. We got down to business. "What do you know about the present state of sight-by-touch, Engineer Vilenskaya? Didn't it all begin with this Rosa Kuleshova?"

Rosa Kuleshova's story is well-known, even in America. The epileptic schoolteacher from Nizhni Tagil made Soviet headlines in the early and mid-1960's. Briefly, she was found to possess the ability to see with her hands. She could read newspaper headlines and even, slowly, smaller type. Blindfolded, she could identify by touch of hand, the color of objects, and could describe drawings and photographs either by touch or by "sensing" them with her fingers, even through metal plates.

Engineer Vilenskaya smiled and accepted a cigarette. Then, puffing on it, "Rosa Kuleshova is gone, a bitter and disappointed woman. We don't know where she is, and it's just as well." She paused, then continued with emphasis, "Rosa has served her purpose. Maybe if it weren't for her, the research we are conducting right now would be nonexistent. Ironically, she triggered a scientific initiative of tremendous dimensions. It involves scientists and hundreds of trainees in at least six Soviet cities.

"We have come a long way since Rosa. Thanks to new research, we are now deep into using sight-by-touch, which may well prove a solution for those whose eyes are dead."

She waved her cigarette. "This takes us back quite a few years, to 1962. It all came out during Rosa's stay at the Nizhni Tagil City Hospital, where she was being treated by Dr. I. M. Goldberg for epilepsy. When she showed him what she could do, he became so excited that he brought in colleagues to watch her identify colors blindfolded. Word spread. Before long, she was asked to demonstrate her abilities to a group of scientists in Nizhni Tagil and this led to tests and more tests, in Nizhni Tagil, in Sverdlovsk, the capital of the Ural mountain region, finally in Moscow. She became a very famous person.

"Unfortunately, Rosa Kuleshova's fame also proved her undoing. She began to develop complexes resulting from exposure to strangers, usually scientists who came to subject her to various experiments. Had she been kept out of reach of these visitors—and above all, had she been kept from going to Moscow for additional tests—she could very well be an active and valuable subject today. The Moscow experiments were conducted in an atmosphere of total distrust which she felt painfully and to which she reacted by slowly losing her special talents.

"In self-defense, she began to cheat, too confused to realize how foolish this was. She was caught peeping and using all sorts of subterfuges, including trying to guess the right answers. The tests became less and less conclusive. She grew more and more unsure of herself. Then came the climax

—a demonstration of her abilities at the Moscow office of the *Literary Gazette*. It was a disaster. She failed miserably, was caught cheating, and the newspaper labeled her a fraud."

We glanced at each other. Some days earlier we had been given an interesting insight into the episode that ended Kuleshova's usefulness. The story came, in fact, from Ladyshev, a member of *Literary Gazette* who was there at the time. He recounted to us how he saw the provincial schoolteacher perform, and that her ability was, in his own words, "truly remarkable."

Indeed, the "official" examination had not gone well. Distrust, suspicion, hostility had driven Rosa to despair. It was evening. The members of the examining panel had gone.

"She was sitting in an armchair when I came in," Ladyshev recalled to us, "a plain woman in her thirties. She glanced at me inquiringly. I was a new face to her. In fact, I was just a visitor. This was before I joined the staff of the newspaper. We started talking."

The young man's friendly face apparently took her off guard. Obviously he was not one of her torturers. As they chatted, she started telling him about life in the Ural Mountains and relaxed, regained her composure and self-confidence. When he asked innocently what she did, she told him proudly. She must have felt her powers returning to her.

"I suggested that she show me how she does it," he went on. "She said, 'Fine. Why not?' She was very much at ease. I asked her what I should do and she said, 'Blindfold me,' and she pointed to a piece of black cloth on the table.

"After I put the blindfold on her, she said, 'Take me to some books.' I led her to a bookcase in the corner, pulled a book off a shelf and opened it on the title page. I told her what I had done. She said, 'Fine!' With that she raised her left hand, with the fingers spread out, palms forward. I raised the book so her hand could find the open page.

"She then withdrew her hand to perhaps 10 centimeters from it. Suddenly two fingers, the third and fourth, bent forward toward the open page, like two antennae searching out an object. Then, moving them left to right, as though tied with an invisible string to the words on the page she could not see, she began reading aloud—very, very slowly. To my amazement, I recognized the words of the title, then the subtitle. Then the bottom line: 'Moscow 1963.' I was dumbfounded. She was actually reading with her fingertips. I remember it all as though it were yesterday."

He shook his head. "I was sure I had been tricked, but I didn't know how. Years later, I still don't know."

Was he tricked? He could have been. He was, according to a group of Russian stage magicians who had been summoned to the newspaper office and who upon watching Kuleshova perform successfully, announced that they could do so, too. But for "ethical reasons," they wouldn't reveal the secret. Magicians don't tell!

But if she was caught "peeping" during this Moscow experiment, she certainly did not cheat on other occasions—back in Nizhni Tagil and

Sverdlovsk where, before the tests began, the local scientists whom she knew and trusted made a point of putting her at ease.

As Engineer Vilenskaya explained it, after Rosa's debacle in Moscow there wasn't much more to tell. "She was taken home to Nizhni Tagil, where her health rapidly deteriorated. Her epileptic fits resumed. Eventually she grew so irrational that Dr. Goldberg turned her over to another doctor to look after her. Soon after that, she vanished into thin air. To be truthful, nobody went looking for her. It was sad, but it was also an end.

"At least we all thought so. Until we realized this was not the case and while Kuleshova herself was gone, the truth of Kuleshova lingered on. Namely, that if she had these phenomenal abilities—and we knew that she did have them at one point—then others might have them too. Especially since there were obviously varying degrees of ability. Kuleshova's abilities had been increased many times through training."

Engineer Vilenskaya cocked her head to one side to make sure we were listening attentively. We were, and she continued, reassured: "Even before Kuleshova was exposed, in fact, machinery was set in motion in the Ural cities. In Nizhni Tagil, in Sverdlovsk, in Magnitogorsk, local scientists like Sudakov, Novomeisky, and Fishelev set out to experiment with individuals they thought could be trained to develop sight-by-touch abilities. Before long, this led to the creation of two categories of trainees, the first made up of young children and high-school students who had reported an affinity to increased tactile sensitivity, and the second made up of blind people of all ages. Some of the blind were blind at birth; others had lost their sight at some time in life. These experiments have since overshadowed the findings of the Kuleshova case. Some of the trainees have actually learned to read by touch and to distinguish colors as a preliminary to the next step.

"By latest count, several hundred subjects have participated in the more recent experiments under the supervision of a dozen or so scientists now considered the greatest authorities on the subject in Russia. Whatever we here in Moscow do now, they can still do better—but we aren't doing so badly either," Vilenskaya insisted. "Even though our Moscow experiments are on a smaller scale and are less sophisticated, we think we've arrived at certain valid conclusions. We have found a link between the Kirlian Effect and sight-by-touch, namely that the same radiation of bio-energy is involved. When you take photographs of objects placed behind a black screen and you photograph the effort, so to speak, of sight-by-touch, you get remarkably similar pictures."

She got up and walked to the window. For a moment she stood there to take in the sight of the majestic city blanketed in snow that had fallen during the night. "Beautiful, isn't it?" she said proudly. "I rarely see Moscow like this, from so high up." We offered to take her down to lunch. She politely refused—she was too busy—and left shortly thereafter. Vilenskaya's visit left us with a feeling of slight frustration. We had overlooked an important facet of Soviet parapsychology.

During the rest of the day we did all we could to set a machinery in motion to track down Rosa Kuleshova, last heard of in Nizhni Tagil, but we hit a blank wall. As one of our Russian parapsychologist friends expressed it, "Rosa was a broken, sick woman when she went home. She had resigned from the human race. She has to be dead." But that wasn't the reason we failed to trace her. The point was that they did not want us in Nizhni Tagil, once a mining settlement on the northeastern slopes of the Ural Mountains, a city of some 350,000 people and a center of industries that outsiders must not know about. Clearly out of bounds for foreign tourists, it was a place even our Yuri shrugged off with a meek "Now you are asking too much!" In fairness to our Novosti hosts who, when asked, even took us to an atomic reactor in another "forbidden city," we did not press our request.

Yet Vilenskaya was right: we were not concerned with a personal phenomenon. At this point, Kuleshova could offer us little, if anything. Much more important was the present state of Russian DOP, the initials standing for Dermo-Optical Perception, a term used prominently by Soviet parapsychologists.

Not that the mystery of Soviet DOP was going to be much easier for us to unravel. The three main centers of Soviet DOP were totally inaccessible to us because of the unfortunate coincidence of their being military weapons production areas. Nizhni Tagil was *verboten,* as we already knew. But so was Sverdlovsk, where much of the Soviet armament is produced at secret plants. And so was Magnitogorsk, farther to the south, where more tanks and guns are built under the cover of the Ural mountain range.

As we pondered our predicament, a message reached us over the parapsychology grapevine: "Don't despair. The mountain will come to Muhammad."

Two days later, the "mountain" arrived in the shape of three rolls of 35-millimeter film. They were delivered rather casually by a Soviet parapsychologist who said, in handing us the little parcel, "This film contains two assortments of reports from members of the Ural Group on DOP. As you will see from the attached, this is not illegal material. You may safely take it out of the country."

The "attached" was a note in Russian, saying, "To Whom It May Concern" and then going on to specify the contents as 128 pages of "Problems of Dermo-Optical Sensitivity," papers published in Sverdlovsk, and 65 pages of "Materials of the Investigation of Dermo-Optical Sensitivity" published in Chelyabinsk, another Ural city. "Should they ask you at the airport," the man said pleasantly, "just show them this. You'll be okay. Don't worry."

We agreed not to worry. It was much later that we realized how useless this authoritative "To Whom It May Concern" really was. We could have landed at Lefortovo Prison as easily as did the man from the *Los Angeles Times,* Robert Toth, who was ruthlessly interrogated by the KGB for accepting allegedly secret information on parapsychology. Blithely, we put the film into a suitcase, and eventually carried it through Sheremetyevo

Airport without anyone demanding to know what the film contained. In fact, we wouldn't be surprised if whoever surveyed our movements and meetings knew all about those three rolls of film, or that we were allowed to take the information out with full knowledge and approval of the powers that be.

Subsequently, out of the country, we had the film developed to find exactly what it showed. Blown up to 8 x 10 size, each frame turned out to be two pages of the original reports by the Ural Group on what they've been doing. This, then, is the gist of the voluminous material we were allowed to take home with us, published in the Western world for the first time.

Vasili Borisov is a totally blind man having lost his sight in a plant accident. Genady Grigoriev, a worker at the same plant, is near-blind; his sight had deteriorated for "work reasons" to one percent of normal vision. Both are members of the Society for the Blind in Nizhni Tagil. Both were recruited for the series of experiments designed by Dr. A. S. Novomeisky, who spent weeks interviewing and testing the blind members of the Society, then formed a working group, an operational nucleus out of which these two men were eventually picked.

After three months of tutoring in a specially equipped room of the Nizhni Tagil Pedagogical Institute, where they were trained with the help of sheets of colored paper, both men learned to recognize by touch of hand all the colors of the spectrum—red, orange, yellow, green, light-blue, deep-blue, and purple, as well as mixtures of these colors and the achromatic shades of black, white and gray.

At the conclusion of the three-month period, they were given a major test. One hundred sheets of colored paper were brought out, and different members of the examining board pulled out sheets at random and handed their selection to a laboratory assistant, who then placed the sheets in front of the two blind men. Borisov wore black goggles, Grigoriev was blindfolded. They were allowed to touch a sheet briefly, then call out the color.

Both passed the test with flying colors. Once when Borisov mistook light-blue for deep-blue, and Grigoriev mistook red for orange, they were angry with themselves for committing such "silly" mistakes. "A child would know better," Grigoriev called out angrily. "These are the easiest colors to see." He actually used the word "see." To him, he "saw."

At the "finals," they were given color sheets of different texture than those used during the training, so as to make sure the men had not grown used to recognizing certain faults in the sheets of paper they had been working with. Some of their "examination papers" were shiny-smooth, others were rough cardboard, still others of a ripply texture. The paper and cardboard had been colored with a variety of paints from watercolor to colored ink to crayons. Every precaution was taken to exclude the possibility that the two blind men could be guided by strictly tactile elements. It had to be the color.

In the concluding tests the members of the examining board, as well as the laboratory assistant, were also blindfolded, so that they would not know the color of the sheet placed in front of the men. This precluded any possibility of voluntary or involuntary mental suggestion. Again the men identified the color correctly.

The size of the sheets varied. The larger the sheet, the more quickly they were able to identify the color. When the paper was cut into narrow strips, they could not proceed, complaining there was "not enough there" to go by. Then, as strips of the same color were placed side by side, they were again able to identify them correctly. Significantly, it was discovered and properly recorded that the two men used different fingers to see by touch. Borisov's effective fingers proved the third and fourth fingers of his right hand, coinciding with the "working fingers" of Kuleshova's left hand. By contrast, Grigoriev used the outside of his right thumb.

Following these tests, the men moved on to a second series: identification without touch. The single week's training consisted of teaching them a "feel" of a given color by trying themselves out from a distance. Before long each discovered the proper distance at which he would "see" a given color. Thus Borisov, "saw" red from a distance of 14 inches, orange from 10 inches, yellow from 5 inches. He "saw" light-blue at 8 inches and deep-blue at 13 inches. To "see" green he had to get his hand closest, a distance of 4 inches from the sheet of paper.

With that, the men graduated to "readin' 'n 'rithmetic." They started with the training aimed at identifying digits. The men were "shown" cards with the numerals 0, 1, 3, 4, 6, 7, 9 printed on them, each 3 inches in size. No matter how hard Borisov tried, he couldn't identify them. But Grigoriev appeared to be at ease, enjoying every minute of the exercises. The wholly blind Borisov was offered the choice of continuing, at a very slow pace, or to take a rest. He chose the rest and was discharged.

The partly-sighted Grivoriev went on alone to make medical history. By the end of a three-hour period he was able to "see" the figures by holding his palm within one inch of the card. During the following session he was able to identify any combination of the seven figures. He "read" 169, 4901, 16904, 669041, 6703416 without a single error. After calling out each digit, he was even able to pool them into figures to read out, "Sixteen thousand nine hundred and four" and then to announce triumphantly from under the blindfold, "I am right, am I not?" At the end of this session, he was taught the remaining digits—8, 2, and 5.

During the third session, Grigoriev was checked out and passed his "arithmetic" reading test. He was now "shown" four letters of the Russian alphabet, B, Zh, M and F. He learned to identify all four of them in less than one hour, his "eyes" being the palm of his right hand.

The fourth session was another major test held at the physics laboratory of the Pedagogical Institute of Nizhni Tagil. Present were Dr. Novomeisky and professors N. I. Kolesnikov and Y. M. Filimonov. Grigoriev was given a succession of figures, each printed on a separate card, the size of playing cards, which were carefully shuffled by the laboratory assistant who, like Grigoriev, was blindfolded. The three scientists could not see the card placed in front of Grigoriev. After he named the figure he raised the card so that they could confirm it. He identified each and all correctly. His average speed was 0.75 seconds per digit. In each case, he identified the digit without touching the card.

At the fifth session Grigoriev was given more figures to "read" and was taught to recognize the letters N, O and Sh. At the end of the session he was tested and two letters from the third session, M and Zh, were added to the test. He failed to identify the letter M and apologized profusely, saying: "Of all the letters, this one I should have remembered!"

Grigoriev was shown more multidigit figures during the sixth session, and he practiced with them all day. The seventh session was the first lesson in adding and subtracting. Grigoriev mastered it easily. A test conducted by visiting Professor K. P. Korolev dealt with multidigit figures in the eighth session. Grigoriev identified six such figures, including one consisting of ten digits. In all, he failed to identify only one digit.

The ninth session was held without a table in a hallway of the Society for the Blind. Cards with digits and letters printed on them were placed on a plate of glass that Grigoriev was told to balance on his knees. The unaccustomed setting and noise disturbed the nearly blind man, but he struggled on and identified each and every letter without touching the cards, his hand remaining at a distance of one inch.

Grigoriev was "shown" eleven letters of the Russian alphabet in the tenth session, then asked to "read" six words—*ruka* (hand), *son* (dream), *tok* (current), and so on. Five of them were three-letter words and one consisted of four letters. He "read" all six correctly.

"Incredible success," Dr. Novomeisky entered in his log. "A blind man has been taught the rudiments of reading in ten lessons." The Nizhni Tagil physician recorded additional observations. The lessons in reading and arithmetic had been, he felt, rightly preceded by meticulous training to identify color. Color was a prerequisite in a blind person's return to the sighted. He noted that Grigoriev had to bring his hand to within an inch of the board to "read" letters and digits printed in black, but he could already "see" red letters at a distance of 5 inches. Each time, his hand appeared to follow the outline of the letter he "read" to tell him what it was. When he was made to stop moving his hand, he could not "see" the letter any more. Grigoriev explained that the outline of the letter imprinted itself on the palm of his hand as if with a branding iron and that he could actually feel a burning sensation. Subsequently the burning disappeared and his hand, to quote Grigoriev, "simply read aloud to me."

In subsequent tests, it was discovered that a sheet of transparent glass placed between his hand and the card impeded reading. Conversely, reading improved when the cards were put on a metal base with up to 80 volts of electricity passing through it.

As time went on, the Nizhni Tagil physician found that prolonged intervals set his "students" back. Nine days of absence had brought Borisov back to Square One; two weeks of absence caused Grigoriev to "forget" what he had done to recognize color. On the other hand, they remembered quickly. In subsequent experiments, Grigoriev was given forty-five days of rest. When he resumed, he could not recognize a single color, but it took him one third of the original time to go through the entire course again. Borisov, who never went beyond color recognition, was recalled after seven months. He had forgotten everything he knew, but it took him only 50 minutes to relearn the colors of the spectrum.

"Both proved unusual students," the Nizhni Tagil physician wrote in his conclusions, "but Grigoriev stood out like a giant among two hundred blind tested by us. Unfortunately, his hand developed arthritis. This had been expected, as he was already suffering from arthritis when he began training. With arthritis moving into his hand, his working thumb quickly lost all the sensitivity it possessed. He was forced to leave the ranks of our trainees and this proved a heavy blow to our research. We have yet to find another Grigoriev. However, he has given us invaluable knowledge that is now being applied to others. Our next objective is to train the blind to describe pictures they see and to read normal-size type. We firmly believe we can accomplish this within the foreseeable future."

What appeared significant and encouraging to him was that both subjects were grown men in their late thirties. Grigoriev's success meant that a blind man can "learn to see" even at a mature age, well past the formative years. True, neither had been blind from birth. Both knew what seeing and, above all, what color meant. They could reconstruct natural images before their inner eye. Novomeisky, however, swears he will not rest until he finds someone blind from birth, Grigoriev's age or older, to confirm the findings. In the meantime, the doctor is quite content with his discoveries to date. As first steps go, his findings are truly a giant step forward.

In contrast to the two blind men of Nizhni Tagil, the hundreds of others tested were high-school and university students. In all experiments they fell into three groups: blind at birth, blinded, and near-blind. These were pitted against blindfolded students with full vision. On the average, the number of males equaled that of females. One of the interesting conclusions was the fact that females did slightly better than males, at a ratio of 53 to 47.

Wherever they were conducted, all experiments invariably began with teaching to recognize color. On this the Ural Group proved unanimous: color identification has to be Step One. Even if subsequent "reading" would be of black letters on white paper, learning to distinguish color was still a prerequisite. The scientists agreed that some of the blind may subsequently be aided by a color aid, such as reading in red or orange rather than black on white. Novomeisky demonstrated this when he discovered that Grigoriev "read" more easily in red. He was planning to have Grigoriev study from books printed in red when Grigoriev's arthritis put a sad end to his "education."

While there was agreement on the basic approach, the methods of the study used by the Ural researchers have differed considerably. Similarly, the researchers have agreed to disagree in their hypothesis on what sight-by-touch actually is. The theory offered by Dr. A. S. Novomeisky sees a definite connection between dermo-optical sensitivity and the effect of invisible rays emanating from every object in the universe. But Dr. Y. R. Fishelev, the Sverdlovsk scientist, leans toward the theory of photoreceptivity of the skin and its ability to reflect light.

Professor N. I. Kolesnikov, another Nizhni Tagil scientist, has endeavored to explain sight-through-skin with a polarization process. Dr. D. K. Gilev of Ishim believes that DOP is a result of mechanical and temperature influences of different coloring on the "receptors" of the skin of the human finger, not necessarily the fingertip only. Finally, Dr. M. M. Kozhevnikov and his group theorize about the existence of certain electromagnetic qualities which the human skin "translates" into vision. In the absence of a definite proven explanation of the phenomenon of DOP, they all agreed that they would do best to continue their explorations separately, comparing notes every so often in the hope that a common denominator might emerge.

It was on this basis that experiments—all triggered, as it were, by the Kuleshova case—have been in progress. The cities involved are Sverdlovsk, Chelyabinsk, Nizhni Tagil, and Magnitogorsk, clustered along the eastern foothills of the Urals, and Verkhnyaya Pyshma and Ishim beyond the mountain range. Of these, the largest is Sverdlovsk with a population of 900,000 and corresponding medical and educational facilities.

The smallest is Ishim, 400 miles due east of Sverdlovsk, a town of some 35,000 people on the edge of the Yarovskoye marshland, not much more than a whistle-stop on the Trans-Siberian Railroad. That the town of Ishim, plagued by deadly marsh mosquitoes in the summer, fighting the bitter Siberian cold in wintertime, could become one of the most advanced clinics researching Dermo-Optical Perception is a typical incongruity of Soviet life. Its head is the aforementioned Dr. D. K. Gilev, who communicates with his colleagues of the Ural Group by radiotelephone and in order to visit them, hitches rides aboard the service planes and helicopters of the headquarters of the West Siberian Oilfields Combine in Tyumen, the oil city halfway between Ishim and the Urals.

Unlike his colleagues, Dr. Gilev has only recently started using the blind and blinded, all recruited from a center for the blind in Tyumen. He has also concentrated on sight-by-touch of fingertips only and in the past limited his exploration to color only. Over the years this specialization has given him a better insight into the faculties of color-by-touch than that gained by the other researchers. His is the "foundation" then, of the beacon for the blind that the Ural Group is trying to erect.

In his original experiment which has since become a textbook example used by his colleagues elsewhere, Dr. Gilev screened some 200 student volunteers from the faculties of physics, mathematics and philology of the Ishim Pedagogical Institute and chose 22. All had perfect sight. His choice was based on the degree of tactile sensitivity shown by the students. The experiments called for daily sessions, six times a week, each lasting 90 minutes. Once the volunteers started, Gilev reported, not one of them dropped out despite the monotony of their "color training." which went on for six months.

The courses began with teaching the volunteers to identify two colors only: red and light blue. First the students were made to identify themselves thoroughly with the room they would be working in: the position of tables, chairs, also the source of light—the windows. They were shown the sheets of colored paper—actually smooth drawing paper colored evenly by crayon—that they would have to identify, and shown how the sheets would be placed in front of them on plates of glass mounted on tiny legs. The first session took them visually through all the motions they would be carrying out blindfolded: stroking the colored sheets slowly with their fingertips, first to and fro, then up and down. They were told they were expected to report the sensation of touch, describing it in detail, indicating any warmth emanating from it, or lack of it. At the end of the first session, they were blindfolded and left to practice for a few minutes.

Actual training began with the second session. The subjects were allowed to take the same seats they had occupied on the first day. Then they were blindfolded and each was handed a sheet to place before him on the plate of glass.

Teaching to distinguish between red and blue took up two full sessions. By the second evening, all 22 could distinguish between the two colors without a single error. They were then handed yellow to add to the red and blue, and after the students had learned to distinguish between the three, they were handed orange as color number four. Then came green, dark blue and purple, in that order. Numerous sessions followed as the students were taught to identify colors, first by comparison, eventually without. Some time later, black, white, and gray were added to make a total of ten colors.

"Five of our students," Dr. Gilev reported, "mastered color identification without need of comparison. In other words, they could identify a color singly, one sheet at a time. Eight learned to identify some colors without comparison, but needed a second color placed in front of them before they could identify the others. The rest learned to identify by comparison only."

As they were asked to describe the touch sensation of each color, these were compared and were found to agree. As a result, Dr. Gilev was able to come up with touch-description of color. It was subsequently compared to descriptions recorded by other test groups in Sverdlovsk, Magnitogorsk, and the rest of the cities where experiments were conducted, most of them with blind and nearblind subjects. The descriptions tallied, ostensibly proving that via some mysterious ability yet to be determined, we know how color "feels." Gilev's students agreed that red feels sticky, rough, and heavy-grained on touch, also warm. Light-blue is cold, slippery, dense, and small-grained. Yellow is soft, smooth, porous, and dusty, and warm. Orange is heaviest-grained, also sticky, but less so than red; it is cooler than red but warmer than yellow.

Green has an adhesive graininess, feels thicker and a little warmer than light blue. Deep blue is cold and hard, but also somehow sticky and sleazy. Purple is cool and thick, is rougher than deep blue. Black is evenly coarse and has definable friction. It is also warmer than white or gray. Gray is smooth, cool, and slippery. Its surface has miniature ridges all running in the same direction. White is smooth-grained, but has some coarseness, and feels cool.

Asked to vote for their favorite color, most elected light blue, since it was the most pleasant color to touch. All the women picked light blue. Student Sonya Narushevich, who was one of the top five, became the subject of some special tests. During one such test she was deliberately misguided. Unable to identify quickly the color of an orange sheet handed her, she asked to be given a red sheet so that she could compare the two by touch. Instead she was given a yellow sheet. She touched it, instantly exclaimed, "This is not red; this is yellow. Give me red."

She was then handed a green sheet. She touched it and exclaimed angrily, "You are not doing what I have been asking you. Why did you give me green?" When finally given a red sheet, she was able to identify the original sheet as orange.

Of the five who fared so well, two were women and three were men. Of the latter, student Ivan Karaoulshchikov mastered the art of identification of all ten colors within two weeks—a record still unsurpassed, Dr. Gilev wrote.

Siberian weather conditions helped him, he says, to test the dermo-optical sensitivity of his subjects in extreme cold and irritating humid heat. On one occasion, the cold made his subjects totally insensitive to sight-by-touch. On another, heavy rain coming down outside the windows had the same effect. On a third, a lonely buzzing mosquito flew in through a hole in a window screen and wreaked havoc with the 22 trainees.

Additional experiments showed that the tactile sensitivity of the students diminished during rainy weather. Narushevich, who scored 100 percent in warm and dry weather and led the class along with Karaoulshchikov, was the first to lose her perception when it rained. She mistook deep blue for purple, orange for yellow, black for gray. Yet she could not know it was raining—the downpour began after class had convened, and none of them could hear the rain through the blindfold that also covered their ears.

The following day it was already raining when the students arrived. The result proved as poor, but no poorer than the previous day. A thunderstorm darkening the sky outside the windows had a similar negative effect on their tactility, yet behind their blindfolds they could not know the room had darkened. Then the good weather resumed and pretty Sonya Narushevich was back in top form, scoring 100 percent.

Even as Dr. Gilev was conducting his first experiments in tiny Ishim, a colleague of his, Professor N. I. Sudakov was conducting his own slightly different tests under the belching chimney stacks of the steel foundries of Magnitogorsk, some 700 miles to the southwest. He knew about Gilev's thorough experiments, but decided not to take advantage of his findings. He would start from scratch. It was just as well. Not knowing the details of the Ishim tests would help him formulate his own *modus operandi.*

Sudakov had set for himself a triple task. "Check out," he wrote, "whether all people can learn to distinguish colors by touch of fingertip.

Ascertain the exact elements that help one to distinguish different color this way. Explore how to teach the blind to distinguish different shades of color as well as geometrical figures and letters."

Within days, an announcement by Sudakov calling for volunteers appeared on the bulletin board of the Magnitogorsk Pedagogical Institute. As Sudakov reported later, he recruited a total of 150 students—freshmen and sophomores of the Institute.

Indeed, Sudakov's tests proved different from the very start. He separated his volunteers into groups of 30, all to work simultaneously in five different labs. His researchers started by giving them two colors—red and orange—to work with, but instead of handing out identical sheets of colored paper, they distributed different objects of the same color: red pencils, red ribbons, pieces of red glass, plastic toy wheels, colored glass tubes. Then they handed out identical objects colored orange. The students were first shown the objects, and were instructed how to rub gently across their surface with their fingertips. Then they were blindfolded and class began.

The groups assembled every day and stayed for 90 minutes. The researchers moved around keeping tabs on the students' findings. After two weeks the students had learned to distinguish between red and orange. They found it easiest with paper, hardest with the glass tubes. It took the best student an average of 42 tries to learn to distinguish the color of a sheet of paper, as against 86 tries to identify that of a glass tube.

Five finalists were then subjected to a color-light test. They were stationed in front of specially built reflectors whose opaque glass screens were lit from behind by a projector equipped with color filters. The students were to identify the color by touching the reflectors' glass screens.

The first test was to distinguish between red and yellow, but eventually blue was added. The three different colors were flashed on the screen without warning or order. Students, their fingers stroking the glass, were asked to determine the moment of change as well as the color.

In all, each student was subjected to 200 color changes to acquaint himself with the elements pertaining to the three different colors. The students were then tested with a succession of ten colors passing through the reflector. One student identified the colors correctly nine times, three identified them eight times, and one named them correctly six times. The students agreed that they acquired no visual concept of the different colors but were instead guided by the amount and direction of a certain resistance they felt on the glass surface.

These tests were followed by a series of experiments with sheets of paper painted partially black and partially white. The same five students were asked to determine the dividing line between the white and black areas.

The tests proved a total success. At this point, Sudakov concluded he was ready to bring in the blind. Of the six previously chosen, two were born blind, two had lost sight, and two were nearly blind. They were taken through the paces of the experiments with the seeing students. The blind took six weeks of daily 40-minute exercises to learn to distinguish the color as effectively as the seeing students. They were then given the black-white border-line exercises. Inside of two weeks they learned to find the border lines. In all, they fared better than the seeing students at a ratio of 5-3.

Then came the crucial tests with the large pictures, actually illustrations from childrens' books—geometrical figures in sizes not less than an inch each, and finally letters of the alphabet in sizes of 2-3 inches reproduced typographically. All these were placed under a plate of glass so that their fingertips would not touch the actual pictures or letters. The blind had to "see" them through the glass.

"We were happy to record total success," Sudakov wrote in his conclusions. All blind subjects after mastering the basic border-line problems eagerly took to defining the outlines of the geometrical figures. Before long they were drawing triangles, squares, and circles on the surface of the glass plate—exactly corresponding to the outlines of the geometrical figures underneath. The typical scientist, Sudakov refrained from registering his jubilation in the journal. He wrote matter-of-factly: "Following this, three of the blind subjects learned to trace the outlines of several large letters placed under the glass and to identify them. Subject V. Shaposhnikov mastered this to such perfection that three exercises later he read aloud a five-letter name that was printed on the sheet under the glass. The name was Lenin."

Ah well! It was not such a big price Professor Sudakov had to pay in choosing this particular five-letter name. It was part of the privilege of conducting his experiments at the expense of the Soviet Government.

Sudakov did not mention what happened next. One assumes that the experiments are progressing and that by now, blind V. Shaposhnikov has learned to "see" more. Importantly, he is another adult taught to read without eyes. Sudakov concluded his report by discounting the theory that fingertips of certain people serve like the retina of the human eye—a theory some have applied to the Kuleshova phenomenon. His experiments, Sudakov wrote, confirmed the conclusions reached by the Nizhni Tagil scientists that dermo-optical sensations are not caused by light *per se*, but by certain light-connected elements, a mystery ray affecting our psyche.

Experiments were also conducted in Sverdlovsk by Dr. N. I. Buskov and Dr. V. P. Suzev with a group of high-school seniors. The following are some excerpts from the minutes.

Following a number of tests, two girls, Natasha T. and Lila K. were singled out as almost infallible in determining the color of paper held up by a laboratory assistant behind their heads at a distance of about 6 inches. The girls were made to wear goggles pasted over with black paper and hoods over their heads.

Each colored sheet, about 8 x 10 inches in size, was picked from a desk in the next room and inserted between two steel plates by a laboratory assistant stationed behind the subject. No one in the room knew what the color was.

In all, the experiment was repeated 17 times with Natasha and 18 with Lila. Natasha identified the colored sheets by announcing the color within 10 seconds after the sheet was held up against her neck. She was right

14 times, wrong 3 times. The colors were presented at random, without order, yellow occurring three times in succession. Natasha stumbled only when it came to black and gray. Lila identified 15 color sheets correctly and also made three mistakes.

The objective of this experiment was to prove that not only are fingers tactilely sensitive, but the skin of the nape of the neck is sensitive in a way similar to the fingers, yet without touching.

Footnote from Dr. V. P. Suzev: "Earlier, successful experiments with our high-school subjects consisted of recognition of color by touch with a metal plate covering the colored sheet. The subjects were able to identify the color through metal one millimeter thick.

"Similar experiments have been and are being conducted with positive results by my colleagues in Nizhni Tagil and Magnitogorsk. While we have no conclusive theories yet, we are of the opinion that tactile kinesthetic, thermal, and quasi-visual images can be triggered even through metal and over a short distance. We have yet to determine what it is that does it. We have both adopted and discarded a great number of theories since we were first brought into this field by the experiments with Rosa Kuleshova."

In experiments conducted in Sverdlovsk by Y. R. Fishelev at the Institute for the Blind, 15 blindfolded sighted subjects were pitted against 18 blind subjects. All were teenagers. Most of the blind learned to distinguish the color of light from a lamp or spotlight. In these experiments, the backs of their heads were exposed to the light emanating through color slides. In their case, the training period took from one to three months while the blindfolded sighted volunteers took twice that long.

Experiments with blind people were conducted by Dr. N. I. Sudakov at the City Hospital in Magnitogorsk and by A. S. Novomeisky in Nizhni Tagil and Verkhnyaya Pyshma. Following three months of sustained training, the group of blind men, totalling 24, worked extremely well in recognizing color by touch. "We took 75 sheets of colored paper which we shuffled at random. We then pulled them out one by one, giving the blind men not more than five seconds to identify the color. Their accuracy was about 85 percent. They identified the color by touch.

"The blind subjects started out by recognizing no more than 3 percent of the colors, but then probably developed sensitivity to color. Significantly, the colors they were first able to identify were those of the middle portion of the spectrum—an ability which with additional training gradually expanded to the fringe area of the spectrum."

The experiments in Nizhni Tagil have been the longest in duration, taking in as much as a full year of work with individual blind subjects. During the first five months, these experiments showed, in the case of Nikolai A., 370 positive identifications and 219 erroneous identifications. Toward the end of the year, the number of accurate identifications was 134 against 48 erroneous ones.

Early experiments conducted in Verkhnyaya Pyshma produced one blind subject, 14-year-old Nadya L., whose margin of error eventually fell to

5 percent. In her case, different materials were used in the making of the colored sheets. After two months of training, she learned to identify colors not only on paper, but also on leather and fabric.

Experiments in Magnitogorsk with blind subjects produced an additional facet. There, subjects learned to identify border lines between different colors placed on the same sheet, such as yellow and blue, which formed vertical and horizontal lines on the paper. The blind subjects were not allowed to touch the paper itself. The paper sheets were covered with plate glass and the blind were requested to run their fingers across the glass.

Two blind subjects, Valya S. and Nikolai A., not only learned to identify the border lines but also to point to the direction in which the colored lines ran on the original drawings. After three months of experimentation, the ratio of error was less than 15 percent. Interestingly, triangles proved more easily identifiable than circles or squares.

Yes, Vilenskaya was right: it didn't matter that a strange, unique Rosa Kuleshova lost her powers within six years of their discovery. What might ironically be called the Kuleshova Effect fired the imagination of some genuine, down-to-earth, dedicated scientists in her very own hometown and in the towns nearby. A chain reaction set in. On those three rolls of 35-millimeter film was the proof—the Ural Group's minutes of sessions with the blind, near blind, and sighted people. They gave hope that one day, loss of eye function will not necessarily mean the loss of the ability to see.

22.
DR. VIKTOR INYUSHIN—
MOBILIZING THE KIRLIAN EFFECT
AGAINST DISEASE

The voice emerging from the crackle and hum of the long-distance telephone call was clear, if not particularly strong:

"Semyon Davidovich is right, of course. Cancer-affected cells give themselves away by producing a very muddy Kirlian picture. The point is that conventional Kirlian photography offers few details. Here in Alma-Ata, therefore, we set out to determine the presence of cancer with greater precision. This has been accomplished. Now we know for sure when it's there. But we want to catch it early, ideally as the very first cell becomes affected by the disease."

Alma-Ata is some 1,950 miles away from Moscow as the Soviet crow would fly, and this time our connection was by radio telephone rather than satellite It was remarkable that we could hear each other at all, for even the Soviets themselves admit they do not have the best telephone equipment in the world. The man on the other end of the line was Dr. Viktor Inyushin, a brilliant biophysicist and doctor of medicine, whose newly developed scientific approaches to the evaluation of bio-energy has brought him international prominence. Knowing how much we liked to get a glimpse of a person we were to interview by telephone, Yuri had scrounged up for us the only picture of Inyushin he could find on short notice. Taken a few years earlier, it showed Inyushin in a group of Soviet scientists on a field trip in Kazakhstan: a slender man in his late thirties, boyish face, a clump of dark hair overhanging his left eye, stooping broad shoulders, crumpled suit. While all others faced the camera, he looked to one side as though to assert his independence. He was younger than we thought, less studious in looks, less conspicuous.

It was some time after we saw Kirlian, but his praise of Inyushin still rang in our ears. In fact, it was his obviously boundless admiration for the Alma-Ata scientist that tipped us off to the significance of the Inyushin operation.

"Happily for science," the mild-mannered Kirlian said, a twinkle in his eye, "the latest equipment has been taken out of the hands of *amateurs like myself* and nowadays is supervised by such professionals as Dr. Viktor Inyushin and his team. Now there's a *man*—Inyushin, Viktor Mikhailovich," we remembered him saying, awe written all over his face. "Incredibly clever. I am so gratified that he became interested in our work and turned it into a tool of his own. As a result, we are collaborating on several projects, all new machinery that is giving aura photography new dimensions and vastly expanded applications. Inyushin is the man who is giving a scientific meaning to our discoveries."

Yuri provided us with Inyushin's home phone number in Alma-Ata. Since it was Saturday morning, we insisted that he needn't be present when we placed the call. If anyone needed a rest from us, it was Yuri Shevyakov, our tireless jack-of-all-trades. Even he had his limits. We had begged him not to bother, to stay in his little suburban apartment and get reacquainted with his wife, a young, pretty schoolteacher. He seemed to appreciate the thought.

On all our many visits to the Soviet Union, we never asked whether it was legal to tape record phone conversations. We strongly suspected it was not. However, the Novosti people at least—and they represented the authorities—were aware that we were doing it and never objected. We never told the people we were interviewing that the conversation was being recorded, nor did we make a point to hide our equipment. It was there in our hotel rooms, in full view of whoever cared to drop by to check on us. The only mild rebuke we received was on the day when one particular floor maid, a thin, sharp-eyed woman in her thirties who had just come on duty, spied the tape recorder with its suction monitor firmly attached to the telephone earpiece. She shook her head, and clucked reproachfully. Obviously, she knew what it was for. Still, nothing happened later, even after she reported what she saw, as they all do when discovering anything suspicious in a foreign visitor's room. We concluded she had been told that we were okay, and that they—whoever they were—knew all about us.

On at least one occasion, we taped a conversation at the Novosti's Moscow office in the presence of a Soviet telephone engineer who asked to be allowed to see how it's done. Most times, though, we taped the calls from our hotel room, making it a routine to have a curious Natasha or a not-so-curious Yuri present—and listening in. But on this trip, neither he nor she stipulated that they sit in as Natasha had done early on our trips.

Because we were able to speak to our subjects in impeccable Russian, the various people we phoned were completely at ease. Although aware that we were visiting Western newspapermen, they did not regard us as strangers. We used a warm, respectful approach, and invariably our subjects ended up sharing their innermost thoughts with us. It seemed that they loved to talk to someone from the West who was not that much different from them. And most, of course, had been properly briefed beforehand.

But we doubted that Inyushin had been similarly coached on what to say and how to treat us. A leading scientist, he was too respected to be subjected to that. It was his rightful pride in his achievements that made him reveal the secrets of his research.

"If anyone will find a way of diagnosing danger signals flashed by affected tissues in the shape of flickering auras," the dapper old Kirlian had said with conviction, "it will be Inyushin." Apparently Kirlian knew what was going on in Alma-Ata. But then over the years, Inyushin has made quite a few pilgrimages to Kirlian's makeshift laboratory in Krasnodar to fill him in on his own progress and seek advice. Yet it took our phone call to show us that Inyushin had made the expected breakthrough with the help of Kirlian's methods.

We were in Gris's room at the Intourist Hotel, overlooking Gorky Street and a sea of roofs all white with snow. It was mid-Saturday Alma-Ata time, early morning in Moscow, and he was at home to pick up the phone personally. "In about five years," Inyushin acknowledged, "we'll have reached the stage where we'll be able to diagnose cancer at a stage early enough to prevent it—in fact, we will be able to detect that very first diseased cell." While there were yet many problems to solve, a new machine, the "Kirlian Scanner 75," built in the workshops of the Kazakh State University in Alma-Ata was ready to diagnose various types of cancer with 100 percent accuracy.

"I am very excited about our findings," Inyushin told us, "but I refuse to go out on a limb and say we already have all the answers. I am very happy that our system will put an end to such things as biopsies of tissues, often requiring difficult surgical incursions. No more biopsies. We'll diagnose without them." Still, this was only a first step. "We're already well beyond it in the area of precancer, but we have to study many cases and interpret them before we establish a *modus operandi*. I am reasonably confident that in five years, as I said, we will know exactly how to diagnose approaching cancer at a very early stage and then proceed to effectively treat it, with the help of chemotherapy, laser beams, and radiation."

That such an important breakthrough would take place somewhere in Central Asia rather than in a metropolis like Moscow is probably another sign of the times. In Russia, this decentralization of the creative mind as psychic research goes on is conceivably greater than anywhere else. Thus Krasnodar, in the northern foothills of the Caucasus, remains an agricultural station where diseased seed and plants are examined. The local agricultural research institute will continue to serve as a national base of study of the auras of plants. Leningrad, having come up with Ninel Kulagina, has stayed with telekinesis as a speciality of its own and has also laid a major claim to hypnosis research. The Ural Mountain cities such as Sverdlovsk (where the last Czar and his entire family were massacred at the height of Russia's Civil War), identify with sight-by-touch. As described in the previous chapter, following the Rosa Kuleshova case, a chain reaction fired the imagination of local scientists, and the entire area does nothing else.

Tbilisi, the capital of Georgia, is "psychic healer land," thanks to Aleksei Krivorotov and his son and their gift of healing by the 'laying on' of hands. Graduate students of Tbilisi University's Medical Institute make it the subject of their master's theses. Gorky and Byurkan outside Yerwan have laid claim to a search for extraterrestrial civilizations. And then there's Alma-Ata.

Alma-Ata reminds one from the air of a gleaming white bastion standing guard over a brown wasteland, with China looming 150 miles to the southeast behind the forbidding Tien Shan mountain range. To Russians, this city in the middle of nowhere is truly a mirage come to life in Kazakh land. They flock to Alma-Ata, having heard of readily available vacant apartments and good jobs in a number of new industries and, unbelievably, get both. The same applies to students, at new universities with vast new laboratories and research facilities. Word has it that there's nothing new and daring that Alma-Ata's giant Kazakh State University won't tackle. It's the home of the pioneers seeking new frontiers in learning.

A rapidly mushrooming city of some 850,000, it is modern in appearance, yet like all Soviet cities it seems to lack modern comforts. Lining its wide boulevards are nine-story apartment houses all built with the identical floor plan. In the last twenty years, Alma-Ata has acquired the prestige of a center of industrial and scientific research second to none. It is the home of the Soviet space industry. Baikonur, Russia's Cape Canaveral, is in Kazakhstan. Some of the most advanced books on Soviet scientific progress are written by Alma-Ata scientists and published in Alma-Ata. Indeed, the most important Soviet books on parapsychology are edited and printed here. Behind them looms the prestige of what is colloquially referred to as the Alma-Ata Group. The identification *Almaateenets*, "Man of Alma-Ata," denotes a Soviet scientific visionary.

The Alma-Ata Group, Viktor Adamenko will tell you in awe, stands for Inyushin and his colleagues, theoreticians and researchers without peer in the Soviet Union. Having come there from all over Russia, they now make up a formidable outpost of scientific pioneering that is so far ahead in parapsychology alone, for instance, that as the Group forges into the unknown it is forced to invent new scientific terms.

Not so surprisingly, then, Inyushin and the Group have been declared out of bounds for even the officially-inspired baiters and detractors. Unlike many of their colleagues in Moscow and Leningrad, they have a home of their own—rather sumptuous quarters at the Kazakh State University—their own labs, and a staff. Treated with respect, they enjoy special privileges accorded scientists whose work benefits the Soviet Union, such as good apartments with private telephone, cars, and no standing in line for travel to Moscow. But then, they have tackled a slice of science that even a slow-witted bureaucrat will be able to comprehend: they are rewriting medical diagnostics, opening new vistas to medicine.

Within the wide spectrum of man's fight against disease, Alma-Ata is using the latest, most sophisticated and still secret—for more reasons than one—machinery to pinpoint the beginnings of deterioration in body and mind. In more practical terms, they are setting down new means of identifying cancer long before it has done any harm. In a sense they are revolutionaries, and their main weapon is Kirlian photography. Hospitals in Russia are beginning to experiment with equipment developed in Alma-Ata five years ago. There is only one "Kirlian Scanner 75" in existence, and it has been in use in Alma-Ata since it was built locally in 1975. It allows observation—with or without simultaneous recording on film—of any part of the human body, and is capable of surveying vital functions. An attached computer translates the visual into charts that can be read, like those of a cardiograph machine.

The "Kirlian Scanner 80," currently in development by Inyushin's engineers, will magnify the human cell many thousands of times, enlarging the elements of its "Kirlian Effect," its vibrant luminosity, to a size in which its revealed components will begin to tell its story—resulting in fast and accurate diagnosis. Yet it is not the ultimate as equipment goes, nor is this the final goal. "We are exploring several different theories," Inyushin was saying, "and many different techniques are being tested. It is merely a question of which will prove the most effective.

"As I said, we are getting there. We have over one hundred men and women—doctors, researchers, bio-engineers, laboratory technicians—all working on this project in our research laboratories. We work hand in hand with the staff of our medical institute, where we observe patients at various stages of the disease. But we are also on the lookout for subjects at the precancer stage whose aura can offer us invaluable studies of a progressing disease. The data are fed into computers, for analyzing and recording. All this is time-consuming and infinitely complicated.

"In addition, purely human and moral issues are involved. What do you do with a cancer patient whose disease had been diagnosed during the precancer stage? You must treat him with the best method available. The treatments, obviously, deny us the observation of a progressing disease. Hence we have to look for *other* patients whose precancer is at a different stage. It becomes a matter of continually correlating data obtained from different sources. The deciphering of Kirlian Effect images itself is easy by comparison."

As he spoke, expressing his thoughts in the exact and specific terms of a scientist, we had the same sensation as we had when facing Kirlian in Krasnodar. Here was a totally dedicated man. While cancer is clearly the Alma-Ata operation's first objective, Inyushin has not overlooked other diseases of the body nor, for that matter, of the mind.

"We have no doubt whatsoever that mental illnesses—specifically schizophrenia—can be diagnosed at an early stage," he said simply. "I could mention a long list of illnesses that we are in the process of tabulating and identifying. Make no mistake about it, the application of Kirlian photography in medicine has only just begun. Its possibilities are enormous. As a few examples, we have found the Kirlian Effect invaluable in indicating the initial condition of patients before we treat them with helium-neon lasers against hypertension, disorders of the joints, enteritis, and metabolic disorders. We are using it to assess the effect of radiation objectively. I can go on and on."

If anyone, then, could answer a question that had been bothering us since Krasnodar, it would be Viktor Inyushin.

Have scientists who have stepped in to take over from an old former X-ray machine repairmen been able to explain a phenomenon that has staggered imagination? Have they been able to unravel the mystery of the forces that, harbored in every living being from plant to man, appear to belong to another world that is superimposed on our present visible, physical world? Or have they simply accepted the opportunities the Kirlian Effect offers them to make fullest use of a latest service to mankind?

We could hear him chuckle on the other end of the line. "It is my conclusion," he said, "that living organisms are endowed with an integral system of elementary charged particles, and that this is a dominant factor in all biodynamic relationships within these organisms. Such a system of elementary particles has been called biological plasma. Biological plasma, in contrast to inorganic plasma, is a structurally organized system. In it, the chaotic heat motion of particles has been reduced to a minimum. That is, the entropy of the system is minimal.

"Moreover, biological plasma in its thermodynamically unbalanced state is notable for considerable stability in varying temperatures and other environmental conditions. Electrons must comprise a considerable proportion of biological plasma and for this reason, electrical and magnetic forces in the environment are likely to impair the structure of such a plasma. This, then, would bring about an energy discharge which cannot but affect physiological processes.

"Naturally, if bioplasma exists in living systems, it is bound to be luminescent in certain conditions. However, concrete proof of the presence of quantities of free electrons in living systems is still forthcoming. Therefore, the presence of the fourth state of matter in live organisms remains so far a hypothesis."

He stopped for a brief instant to let his mention of a fourth state of matter sink in, then went on: "What the Kirlian Effect amounts to, then, is a demonstration that the plasma state can be produced artificially in the living organism without impairing its vitality. To this end, it is sufficient to apply strong-pulsed high-frequency fields." He paused to ask, "Is this too technical?" We were able to reply, "We are all right so far."

"Good. Investigations have revealed that the cause of the Kirlian Effect is the cold or autoelectronic emission of electrons from a live object into the atmosphere in a strong high-frequency electrical field. Observation or photography of a live object in the high-frequency field becomes possible when the field is formed with the object itself serving as one of the plates and a dielectric-coated electrode serving as the other. Auto electrons 'extracted' from the live object ignite the microchannels of the high-frequency discharge. And so, a uniform discharge field is obtained as it passes through the dielectric covering of the electrode. In the high-frequency field, the dielectric is polarized, thus taking on the role of the electrode.

"Now I know that it is not easy to follow, but I cannot put it in simpler terms. In the system of a flat capacitor formed by the observed object and the metallic dielectric-coated electrode, the high-frequency plasmic microchannels interconnect every pair of dipole molecules lying opposite each other. Moving along these microchannels are electrons and ions carrying information about the object that is under observation.

"Electric field intensity depends on the object's geometry, while the work function of the electron depends on numerous physiochemical factors that account for a variation of the energy levels in the electron.

"Taking place continuously in the living organism are physiochemical reactions that bring about changes in electric parameters of the cells as well as in work functions of electrons. And it is these variations that find reflection in the brightness, color, and dynamics of the microchannels."

He paused again to give us time to absorb the information he had just passed on to us. "That is it, fundamentally, except that there are a few random points worth making. Here in Alma-Ata, we have conducted a special spectral study of the high-frequency discharge luminescence which has brought out that in plant leaves there are a great number of luminescence maxima and a few small peaks in the red spectrum.

"Laser irradiation of the plants brought about changes in the blue-green luminescence spectra." The shortwave portion coincided in maxima arrangements with luminescence of leaves, he explained: "The Kirlian method can be used for an objective appraisal of the state of living organisms and how they are affected by various environmental factors, including those of electromagnetic origin.

"Another point: When a living organism is subject to the effect of electromagnetic waves, skin is the first line of defense to be overcome. Consequently, the knowledge of electric parameters of this barrier is of great interest to us. We have carried out a detailed study that has revealed, for instance, that electric conductivity varies solely at high conductivity points, rather than *throughout* the skin area. And the cause of variation was found to be emotional—namely, emotional reactions and oxygen consumption changes brought on by them.

"We found out that in the case of emotional excitation, the points varied in diameter, and so there is a possibility of the points' overlapping one another to form high-conductive spots. This certainly reduces our area of search and, conversely, of observation. Curiously, our measurements were correct on dry skin only." What this amounted to, then, he seemed to say, is that emotions are as much "matter" as matter itself, and they produce bioenergy—a measurable substance.

"A last thought," he added, "because I can go on and on. When we put hypnosis to work in our studies, our findings showed that when emotional reactions were controllable under hypnosis, it was possible to carry out an objective registration of emotions by measuring conductivity between two points.

"I don't know whether I've answered your question," he reflected pensively after a brief pause. "Let me sum it up for you. In terms of bioplasma, and very much in line with the manifestations of the Kirlian Effect, I see man as a ball of lightning. A living organism is nothing but a giant liquid crystal, a semiconductor composed of an intricate system of conductors of various stages of conductibility. Hello. . . . Can you hear me?"

The connection grew better again, and we threw some other questions at him. It went without saying, that there was much more to it: that the work of the "Alma-Ata Group" went beyond its official medical designation was something we simply felt—with that additional sixth sense of a newsman on a job—without being able to put a finger on it.

Much later, in the wake of the disclosures in the summer of 1977, Alma-Ata became the object of much speculation as to its role in secret Russian parapsychology programs. When we thought back to our conversation with Inyushin, we *knew* that our instinct was right. But on this Saturday in Moscow we made sure we stayed away from questions we sensed would not be appreciated—either by Inyushin or, even more importantly, by those listening in. So, instead it was small talk. Was he planning trips to international parapsychology gatherings? To Moscow? To Krasnodar? We had recently visited Semyon Davidovich, we said, and he looked fine, brimming over with new ideas, seemingly indefatigable at seventy-eight.

Inyushin chuckled across 1,950 miles of Russia. "I won't put it past him to be able to solve our mechanical difficulties for us as quickly as it would take us to tell him the problem. He is a genius." As for traveling, "No time," he reflected. "Too much to do. Unless it's a consultation. Then it's a different matter; then Alma-Ata is only five hours away." We told him we knew from his friend, Viktor Adamenko, that around the Alma-Ata University campus he is famous for the green scooter he uses to shuttle between the different buildings.

He laughed over the crackle of the radio connection. "Tell him it's still doing a good job."

After we replaced the telephone receiver, we turned off our Sony tape recorder and listened through the tape. Not bad. But had Inyushin answered all the questions uppermost in our minds? At the time, we thought he had. But much later, when the summer of 1977 erupted with suggested Soviet plans to use parapsychology as a weapon, we found ourselves thinking increasingly of the man in Alma-Ata. His was the sophisticated equipment, both in his laboratories and on his drawing boards. Surely they would come to him. We should call him again. Hell, why not? The worst that could happen would be the operator saying, "The subscriber does not wish to receive a call from the United States," a retort we had heard before.

And so, one morning we ordered a call to Alma-Ata. "There may be a one or two hour delay," the operator said; the call materialized 1 hour and 20 minutes later. It was evening in Alma-Ata, in Central Asia, and Inyushin was at home. Intrigued, he accepted the call: "Who is that?" We had to talk fast. "Hello Viktor Mikhailovich . . ." We identified ourselves as the journalists who had called him from Moscow some time ago, with greetings from Adamenko and Kirlian. "I remember you," he said haltingly.

"We spoke to Vinogradova the other day."

"She was over to see me in Alma-Ata a while ago . . ."

"She told us that you've made remarkable progress . . . particularly with lasers."

We were not bluffing. We had called Alla Vinogradova in Moscow, got through without difficulties; she had referred to Inyushin's "incredible new advances—especially with laser beams." We're on the right track, alright.

"Well, yes indeed," he said slowly. The typical scientist, he was being cautious, but perhaps it hadn't sunk in fully that we were calling from America.

"In what direction?"

"In both. Theory and technology . . ."

"That's beautiful. Any *particular* area?"

"We've found new uses for lasers in medical science. Very important." He sounded relaxed. "Also in agriculture and in some other areas . . ." He paused.

The "other areas" could be military, but we would get nowhere prodding him about that. Better retreat to safer ground. "By the way, we remember, you've also been working very hard on improving the technology of the Kirlian Effect. . . . Diagnosing precancer among other things."

"Yes, we've been making steady progress in this direction. Still, it should take us another eighteen months to get all the technical bugs out and to perfect it for general use."

"That's pretty close. To return to lasers, what in particular. . . ?"

"Laser acupuncture," he volunteered. "I am referring to the laser ray needle. Tremendously effective in healing, much more so than the traditional way of using electric charges, and worlds away from the archaic original method of inserting a metal needle. The Chinese thought they had it developed to perfection with their so-called Shanghai method. But I suspect the Chinaman will not be able to compete with our ray. . . ."

He gave out a good-natured chuckle, slightly contemptuous. A political connotation was obvious. The People's Republic of China had better beware. The Inyushin Ray may hit them elsewhere, too. Our satellite connection was loud and clear, though it spanned half the world. So this was it: He has come up with a new powerful ray that heals, that also changes the genetic structure of seeds and which, in different circumstances, might well become the "death ray" for use, first, maybe in a war with that Chinaman. We would have given anything to find out more, but we didn't press him, knowing full well that whoever was monitoring our conversation on the Russian end might already have taken a dim view of our call. "We may visit you in Alma-Ata," we concluded on a cheery note.

Milosti prosim, he said pleasantly. In translation it meant, "You will be most welcome."

When we make our next trip to Russia, we'll find out if he really meant it.

23.
PSI TECHNOLOGY:
The Latest Breakthroughs

We should have been tipped off by Yuri Shevyakov's behavior. We were having breakfast in the Astoria dining room when he came over, triumph written all over his face. "She" would see us, he announced proudly. We were being granted an audience. Tomorrow—four o'clock.

Who was "she"? He apologized: he was too excited. She was the great Bekhtereva who, following in the footsteps of a giant of science, her grandfather, Vladimir Mikhailovich Bekhterev, founder of the Brain Institute, was currently heading the internationally famous research center, with an army of seven hundred doctors under her command. She was also a Member Correspondent of the Soviet Academy of Sciences and a celebrated neurologist in her own right, whose work had attracted the attention of the international scientific fraternity. Above everything else, she was a Bekhterev continuing a Bekhterev tradition.

The next day we made our way to the Institute in the darkness of a wintry afternoon and we had trouble finding Bekhtereva's office, tucked away in a far corner of an inner courtyard. However, the orderlies in the crowded outside office knew about our coming. Within seconds we were being ushered into her private office to confront her.

We had been prepared to meet a Soviet woman-scientist in her natural environment of utter austerity, a woman in a white smock, with ball-point pens stuck into the rim of her breast pocket, a pale face that had never felt the need of makeup, topped by hair pulled back in a severe knot, and flanked by unsmiling, white-clad colleagues. That was the familiar figure we had confronted on so many previous occasions. Somehow it never occurred to us that status distinction of sorts went with her being the granddaughter of Vladimir Bekhterev.

As it turned out Natalia Petrovna Bekhtereva's study had all the accoutrements of the inner sanctum of a woman president of a big European corporation. Were it not for a large portrait of Lenin facing her desk across the entire length of the mahogany-paneled, oversize office, we could be anywhere, from Paris to Zurich to Athens. Here it was staring at us, status Soviet-style, from the sophisticated modernistic rendering of the obligatory Lenin portrait—she later divulged she had personally picked the artist—down to the elegant dining alcove and frilly organdy curtains. There even was a faint smell of perfume in the room.

Bekhtereva could go to a reception at Claridge's and fit perfectly into the most discriminating crowd. The boss of the prestigious Brain

Institute on Leningrad's Kirov Prospekt fitted the woman executive image to a T as she sat there, behind the large tidy desk. A short, somewhat plump woman in her early fifties, she sat motionless, imperious, and slightly impatient, carefully coiffed, her hair teased into a gleaming pompadour to frame her face in flaming red. She was wearing a rather elegant long-sleeved dress that most probably was bought abroad.

Nods, introductions, handshakes. She looked us over, then motioned us to take the seats across from her desk. The door, heavily padded on the outside, had closed behind us, to leave us alone with her. These, obviously, were her instructions: no kibitzers. As she eyed us in a posture of cool, detached efficiency, we realized that she could handle us.

We could easily guess that her position paid well, warranting a large, well-appointed apartment on Mars Field or some other exclusive area in Leningrad where the local elite of scientists and artists live. It went without saying that a chauffeur-driven car was at her disposal day and night. A dacha? Probably two, one outside Leningrad somewhere near the old Imperial palaces of Pushkin, where the same elite has its summer homes, another outside Moscow for a Soviet status symbol. But then, we figured, she deserved it. After all, she was continuing the Bekhterev tradition inside Russia rather than outside it. She contributes to Soviet prestige and upholds it at international gatherings of scientists. One may call it a fair exchange.

In a precise, metallic voice, she got straight down to business.

"Would you state your case? What do you want to know? I will talk to you in English." Her English was heavily accented, but good. She sat back and waited. Her hands—small, sensitive and expertly manicured—were folded on the desk in front of her.

In these very dainty hands, ironically, this woman may well hold the future of parapsychology, something she scorns with a passion. For to all intents and purposes, this very office is the captain's bridge from which her commands go out to the largest team of brain surgeons, doctors, and technologists in the world as it probes the mysteries of the mind. It could be tomorrow that they come up with the breakthrough that parapsychologists are waiting for to put telepathy, ESP, and telekinesis on a clear-cut scientific basis, to define bio-energy as simply as Einstein's equation of relativity. Yet if she knew she was helping parapsychology, she would probably call a stop to the research right there. That's how much she hates the subject.

"Well?"

The "well" was thick and heavy. Even though only seconds had ticked by, she had grown impatient. It was then that, fitting ourselves into her surroundings, we first thanked her for allowing us to visit her in her impressive office. We would take up only minutes of her precious time. We addressed her as "Madame Bekhtereva." It seemed appropriate.

She nodded, accepting it as a title due her, more appropriate than the Soviet common denominator of "Comrade." It clearly pleased her. "All right, gentlemen," she said, thawing somewhat. "Your questions, please."

We had found a common plateau. The introduction was flowing

easily now, and on target. "Madame Bekhtereva, now that you have reached a point where your Institute has started decoding electrical impulses in the human brain caused by sound—"She gave out a pleased smile: we had done our homework. "What is your great ambition in life?"

"I have two ambitions in life," she said, enunciating every word. "One in general terms, is to match the contribution of Vladimir Mikhailovich. The other is not to merely code and decode words as registered acoustically by the human brain, but to transcribe electronically the entire range of the intellectual activity of the human mind." She paused for emphasis.

Once this is accomplished, would it not be feasible to feed a superior intellect into a lesser brain?

"This would not be ethical," she shot back. But she admitted they can already send the codes for certain words back into the brain through electrodes.

"Isn't parapsychology concerned with this, too, among other things?"

Her eyebrows shot upward at the sound of a word, obviously taboo in her presence. "Don't mention parapsychology to me."

"But wasn't your grandfather among the first to conduct research into it?"

Some seventy years ago, an Imperial Russian neurologist named Vladimir Mikhailovich Bekhterev evolved a theory that psychic phenomena were actually of a down-to-earth, physiological nature. In other words, the phenomena were *matter*. His study attracted international attention. Unfortunately, he did not pursue these studies, sidetracked by his associate Dr. Ivan Pavlov into work on what became known as the theory of conditioned reflexes.

Just then an orderly arrived with the coffee on a silver tray, giving her the opportunity of delaying her reply. She busied herself with the silver coffeepot. "Black or white?" We played the game and took the coffee.

"I will be the first to applaud parapsychology," she said unexpectedly, returning to the subject on her own, "if and when telepathy, for instance, is proven beyond a shadow of a doubt to be a viable means of mental communication. I myself can't see it, but if and when this happens, I am willing to have a look at the facts." Nevertheless, that was not her job for now. Bekhtereva's precise mind, picking up where she had stopped to pour the coffee, went on to formulate her stand.

"I have dealt with the brain all my adult life. I look into the brain. Its capacity is infinite, its secrets complex. There are at least 14 billion cells. The number of connections, groupings, interactions, and interdependencies are in the millions. We can unravel its secrets only by careful reconnaissance, area by area."

In the last eleven years, she went on, researchers of the Brain Institute have pinpointed and explored two thousand zones of the brain, each serving a different purpose. This was accomplished parallel with the Institute's hospital work of diagnosing and treating patients. The discovery of one particular zone that becomes affected by Parkinson's Disease, for instance, led to an effective means of dealing with it: deliberate destruction of nerve cells of the zone found in a microscopic section of the brain. Other explorations of the human brain have located zones responsible for various emotions. Some were found to be protected by others, thus preventing the emotions from becoming overpowering. Some are positive, others have a negative effect, and they balance out to protect man, as in the classic example of laughter to tears. "We know all these zones," she said matter-of-factly. Still other explorations of the brains of patients have led to the use of electric stimulation. Electric current fed into a distinct area of the brain helps it to mobilize its own resources and so to reorganize itself following an operation.

This is where Bekhtereva's gold electrodes come in, bunches of six to eight coated wires 50 to 100 microns in thickness. They are passed into the exact spot, a minutest area of the brain, through tiny holes bored in the skull. Each electrode is about one twelfth of an inch shorter than the next. As a result, each then monitors a different level of cells. The electric current may be an irritant or may be wanted for a soothing effect.

The electrodes are attached to an electroencephalograph. In this way, the researchers can "see" the bioelectrical exchanges between the cells. By painstakingly logging these interactions, the researchers have been able to trace intricate patterns as information, received by the brain, is directed to the appropriate "command center" and is stored for future use or is used in a decision-making or emotional response situation. There are thousands and possibly millions of zones such as those already explored, each and all serving a definite function.

"What will we find? We do not know. When will our search end? Perhaps never." But already they are making remarkable advances. They can now trace a single word from the time it is picked up by the ear to where it triggers the proper response in the brain."

Bekhtereva explained, "There is a vast matrix, linking groups of brain cells, all powered by bioelectricity. Each group of cells has a different function and shows different outputs of these electrical impulses as it reacts or does not react.

"We know that when we hear a word or sound, this is basically what happens—a simple word or sound becomes a complex code which is handled and reacted to by a computer more complex than any we can build—the brain. The responsible cells instantaneously turn it into an acoustical code. Every word or sound has a different code. Then it is passed on to another group of cells, which instantly analyze what 'routing' the code should be given. The code is then passed to the appropriate cell groups, which respond to it, sending action suggestions to cell centers, or merely filing the knowledge in long- or short-term memory banks.

"Let me give an example. You hear a shot. The acoustical code is sent to the long-term memory, which will indicate that the code for shot indicates 'danger.' At the same instant, other cell groups will be analyzing whether the shot is near or far, whether there is a reason for you to expect to be shot at, what evasive action you can take. All this, remember, in a micro-second. The net result is, you duck your head almost at the same instant that you hear the shot. This is simplifying what is taking place, of course."

Her eyes narrowed as she hammered home the thought: "We can now, by using electrodes, trace this chain reaction through the cells of the brain, pinpointing the cell groups to which the code has been sent, what we call the areas of responsibility.

"We can now actually see a word traveling round the brain on its various routes, and we are now trying to find out how the groups of cells make logical deductions based on these codes. We believe we will soon be able to isolate what zones of the brain deal with emotions. By inducing reflexes and emotions in a person and monitoring the bioelectrical activity with the electrodes, we are zeroing in on various areas. But keep in mind the billions of cells we are dealing with! It is like trying to find a needle in a hundred thousand haystacks."

She unfolded her hands slowly and sat back: "The important thing is that we now have the ability to measure at what time a nerve message or an acoustical code appears in the brain, keep track of it in general terms, and tell when a decision has been made. We can now duplicate many of these acoustical codes."

The great Bekhtereva raised a hand rather imperiously, and like magic, her aide was by our side, handing out chocolates. We sipped her coffee and complimented her on the excellent service. She nodded. It was expected.

"Madame Bekhtereva, you have just said you could duplicate these codes. Could you do it in the brains of animals, allowing them to understand human instructions?"

For a moment we thought she might not answer. But she did. "Of course!" She shrugged. "We could implant electrodes in the brain of an animal and give it simple instructions. To come or go away or drink milk, if you were dealing with a cat. It would understand. You could also do it with larger animals. And the possibility is there, if we conducted lengthy experiments, to work out and electrically code animal languages so that in effect we could 'talk' to them. But you forget: man comes first."

Wouldn't the control of animals also have great benefits for mankind?

"I have already answered that question," she snapped. "In any case, what would be the point with animals? It is easy to teach them with a system of rewards. You could never instruct them in human qualities such as truth, which has no meaning to a cat. We would be wasting our time and spending a lot of money for very little reward. We are trying to help people with serious mental illnesses. We must direct all our efforts to achieve that goal."

All right, then, could such a technique be used to implant thoughts in people? She shook her head. "Ethically, I do not believe that should ever be done." A frown crossed her face, she looked at us quizzically across the desk, as if wondering what we were up to. Then, with a shrug, the scientist took over: "Anyway, the technology of doing it is a long way off. It may be possible in seven to ten years."

She was obviously not comfortable with the thought and its implications, but in another instant she was back to her old commanding self. Did we have any other questions?

Well, yes, could she reveal more about those 2,000 zones of the brain her teams have explored?

"Too complicated for the layman and too time-consuming."

Then, suddenly, she softened. "We are currently investigating an area of the brain where groups of nerve cells perform the unique function of standing by totally inactive while the human mind is behaving rationally. But the moment we do something wrong, the moment we forget something vital to us, these cells spring into action and touch off an alarm.

"This in turn mobilizes other cells in a 'command post' of the brain. And they then issue an order that the mistake be corrected. For instance, this is what makes us remember to turn around, while already halfway through the door, to pick up a forgotten umbrella. After the correction is executed, the area in the brain returns to its silent state, until it springs into action as the next error is committed.

"If we were to eliminate this area via microdestruction of cells— which we can do since we know its exact location—we could turn you all into absent-minded professors." For once her face lit up and she laughed heartily at her own joke. We quickly moved into the breach. One last word—about parapsychology?

"What can I say?" She sounded a compromising note. "We are scientists at work, daily probing a new frontier. If on one such day we happen to unlock a door in the mind that will confirm ESP, then well and good. Mind you—I must not be rash—I have personally had instances of intuition when I foresaw something happening. I am sure there is a perfectly rational explanation for that, which we have yet to uncover. Meanwhile, we have too much to do that is scientifically sound to even think about deliberately trying to seek out this door." She didn't say it, but it seemed she realized that they might hit their heads against it one of these days, and then they'll be forced to pry it open whether they like it or not.

Later at the hotel, going over our notes, we were struck by an obvious conclusion: despite her refusal to endorse parapsychology, she has been moving in the direction of the same goals as the Russian parapsychologist researchers, but along a different, parallel road. It was the same bio-electricity or bio-energy that she has been discovering while probing the mystery of the human brain. And even more significantly, whether she will acknowledge it or not, here too she was proceeding in the footsteps of her famous grandfather, the man who was one of the first to postulate that parapsychology was a potential science—all of seventy years ago.

We thought we could detect a hidden message in what she was saying—namely that ESP, telepathy, telekinesis should come of age in a sophisticated research center like the Brain Institute. It has the technical means and the scientific brain power to solve riddles of this complexity. Obviously she was in a better position to forge forward, backed by some of the finest potential PSI technology in the Soviet Union. To be sure, there isn't any machinery probing the human mind anywhere in the world that isn't also available to the scientists in this complex of buildings on Kirov Prospekt, No. 69, Leningrad. There is probably other equipment there, not known to us in the West. In its research of the human brain, the Brain Institute—also known as the Brain Pantheon of Leningrad—is determined to lead the world. How fitting, we thought, if Bekhterev's formidable granddaughter, who doesn't give a hoot for parapsychologists, were to pick up where he had left off.

A day later we found ourselves facing PSI technology again, when we met once more with Dr. Genady Sergeyev. We shook our heads as we thought how close these two were, and how much Bekhtereva could do for him and his experimental, makeshift equipment. He had told us over the phone that he wanted to take advantage of this last meeting to show us his "time machine."

Sergeyev's amazing device has been described in no less an important publication than *Pravda,* the mass circulation government-controlled daily. He told its reporter, "I have given years to the study of biological energy of man, and how to be able to measure and analyze rhythms of all kinds of biological information that we emanate." *Pravda* had printed his observations and the details of his device without comment.

It was now suddenly much colder. A blistering wind was blowing across the city and the broad, menacing Neva River was reaching to the very rim of the quaysides and threatening to break out of its concrete casing. The palazzos on the opposite side were shrouded in a heavy mist, the ice was floating by in a hurry to go nowhere. We were happy to be inside a car as our driver cautiously piloted us along the river embankment, the wind broadside. As usual, Yuri was sitting next to the driver. In the back seat, flanked by the two of us, was Sergeyev gingerly holding onto a contraption sitting on his knees. If we were worried about out car going out of control, all he was concerned about was his machine.

"Is that it, Genady Aleksandrovich?"

He grinned. "It is, it is. My most precious possession. My time machine."

Up front, Yuri turned around to catch sight of Sergeyev's time machine. If he was disappointed by what he saw, he didn't show it. "Don't worry," he smiled, "we'll make sure nothing happens to it. Guaranteed."

Nothing did. We had settled down by a little table under the giant blue-and-gold ornaments of the heavy drapes in the Novosti conference room and both of us tried desperately to follow what Sergeyev was explaining. However much we had already learned about Soviet parapsychology, he hadn't been an easy man to follow on previous occasions. Now he was spouting terminology that wasn't in any of the latest scientific encyclopedias and he was combining it into sentences that obviously had a deep meaning to him. If only he would throw in at least a few ordinary words and terms from a regular physics textbook.

He caught our bewilderment and actually stopped in the middle of a sentence. "I am sorry. Your being here and listening to me is such a pleasure that I forgot I am not talking to my Russian colleagues in parapsychology. Shall I reword, and start from the beginning?"

We breathed a sigh of relief.

"Yes. Please. Thank you."

"All right, let me put it this way. We've just had emotional problems, both you and I, and however minor, it was emotional. That's good, because even if we don't have any of that again before we leave here, this little emotional clash caused each of us to leave something of ourselves behind. Call it, if you will, an imprint of yourself. You may not see it or feel it, or smell it, or hear it. But it is here all right and, theoretically, should remain in this spot forever."

He had slowed down his speech and was carefully choosing his phraseology as if now lecturing to a high-school class. "Every human being makes an imprint on his surroundings, because we are at all times radiating energy, which is soaked up and stored by items around us. Energy can never be destroyed. Therefore, our energy imprints are preserved—technically for all eternity—along with the imprints of other people who have been in this room.

"Quite simply, what I have done is to develop a machine that uses liquid crystals—the same crystals used in those fashionable digital watches—to recover such energy from the surface of these objects. It can record and turn into electrical impulses 'memories' of the past which, we have found, are stored in every object. We have a long way to go before we'll be able to record and translate accurately such imprints of ourselves, left behind in the void of time. But my machine is a beginning in the right direction."

Although he displayed his machine openly and allowed us to photograph it, he was rather reluctant to disclose its working secrets. Perhaps he felt that the technology was above our heads—in which case he was probably right—and that it would lose its impact if reduced to easily digestible explanations. However, it could also be that too detailed a description might allow others to copy it—and Sergeyev was too shrewd to allow a major scientific discovery to be stolen from him.

We can say only that the machine, which is easily portable, is in two parts, connected by wiring. One part, the scanner, looks rather like a microphone and contains the liquid crystals, the basic component of his device. He explained that the liquid crystal is a collection of organic compounds with characteristics close to those of the components that are part of the brain and our blood. They can be made to respond to almost any stimulus—heat, light, ultraviolet radiation, sound, pressure, magnetism, electricity, and even traces of chemical vapor. In the West, we reminded ourselves, liquid crystal electronics, used in watches, calculators, and aircraft instruments, are a whole new industry.

The other part of the device is a meter that gives visual proof that electrical impulses are being picked up by the crystals and records the impulses on magnetic tape. Sergeyev demonstrated it to us, moving the scanner over the table and other objects around him. The meter needle moved higher when the scanner was closest to the object, indicating, he said, that electrical impulses stored by the objects were being radiated, and then recorded by his scanner.

"Soon I will have a more sophisticated machine," he said, a little self-consciously. "I have worked many years to perfect this, and this present device is sufficient to show that the theory is valid. Let me explain more."

He sat back in his chair. "By using very exact analytical methods, we have determined that man can change the electrical conductivity of the area around him. An important part in this is played by the water vapor in the air. In laboratory experiments we have shown that the electrical field of the human brain can affect the contents of this vapor.

"Since thought is energy, the human body can transmit electrical impulses to this medium, the vapor. What happens then is that our thoughts change the structure of the molecules in the vapor, which then becomes a bank or repository of human thoughts."

He paused to glance at us. Could we follow him? Reassured, he continued. "We have proven in tests that a room where there is a reasonable amount of humidity will retain human thought for up to four days in such vapor 'banks.' A person who has been thinking intensely, even for a very short time, will leave these thoughts in the vapor banks.

"After four days this vapor settles. We have shown that the water, as it lands on the objects, leaves the imprint of the thought again, in the form of energy. This was demonstrated using Kirlian photography. The imprint is of course invisible to the eye, but it is shown clearly using the Kirlian technique."

Again he paused to allow us to catch up with him. "We covered clean coins with pieces of plastic, then pressed on the plastic with our fingers. Our fingers never touched the coins. Yet an imprint was clearly shown on them, and remained for four days. The imprints were particularly clear after a person had thought intensely, or had been under great emotional strain.

"From these experiments we have determined that every human being leaves an energetical imprint, as well as an informational imprint, on objects that he touches or is close to. Every object around us has magnetic qualities. When it absorbs energy, it changes the magnetic characteristics of its molecules. It is then that it becomes a natural magnetic recorder."

His device then returns these imprints to electrical impulses. "We are at the stage where we can recover the electrical information. Now all we have to do is decode it." His "we" applied to a small group of Leningrad mathematicians—Sergeyev holds a degree in mathematics. Working with him on the problem, they are currently attempting to determine the amount of emotional stress in actual figures, based on the levels of the electrical impulses picked up from the objects.

He continued, working hard at being explicit: "A person under tremendous stress, facing a crisis or suffering great fear, can increase his electrical output ten thousand times. In this way, man can over a very brief period record the information of his entire life on a nearby object. By brief, I mean in a split second. If you have an object that a man has had for a long time—a favorite book, for instance—you will find that it has already been affected by his electrical impulses. It will contain the thoughts and emotional imprints of the man.

"All objects have this information of other people, of other times. That is why I say that I may well be able to explain the mystery of whether people have a soul. Energy does leave the body when a person dies, and it carries off all the information, all the history, of that person. Perhaps that can be regarded as a soul. Once my machine finds and records it, and we interpret the energy signals, we might have a complete record of someone long dead.

"In fact, I believe that this is what may make ghosts possible. There must be cases where the energy does not become assimilated into other objects. Perhaps all this energy, this information, of a dead person is just contained in a room or an area, and, through some process we do not yet understand, becomes visible to a person. It is feasible."

For a moment, he lapsed into silence. Then, looking up, he postulated that all this may explain the theory of reincarnation. The human brain picks up signals from imprints left hundreds or thousands of years ago. The person's thoughts are then influenced by the electrical messages left by the dead. A house in which someone lived will still contain all the information on the person's life. It is very possible, he was convinced, that a person can perhaps even at birth pick up the past information and then regard it as his own—causing the belief that he has been reincarnated.

"I must stress that we can detect these signals with my machine, and we have already managed to give certain characteristics to certain signals—joy, frustration, sorrow. It is only a matter of time before we can decode them fully."

Sergeyev collected his contraption lovingly as he got up to go. "With this, we will be able to find the memory of the world, its people and its history. Can you imagine the importance of that? To be able to know what famous men and women thought and felt, to recreate important events exactly as they happened, to trace the evolution of man?

"Man has always cloaked what he doesn't know in mystery. We are now scientifically examining these mysteries, including ghosts, and they will not be mysteries for too much longer." We nodded in agreement. He might not have the facilities of Bekhtereva and her brain surgeons, but he certainly had the same determination.

Then we left the Novosti office together, back into the wintry gale outside the building and into the waiting car. En route to the hotel we spoke little. Sergeyev was clutching his time machine, a faint smile on his face. He had brought us face to face with too awesome a reality to fully comprehend. We felt as though we had touched eternity.

We parted in front of our hotel, he going home in our car escorted by Yuri. We shook hands, first one, then the other, then impulsively threw our arms around him in the Russian manner of a farewell to a friend. "We wish you success, Genady Aleksandrovich. . . ."

He nodded. "Thank you. Hopefully we shall meet again."

Our meeting with Sergeyev did not end our brush with the ongoing research into the mysterious bioelectricity, or bio-energy. Back in Moscow, when we told Viktor Adamenko how the electrodes of the Brain Institute were really linked with Sergeyev's "time machine" he said, "Add one more to your list."

Adamenko reached into his pocket and pulled out what looked like a stubby aluminum pencil. "This is an 'acupointer,' " he informed us. "I invented it, and basically it does the same as the electrodes and the time machine—it seeks out bio-energy being discharged by the body."

The acupointer, which is powered by three small batteries and is about three inches long, is currently being used in a limited number of research hospitals in the Soviet Union, since only twenty have been produced and they are tightly guarded. Adamenko, who is in the course of getting his invention patented in the USSR, explained that the pencil contains an electronic circuit amplifier, operated by three power cells. The amplifier is attached to a light bulb and to a metal contact point in the sharp end of the pencil. As the pencil is moved over one's skin, the bulb glows when the contact point connects with an acupuncture point. The variation in the glow tells whether the person is healthy or not.

The device, and the principle on which it works, has been accepted by the Soviet scientific community. We were shown a report in the highly respected science monthly *Science and Life,* published by *Pravda,* which said, "At Alma-Ata, the Leningrad surgeon, Dr. M. K. Geykin, was experimenting with Kirlian photography. He had spent some time in China, where he worked on acupuncture. Fascinated by Kirlian's method, he decided to visit him in Krasnodar and induce him to build a gadget that could help physicians find the points of acupuncture on the human body. Kirlian listened to him with great interest. He had already discovered long before that the 695 points on the human body considered to be the points for acupuncture coincided with the points of intense luminosity brought out by Kirlian photography.

"Kirlian was the first, with his photography, to come up with a machine to determine the points of acupuncture. It was a joint effort between Kirlian, Dr. Geykin, and electronics engineer I. V. Mikhalevsky. Later Soviet physicist Viktor Adamenko constructed his own instrument, which had a very original and stable electronic circuit. Adamenko's device not only determines the points of acupuncture but observes the bio-energetic processes in the human organism.

"So the ancient means of healing has been given a completely new, up-to-date, technological presentation. As a result, it is possible that through the very points now clearly defined by Adamenko's invention, the physicians of tomorrow will be able to make deductions on which the ancient medicine, acupuncture, was intuitively based."

Early models of the devices were apparently quite bulky. The one

Adamenko showed us was the smallest yet developed. But he told us he is already working on a still smaller, simpler device. "Acupuncture points in the body give off a weak electrical discharge," Adamenko explained. "This has been shown by using electronic equipment and Kirlian photography. In the latter, the discharges are very clearly shown by bursts of electricity coming out of the skin.

"When the contact point of my acupuncture pencil meets this electric discharge, it relays it to the amplifier, which boosts it into a measurable power. This is passed on to the bulb, and it lights up."

He allowed us to try the device ourselves. A simple press switch on the side of the pencil turned the amplifier on. Adamenko, with his knowledge of acupuncture, unerringly hit each point without searching for it. We found it much more impressive, however, when we just ran it over our skin not knowing the location of acupuncture points. When the pencil point was run over the skin, even though the amplifier was on, nothing happened for most of the time. But when it hit an acupuncture point, suddenly the bulb did light up, often quite brightly! It seemed simple to use, although without a chart we could not judge what was indicated by the different intensities of the glow in the bulb.

Most recently Soviet scientists have found that the strength of the discharge from the acupuncture point is directly related to one's health. If one's liver is bad, the corresponding acupuncture point reflects it. The same applies to the kidneys, or the heart, and so on throughout the body. When a person is not feeling well, there is little discharge from the affected acupuncture point. Even when amplified by Adamenko's device, the power is still low. Therefore, the weak glow from the bulb indicates illness. When the bulb lights up brightly, you are healthy.

"In fact, it is so simple that if these were made available to the public even at this moment, people could check over their acupuncture points in the morning to see what was wrong with them," Adamenko said. He stressed that an ordinary person, having discovered that illness was indicated, should then go to a physician for a full examination. "But, supplied with a chart showing which acupuncture points are connected to which organs, an average person could make a pretty accurate diagnosis."

In America, indeed in most of the Western world, a mass-produced version of this device would become almost indispensable for every household. Imagine getting up in the morning, checking your body out with the pencil, and knowing immediately whether you are completely healthy or whether some organ is threatening illness!

We asked if we could buy one, or at least take one back to be examined by American scientists. We guaranteed to return the device. But Adamenko was strongly negative on both suggestions: "They are not for loan or sale," he stressed. "I have been told if I sold the secret of this to America, I would make a million dollars. But I am not interested. These are for use in scientific research, not for commercial use. It is my invention. I know how it works, and our scientists know that it is effective."

In a paper circulated to the scientific community, a copy of which he gave us, Adamenko postulated: "The body system of a man can be likened to a complicated energetical system in which a tremendous number of transformations and accumulations of energy are taking place at all times. These processes are not haphazard. To the contrary, they are regulated with very high precision. This allows one to explore such energy activity against the whole human mechanism.

"This finding is based on a new area of biology described as the Theory of the Biological Field, first mentioned by the Soviet scientist A. G. Gurvich in 1944. The element of the field itself was assumed to be a molecularly unsteady constellation. Further developing Gurvich's theory, one concludes that the human mechanism is one giant crystal in a state of unsteadiness. The energetical skeleton of the crystal is determined by means of 'zones of conductivity' in a very complicated configuration.

"The skin of animals, man, and plants feature points that are exits of this very conductivity. In the case of man, these points actually coincide with the points recommended for acupuncture by Hindu, Chinese, and Japanese physicians. The human body has the maximum such points (695); the plants, the least number.

"The study of autoelectronic emissions in the area of the points with the help of the high-frequency field of the Kirlian system, shows up two effects. In some points the illumination is higher, and in others much lower. One can assume that some points contain a large number of negative charges, and others, positive charges.

"During the day, the electrical character of the active points changes. By measuring their electroconductivity, we discovered a correlation with the changes of the electroconductivity of the atmosphere. As conductivity of the atmosphere increases during a regular 24-hour period, the electroconductivity of the points decreases. There is a leap in increased electroconductivity from the points during the moment of sunset. The points' electroconductivity changes with the level of the activity of the sun, but also with the change of weather—before a thunderstorm, for example. By the same token, every man possesses his own peculiar electric stability that is higher with some, lower with others. That is why people react differently to weather changes.

"In the course of evolution, living organisms have adjusted their shapes. Similarly, they must also have adjusted to electrical and magnetic fields of the Earth, and are sensitive to their changes. Apparently the active points in the skin actually serve as instruments for an exchange of electric magnetic energy with the surrounding atmosphere.

"The experiments of our scientists have shown that there is a connection between the electrical stability of man and his general state of health. With sick people, the character of certain points of his skin changes radically. It is those people who best react to changes of the electrical magnetic fields of Earth. This is why rheumatic patients can best predict weather changes. These experiments have also shown that the state of the mind of man is recorded through the points of acupuncture."

The Adamenko report seemed to cry out for scientific methods to measure the various phenomena that parapsychology has already uncovered and wants to check out. More instrumentation and more equipment is needed for the experiments of tomorrow. As we read it, we thought of Bekhtereva and her vast technological empire on Kirov Prospekt, and we could see Sergeyev clutching his time machine. Somehow we knew nobody had yet stopped for a rest. Even at this moment, Sergeyev, Adamenko, Inyushin, Kirlian are hard at work on new devices.

24.
CONCLUSIONS:
The Aftermath of the Toth Case

As the 1974 edition of the Great Soviet Encyclopedia puts it, "What is referred to as parapsychology should be subdivided into two areas. One is phenomena that realistically exist but have yet to be scientifically explained. The other is fakery advertised as supernatural occurrences by mystics and charlatans; these people need to be exposed an discredited."

This became evident to us early in our investigation. As we c welled on what we thought to be genuine and moved from the Kulagina expe iments to the tremendous yet disturbing work of Soviet hypnologists, from touching upon the mystery of the "Alma-Ata Group" at its clandestine labora tories to investigating the moving quest for sight-by-touch for the blind (based, incongruously, in a closed military area), we also sensed that there was more to it than met the eye. But we never bothered to get involved with quacks. We could have, for we were given more names of alleged "psychics" than we could handle.

Thus, Vilenskaya knew of a peasant woman named Agrafena Popova, who was famous for the gift of finding missing people dead or alive. Her reputation has traveled far and wide from Chita in Siberia, where she lives.

She was referred to as a female Rasputin, because she allegedly also cured a youngster suffering from hemophilia, just like Rasputin's notorious "healing" of Czarevich Aleksei, only son of the last Czar, Nicholas II. Indeed the average Russian traditionally believes in miracles, visions, premonitions, miraculous cures, spirits, soothsayers and prophets. There are probably more fortune tellers per capita in the Soviet Union than in other countries. Tolerated by police, they operate in the backwoods, where people are more gullible. On one occasion, stopping for a meal in a roadhouse in Georgia, we came face to face with a woman who ran a profitable business in a back room telling fortunes from coffee grounds. When Natasha—who is a card-carrying party member and clearly a nonbeliever—spied the woman, she insisted on having her fortune read. We were in a hurry to catch a plane to Sukhumi, but the opportunity excited her. Later, a blushing Natasha said the woman was cunningly accurate in telling her what her secret problem was, and told her how it would be resolved. The woman also claimed to be clairvoyant, with "references."

Russia has more than its share of quacks, who have spilled over into parapsychology, much to the dismay of scientists like Sergeyev and Adamenko. On one occasion, we asked them for advice on how to handle Dr. Vyacheslav Zaitsev, who had contributed several widely-read articles on paranormal phenomena to Soviet magazines. "Stay away from him," we were told. Why? The answer was mysterious. "He is not what you are looking for." We interviewed him just the same, only to arrive at the conclusion that the Minsk scholar had, to put it politely, lost touch with reality. Among other things, he warned us to beware of beings from another planet who had moved into the bodies of certain Moscow citizens. He even gave us a couple of addresses where we could meet these aliens.

We never used the Zaitsev interview, nor did we travel to meet Agrafena Popova, or any of the many "mediums," oracles, seers, or astral prophets who, at least in the eyes of the Soviet authorities, have given parapsychology a bad name. Still, despite our precautions and clean living, the KGB could easily have arrested us for the material we collected and eventually took out of the country. We did, on many occasions, accept material from people we had just met for the first time: photographs, film, documents, scientific papers in original form and on microfilm, newspaper clippings, and books that they had written, and proudly autographed for us. However highly recommended, at least one among them could have been a recently converted informer. And all it takes is one. We were almost certain that one KGB agent was assigned to us on our many trips. But despite our suspicions about Nikolai Sergeyevich Vitrokhin, we didn't have absolute proof about him, except that the series of coincidences was all too incredible.

The first time we came face to face with him was in the north wing lobby of the Rossiya Hotel in Moscow, on our very first trip. "Vitrokhin, professor of philosophy," he announced, his voice oozing with friendliness. He was rather rotund, and in his early forties. He explained that he had learned about us from the people at Novosti and wanted to discuss science articles he might be able to write for us in his spare time. He sounded harmless enough to be invited up to the room. After a while he said anxiously that his young wife was waiting for him downstairs. Might he bring her up? Certainly, we said.

A few minutes later he reappeared with his wife, a rather attractive young woman. It was lunchtime, and we agreed to have lunch with them, provided we paid. He probed us with questions about the type of information we wanted. We answered carefully, so that there could be no misconception about our reason for being in Russia. We were there to conduct interviews on popular scientific research, nothing else.

After lunch we parted company, and we didn't hear from him again. But a full year later, while in Leningrad on another reporting trip, we were suddenly stopped in the lobby of the Hotel Leningrad. "Hello, Mister Henry and Mister Bill," a voice called out, and the beaming face of Nikolai Sergeyevich Vitrokhin came into focus. "What a pleasant surprise!"

We had no doubt in our minds that he had been sent to Leningrad to check on us again—presumably by the KGB. He reminded us of a Russian Peter Lorre, definitely up to no good. But if so, and he was with the KGB, we had nothing to hide. We invited him to our rooms to give him a chance to look around. He claimed he had learned about us from Professor Ryrik

Melnikov of the Petrov Cancer Institute, whom we had interviewed the day before. Again his references were perfect. And once more his young wife was brought in a quarter of an hour later to chat amiably, then leave.

Another year went by, and—yes, there he was, beaming at us in the lobby of the Intourist Hotel in Moscow. "What a coincidence," he called out with apparent surprise. This time we were on our way out, and asked him to call us later. But we did not hear from him again, even though we assumed he kept us in the corner of his eye from behind whatever pillar he was hiding.

By then, we had become so used to Vitrokhin that we considered him part and parcel of our Russia trips, a mascot of sorts. He would bring us luck. Then, on our last trip he didn't show. We didn't think we had covered our tracks that well. What was wrong? We almost worried about the poor man.

On the day we were ready to leave, we had just come into the street in front of the Hotel Berlin. Zhdanov Street was empty, a pall of sadness hanging over it as it hangs over so many Moscow streets. Our car, a black Volga that was to take us to Sheremetyevo Airport, had just stopped in front of the entrance to the gray neobaroque facade of the old hotel.

A lonely figure, short and squat, in a heavy coat, a brown fur cap pressed down deep to reach the coat collar in the back, was turning the corner. Something struck us at the same time. The cloth coat with the dainty fur collar and the fox hat were terribly familiar. "Vitrokhin the Spy" we thought.

We called out in unison, "Why, Professor Vitrokhin, what a pleasant surprise." The figure ignored our shouts, turned the corner and was gone. Was it Vitrokhin? We could have made a dash and caught up with him, but we were eager to get out. We had completed our job. Why ask for trouble? We both reached the same conclusion: "Let's go home."

Fortunately for us, the Soviets, for whatever reasons, did not want us harassed. The luggage search at Sheremetyevo's hall of departures, their last but most effective opportunity, passed without incident. We headed home, very satisfied with our achievements.

Time went by. We were back in America writing this book when, one summer morning in 1977, KGB agents arrested 48-year-old *Los Angeles Times* Moscow correspondent Robert Toth. The arrest took place on Moscow's busy Kutuzov Prospekt in full view of passers-by who pretended to pay no attention. The scene, obviously, was not unfamiliar. Toth was taken to a police station and charged with gathering secret information of a "political and military" character.

"On the 11th of June of this year," the Soviet Ministry of Foreign Affairs stated officially, "Robert Charles Toth was apprehended at the moment of meeting with a Soviet citizen, Petukhov, Valery Georgievich, which took place under suspicious circumstances. When apprehended, the American journalist was found to have materials given to him by Petukhov containing secret data.

"The Ministry of Foreign Affairs informs the American Embassy in

Moscow that in conformity with established procedure, Toth will be summoned for interrogation by the investigatory organs, in connection with which his departure from Moscow until the end of the investigation is not desired." Although his three-year stint in Moscow had just been completed, Toth was effectively barred from leaving the country.

What had happened was this. In late 1976, a dissident scientist had asked Toth if he was interested in parapsychology. When Toth replied he didn't believe there was any scientific basis for it, he was informed there was a scientist who thought he could prove a solid basis for extrasensory perception. Several months later, Toth was introduced to Petukhov, but could not understand his involved explanations. He wrote no story about the encounter.

On the morning of Saturday, June 11, Petukhov phoned Toth, insisting that the two men meet almost immediately across the street from Toth's apartment. There, Petukhov handed the newspaperman a document. Toth later said he held the document for only a few moments before five KGB men appeared, bundled him into a car, and took him to a nearby police station. There Toth came face to face with a police inspector who then interrogated all involved. The inspector also took a deposition from one L. M. Mikhailov, identified as senior research worker of the Soviet Academy of Sciences who appeared seemingly out of nowhere to examine the typewritten pages Toth was holding when detained. His verdict: the material, at least in part, was "secret." Eventually, Toth, who refused to sign a hand-written Russian account was allowed to leave, accompanied by a U.S. vice-consul. But a few days later, Toth was questioned as a "witness" at the KGB headquarters, the infamous Lefortovo prison.

Toth's first summons was for 2 P.M. at Lefortovo on Tuesday. He was allowed to arrive under his own power, was ushered first into a small waiting room, then up some stairs and through a long corridor into the office of Maj. O. A. Dobrovolsky, a member of the KGB investigating elite. The Major, a casually dressed, slightly paunchy man in his thirties, informed the American newsman of his alleged offenses: He had received from a Soviet scientist a document which purported to prove that parapsychology, particularly ESP, was a scientific fact.

"I asked how parapsychology could be considered a secret," Toth said in later interviews.

"Parapsychology as a whole may not be a secret," Maj. Dobrovolsky replied. "But there could be fields of science *within* parapsychology that are secret. It's not for me; it's a matter for the experts to say what is secret. And L. M. Mikhailov of the Soviet Academy of Sciences has stated that the materials you received are secret."

The following day Toth was back at Lefortovo to answer more questions, this time put to him by a different KGB interrogator, a Col. Volodin. Questions ranged from his interest in parapsychology to his involvement with Soviet dissidents. In all, Toth was interrogated for 13 hours, was told at the end of the second day to remain at the disposal of the KGB, but the next day was informed by telephone, *"bolshe ne nado,"* he was not needed any more. A query via the U.S. Embassy brought the amplification, "There is no obstacle to Mr. Toth's departure." And so the Toth family left for home: a happy ending to a nasty experience that could have been much worse.

Who was Petukhov? We had never heard of him, much less of his momentous discovery. One day in August 1977, we finally caught up with that brilliant figure of American parapsychology, Dr. Thelma Moss, whose base of operation is an office and laboratory at UCLA. She had only three minutes at her disposal, but they proved quite sufficient for our purpose. "In our dealings with Russian parapsychologists, we have never come across this man Petukhov. Nor have we heard his name mentioned or seen it in scientific papers. How about you?"

"Never heard of him," she replied, "and neither have any of the people I know. Very strange, isn't it?" She grew silent, the silence seeming to echo her thoughts: Petukhov was not what he was purported to be.

We felt that Dr. Moss, who is continually in contact with parapsychologists throughout the world, would have heard of Petukhov had he contributed the minutest piece of valid work in this area. Dr. Moss not only knew of Adamenko, Inyushin, Sergeyev, and the rest of the Russian parapsychologists we had talked to, but she had also met some of them personally, and has steadfastly tried to maintain correspondence with them. That she had not heard of Petukhov was confirmation by default that the alleged parapsychology researcher—although officially in biological research—who handed over the documents that resulted in Toth's arrest, was a phoney. The incident was a thoroughly planned and executed setup.

The motive seemed obvious. The Soviets wanted to intimidate Toth because he had reported the activities of dissidents. In fact, the KGB subsequently spent much more time questioning Toth about his connections with the dissidents than they did about parapsychology. Whatever Petukhov's motive—hunger, harassment, hopelessness—he had infiltrated the circles of dissenters so as to gain access to the foreign press in Moscow. He was a *"provokator,"* a well-used term in post-revolutionary Russia, an *agent provocateur* recruited by the KGB. After ostensibly spending four days in custody, Petukhov—according to Tass—was allowed to go home because he had helped the KGB to "expose an arch-intelligence agent from one of the imperialist countries." He will never be heard of again.

Why did the Soviets choose parapsychology to justify their harassment of Robert Toth? There seems only one clear answer: Since our last visit to the USSR, parapsychology has become a very important matter, ranking with nuclear, rocket, and other strategic secrets. In line with this, early in 1977, Soviet authorities launched a drive to stop the flow of psychic information to the West.

On June 13, 1973, almost exactly four years prior to Toth's arrest, Soviet leader Leonid I. Brezhnev rose in the Palace of Congresses in the Kremlin. It was Brezhnev's first public speech in more than five weeks and at first Western observers concentrated mainly on analyzing his appearance for signs of the illnesses that had reportedly sidelined him. Since he pronounced his words rather indistinctly, they concluded that he had undergone treatment for his left jaw or his throat. But his voice was strong and clear when he urged the United States to agree to a ban on research and development of new kinds of weapons "more terrifying" than existing nuclear weapons. "The reason and conscience of humanity dictate the necessity of erecting an insurmountable barrier to the development of such weapons," Brezhnev warned.

His statement took Western military observers totally by surprise. What did he mean? Agreement had already been reached on outlawing chemical and biological warfare. What weapons systems was he referring to? Could he mean that the Soviets were far advanced in focusing the searing rays of the sun into a viable instrument of war? Were the Russians close to perfecting the long-range laser beam weapon that had been long talked about but never developed in the West because of the immense technological problems? The Soviets would not explain.

The controversy over Brezhnev's statement raged wherever the gathering of secrets was of paramount importance. Every·Western intelligence agency tried to find the answer, particularly the Central Intelligence Agency. Although the Americans had won the race for outer space, they feared the Russians might win the race for inner space—the mind of man.

From CIA agents stationed behind the Iron Curtain came reports that the Russians were able to influence telephathically the behavior of people, alter their emotions or health, and even kill at long distance by using only psychic powers.

A U.S. Defense Intelligence Agency report stated, "Other Soviet tests included inducing the subject with anxiety associated with suffocation and the sensation of a dizzying blow to the head. Some Western followers of psychic phenomena research are concerned, for example, with the detrimental effects of subliminal perception techniques being targeted against the U.S. or Allied personnel in nuclear missile sites. The subliminal message could be carried by television signals or by telepathic means." There were other fears that our national leaders might be targeted for telepathic mind control, "The political applications of focusing mental influences on an enemy through hypnotic telepathy have surely occurred to the Soviets. Control and manipulation of the human consciousness must be considered a powerful goal."

For confirmation that the Soviets were, in fact, earnestly researching parapsychology, the CIA had only to turn to the *Great Soviet Encyclopedia,* Volume 19, 1974, which carried a lengthy description of parapsychology giving it scientific credence. The report, compiled by V. P. Zinchenko, author of *Parapsychology: Fiction or Reality,* and A. N. Leontyev, concluded, "The basic hopes and efforts of a number of parapsychologists are currently concentrated on the study of the electromagnetic field of organisms as a means of biological communication and a carrier of information. This research is carried out on insects, animals, and on humans, but there are many researchers who, at least on the surface of it, do not associate their work with parapsychology. A physical basis for these phenomena has thus far not been found."

After defining in simple terms the various types of phenomena grouped under the heading of parapsychology, the *Soviet Encyclopedia* states, "In essence, the only basis for parapsychologists to connect these phenomena together is the mystery and enigma common in these occurrences. However, to consider such a basis as warranting the setting aside of a separate research area in science would, in principle, not be justifiable or correct.

"In the European culture, parapsychology as an object of systematic research and observation dates back to 1882, when a Society for the Study of Psychic Occurrences was founded in London. It still exists. Ever since, numerous such organizations have been formed and disbanded in many countries. According to statistics kept by parapsychologists, more than 200 laboratories and societies, mostly in the USA, existed in 30 countries in the early 1970's. Many of them were united within the International Parapsychology Association in New York. On a small scale, parapsychology research is also conducted in a number of American universities, mostly private, and in other science research centers financed by the state or by large firms. In 1969, the American Parapsychology Association was accepted as a member of the American Association of Sciences.

"Parapsychology research is published as a rule in special periodicals in a number of countries. The same applies to reports on conferences and symposiums.

"In the USSR, beginning in the 1920's, L. L. Vasiliev, a pupil of V. M. Bekhterev, carried out research in the area of telepathy and clairvoyance. In 1965, a Department of Bio-Information was organized at the Moscow head office of the A. S. Popov Science Society of Radiotechnology and Electrocommunications. In 1967, a Department of Technical Parapsychology and Bio-Introscopy was created at the central headquarters of the Scientific Technical Society of the Instrument-Building Industry.

"In the beginning of parapsychology, rather primitive means of research were used—such as guessing the symbols on cards and recording dreams and thoughts. Criticism and exposure of claims by parapsychologists caused them to search for new proof. An influx of engineers and physicists, who brought along scientific methods, had a great effect on parapsychological research. The new arrivals advanced the theory that the human brain operates like an electronic installation and that therefore, concepts taken from corresponding areas of physics are applicable. As a result, contemporary parapsychology makes use of latest technological means, computer technology in particular. Some parapsychologists erroneously consider the effects under study as conventional physical phenomena that can be explained with electromagnetic radiation.

"Research and attempts at measuring electromagnetic fields, called variously bio-plasma, electro-aurogram, and bio-potential, in conjunction with traditional methods, such as guessing Zener cards and suggestions at a distance, are continuing. Newly developed instrumental methods now available to evaluate the functional state of the individual have changed the face of contemporary parapsychology.

"Certain private research methods used in parapsychology, while not explaining the nature of the parapsychology phenomena, have on occasion proven useful for psychophysiology and experimental psychology. However, the absence of methodical accuracy in conducting parapsychological experiments has, naturally, caused skepticism and irritation among scientists. This is further compounded by the all too frequent cases of mystification and deception.

"One of the reasons for distrust is also the fact that parapsychological events are not reproducible, that is, they do not fit into the pattern of demands made to prove them to be scientific fact. Parapsychologists explain that parapsychological phenomena originate in some special conditions of the psyche. They cannot be produced at will, are extremely unstable, and disappear as soon as outer and inner conditions prove unfavorable. This, then, makes interpretation of parapsychological phenomena very difficult. Some psychic occurrences it seems, do take place. However, recognition of their existence is prevented in view of an absence of information about the channels over which information is transmitted."

The very official *Soviet Encyclopedia* had, in fact, answered many of the questions being asked by Western observers. It confirmed that in facilities all over the country, Soviet researchers are at work probing psychic phenomena, often disguising their efforts under the cloak of a more legitimate science. Despite the difficulties in duplicating the phenomena in controlled tests, they are making headway. The Toth incident triggered renewed speculation concerning the hidden meaning of Brezhnev's 1973 statement.

Discussing the question a few days after Toth's arrest—the Soviets called it "detention"—*The New York Times* reported, "There is no evidence that Brezhnev was referring to something in the field of parapsychology. But it is a possibility that has occurred to some observers, because of the vacillating treatment of parapsychologists, the evident involvement of the KGB with the subject, and what some regard as a traditional Russian interest in mysticism."

The *Times* reference to the KGB involvement in parapsychology came shortly after August Stern, a Russian émigré now living in Paris, revealed in press interviews that in the late 1960's he spent several years in a secret laboratory in Novosibirsk's Science City in Siberia trying to find a physical basis for psychic energy. He stated that he had been told that in Moscow an even more secret laboratory had been set up under the direction of the KGB. A CIA report made public at the same time estimated that a single special Soviet parapsychology laboratory had a technical staff of three hundred physicists, doctors, biochemists, and electrical engineers.

Stern's reference to the KGB psychic research laboratory became even more plausible when the full details of our own CIA's involvement with psychic research became known.

In 1977, the newspapers gained access to CIA's once secret files through the Freedom of Information Act. A vast research program involving the use of psychics, drugs, hypnosis, regression, electric-shock radiation, ultrasonics, psychiatry, and psychology was revealed. Top universities, hospitals, and research institutes were involved, disguising the experiments under innocuous code names. For years, unknown to the American public, they have been experimenting with mind-control techniques because they feared that the Russians were already well ahead of us.

In 1973, for instance, the CIA carried out tests of "astral projection," or "out-of-the-body experiences" with two noted U.S. psychics, Ingo Swann and Pat Price. The experiments, conducted by physicists Harold E. Puthoff and Russell Targ at the Stanford Research Institute in California, produced amazing results. In controlled tests, the psychics projected their minds over long distances, apparently accurately describing supersecret military installations and even the contents of confidential files in these bases. During one experiment, Price described in minute detail a Soviet installation hidden in the Ural Mountains. CIA agents in Russia confirmed his description. The two psychics "spied" on China and once again, "ground truth" agents—CIA contacts in the People's Republic—were able to confirm their accuracy. United States government officers were astounded. When he saw the results of the tests, a security officer exclaimed, "Hell, there's no security left!"

By the time of Toth's arrest, Soviet parapsychology was so significant to the Kremlin that whoever acted to entrap Toth did not realize that the "scientific" nature of parapsychology will still largely a *Soviet* conclusion. Suddenly, the cat was let out of the bag. And then to compound the original goof, a Soviet scientist of Academy status, Prof. Mikhailov, was made so conveniently available at a moment's notice on a Saturday morning to publicly finger culprits Toth and Petukhov. It could only mean that the Soviets regarded parapsychology very, very, seriously.

Western observers were surprised when the following letter appeared in the January-February 1977, issue of *Psychic,* a magazine published in San Francisco. The writer, Eduard Naumov, had just completed a full year of a two year sentence in exile, ekeing out a bare existence as a night watchman in a railway yard in Vologda. He was found guilty of unlawful collection of admissions to unauthorized lectures on parapsychology he gave in Moscow and other cities. His so-called accomplices who printed and sold admission tickets testified against him and were sentenced to unspecified terms in mental institutions. But they reported and were promptly discharged on one and the same day, while Naumov was sent off to banishment. He was allowed to return to Moscow when a supreme court ruling voided his earlier sentence. Naumov's letter to America read as follows:

> Editor: Herewith I want to inform you of the fact that everything is more or less all right with me and to convey my best regards to you for the coming year. Through your journal I would like to thank all your colleagues who had always remembered me, even if the times were hard, and supplied me with the valuable scientific information. I am looking forward to a time when the cooperation between our scientists will reach a much better state. Personally, I am going to continue my research activities into parapsychology, as this is the

sense of my life. Any new ideas demand a lot of effort to be pushed through, and such a struggle is only natural to me. I would appreciate very much if you would inform our colleagues through your journal that I am willing to continue cooperation as we used to have previously. The complications I had are no longer relevant, and there is no obstacle to renewing the former contacts. I am very much interested in learning what my colleagues are doing, and how the research is going on in general. My address for the time being should be Moscow G-19, General Delivery, Eduard K. Naumov.

"We have not heard from Naumov since that letter," Allan Vaughan, an editor of the magazine (which has now changed its name to *New Realities*) informed us in late 1977. "We have heard only through other sources that he is having a very tough time of it in Moscow. He has not been given a job, and the authorities are threatening to take his apartment away. As far as we can gather, he has not been able to carry out his intention of picking up on his parapsychology research. It is very unfortunate." Vaughan, who is himself a gifted psychic and psychic instructor, said the information on Naumov came from a contact in Vienna who had recently visited Moscow.

Dr. Stanley Krippner, a noted researcher and former head of the Maimonides Dream Center in Brooklyn, New York, is highly regarded by Soviet parapsychologists, and frequently corresponds with them. Viktor Adamenko regarded him as a friend as well as a fellow scientist. When we called Dr. Krippner in August 1977, he too had heard that Naumov was still in serious trouble with the authorities. "In fact," he said, "I have not heard from any of the Soviet parapsychologists for many months—even long before the Toth case. There has not been a single word from Adamenko, Sergeyev, Inyushin, or any of the others. Something has obviously happened. I fear it indicates there has been a clamp down on their work."

When we spoke with Dr. Thelma Moss, she had just returned from the Third International Psychotronic Conference held in Tokyo in the summer of 1977. The first had been held in Prague, attended by several Russian parapsychologists including Genady Sergeyev. Even Tofik Dadashev was there, to demonstrate before baffled international scientists his incredible ability to receive and read human thoughts, even of people thinking in a foreign language he did not understand. Other delegates from Russia attended the second conference, held in Monaco.

Naturally, we were eager to hear Dr. Moss's reports of the third international gathering. "Whom did you see of our Russian friends, Dr. Moss?"

"Nobody," she replied. "I am very disappointed, because I and the other delegates were looking forward to the reports from our Russian counterparts." She stopped to reflect: "This summer we attended yet another international conference, devoted almost entirely to acupuncture and applied techology. It was held in Rumania. At that conference, there were some people whom I did not know—a small group from Moscow. A woman whose name I don't remember. They were from the Institute of Unorthodox Medicine. They said they were expecting Viktor Inyushin, but he did not come. In retrospect, this was not significant, since the Rumanian conference took place one month before the Toth incident. But at the Tokyo conference, there was no one from the Soviet Union and that was after the event," she said. "I think the Toth incident affected the Tokyo conference in more ways than one. There was certainly a sharp decline in people who attended that conference, anyway. And nobody, absolutely nobody came from Moscow."

Well, had she heard from Adamenko? "No, the only person I have heard from indirectly is Larisa Vilenskaya. She apparently is doing okay."

The new categorizing of parapsychology as being of political and military importance, we agreed with her, may have led to severe repercussions for these men and women so totally dedicated to a scientific crusade of their own. We knew that the Toth incident was widely reported by the Voice of America and the British Broadcasting Corporation, both eagerly listened to by Russians on shortwave radios. On the basis of our own experience, we assumed that the parapsychologists first curtailed their activity to figure out which way the winds were blowing.

We also assumed that, having been denied visas for Bucharest—probably without explanation—they had reached their own conclusions: namely, that their research had become too delicate. None of their knowledge, however innocuous at first glance, should get into wrong hands. In these circumstances, then, it made sense to us that Viktor Inyushin did not make it to Bucharest, and that none of them made it to Tokyo in the hot and pregnant summer of 1977. We could only guess how they reacted, realizing under what ironic circumstances they had won that official recognition they had been dreaming of for years. And getting even with the *Literary Gazette*—surely a Pyrrhic victory. But one thing is deadly certain: We had gotten our parapsychology probe out just in time, just before the Iron Curtain slammed down, tight . . .

It is a foregone conclusion that Soviet authorities have since been reevaluating their parapsychologists. The rule of thumb hinted at by the *Soviet Encyclopedia* has been put in force. "Mystics and charlatans" to one side; genuine researchers to the other.

Late in 1977, using contacts inside Soviet Russia, we sent word to them and got word back accounting for almost all of them. We learned that Viktor Adamenko, having lost his job with the Institute of Normal Physiology in Moscow, and after spending some time in Krasnodar, was back in Moscow about to be assigned a new project of "considerable significance." Alla Vinogradova had been allowed to continue to practice telekinesis and has "important developments" coming up as well. Semyon Kirlian is in good health and has never been held in higher esteem, following a significant report on the role of the Kirlian Effect in acupuncture he delivered at the All-Union conference on acupuncture in Taganrog in mid-1977.

Word from Genady Sergeyev was a defiant, "I am not doing so well," following an attack on him and his latest book on bio-energy by the authoritative magazine *Science and Life*. It cost him a job, but he was fighting back, pinning his hopes on a positive article about him and his "time machine" in the December 1977 magazine *Science and Technology*. He was reached in Moscow where he was rebuilding his scientific reputation. Word was "not to worry" about him. He was too valuable a man to cast aside.

Aleksei Zolotov's lush black beard had grown a few more inches while he forged ahead on the Tungusky site. He spent all of October 1977 in the "telegraph forest." He and a crew of six sighted a UFO which overflew the forest but did not land. Nikolayev was well, and had been allowed to continue his telepathy experiments, his reputation fortified by a highly successful telepathy test filmed in March 1977. Word about him also mentioned a "new assignment" coming up that would curtail his work as an actor. Prof. Zigel, apostle of Soviet UFOs, was hard at work at the Moscow Aviation Institute, instructing cosmonauts. As anticipated, there was no word from or about Ivanova—even the Russians have difficulty tracking her down. But Kulagina was hanging on.

What about their tomorrow? Of course we are worried about them, because the winds in Russia can veer overnight. That's why no one in Soviet society who has a prison record is looked down on—the next time, it could be you. Yes, we keep worrying about them because, somehow, we grew attached to them. When we came, total strangers from the Capitalist world, they received us as friends. True, official clearance had been passed down from above. But this did not commit them to out-and-out friendliness. They greeted us with typically Russian warmth, with an insatiable curiosity that comes with living in the controlled vacuum of isolation, but also dignity that was both simple and endearing. They wanted to like us. Touchingly trusting, they decided we were honorable men worthy of confidence, and they proceeded on this premise. We reciprocated by being honest and sincere, and a Russian senses that better than anyone else. They told us all they knew, but they had almost as many questions for us. And as we exchanged thoughts, we believe we instilled in them a greater self-confidence and a strength of renewed conviction that they were on the right track.

Those we interviewed had been carefully screened for viable contributions to the science of parapsychology. Their credentials since checked out, most should be of considerable value to the State. We don't expect them to defect, nor would they be allowed to leave the Soviet Union for a long time to come. It is their possession of "secret information" that will tie them down to wherever they are. But we can only guess as to what exactly will happen to them.

We may assume that Viktor Inyushin is to be a key person in the coming scheme of things, as he was already masterminding an important secret project when last we spoke to him. Not that he has ever thought of himself a weaponry expert. But then, did our atomic scientists ever think of themselves as the fathers of the horribly destructive atomic bomb? If one were to ask us to pinpoint the type of researcher whom Moscow expects to produce the most far reaching results, we would say the mystery man of Alma-Ata is Candidate Number One.

If Russian parapsychology is ahead of the West, it is through the sheer genius and effort of men lacking in funds and technical facilities. One wonders if their early poverty, their being the low man on the Soviet scientific totem pole until the recent upsurge of official interest, their being denied so much that we in our own world take for granted, contributed to their single-minded resolve to succeed. Their shortcomings and privations, so taken in stride, are also a source of their strength.

A Naumov returns from exile, totally undaunted, to shrug off a prison conviction and to take up where he had left off as if nothing had happened. Adamenko worked out of a cubbyhole, a tenant in an institution he actually had little connection with, just enough to qualify for minimum space. Sergeyev, once fully attached to a permanent position with the Leningrad Physiological Institute, is now, since his adamant stand on telepathy, a mere wandering consultant. Ivanova defies the police to close her down. We would not put it past Leningrad's Dr. Bekhtereva to make us believe she thought nothing of parapsychology while actually experimenting with it at her sophisticated Brain Institute. After all, her grandfather did start it all off, and Russians are old-fashioned enough to believe in family traditions.

But however dedicated, the Adamenkos, Vinogradovas, Kirlians, Nikolayevs, and the rest of them are obviously not a breed unto themselves. They were reared in Russia; that has been their home since A.D. 862, when a Viking called Rurik was called in to bring order to a land that had suffered centuries of invasion by Tatar hordes (which is how the fortress of Kremlin came into being). Although called scientists and researchers, they identify with the rest of the Russian people who endured a police state under Ivan the Terrible, a police state under Nicolas I, and a Soviet police state under Stalin. Yet is is also their Mother Russia. They may disagree with much that their regime stands for, but at no time in our dealings with them were we allowed to lose sight of the fact that we were dealing with Russians. Viktor Adamenko's eyes never let us forget that he was determined to succeed, but also that he was prepared to accept all the disillusionment and pain that might come his way. Should he fail, some other Russian man or woman would take his place in the lab.

That dear old man, Semyon Kirlian, may have had his misgivings about the way he had been mistreated for lack of an academic degree or formal education, for that matter. But that was his business, he seemed to tell us, not ours. All, including a failing Kulagina, seemed to show strength in their weakness: They had been cast in the same mold as so many famous Russians. If they triumph, they will want it to be a Russian triumph. If they fail, they will, unhappy and disillusioned, ask their own people to judge them and pass a verdict. They are philosophical about the morrow the way only Russians are. But in the meantime, their convictions and their endurance are one.

INDEX